CURRENT ISSUES IN
SCHOOL LEADERSHIP

Topics in Educational Leadership

Larry W. Hughes, *Series Editor*

CURRENT ISSUES IN SCHOOL LEADERSHIP

Edited by

Larry W. Hughes
University of Houston

2005

LAWRENCE ERLBAUM ASSOCIATES, PUBLISHERS
Mahwah, New Jersey   London

This book was typeset in 10/12 pt. ITC New Baskerville, Bold, Italics
The heads were typeset in ITC New Baskerville Bold

Lawrence Erlbaum Associates, Inc., Publishers
10 Industrial Avenue
Mahwah, New Jersey 07430
www.erlbaum.com

Library of Congress Cataloging-in-Publication Data

Current issues in school leadership / edited by Larry W. Hughes.
    p.   cm.—(Topics in educational leadership)
  Includes bibliographical references and index.
  ISBN 0-8058-4964-5 (pbk. : alk. paper)
  1. Educational leadership—United States.   2. School management and
organization—United States.   3. Education—Political aspects—United
States.   4. Education—Social aspects—United States.   I. Hughes, Larry W.,
1931–   II. Series.

  LB2805.C857   2005
  371.2′00973—dc22   2004021590

Printed in the United States of America
10 9 8 7 6 5 4 3 2 1

With much love to
my grandchildren
Kymberli Jordan
Scott Larry
Ashley Jane
Rebecca Danielle
and
John Harrison

Contents

Foreword

Every 5 years or so, we need a new book like this one. That's because the contextual forces that have an impact on schooling shift and reform just that often. *Current Issues in School Leadership* is a timely volume.

Current Issues covers the ABCs from art education, to school budgets, to censorship, and editor Larry Hughes adroitly clusters the chapters under three broad themes: social and political issues, curriculum and learning issues, and organization and management issues. In addition, Hughes has, as he claims in the Preface, recruited a broad range of authors who are experienced with their topics.

That said, *Current Issues* is hardly a one-way street. This book certainly does inform us, as such an update should, but *Current Issues* requires us to react, to interpret its commentaries from our vantage point of school principal, teacher leader, or interested citizen.

Current Issues also provokes us into being its second editor. Made aware of the tensions and contentions that surround school issues, we are coaxed into parsing the debates set off by the issues. Our engagement leads to looking for new ways to group the issues—this time according to the values that underlie them. I was struck by how easily school finance issues can migrate out of the category "organization and management" and relocate under "curriculum and learning" because of the influence that budget allocations can have on what gets taught. Similarly, the effects of class size have implications for "curriculum and learning" (which is the heading under which Hughes placed this issue), but class size doesn't deliver an automatic payoff in learning unless it is explicitly on a school's "organization and management" agenda. And isn't the range of applications for instructional technologies, aptly grouped in this book with other issues in "curriculum and learning," often a function of community wealth and parental worldview—phenomena that push it toward the domain of "social and political" forces?

Whatever the sorting mechanism, preordained by the editor or invented by the readers of this tidy volume, I think that the issues that Larry Hughes has selected can be projected onto a couple of larger, more abstract levels. Hughes anticipated the first of these meta-considerations when he asked his focus group, in preparation for this book, "What is interfering with schooling processes?" As a student of the politics of education, I am reminded of the age-old contest between the outside world of the parents and public electorate, on the one hand, and the inside world of the school specialists, on the other. Here we have the actions of the people (polis) creating *issues* for the professionals. Messy democracy challenges elite control. Case in point: in *Current Issues* we get a treatment of the social studies that portrays it either as exercises in "social justice" or rote lessons in civics and history. Which version of this subject would the well-prepared and certified teacher elect? Which way would socially conservative parents or the local patriotic league have it? And the school principal: Whose job is she to carry out—the one that her parents or district superintendent bid her do or the one embedded in the syllabi of her academic preparation in educational administration?

A second way to encounter many, if not all, of the issues presented in this book is to revisit one of our perennial questions: What's the purpose of schooling? Is schooling meant to facilitate the transfer of knowledge or is it about opening children and youngsters to the worlds of inquiry and rapport? A whole list of school topics can teeter on this fulcrum—topics like religion, censorship, testing, ethnicity, and school culture. Pitting knowledge against inquiry, we may bump into the ultimate issue for schooling in the 21st century: It's not a matter of what you know, but who else knows it.

—Robert K. Wimpelberg
Dean, College of Education
University of Houston
Houston, TX

Preface

What is an "issue"? An issue derives from tension, or cognitive dissonance. Research or law may be reasonably clear on something but different collections of people—a community, a pressure group, political blocs, academicians—take a position contrary to the research or current practice. Or, there may be insufficient research and an ongoing argument about "what is right." Think of the controversy that continues to surround the selection of textbooks, or prayer in schools, or retention of students, or school vouchers, and so on. In other words, the controversy has a reasonable basis for solution, but many do not accept this reasonable basis.

This book is about matters of importance in how schools are conducted. The particular issues making up the book were identified after some brainstorming sessions that focused on two questions: What is important to today's school leaders? and What is interfering with schooling processes? Contributors were selected with care and include a broad range of individuals who have demonstrated their interest and abilities with the subjects in question by experience and previous writings.

The book comprises three parts: Social and Political Issues, Curriculum and Learning Issues, and Organization and Management Issues. Contributing authors were encouraged to focus on the issues *as* issues that is, to focus on matters for which positions can be taken and arguments waged. They were asked not only to explore the issues but also to take a position on the issues they are exploring. The structure of the book flows from context issues to curriculum and organizational issues. Each chapter concludes with a case study or a series of questions or both to help readers understand the concepts that have been presented.

Fundamental to the nature of this work is that teachers are an important part of the leadership structure of schools. This is even more so in the current ways of organizing but, really, teachers have always been important players—even if not formally recognized as such—in the drama of formal schooling. Anyone who has ever performed as a school administrator recognizes the power to lead that many teachers possess *and* use!

Part I, Social and Political Issues, contains discussions about those general societal conditions that continually impinge on operation of the schools. Larry Hughes begins the discussions in chapter 1 in which he describes the nature of political pressures on schools to either change what is going on or to respond to this or that societal need. He completes his chapter with a discussion about ways in which the public can be better informed.

Five chapters follow, each identifying a force. In chapter 2 Ronnie Casella writes about violence in school settings. He points out tellingly that "school violence encapsulates a range of policies and disciplinary actions ... to respond to threats of violence." How leaders deal with violence is critical to the solution of violence in schools.

There is probably no more contentious an issue today than the role of the school in promoting social justice. Jaime Romo and Michael Roseman and Cameron White and Tony Talbert confront the issue of social justice in two chapters. In chapter 3 Romo and Roseman report cases of several teachers as they come to grips with teaching about social justice. Then White and Talbert follow in chapter 4 with a further exposition of the social justice issue and what that means to teachers of social studies. White and Talbert bring spirit to the debate about how social studies should be taught and for what purpose. Suzanne Rosenblith, in chapter 5, covers the seething controversies about the role or nonrole of religion in public schools. Richard Fossey continues the examination of social and political forces in chapter 6 by discussing the influence of censorship and school practice. He details the conflicts between citizens and schools regarding what can be taught and what should be taught. Chapters 5 and 6 link nicely to provide a solid legal context as well as an historical perspective.

Part II, Curriculum and Learning Issues, contains seven chapters and becomes specific about continuing controversies affecting classroom teaching. This part opens with Charles M. Achilles examining, in chapter 7, the implications of class size and learning efficiency. His observations about the efficiency of teaching smaller groups of students fly in the face of so-called common knowledge about how to most economically organize for instruction. In chapter 8, Patricia Holland and Joy Phillips discuss the evaluation of schools from a perspective that is, at once, challenging and informative. In chapter 9 about evaluating students, Richard Meyer indicates little positive regard for today's movement in the direction of high-stakes statewide testing programs as a way to help teachers help learners. He illustrates his reasons with two compelling case studies.

In chapter 10, Reyes Quezada and Keith Osajima bring new insights to the schooling of children and youth who are from different ethnic groups and different cultures. The curriculum and teaching practices for children who are intellectually, emotionally, or physically disabled is the subject of chapter 11, by Judy Mantle. Mantle bases her chapter on three basic assumptions: (a) that school leaders value persons with disabilities; (b) that school leaders are committed to helping disabled persons achieve the highest levels of success possible; and (c) that leaders are dedicated to their own personal and professional growth to make them better able to maximize the development of the disabled.

Fine arts are Sara Wilson McKay's focus in chapter 12 as she examines specific neglected aspects of the curriculum. The author draws on multiple resources and perspectives. Part III concludes with chapter 13 by Melissa Pierson. Pierson explores the effective use of technology in the classroom. She writes that the effective use of technology depends on the leadership of teachers and the solid support of administrators. She contends that leaders must "think beyond the machines."

Part III, Organization and Management Issues, contains six chapters. William Greenfield and Joseph Flessa lead off this section with chapters that focus on the building administrator. In chapter 14 Greenfield examines the administrator's role in leading teachers to persisting pinnacles of excellence. Flessa, in chapter 15, describes principal behavior in three very different inner-city schools. In chapter 16, Angus MacNeil focuses on the relationship of school culture and climate to school outcomes. He notes that strong school cultures have more highly motivated teachers and highly motivated teachers have more success with student performance and student outcomes. His chapter is a discussion about how a school leader can achieve a better learning climate and stronger school culture.

In chapter 17, Charles Achilles and Christopher Tienken reach some interesting conclusions that raise serious questions about the efficacy of professional development programs. There is a description of what relationship, if any, exists between staff development programs and the effectiveness of the school.

Financing schools is the issue in chapter 18, where Augustina Reyes and Gloria Rodriguez confront and develop interesting arguments about how this might best be done. They relate the development of school finance programs to a Russian novel: "It's long and tedious." In a well-documented chapter, they present the fundamentals of school budget development and school finance programs.

In chapter 19, Liane Brouillette offers another and final perspective to the school support issue. This chapter concludes Part III. Brouillette discusses the charter school movement, a movement that increases the schooling choices of parents and caregivers. She concludes by asserting "Through the charter school movement new ideas, new energies, new perspectives have been brought into the nation's public schools."

As the editor of this volume, I know I speak for each of the authors when I write that we hope you are challenged by our discussion and moved to think carefully about each of the issues. We hope that thinking will cause positive action and leadership on your own part. Best wishes in all of your professional endeavors!

Author Biographies

C. M. ACHILLES, EdD

Chuck Achilles holds joint professorial appointments at Seton Hall University and at Eastern Michigan University. His most recent books are *Let's Put Kids First, Finally: Getting Class Size Right* (Corwin, 1999) and *Problem Analysis* (Eye on Education, 1997). His several areas of research interests include class size and student outcomes, student behavior, public confidence in public schools, and preparation of school administrators. In addition to authored and coauthored books and chapters on these topics, he has more than 300 contributions in the professional literature.

Dr. Achilles began his professional education career in 1959. He has teaching and administrative experience in private and public schools and universities. He has been a professor at the University of Tennessee and at the University of North Carolina-Greensboro. In 2000, he received the coveted Living Legend Award from the National Conference of Professors of Educational Administration.

His doctorate in education is from the University of Rochester.

LIANE BROUILLETTE, PhD

Liane Brouillette is associate professor in the Department of Education at University of California, Irvine. Her research interests focus on site-based school reform. Her most recent book, *Charter Schools: Lessons in School Reform* (Lawrence Erlbaum Associates, 2002), is an intensive study of seven schools in three states. An earlier book, *Geology of School Reform: The Successive Restructurings of a School District* (SUNY Press, 1996), was an examination of how successive waves of reform have affected a single school districts. She also is well published in professional journals with recent articles in *The Chronicle of Higher Education, Phi Delta Kappan,* and *Educational Administration Quarterly.*

She has her PhD from the University of Colorado at Boulder.

RONNIE CASELLA, PhD

Ronnie Casella is assistant professor of educational foundations and secondary education at Central Connecticut State University. His research interests include youth violence, public use of security technologies, and globalization. His current research focuses on the use of security technologies in public schools. He is the author of *Being Down: Challenging Violence in Urban Schools* (Teachers College Press, 2001) and *At Zero Tolerance: Punishment, Prevention, and School Violence* (Peter Lang, 2001). He has conducted research under the auspices of the Violence Prevention Project at Syracuse University and the National Institute on School and Community Violence at George Washington University.

Dr. Casella received his PhD from Syracuse University.

JOSEPH J. FLESSA, PhD

After completing his bachelor's degree at the University of Virginia, Joe Flessa taught for 3 years as a sixth-grade teacher in Houston in the Teach for America program. He received his master's degree from the University of California–Berkeley. Then, he served for 3 years as a teacher, program coordinator, and headmaster in Pachuca Mexico.

He has presented research papers about the urban principalship at annual meetings of the American Educational Research Association and the University Council for Educational Administration. He is currently assistant professor of educational leadership at St. Mary's College of California.

The University of California-Berkeley awarded his PhD.

RICHARD FOSSEY, JD, EdD

Richard Fossey is professor of educational leadership at the University of Houston. He is also Fondren Research Fellow at the Center for Reform of School Systems in Houston. He teaches courses in school law, higher education law, and personnel management. Before arriving at the University of Houston, he was associate dean and professor in the College of Education at Louisiana State University. He has practiced educational law in Alaska, representing several Alaska Native school districts. He is coeditor of the forthcoming book *Mapping the Catholic Cultural Landscape* (Sheed and Ward, 2004).

Dr. Fossey earned his doctorate of jurisprudence from the University of Texas Law School and his EdD from Harvard University.

WILLIAM D. GREENFIELD Jr., PhD

Bill Greenfield is professor and chair of the Department of Educational Policy Foundations and Administrative Studies at Portland State University. He teaches and studies organizational leadership and school improvement with an emphasis on the role and challenges of the contemporary principalship. Among numerous publications are multiple editions of *The Effective Principal*

(Allyn & Bacon, 1980, 1987) coauthored with Art Blumberg; an edited volume, *Instructional Leadership: Concepts, Issues, and Controversies* (Allyn & Bacon, 1987); and numerous conference presentations, articles in leading professional journals and chapters in books on the moral dimensions of leadership and the socialization and preparation of school principals.

During his 30 years in the professorate, he has served as a tenured faculty member at Syracuse University, Kent State University, and Louisiana State University. He received his PhD from the University of New Mexico in 1973.

PATRICIA E. HOLLAND, PhD

Pat Holland is associate professor of educational leadership and cultural studies at the University of Houston. Her research and publications are in the subjects of instructional supervision and teachers' professional development. Recent publications include articles in the *NASSP Bulletin Journal of Curriculum and Supervision*, a chapter in *The Principal as Leader* (Prentice Hall, 1999), and a forthcoming edited book, *Beyond Measure: Neglected Elements of Schooling in an Age of Accountability* (Eye on Education).

Her PhD was awarded by the University of Pittsburgh.

LARRY W. HUGHES, PhD

Larry Hughes is Professor Emeritus at the University of Houston. He came to the University in 1977 as chair of the Department of Educational Leadership and Cultural Studies and served as well as associate dean of the College of Education in the early 1980s. He has held teaching and administrative positions in Texas, Tennessee, Ohio, and Michigan. Hughes served as a principal in Michigan and school superintendent in Ohio and, for 10 years, was a professor at the University of Tennessee. He received his PhD from The Ohio State University.

Dr. Hughes is the author, coauthor, or editor of 17 books and revisions, 3 of which are still in print and in multiple editions. His most recent books are *The Principal: Creative Leadership for Excellence in Schools*, 5th ed. (Allyn & Bacon, 2004); *Public Relations for School Leaders* (Allyn & Bacon, 2000); and *The Principal as Leader* (Prentice-Hall, 1999). He currently serves as editor of the Leadership Series for Lawrence Erlbaum Associates.

ANGUS J. MACNEIL, PhD

Angus MacNeil is associate professor of educational leadership and cultural studies at the University of Houston. Prior to beginning his professorial career at the University of Houston–Clear Lake, the Canadian-born and -reared MacNeil served for 25 years in the public schools of Nova Scotia, 21 of these as a school administrator. He was a principal in five schools including middle schools and rural high schools and two large urban high schools. His major research interest is the principalship and the relationships principals need to improve student learning and achievement.

He received his PhD from the University of South Carolina.

JUDY A. MANTLE, PhD

Judy Mantle currently sits in the Deforest L. Strunk Endowed Chair in Special Education at the University of San Diego. She also serves as coordinator of University of San Diego's Special Education Teacher Training Programs. She has taught in a variety of programs for individuals with special needs from birth through the lifespan. Her research interests are in the leadership and management of special education programs, early intervention practices, and parent and community involvement in special program for disabled individuals. She diverges from this focus with an interest, also, in the challenges faced by women in leadership positions in higher education.

Dr. Mantle earned her PhD at the University of Kansas.

SARA WILSON McKAY, PhD

Sara McKay is assistant professor of art education at Texas Tech University. Her research interests include theories of vision and perception and art and democracy. She advocates critical thinking in education through art experiences that emphasize the value of diverse points of view and multiple interpretations. She was a member of Teach for America and taught in the sixth grade in Houston. Later, she served as curriculum coordinator for a bilingual and bicultural school in Mexico. Most recently, she has published "Dialogic Looking: Beyond the Mediated Experience," in *Art Education* and "Content, Subtext, Schooltext: Building an Art-Centered Curricula" in *Contemporary Issues in Art Education* (Gaudelius and Speirs, Eds. Prentice-Hall, 2002).

Pennsylvania State University awarded her PhD.

RICHARD J. MEYER, PhD

Rick Meyer is associate professor of language literacy and sociocultural studies at the University of New Mexico. He taught young children for almost

20 years before earning his PhD in reading from the University of Arizona in 1989. His research interests include young children's literacy development, beginning teachers of reading, and the political implications of teaching and learning. He believes every act is political, including acts of learner assessment.

KEITH OSAJIMA, PhD

Keith Osajima is associate professor and director of the Race and Ethnic Studies Program at the University of Redlands. He also has taught preservice multicultural studies courses at Colgate University and the University of California–Davis. Much of his professional writing has been focused on challenges linked to teaching about racism. He has also written about the development of Asian American studies, from theoretical and pedagogical perspectives, and about the experiences of Asian Americans in higher education.

He received his PhD from the University of California, Berkeley, in social and cultural foundations in education.

JOY C. PHILLIPS, PhD

Joy Phillips is assistant professor of educational leadership and cultural studies at the University of Houston. From 1999 to 2002, she served as associate director of the Houston Annenberg Challenge Research and Evaluation Project at the University of Texas.

Dr. Phillips' research interests focus on education leadership, policy development, and school reform in urban settings. Recent publications include "Powerful Learning: Creating Learning Communities in Urban School Reform (*Journal of Curriculum and Supervision,* 2003) and "Building Constructive Partnerships in Urban Schools Reform" (Annenberg Institute for School Reform, 2003).

She received her PhD from the University of Texas. Her major area of concentration was policy and planning.

MELISSA E. PIERSON, PhD

Melissa Pierson is assistant professor in the Instructional Technology Program at the University of Houston. Teaching in the primary grades in schools led to research interests that include selecting and using appropriate technology in K-12 settings, the relationships between teaching experience and expertise with technology, the use of portfolio assessment, and technology integration in the education of future teachers. Most recently she received a $1.4 million grant to "Prepare Tomorrow's Teachers to Use Technology." Upcoming books include *Using Technology in the Classroom*, 6th ed. (Allyn & Bacon, 2004) and *Using Technology for School Leaders* (Allyn & Bacon, 2004).

She received her PhD in curriculum and instruction from Arizona State University.

REYES QUEZADA, EdD

Reyes Quezada is associate professor in the Learning and Teaching Program at the University of San Diego. He has been on the faculties of the University of Redlands and California State University, Stanislaus. He has taught undergraduate and graduate degree courses in multicultural and bilingual education, school-community partnerships, and physical education for elementary school teachers and student teaching seminars. His areas of publication include recruitment, retention, and promotion of faculty of color, and effective parent involvement of ethnically diverse families.

He received his EdD from Northern Arizona University.

AUGUSTINA REYES, EdD

Tina Reyes is associate professor of educational leadership and cultural studies at the University of Houston. She is also director of the S. W. Richardson Urban Principal's Center at the university. Her instructional role includes principal preparation classes, school finance, and public relations. She is a former teacher, central office administrator, and school board member in the Houston Independent School District. Her recent publications include articles in *The National Association of Secondary Schools Bulletin, Education and Urban Society*, and *The Fordham University School of Urban Law Journal*.

She received her EdD from the University of Houston.

GLORIA M. RODRIGUEZ, PhD

Gloria Rodriguez is assistant professor in the Department of Educational Leadership at California State University, Hayward. She began her professional career in the public arena as a fiscal and policy analyst with the California Legislative Analysis Office. She currently teaches courses in school finance and educational leadership for equity. She conducts research on school-level resource allocation practices and broader school finance policy issues, as well as the equity status of Latina/o students in the United States. A recent publication, coauthored with Russell Rumberger, is "Chicano Dropouts: An Update of Research and Policy Issues" in *Chicano School Failure & Success* (Falmer Routledge, 2002, 2nd ed.).

She received her PhD from Stanford University, where she majored in educational administration and policy analysis.

JAIME ROMO, EdD

Jaime Romo is assistant professor of education at the University of San Diego. Prior to joining the faculty there, Dr. Romo taught about multicultural education in the teacher education department at National University. He has taught and served as a school administrator in middle and high schools in Los Angeles and San Diego.

Dr. Romo's primary interests are in promoting multicultural competency development and cultural democracy. His research ranges from transformational teaching to staff and community change. He has been a consultant to the Anti-Defamation League and to private industry.

He has degrees from Stanford and UCLA and a doctorate from the University of San Diego.

MICHAEL ROSEMAN, MA

Mike collaborated with Jaime Romo on the chapter about "warriors" for social justice. He just completed his masters degree at the University of San Diego. He specialized in "character education." Roseman teaches at Pioneer Day School and Learning Center in San Diego. He has just received a grant to redesign an ESL Web site for the university. His undergraduate degree is from Washington University in St. Louis.

SUZANNE ROSENBLITH, PhD

Suzanne Rosenblith is assistant professor of educational foundations in the Eugene T. Moore School of Education at Clemson University. Prior to accepting her position at Clemson, she was a lecturer at the University of Wisconsin-Whitewater and at the University of Wisconsin–Madison. Her particular research interests are religion in public education, epistemology and religion, and philosophy of education. Recent publications include "Religion and Public Education: Rival Liberal Conceptions" (University of Illinois, 2002).

She has her PhD in educational policies studies from the University of Wisconsin-Madison.

TONY L. TALBERT, EdD

Tony Talbert is an assistant professor at Baylor University. His research, service, and teaching is committed to collaborative development and facilitative leadership. His qualitative and ethnographic research interests include social justice and education in democracy including the right of dissent within a democracy.

He received his EdD from the University of Houston.

CHRISTOPHER H. TIENKEN, EdD

Chris Tienken is currently assistant superintendent for the Monroe Township School District in New Jersey. He began his professional career as an elementary school teacher and later held posts as an assistant principal and as district curriculum coordinator. His doctoral research focused on the effects of professional development on school achievement.

He completed his EdD at Seton Hall University.

CAMERON S. WHITE, PhD

Cameron White is associate professor of social education at the University of Houston. His areas of research interest include education for social justice, global and international education, youth culture, and critical pedagogy. His recent books include *True Confession: Popular Culture, Social Efficiency and the Struggle in Schools* (Hampton Press, 2003) and *Issues in Social Studies: Voices from the Classroom* (Charles C. Thomas, 2000). A text now in press is *Democracy at the Crossroads: International Perspectives on Critical Citizenship Education* (with R. Openshaw as coeditor, Peter Lang, in press). He is also well published in the appropriate professional journals. Dr. White is co–project director of two Teaching American History Grants for approximately $2 million. He has 15 years of social studies teaching experience in secondary schools.

The University of Texas awarded his PhD.

SOCIAL AND POLITICAL ISSUES

Six chapters comprise part I. The focus is on society and the political framework within which society functions. Although each chapter is independent and the authors present diverse viewpoints, there is a common framework and a common organization to the chapters. Moreover violence and social justice are closely related. Can one be studied without considering the other? What are students learning in schools that are disrupted, in schools with "zero tolerance," in schools that fail to express common decency? And, what has been the effect of religious practices and belief systems on the environment of the schools? All of this occurs within communities that are impacted by cultural pluralism and political pressures from a variety of sources.

Readers will be challenged about their own positions on educational matters that are curricular as these are manifest in beliefs about social and political issues.

Chapter 1

Politics, Pressure Groups, and School Change

Larry W. Hughes
University of Houston

"Slippery and scheming politicos" goes the charge. Schools are a public business and fair game, the response may be. And, so? How did it all start? And why?

There is a national, state, and local interest in the operation of the schools. All three scenes are locales for pressures and enactments that influence how children get schooled and how teachers teach.

This chapter begins with an historical examination of the national interest in schooling and then develops a state and local thesis with an emphasis on school operation in the local setting. An analysis is made of the nature of communities and of the nature of pressures and protest. The good, the bad, and the ugly are examined.

There is a discussion of the nature of informal power structure in communities and the way it gets manifested. Informal power is distinguished from the formal power that occurs when individuals hold particular offices.

The chapter concludes with some propositions for strategies for doing business with pressure groups and ways school leaders can utilize community resources and mitigate negative influences on schooling and the organization of schools.

THE NATIONAL INTEREST

This chapter is about community pressures and influence but it is appropriate to begin by briefly presenting the historic nature of federal influences on local decision making and local school practices. Even though schools in the United States are conceived and held to be "local" and state creatures, there has long been a federal interest. From the beginnings of nationhood, schools have not been free of controls and acts at local, state, and federal levels. More formal, perhaps, than the pressures and politics at the school community level, the effect of federal governmental actions—legislative and court—has been markedly pronounced.

In May 1795, the federal government established its interest in public education. Under the presidency of Thomas Jefferson, the Northwest Ordinance was enacted by the Congress, and although at the moment there was no thought about it, the federal government became a partner in public education in the United States. What happened to do this?

The Ordinance provided for land surveys for that part of the country known as the Northwest. Thirty-six square miles became a township and land was surveyed accordingly. There were 640 sections in a township. One section—a square mile—was given to each state. The money from the sale of this section provided for the establishment of state universities. The influence of the federal government on education began quietly but because of court actions and congressional enactments throughout the years has been continuous and, most often, for greater social good. So then, the federal role in school practice is historic and pervasive—and both specialized and general.

Federal legislators have often passed into law efforts to mitigate social and economic problems that they thought the schools might help solve. The Smith–Hughes Act in the early 1900s, really was to address labor issues; the federal lunch programs began in the 1930s at least partially in an effort to address the problem of farm surpluses; and, leaping ahead historically, what of the National Defense Education Acts in 1958? This latter was to help schools improve what was perceived to be a deficiency in science and language instruction that had placed the nation behind the former USSR. The way to get a "man on the moon" was to improve the teaching of science. The Education for All Handicapped Children Act (1975) brought equity to a million children who had been excluded from proper schooling because of the nature of their handicapping condition. Similarly, the Americans with Disabilities Act (ADA; 1990) provided equity in employment for adults. These are but examples in a rich array of legislative acts.

More recently, in 2002, President George W. Bush signed into law (PL 107-110) legislative enactments that reauthorized the Elementary and Secondary Education Act of 1965. This enactment, labeled the No Child Left Behind Act, redefined the federal role in K–12 schooling. It included school options for parents as well as a focus on teaching methods, among other reforms. And it included rewards and punishments for schools based on student performance on statewide approved tests that would determine such things as whether children were at "grade level." The tests would focus on literacy and mathematics.

This has provided much controversy among teachers and administrators and a tremendous press on test taking, the use of classroom time, and curriculum adaptation. Fine arts persons are distressed and so are those who favor a broadened curriculum that is focused on needs less subject matter oriented and directed instead on the needs of children. Yet some are quite supportive of the move to more stringent testing, claiming that it sets standards higher and will result ultimately in programs that enhance the learning of all children irrespective of ethnicity and economic place.[1]

The federal courts, too, have played a significant role in influencing the operation of the schools. *Plessy v. Ferguson* (1896) established that school attendance by race was constitutional (the separate but equal doctrine); *Brown v. Topeka*, some 58 years later, established that it was not. *West Virginia v. Barnett* in 1943, *Tinker v. Des Moines* in 1969, and *Goss v. Lopez* in 1975 among many other cases decided by the Supreme Court clearly circumscribed the powers of local school officials and boards of education.

But this chapter mostly is not about official governmental influence on schooling, as omnipresent as that is. It is about the political and social influences that exist and within which all school systems—particularly public schools—operate. I opened this chapter with some comments about the governmental scene to highlight the historical influences the federal governments has had on schooling.

Schools are local and state functions, as well. State governments and state courts have had great impact on schooling and so have school boards on the local practices and policies of the school. And the relationship with the publics is often strained at all levels of government.

The remainder of the chapter is about the informal structures that exist, sometimes latent, sometimes highly visible, and frequently very loud. The influence of these groups and individuals within groups is also pervasive and has been responsible for change of great magnitude, often for great good, sometimes not, but always at the price of controversy and much discussion.

LOCAL POLITICS AND PRESSURE

Multiethnicity and cultural pluralism characterize society and the many groups and individuals that comprise a community, a neighborhood, a city reflect widely varying points of view and hold diverse opinions about the several agencies that are established to deliver services to them.

Interfering with it all are the actions and interactions of *vox populi*. Special-interest groups, old-time conservatives, wild-eyed fanatics, concerns of the

---

[1]Authors of several subsequent chapters in this book speak to this issue. See especially chapters 8, 9, 10, and 12.

commercial enterprises, shifty-eyed politicos, moms with axes to grind, and the rights and interests of all—the good and the bad—are the issues that clarify extralegal intrusions on the operation of the school. What happens on the national, state, and local scene is the product of organized efforts of unified groups of people arguing for this cause or against that school policy.

Schools are the closest community agency, geographically, psychologically, and economically. Geographically, the school is "just around the corner." Psychologically, everyone has gone to a school and may have children who are or have gone to a school, and all pay taxes to support the school. Opinions about what schools should look like, should do, and how much they should cost are wide and rampant.

There are many local groups and individuals whose attitudes and opinions influence the nature of school approaches and practices. The focus is on the informal political dimensions of school policy development. In this chapter, I address the nature of pressure groups and the nature of political pressure. And I establish some guidelines about how to deal positively with these pressures.

POWER AND INFLUENCE

Power and influence in a community are not haphazard. The exercise of power and influence requires organized and patterned relationships of groups and of individuals. But individuals and groups vary widely in the amount of influence they are able to exert on schools and other public services.

In many communities only a few persons may participate to any great extent in local issues and actions other than voting in formal elections, but on any given issue there may be broader participation depending on the nature of the issue and the psychological press the issue causes. Consider, for example, issues of school prayer or location of schools, or alleged racism, or creating barrier-free learning environments. Issues such as these often cause a great outpouring of community opinions and significant influence placed on school board members or legislators. These issues affect the children of the community and the pocketbooks of the citizens of the community.

Control of Resources. Having large resources at hand is a determinate of how much influence an individual or group may possess. Certainly high income or access to income, occupational standing, social standing, and so on are measures of how much influence a person may have. (Although some groups or individuals may not be wealthy, they often do have access to wealth.) This is a visible and acknowledgeable indication of potential for control, but potential for control is not control.

Potential for Unity. A high potential for control must be coupled with a high potential for unity for there to be power. Power is a function of a group's potential for control plus its potential for unity. Being able to unify a group about a single issue may overcome, in fact, the lack of material resources that the group has as it seeks to do or to undo a perceived right or wrong.

Generalized or Specialized? One can distinguish between members of the power structure by examining the nature of a member's influence. In some communities or on certain issues the ability to influence the opinions of others or the direction a particular public policy takes may be "specialized," that is, restricted to the issue or policy itself. For example, those members who are effective when trying to bring a professional athletic franchise to town or the members who are effective when attempting to establish a new public transportation system or the members whose interest is in locating a school in a particular area may differ widely, depending on the issue. Or, those who are powerful may influence decision making in all of those areas and most others of a community nature and thus would be "generalist" in their influence.

School leaders need to know this because it helps determine strategies for working within the community to get done what needs to get done.

Formal Political Power. The discussion to this point has been on informal power—the power individuals and groups have who have not been elected to anything or who do not hold any kind of public office. But aren't mayors important? Aren't police chiefs important? Aren't directors of public health important? Aren't school superintendents important? Aren't board members of various policy-making bodies important? Of course, and the powers of these respective offices are many. This is "official power," formal power. The question is often, though, what have been the characteristics of the nomination and selection process? How did these folks get those jobs and who might have been influential in that process?

But, I write in this chapter mostly about informal power at the local level. That's where the intensity and emotion so often manifest themselves. And, that's what causes the most intense headaches in school personnel.

The task confronting school leaders when confronted with groups or individuals who are interested in fomenting a change or addressing a perceived wrong is a complex one.

WHO ARE THESE PEOPLE?

What generally describes our society and most of the communities within our society—certainly, all well-populated areas—is *gesselschaft*. Gesselschaft, what on Earth is that? It is possible to distinguish communities by the nature of interactions that occur within that community. In the gesselschaft community, people are unified largely by civil units rather than by kinship ties. There is a proliferation of organizations—some for social reasons, some for political reasons. There is a general lack of knowledge about one's fellows and general anonymity. Formalized social controls—laws—are established to keep order.[2] Some have labeled this the "secular community." So, the people are many indeed and have multiple memberships and a plethora of beliefs and attitudes. Ideological unity does not describe our society.

Even within a specific issue, differences of opinion exist and complicate arriving at a just solution. It is common for one to hear the phrase: "Let's look at both sides of the issue." Okay, that's a start, but the reality is that many issues have more than two sides and that's where it begins to get complicated. The harried school person when faced with a conflict in the community that involves or revolves about the school often wishes there were only two sides—one side or another to choose from—but that isn't often the case.

For example, one might examine the issue of equity. What does achieving equity mean? Does it mean fair employment or equal opportunity? Does it mean affirmative action? Does it mean, simply, barrier-free schools and help for the disadvantaged? One gets answers on that issue that will be along a spectrum. Think of the statement "Yes, I'm for 'equity,' but that simply means a fair chance; but I'm not for giving some individuals an unequal shot at a job just because of their race or ethnicity." And, at this point, the arguments may really intensify. Similarly, the implementation of PL 94-142 presented a multitude of dilemmas. Educating all children irrespective of the nature of the handicap presents a host of conflict situations, from the development of an individual education plan to specific compensation for attendance at specially developed educational institutions.

Or, issues of what shall be taught, and the way it shall be taught, and when it should be taught present continuing problems not only within the education profession but also within communities. Are fine arts programs and physical education really necessary, especially when there is a budget crunch? Of what real value are such programs? And the selection of

---

[2]The opposite of gesselschaft is *gemeinschaft*. Gemeinschaft is at the other end of a continuum. It depicts a community wherein there are strong kinship ties and a general lack of special-interest groups. (There are few special interests; people see things similarly.) There is self-sufficiency and a strong sense of community identity. Of course, in any urban area one may find vestiges of the gemeinschaft. Early residents would house themselves in neighborhoods of their fellows. There are "little Italys," "little Saigons," "Chinatowns," and ghettos and barrios to be found in any city. These are manifestations of the gemeinschaft. But Western society as a whole must be characterized as gesellschaft and that is at the basis of many, if not most, community conflicts involving community agencies. Interested readers might enjoy reading the works of German sociologist Ferdinand Tönnies first published in 1887 in which he describes the derivation of the distinctions.

educational materials, including textbooks, creates situations that imperil good relations between the school and this or that community group. Is phonics the best way to teach children to read? When should books that discuss sex education be available? Should books that teach about sex education be available? Are the textbooks "Godless"? Should the textbooks be "Godless"? If not, would that mean no adequate presentation and discussion of the evolution of humankind? Or, does that mean "Creationism" must be taught? Or, does that mean neither of those but that the schools are simply too secular? And, what is "Godless" anyway? And on, and on. How many positions might one face about these issues? Clearly, many.

Official State Influence

Some states imbue official bodies such as an elected state board of education with broad powers; others imbue a regulatory agency such as a state education agency headed by an appointed commissioner or someone of like title. (Some states do both, but the respective powers and charters differ.) There are problems of influence whichever way is employed. The following is but an example.

Ivins and Dubose (2000) point out some problems that confront Texas schools, problems created by its elected state school board. For some years, the state board of education in Texas has been the target of candidates who, to quote Ivins and Dubose are from the "Christian right."

> Seven of the fifteen members are now Christian right, and they are sometimes joined by one or another of the "secular members" to do odd things. Not just predictable things like pushing phonics and school prayer; the Christian-right board members forced the state to dump its stock in the Walt Disney Company, which had been paying extremely handsome returns to the state school fund, on grounds that they didn't like the company's allowing a gay pride day at Disneyland." (p. 127)

Ivins and Dubose go on:

> For years the Board of Ed [sic] chose textbooks in a procedure dominated by . . . right wingers . . . . Because the state of Texas is such an enormous market, all of the national textbook publishers have to meet Texas standards, which is why a generation of American students never heard of Eleanor Roosevelt or the United Nations, mention of which our Board of Ed [sic] considered prima facie evidence of communist intent. The [state legislature] eventually solved most of the problem by simply taking away much of the board's authority. Vestigial problems keep cropping up, however." (p. 128)

The previous quotation described the downside of outside pressures on school practices. It is not the only "side," however.

IS THERE A BRIGHT SIDE?

Organized pressure and subsequent official action have been responsible for much in the way of positive change. Consider the changes that have occurred in sports activities for young women and girls. Title IX of the Education Amendment Act of 1972 (PL 92-318) did not come about without much organized effort from many local groups to provide equal opportunities for girls to participate in organized interscholastic athletic events.

Similarly, provisions for equity for mentally or physically challenged children only came about because of local community groups discussing the issues with legislators and school persons and ultimately being responsible for legislation and changes in local practices. The Americans with Disabilities Act in 1990 opened up sweeping provisions for students and employees for nonrestrictive learning and teaching environments.

The work of such groups as the American Center for Law and Justice, National Association for the Advancement of Colored People, American Civil Liberties Union, and the Anti-Defamation League among many others with national, state, and local affiliates has helped bring about much positive change. Other, less well known organizations and special-interest groups, some not formally organized and often only issues based, adopt an important watch-dog status on school practices. Each of these organizations— formal and well known or loosely knit and local only—demand loyalty from members and may at frequent times, rightfully or wrongly, demand changes in school policies and practices.

Neighborhood Influence Crowds

As communities have become more complex, influence groups have formed and re-formed in neighborhoods—almost a restatement of gemeinschaft. These have become increasingly influential in some urban areas, particularly in local issues that deal with public services such as schools, or zoning, or welfare delivery questions. Such interested groups may often reflect an ethnic, racial, religious, or economic identity. And such groups, in all but the most anomic neighborhoods, always have a few persons who are more influential and are opinion leaders.

These may be especially important within the school leader's sphere of action. It was noted earlier in this chapter that the specific schoolhouse, in most places, is the nearest community agency in geographic proximity and, for many persons, psychologically. Thus, it is convenient and accessible to residents of the neighborhood who have opinions to express. School leaders are in a particularly good position to sense feelings in the area and to be able to interact with neighborhood leaders.

There is much evidence to suggest that, even in these days of mass-media blitz, an individual's decision to support or not support or even be interested in a public issue is much dependent on his or her friends' and neighbors' opinions rather than on any outside information or data. So, school leaders need to learn about the leadership structure in the neighborhood and develop mechanisms to interact with members of this structure.

But what happens when there is disagreement, even hostility, to certain school practices and policies? How should the school leadership analyze, cope with, and deal effectively with opposition groups?

THE ORGANIZED OPPOSITION

I have written in a previously published work:

> Adversary groups may be the source of much community-school conflict. Moreover, many times such groups are much less formerly organized than [some of the groups] named earlier. In fact, one characteristic of many pressure groups is that they are temporal and amorphous, forming and re-forming around single issues only. These issues, however, are often predictable and negotiable. (Hughes and Hooper, 2000, p. 4)

Should any school person be surprised when there is opposition to certain school policies and practices? No. Public organizations are, indeed, *public* and to expect quietude and compliance always is hardly realistic.

Why should anyone be surprised when a school that has a biracial or multiethnic school population has, from time to time, discord and controversy? And why should the issue of bilingual instruction or that persons in the community are worried about drop-out rates and low test scores, or that some books and teaching materials have language or themes to which some object surprise anyone? Or, that not everyone says "hosanna" at the proposed location of a new school or the closing of another? Or, why should anyone be puzzled about disagreements about capital needs or admission policies or staff selection and assignment? Certain decisions that must be made and certain practices that must be carried out have the power to inflame some members of any community.

Not anticipating these and being unprepared to do something about the controversy is the problem. The answer is to anticipate these and other issues that may arise—and will arise in any active community—and develop policies and procedures to fairly resolve the issue. It isn't easy, of course, but good planning can help avoid the flashpoints.

NEGOTIATING WITH PRESSURE GROUPS

> The problem in an urbanized society such as we live in, with its evident cultural pluralism, is that various groups and individuals will . . . hold different perceptions of what the institutions serving that community ought to look like. The policies of confrontation and conflict within which schools and other social institutions are caught is simply a manifestation of this. (Hughes, 1976, pp. 2 and 3)

Being surprised at the appearance of groups or individuals who are not satisfied with particular schooling practices is an indication that school leaders have not been keeping in touch with the community served. Something is wrong with the feedback mechanisms.

Feedback Mechanisms

There are a number of devices that can be effectively implemented to improve community and school communication. Many schools are making good use of community advisory councils. In some states these are required. Parents, other community members, students, and sometimes school professionals are included in such groups. The group, however selected—and this does vary—meets regularly to examine school policies and discuss schooling issues. The role of the group is policy advising not policy making; it is not a mini–school board.

Review boards are often convened on an ad hoc basis to deal with censorship issues and other temporary kinds of concerns that have raised the ire of this or that community member.

Focus groups also have a role to play from time to time to define issues, anticipate problems, explore reaction to impending issues, develop alternative scenarios, and facilitate plans for the future. Focus groups have proved especially helpful in planning the location and nature of new schools.

Partnerships with community agencies and commercial enterprises have become more and more common. An avenue is provided for shared expertise and cooperation as well as a sharing of information.

Less formal occasional meetings with influential persons in the community—a key communicators group—can often be used to explore controversies, share information, and present arguments for a particular course of action as well as uncover potential problems. Care should be taken to ensure, to the degree possible, that the key communicator's group is indeed representative of the community.

Finally, school leaders should recognize that formal and informal parent-teacher conferences can be a rich source of information about developing community attitudes. Using feedback sheets and having conversations with participants may provide insights not otherwise obtainable.

SUMMARY

This chapter has been about the nature of pressure and politics on school practices. I began the chapter with an examination of the considerable role the federal government plays to influence formal education. Most of the content of the chapter, however, was on the local scene and the interplay of various groups—some specialized, some generalized—on schools and school leaders.

The nature of modern society, multiethnic and culturally plural, combined with an increasing cognizance of the role schools must perform to create the most equitable of social environments has intensified the interference of others in the operation of the schools. Both the positive and the negative aspects of these external forces have been discussed.

The chapter has concluded with a discussion of strategies to ameliorate the negative forces and capitalize on the positive forces. Two-way information exchange processes are recommended.

GUIDING QUESTIONS

1. Collect some demographic information about the neighborhoods your school serves. You will want such things as population patterns, income levels (census data will help with this, as will dwelling types), and ethnic and racial makeup of the adult and the student population, among other relevant demographic data. Now, respond to the following questions:

   a. Currently, what communication instruments are in use in your school? Are there regular newsletters? How do messages from the school get transmitted to the neighborhood? Are parents the group of adults that are receiving the messages? Are there any two-way communication mechanisms (advisory councils, key communicator groups, review boards, etc.)? What means are used to related to those in the community who are not parents of schoolchildren?

b. Identify any recent or existing issue of conflict that has occurred in your school and school community. How was this resolved or is it being addressed?

c. How would you evaluate the quality of school-community interaction at the present time? Could there be improvement? What would you suggest as changes?

2. Case Study

You sit as a member of an in-school professional advisory team that is now having its twice-monthly regular meeting. Your middle school has an enrollment of 1,200 students, about a third of whom are bussed in. The school enrollment is 35% Anglo, 30% African American, 25% Latino, and 10% Asian.

Among the issues on the agenda today is a charge by two prominent members of the PTO that the required reading lists of two of the eighth-level teachers contain books that are "offensive and inappropriate" for students. The particular books in question are *Huckleberry Finn*, *Lord of the Flies*, *Go Ask Alice*, and *Catcher in the Rye*.

The charges include that the books use profane, vulgar, and offensive language; focus on inappropriate behavior including drug taking, suicide, and disrespect of government; and are antireligious.

One of the protesting parents is Anglo, the other is African American. They are not together. They have appeared separately and filed their protests separately, and they disagree about which of the books are offensive.

a. Make and state any assumptions about the school and situation that are consistent with the information above but are important to your consideration of a solution.

b. What do you believe are the main issues in this problem?

c. What procedures will you encourage your fellow group members to develop to resolve these issues?

d. How would you resolve this case?

SELECTED READINGS

Duke, Daniel L. (2004). *The challenges of educational change.* Boston: Allyn & Bacon. See chapters 7 and 9, especially.

Hughes, Larry W. (1976). *Informal and formal community forces: External influences on schools and teachers.* Morristown, NJ: General Learning Press.

Hughes, Larry W., & Hooper, Don W. (2000). *Public relations for school leaders.* Boston: Allyn & Bacon.

Ivins, Molly, & Dubose, Lou. (2000). *The short but happy political life of George W. Bush.* New York: Random House.

Spring, Joel. (2002). *Political agendas for education* (2nd ed.). Mahwah, NJ: Lawrence Erlbaum Associates.

St. John, Edward P., & Clements, Margaret M. (2004). "Public opinion and political contexts. In Theodore J. Kowalski (Ed.), *Public relations in schools* (3rd ed., chapter 3). Columbus, Ohio: Pearson Prentice-Hall.

Wayson, William W., Achilles, Charles M., Pinnell, Gay Su, Lintz, M. Nan, Carrol, Lila N., & Cunningham, Luvern. (1988). *Handbook for developing public confidence in schools.* Blooming-ton, Indiana: Phi Delta Kappa Educational Foundation. Don't let the copyright date be misleading. This is still the best single guidebook that is published. It is up to date and it is penetrating and practical.

REFERENCES

Brown v. Board of Education of Topeka, 347 U.S. 483, 493 (1954).

Goss v. Lopez, 419 U.S. 565 (1975). Suspension of students from school was the issue in this case.

Hughes, Larry W. (1976). *Informal and formal community forces: External influences on schools and teachers.* Morristown, NJ: General Learning Press.

Hughes, Larry W., & Hooper, Don W. (2000). *Public relations for school leaders.* Boston: Allyn & Bacon.

Ivins, Molly, & Dubose, Lou. (2000). *The short but happy political life of George W. Bush.* New York: Random House.

Plessy v. Ferguson, 41 L. Ed. 256 (1896). "Separate but equal" publicly supported schools are permitted in the instance of race.

Tinker v. Des Moines, 89 S.Ct. 733 (1969). The issue was the first amendment rights of students.

Tönnies, Ferdinand. (1887). *Fundamentals of sociology* (Translated and supplemented by C.T. Loomis [1940] from *Gemeinschaft and gesselschaft,* 1st ed.). New York: American Book Company.

Ubben, Gerald C., Hughes, Larry W., & Norris, Cynthia J. (2004). *The principal: Creative leadership for excellence in schools* (5th ed.). Boston: Allyn & Bacon. See chapter 15, especially.

West Virginia v. Barnett, 319 U.S. 624 (1943). This decision applied the 14th Amendment to "States and all of its creatures—school boards not excepted. These boards of education have, of course, important, delicate and highly discretionary functions, but none that they may perform except within the limits of the Bill of Rights."

Chapter 2

Violence and Threats of Violence

Ronnie Casella
Central Connecticut State University

In a school district meeting, officials discussed an incident that had occurred in a high school. An African American boy had fought after school but on school grounds with a white student, and though nobody was hurt, both of the boys had thrown punches. The white student was on the honor roll and a star athlete. The African American student was new to the district and was one of only a handful of black students in the school; he was also in special education classes, having been diagnosed with a behavioral disorder in his previous school. After the fight, the African American student claimed that the white student had taunted him in the past. The white student claimed that he had never spoken to the African American student, let alone taunted him.

When the district officials discussed the incident, important issues were raised about youth violence and responses to violence in schools. One official wanted to suspend the African American boy for starting the fight, and another insisted that both boys be expelled because each had violated the school's zero-tolerance policy. One official felt that the boys should be required to attend peer mediation and perform some type of community service but not be suspended or expelled. Another felt that they should be arrested and charged with "breach of peace." The one who recommended peer mediation and community service felt that the African American student should be given a second chance because he was "disadvantaged" and "special ed," and a second official responded that the boy would never "learn his lesson" if he "got away with it." Some officials wanted to explore whether the white boy had taunted the other boy, and if these were "racial taunts." One official wanted to let the whole thing blow over, stating, "it was only a tussle between two boys."

How should this incident be interpreted? Certainly, more information is needed: What were the circumstances leading up to the fight? How old were the students? If one or both were suspended or expelled, what would happen to them? Do they have a history of fighting? However, even if we got the so-called facts of the incident, we would still face ambiguities based on our own thoughts about the situation and may disagree on how the problem should be solved. This occurs partly because we all have different ideas about violence (even different definitions of what is and what is not violent); we have different feelings about youths and how they should be treated; and we also have different levels of understanding about the responsibilities of school officials.

   This chapter is meant to provide some background information and context relating to school violence. It should help you to understand the complexities of the issue when making your decision about what to do about the situation involving the two boys—or other situations you may encounter.

THEORIES OF VIOLENCE AND THEIR INFLUENCE ON VIOLENCE-PREVENTION EFFORTS

There are several theories of violence that can influence your thinking about a violent situation. At one level, these theories are ways of thinking about why individuals act violently. Not only do they represent a theoretical perspective, but they also shape officials' responses to violence. For example, if violence is viewed as a manifestation of a youth's economic background, an intervention addressing poverty and other social problems may be developed. However, if violence is viewed as a manifestation of poor decision-making skills, an entirely different type of intervention based on education may be implemented. The following four theories of violence are the most common and influential in shaping school officials' responses to violent behavior.

Cognitive Theory of Violence

One theory views violence as "learned behavior," an outcome of students appropriating from their peers and popular culture aggressive behavior and then considering violence a norm that they then replicate in their own interactions with others. In this case, the individual is viewed as lacking the skills necessary to solve conflicts peacefully. To eradicate violence, then, individuals propose various forms of educational activities, such as Drug Abuse Resistance Education (DARE) or character education, to teach individuals that violence is wrong and then to work with them in order to change their behaviors. These attempts draw from ideas associated with cognitive development, social psychological balance theories, and conflict theories, and attempt to give students the skills, education, and reasoning needed to avoid conflicts. In many schools, for example, peer-mediation programs are viewed, in part, as a means of teaching mediators conflict-resolution skills that would help them not only in school but also with their families and peers outside of school. Character education programs such as Second Step also intend to teach students how to behave properly.

Rational Choice Theory of Violence

Another theory, called rational choice theory, could be renamed the "crime pays" theory and was given impetus by strains of criminology, political science, law, and the economics of crime. Those who adhere to rational choice theory believe that individuals weigh the consequences of a violent crime against the possible benefits and make the rational choice to be violent. In a sense, individuals determine that "crime pays." This theory originated from the classical school of criminology in 18th-century Europe and England with Cesare Beccaria and Jeremy Bentham and has continued today in the actions of those who, for example, espouse the building of more prisons and who advocate for stiffer punishments—and in schools, specifically, by those who espouse zero-tolerance policies and greater use of security technology. To address violence in this case, one would not attempt to teach students how to behave; one assumes that the youth already knows how to behave. The point is to sway the student to behave properly through threats, sanctions, and other actions that would convince the rational thinker to act appropriately. According to rational choice theory, because people make the rational choice to be violent, society must make violence a less desirable option. Hence, the logical deterrent to violence is to punish violent individuals more severely and to prevent violent crime through surveillance, which makes violence—to the rational, economic mind—simply not worth it. School policing is also a form of violence prevention that is motivated by rational choice theory.

Biological Theory of Violence

With the resurgence of biological theories in the social sciences in the latter part of the 20th century—which was spurred on by DNA and brain research as well as certain publications such as the *The Bell Curve*—the biological theory views violence as innate to particular individuals. At times, biological theories of violence are not unlike eugenic explanations of criminal behavior put forth by Cesare Lombroso in the 19th century. According to Lombroso, criminal tendencies could be identified in people's physical and psychological "stigmata"—essentially, in ones natural makeup. The biological theory of violence would not blame youths' poor reasoning or lack of education; adults would put the onus of the blame on the genetic constitution of particular youths. They'd be able to identify the problem through science, brain scans, and genes. In this case, people are "born criminals," and violence prevention would have less to do with skills building and police and more to do with gene therapy and medication. Hence, those combating violence may turn to the health sciences for cures. The extent to which some individuals at schools subscribe to this view is made evident in their use of prescription drugs on students (Ritalin, for example) and their belief that some students are destined not only for prison, but also for inferior lives as poor laborers or welfare recipients.

Structural Theory of Violence

With a history closely linked to the New Deal, War on Poverty, Great Society, and other social meliorism efforts, structural theory views violence as a consequence of one's economic and cultural background. Drawing its ideas from liberal ideologies, social ecology, and in some cases deficit theories, violence in this case is viewed as a systemic problem having to do with inequities in the world and a general breakdown of relations between people. In this case, violence has structural roots—it is not a disease located in the body or the mind, but rather it is a discordance in the community, where long-term and ingrained social and economic factors produce violent behavior. When school officials seek community involvement, or aim to solve problems associated with racism, poverty, and other social ills, they are often working from a structural point of view. According to structural theory, one must revitalize communities, improve the lives of individuals, and provide basic necessities in order to solve problems of violence. Though school officials often see the legitimacy of structural theory, they often consider structural solutions outside the bounds of schooling: According to many school officials, this is the realm of social work and community activism, not schooling.

When we think of the range of measures that are taken in schools to address aggressive and violent behavior, we can see how each is linked to one or more theory bases. For example, when a school official believes that conflict-resolution classes for youths are the best way to address aggression in schools, she is working from a cognitive theory base, following a belief in the possibility of "teaching" youngsters how not to be violent. When this is dismissed by another official, who may feel that surveillance cameras in all classrooms should be mounted (as a school did in Biloxi, Alabama, in 2003), it is likely that this official is in favor of a rational choice theory, one that states that surveillance will convince individuals not to act inappropriately. Others who believe the problem is biological may wish to have aggressive youths tested for disorders. And others may believe that the root of the problem can be found in the circumstances and environment of the youths and may seek to create partnerships with community groups and to support aid to poor students. Most people believe in more than one of these theories and may advocate for surveillance cameras and medication, for example. In addition to shaping the way we interpret situations and how we respond, the theories also influence the nature and environment of schooling; certainly the school in Biloxi that opened in September 2003 with more than 500 security cameras in the building is going to look different than the school that has yet to buy into surveillance technology but has developed well-institutionalized peer mediation and restorative justice programs.

However, while theories may give us the rationale for the choices we make about prevention strategies, no individual is simply guided by theories. School officials also respond to policies and federal and state mandates. In the next section, we examine some of the more recent and well-known federal policies related to school violence.

OVERVIEW OF SCHOOL VIOLENCE POLICIES

Concerns about violence have a long history. The first 19th-century common schools were developed partly to curb teenage delinquency—to "tame" new immigrants and "savage" American Indians. Later in the 1960s and 1970s as greater numbers of students rebelled against injustice and authority, discussions about school violence became more heated, culminating in 1977 with the *Safe School Study* (National Institute of Education, 1977) mandated by the U.S. Congress. More recently, crime prevention legislation that has focused specifically on schools has been passed by the federal government, including the Drug-Free Schools and Communities Act (1986), Gun-Free School Zones Act (1990), Safe Schools Act (1994), the Gun-Free Schools Act (1994), and the Safe and Drug-Free Schools and Communities Act (1994). Sometimes funded or mandated through this legislation, many schools in the United States have also made greater use of school police (sometimes called "school safety officers" or "school resource officers") and various forms of security technology (metal detectors, surveillance cameras, biometric equipment, and automatic locking doors). In many cases, violence prevention efforts are supported by federal and state appropriations that provide funding (along with mandates) that make it possible for school officials to invest in the efforts.

The 1977 *Safe School Study* was the first major federal study on violence. It found that violence was a significant problem in schools and that lax and inconsistent discipline by school officials can contribute to the problem. Though this was a major $2.4 million quantitative and qualitative study and the document was distributed by the National Institute of Education, federal legislation having to do with violence did not occur until a decade later. The 1986 Drug-Free Schools and Communities Act did not deal specifically with weapons and violence, but its focus on drugs was meant to ameliorate other social problems, including violence. The act appropriated federal money for school districts and police departments to develop liaisons to sustain the DARE program in schools, as well as other antidrug efforts involving the police, community groups, early intervention groups, and ex-drug users.

More specific legislation having to do with school violence began in the 1990s. The Crime Control Act of 1990, which was a very broad crime control policy, included one section called the Gun-Free School Zones Act. This act made it unlawful to carry a gun within 1,000 feet of school property or a municipal playground. Yet although it is not unlikely that one will see signs around schools stating that the area is a "drug-free zone," we do not see signs reading "gun-free zone." This is because the Gun-Free Schools Zones Act was overturned and declared unconstitutional in the 1994 Supreme Court case *United States v. Lopez*, a case heavily backed by the National Rifle Association.

One significant federal initiative of the early 1990s was not a policy or law, but a well-publicized document, *America 2000*, which was released by the National Governors' Association and President's Education Summit (1991) during the administration of George Bush (Sr.). The document included six goals, one of which stated, "Every school in America will be free of drugs and violence and will offer a disciplined environment conducive to learning"(p. 1). In response to *America 2000*, Congress passed the Safe and Drug-Free Schools and Communities Act of 1994, which stated, "Drug and violence prevention programs are essential components of a comprehensive strategy to promote school safety and to reduce the demand for and use of drugs throughout the Nation." This made available funding for training, development, technical assistance, and programs responding to violence in schools. The nature of these efforts was established by the Safe Schools Act of 1994, which appropriated up to $3,000,000 for schools to develop violence-prevention programs that would lead to collaborations between community-based organizations. These organizations needed to demonstrate, according to the policy, a strong local commitment:

> to the formation of partnerships among the local educational agency, a community-based organization, a nonprofit organization with a demonstrated commitment to or expertise in developing education programs or providing educational services to students or the public, a local law enforcement agency, or any combination thereof; and a high level of youth participation in such projects or activities.

Because the focus of the Safe Schools Act was on partnerships and violence-prevention programs (and not security), only 5 % of a grant could be used for metal detectors and security personnel. But in 1998, U.S. Representative Martin Frost (D-Texas) introduced a bill through the Safe Schools Act that would establish a $175 million initiative to help schools hire police officers. Also in 1998, police officers got their own boost with an amendment to the Omnibus Crime Control and Safe Streets Act of 1968. The amendment established school-based partnerships between local law enforcement agencies and local school systems "by using school resource officers who operate in and around elementary and secondary schools to combat school-related crime and disorder problems, gangs, and drug activities."

Like the Safe Schools Act, the Gun-Free Schools Act of 1994 was part of President Clinton's Goals 2000: Educate America Act. But unlike the Safe Schools Act, which awarded grants for violence-prevention initiatives, the Gun-Free Schools Act was a disciplinary mandate, stating:

> No assistance may be provided to any local educational agency under this Act unless such agency has in effect a policy requiring the expulsion from school for a period of not less than one year of any student who is determined to have brought a weapon to a school under the jurisdiction of the agency except such policy may allow the chief administering officer of the agency to modify such expulsion requirement for a student on a case-by-case basis.

Since the enactment of the Gun-Free Schools Act, amendments have been made to extend the legislation's application. In 1995, the word "firearms" was amended to read "weapons." This made it possible for school personnel to expel students in possession of not only the broader category of "weapons," but also items that can be used as weapons, such as nail clippers, files, and pocket knives. In addition, in 1997, Senator Jesse Helms introduced an amendment that enabled local educational agencies to expel not only students carrying weapons, but also students in possession of an illegal drug or drug paraphernalia. As decision makers in states and municipalities adopted the policy, they too included less serious violations punishable by zero-tolerance standards.

Under George W. Bush, violence-prevention policy was incorporated in far-reaching education law: the No Child Left Behind law, passed in 2002. This law enables students to transfer to another school if their school is determined to be a "persistently dangerous school": in 2003, two schools in New York City were determined "persistently dangerous schools" and the students starting the school year were allowed to apply for transferals to other schools. The law also provides funding for the School Security Technology Center (SSTC) at Sandia National Laboratories. Located in Albuquerque, New Mexico, Sandia employs more than 8,000 scientists, engineers, mathematicians, technicians, and support personnel; the laboratory was established in 1941 by the U.S. Department of Energy to support its nuclear weapons program. SSTC distributes information about school security and trains school employees on choosing and using the right technology for their schools (Green, 1999). SSTC is also involved in several security initiatives, including working with Albuquerque public schools to implement a system that uses hand geometry to identify parents and guardians of children. When parents or guardians register their children, they are assigned a personal identification number (PIN) and are asked to place their hand on a pad that uses biometric technology to record their hand features. Each time someone goes to school to pick up a child, he or she enters the PIN and places a hand on the pad. If the PIN and the hand geometry match the information in the system, the person is allowed to take the child.

Beginning in 2003, when schools were identified as potential sites for terrorist attacks, the newly created U.S. Department of Homeland Security made funds available to schools to purchase the biometric equipment being used in the Albuquerque schools or the surveillance equipment in the classrooms in the Biloxi school. The U.S. Department of Homeland Security appropriated over $350 million for, among other things, hiring high school police officers and buying security equipment through its Public Safety and Community Policing Grants program. Other departments that offer funds for similar goals include the U.S. Department of the Treasury (through its Safe Schools Initiative, which also funds research conducted by the U.S. Secret Service), the U.S. Department of Education (through its Emergency Response and Crisis Management Grant Program and its Safe and Drug-Free Schools and Communities Act), and the U.S. Department of Justice.

There has been much disagreement about the nature of violence-prevention policy: Should we mount surveillance cameras in all classrooms, and should it be public tax money that pays for this? Is peer mediation enough or is money and time wasted and better spent on police and greater security? How effective is federal policy, and is it always fair? In some cases, policy disagreements involve tensions between the rights of students and the rights of school administrators. A major criticism of zero-tolerance policy, for example, involves whether it is overly punitive and denies young people the right of an education. As mentioned earlier, zero-tolerance policy has been an influential force on discipline policy. Originally intended as a means of dealing with gun violence (through the Gun-Free Schools Act of 1994), many schools have adopted a zero-tolerance policy for fighting, threats, absenteeism, and other less serious violations, raising the question about whether it is too draconian (Ayers, Dohrn, & Ayers, 2001). Also, there is mounting evidence that suggests that the policy can potentially single out minorities and those who are not doing well in school. Individuals wonder if it makes sense to expel students—does expulsion solve the problem, or make the problem worse? And are there alternatives to zero-tolerance policy that are not detrimental to students, but also force students to be responsible for their actions?

Whereas this section has provided a general overview of violence policy, the next section hones in on one of these policies: The Gun-Free Schools Act, and more specifically, zero-tolerance policy. The section discusses the rationale behind zero-tolerance policy: It lays out what advocates claim. It also discusses potential consequences, and because the policy can have serious consequences for students, the section also discusses alternatives to the policy.

ZERO-TOLERANCE POLICY

The implementation of zero-tolerance policy in schools has caused much controversy. Although considered overly punitive by some, the "get tough" policies are hailed by others as a significant factor accounting for reduced rates of crime and violence in the 1990s. An outcome of the Gun-Free Schools Act of 1994, which mandated that students bringing firearms to schools be expelled for at least one school year, zero-tolerance policy represents a form of discipline based on preventative detention. The idea of preventative detention has played a significant role in national crime policy in the 1990s: the idea is that you isolate or "detain" individuals as a way of preventing serious crime. Harsh sentencing for drug offenses is an example of this; so is expulsion for relatively minor school violations. Although zero-tolerance policy may have been a rational, short-term response to what appeared to be an epidemic of lethal violence in schools in the 1990s, the implementation of the policy reveals consequences that were not intended by legislators and administrators who wanted to put a halt to school shootings.

There are several aspects of zero-tolerance policy that provide its rationale. Supporters will claim that zero-tolerance policy was never meant to be the sole means of disciplining students and is not just a punishment, but also a deterrent. The rationale for zero tolerance includes the following:

- Many forms of violence prevention are needed in a school, and zero-tolerance policy is one of them. It can be used as a last resort or as a whole-school violence-prevention package that includes peer mediation, counseling, and conflict-resolution programs. The policy aims to prevent trouble by identifying potentially dangerous individuals; it is proactive, rather than reactive.
- Zero tolerance concretizes discipline policy for schools where enforcement of discipline has become lax; these are schools that are made more dangerous and chaotic by school personnel who have given up

on trying to control students. Supporters of zero-tolerance policy understand that discipline should not be overly punitive and unfair, and point to zero-tolerance policy as a way of bringing uniformity to disparate and sometimes racist discipline polices in schools.

- Like minimum sentencing laws and habitual-offender statutes, zero tolerance is based on preventative detention. This is a criminal justice paradigm that has been used nationally to combat drug dealing and other forms of street crime. The policy acts to apprehend, separate, and detain those who display dangerous behaviors in order to protect innocent people.

- The underlying theory for zero-tolerance policy is rational choice theory, which states that individuals choose among a number of options of behavior before acting. In a rational sort of way, zero-tolerance policy convinces students that they will be punished severely if they misbehave, therefore it is a deterrence.

Supporters of zero-tolerance policy will also cite research and anecdotal evidence that demonstrate that students become accustomed to the new expectations and strict responses to misbehavior that zero-tolerance policy introduces to schools. There is evidence that suggests that violence and criminality decreased across the United States after the implementation of zero-tolerance policy as both crime policy at the national level and school policy through the Gun-Free Schools Act. Additionally, zero-tolerance policy is viewed as a necessary policy in the event that other forms of discipline and violence prevention do not work.

However, when zero-tolerance policy is implemented, potentially there are long-term consequences that exceed the duration of a suspension or expulsion from school. Those who are critical of zero-tolerance policy are usually those who have had opportunities to see how the policy is sometimes implemented in schools and are therefore familiar with consequences involving the following:

- If discipline policy calls for punishing all individuals caught in confrontations, then poor youths will be punished most, because they are more likely to be involved in confrontations than middle-class youths due primarily to structural factors involving high rates of violence in neighborhoods and families, social isolation, and lack of opportunities leading to economic and social success. In addition, punitive discipline negatively affects poor students because it supports practices that can be, at the very least, biased and sometimes racist.

- Zero-tolerance punishment negatively affects those who are already negatively affected by poverty, racism, and academic failure. Tied to this is the greater difficulty these youths have when trying to recoup after being expelled or suspended from school. Ultimately, due partly to their circumstances and their lack of social capital, these youths are penalized more severely than those who can bounce back from a suspension or expulsion.

- Since the enactment of the Gun-Free Schools Act, amendments have been made at local and national levels to extend the legislation's application. This has led to cases involving students who are expelled for minor infractions. As decision makers in states and municipalities adopted the policy, they too included less serious violations punishable by zero-tolerance standards.

- Under zero-tolerance policy, violence is conflated into one category of behavior that encompasses a broad range of conflicts, violations, and confrontations. Confrontations are not the same as violence, and yet those who are involved in confrontations are sometimes punished as if they had acted violently.

Zero-tolerance policy can create blockades for all students. But for some, the policy adds another risk factor to lives that are already overburdened with risk factors, especially for poor youths of color. Though zero tolerance may have a deterring effect, in many cases rather than learn not to break the law, many youths learn to live within the lawbreaker institutions. In addition, though deterred in school, many youths take their troubles elsewhere, usually to neighborhoods or to their homes. Although some students may have the support and knowhow to wrangle their way back to success after an expulsion, suspension, or out-placement, other students cannot. Hence, applying the policy consistently does not mean that all students receive the same punishment.

In order to avoid long-term consequences, discipline policy must be fundamentally different from the criminal justice paradigm of zero-tolerance policy. The alternatives presented in the following initiatives are possible changes that schools can make even within constrained work conditions, but certainly not without the commitment of policy makers, administrators, teachers, and all school staff who must reject the easy acceptance of out-placement and arrest as a means of school discipline. The first two refer to violence prevention, the second two refer to disciplinary actions.

- Make available and publicize mentoring and tutoring programs for all students. Have ongoing peer mediation, student support teams, and other forms of effective conflict-resolution programs. Encourage the study of character and social well-being in academic coursework, and give more time for counselors and teachers to get to know students.

- Have students form a student government that represents the concerns of all students to administrators. Make youths part of the solution through governance councils and interventions participated in by all students. This would have to coincide with other efforts to reduce or eliminate exclusionary practices in schools that segregate students and therefore ferment violent circumstances.

In the event that there is misbehavior or potentially dangerous behavior in spite of the best efforts of school staff to prevent it, the following steps could be taken.

- Institute a program of school service to replace out-of-school suspension, based on a model of restorative justice. Have in-school suspension that is accompanied by academic work, tutoring, or community or school service. In addition, schedule times during the week for school staff to meet with parents or guardians of students who continuously violate school policies.
- Develop "discipline contracts" that students and school staff must abide by. Offer victim services so that victims have opportunities for involvement and input in deciding what actions should be taken by the offender and the school to restore peace. A longer term "problem-solving plan" can also be developed, with a system of "student check-ins," in which the student is required to meet with an adult or older student to discuss weekly progress regarding the problem-solving plan.

These violence-prevention initiatives and disciplinary actions will not guarantee a problem-free school and are meant to address more subtle, yet serious, problems that promote everyday unruliness. Although moderate in scope, the initiatives still may be unrealistic in some schools. However, this is why violence prevention, conflict resolution, and nearly all forms of school improvement need the buy-in of policy makers, legislators, and administrators who can provide the fiscal and organizational support such initiatives require. The initiatives aim not only to hold students accountable and to deter violent actions, but also to keep students in school and on a path to success, which is where zero-tolerance policy falls short.

VIOLENCE AND SPECIAL EDUCATION POLICY

The number of students identified with behavioral problems is a significant proportion of the roughly six million youths (more than one of every eight) who receive special education services in the United States (General Accounting Office, 2001). As students with physical disabilities are increasingly accepted in mainstream classes due in part to the inclusion movement, there is growing evidence that students with behavioral problems are filling the newly vacated special education spaces. The 1997 reauthorization of the Individuals with Disabilities Education Act (IDEA) was, in a part, a response to increased numbers of youths in special education programs due to diagnoses related to their behavior. The amendments focused almost entirely on discipline requirements for aggressive and misbehaving students, the placement and protections of students who are being disciplined because of their behaviors, and regulations involving students caught with weapons in school.

IDEA defines disabilities to include a number of emotional and physical impairments, including mental retardation; hearing, speech, or language impairments; orthopedic impairments; serious emotional disturbance; autism; traumatic brain injury; other health impairments; or specific learning disabilities. Along with its earlier version, Education for All Handicapped Children Act, IDEA includes what are essentially behavioral problems, especially in regard to "serious emotional disturbance" (SED) and "other health impaired" (OHI). These are diagnoses for children who act aggressively, are self-destructive, or possess one of several types of behavioral disorders (BD) or conduct disorders (CD).

It is telling that the most comprehensive and significant form of legislation having to do with special education services is largely about dealing with aggressive and violent children; along with the cost of special education, what is often debated during reauthorizations of IDEA (this was true in 1997 and 2002) has been discipline issues and the related issues of racial and social class disparities involving both suspension/expulsion rates and special education placements. The merging of violence policy (especially the Gun-Free Schools Act) and special education policy (especially IDEA) was seen, as well, in a General Accounting Office (2001) report to the Committees on Appropriations of the U.S. Senate and House of Representatives on school discipline and the Individuals with Disabilities Education Act, which stated in its opening sentences:

Maintaining discipline and safety in America's public schools is a key concern of school officials, parents, and policymakers nationwide. The public expects schools to operate in an orderly environment free from violence. Standards for discipline and safety in schools are set primarily by local school districts. In recent years, however, federal law has required states and local districts to implement certain discipline-related policies in schools—for example, through provisions of the Gun-Free Schools Act and the Individuals with Disabilities Education Act (IDEA).

IDEA defines "serious emotional disturbance" in a fashion that only hints at the possibility that the student labeled SED is aggressive or hostile; rather, the essence of the label is meant to identify students who appear detached, alienated, depressed, or suicidal. A "serious emotional disturbance" as stated in IDEA included five characteristics, one or more of which must be evident over a long period of time and to a marked degree and must have an adverse effect on educational performance. The categories include:

1. An inability to learn that cannot be explained by intellectual, sensory, or health factors.
2. An inability to build or maintain satisfactory interpersonal relationships with peers and teachers.
3. Inappropriate types of behavior or feelings under normal circumstances.
4. A general pervasive mood of unhappiness or depression.
5. A tendency to develop physical symptoms or fears associated with personal school problems.

When acts of misbehavior and aggression in schools are viewed as manifestations of a serious emotional disturbance, special education can become a placement for students who are not disabled in the traditional sense, and not just those with a "pervasive mood of unhappiness or depression," but also those who are deemed hostile or potentially violent. The protections that IDEA provides for these students (generally labeled SED or OHI) have been modified over time. Before the 1997 reauthorization of IDEA, a student with a disability could be removed from school for up to 45 days to an interim alternative educational setting for carrying a firearm. Although this placed a restriction on the Gun-Free Schools Act, which stated that students should be expelled for no less than 1 year for the same violation, the 1999 regulations that were mandated 2 years after the reauthorization modified this provision. When its proposed regulations were made public, and during hearings and through the solicitation of nearly 6,000 public comments on the proposed legislation, school administrators reported that they would be hindered in their efforts to provide a safe environment in schools if they were restricted in disciplining students in the ways outlined in the proposed legislation.

Under the revised law, students in special education programs who have been found with any weapon (not just a firearm), or possess, use, sell, or solicit drugs in school or at school functions, as well as disabled students determined by a hearing officer to be so dangerous that the student's behavior is "substantially likely to result in injury to the child or others"—these students too can also be suspended for up to 45 days. These out-placements can also be extended in 45-day increments if it is determined by a hearing officer that the student still poses a risk. IDEA also states that disciplinary procedures for nondisabled students may be applied to those with disabilities if an Individualized Education Plan (IEP) review determines that a disability did not impair a student's ability to understand the impact and consequences of his or her behavior, or to control the behavior, and if appropriate due process standards are met. In the end, the 1997 reauthorization of IDEA granted much latitude to school districts to discipline students in special education programs for misconduct and to maintain a student's special education placement, (even against the wishes of the student and the student's family) if the student is deemed a behavioral problem.

There has been a similar trend in court decisions as well, where state and federal courts have distinguished between disabilities based on physicality and those based on behavior. Their rulings sometimes suggest differential treatment, whereby students with behavioral disabilities are afforded fewer rights to protest their special education placements. The inclusion movement and the precedent-setting cases of *Daniel R. R. v. State Board of Education* (1989), *Greer v. Rome City School District* (1991), *Oberti v. Board of Education of Clementon School District* (1993), and other cases have been interpreted as supporting the mainstreaming and inclusion of students with disabilities, argued on the grounds that schools must accept and enforce the provision in IDEA of "least restrictive environment." However, in all of the cases that have supported inclusion, the students were not considered a behavioral problem.

The first appellate court decision involving whether a child who was categorized with a "serious emotional disturbance" could be placed in special education against the wishes of the parents was decided in *Clyde K. v. Pulyallup School District* in 1994. In this case, the court ruled in favor of the special education placement after considering the academic and nonacademic benefits of regular education and the effects of disruptive behavior on other children and on the teaching and learning process. In so doing, it supported the right of administrators to keep students in special education placements, and sometimes special education out-placements (in mental health facilities, for example), in spite of the "stay put" provision of IDEA, which states that students remain in school while their cases are being considered and due process is being applied. In the case of *Light v. Parkway School District* in 1994, the courts stated that a court injunction to expel a student beyond what is allowable by law is possible if it is determined that a student is substantially likely to cause injury and the school has made reasonable efforts to ameliorate the problem behavior through the use of supplementary aids and services.

Additionally, public schools can request injunctive relief from the courts to prevent the return of a child to his or her prior placement. In terms of suspension, the reauthorization stated that schools were permitted to suspend a child in special education for up to 10 days in a given school year without providing educational services or an out-placement. If the misconduct is not a manifestation of the student's disability, then the child can be suspended for more than 10 school days, but must be placed in a facility that can provide for his or her education. The final regulations require a "manifestation determination" (to assess whether the student's misconduct was caused by his or her disability), a Planning and Placement Team meeting (to determine a student's placement while out of school), as well as an IEP. Although some have seen these provisions as a way of safeguarding both the school and the student, others feel that they create a bureaucratic system of paperwork that does little to protect students and expands the rights of schools to apply zero-tolerance policy to students diagnosed with behavioral disorders.

SUMMARY

A central point of this chapter is that school violence encapsulates a range of policies and disciplinary actions used by school officials to respond to threats of violence. In other words, a fight between two students is one aspect of school violence; but other aspects include the policies that are in place to deal with the fight and the responses to the fight by administrators (and in many cases police officers and judiciary officials).

Before examining any form of violence, it is important to understand how you understand violence. Before a violent incident occurs, we already have ideas about how to interpret the incident, because we have all been inculcated with various notions about violence. Political ideals, thoughts about crime, feelings about youths, ideas about school, our own experiences, and much more impact how we react to violent incidents. There are different ways of interpreting causes of violence and various theories that become part of our everyday discourse and ways of thinking about crime and violence. Certainly, school officials do not propose violence-prevention efforts by summoning a theory base. Nobody goes around saying, "I'm a rational choice theory type of person, so let's hire more police and expand our zero-tolerance policy." Rather, they see a problem (and in some cases, imagine a problem) and then propose a solution. But the solutions they propose are in some ways based on theories which circulate in our society and shape the way we think about violence, though, in most cases, we are unaware of these theories or their effect on our reasoning.

Responses to violence encompass many aspects of school practices and organization; individuals respond within a school culture and according to the types of services that are available. In addition, school policy influences decisions. Policies also change the nature and look of schools (the installation of security technology); they lead to the development of new professions (school resource officers); and have altered other school-related practices, such as special education programs. The types of services that are available, the extent of a school's special education program, the nature of policies and laws, theories related to violence, and the culture of schools all participate in the choices that are made by school personnel.

Being able to form your own judgments about violence and responses to violence is an important skill. How then would you respond to the incident discussed in the introduction of this chapter? How would you treat the African American boy now that you have some understanding of the role of special education policy related to violence policy? Should it matter to you that a discipline policy may have long-term consequences? What policies should be considered or adopted that may help you to avoid similar situations? The following interview excerpts and questions aim to help school professionals to understand violence in relation to the topics raised in this chapter.

GUIDING QUESTIONS

1. Read the following interview excerpt by an 18-year-old Latina who was the only girl in her immediate and extended family to graduate from high school. What may be the theory or theories that guide her interpretation of high school? What indicates that to you? What theory may she oppose?

What most people don't understand is that most of the kids in there [in the high school] don't have what it takes to be better in life. If you ask anyone who was a graduate and didn't get in trouble, they'd say that they had certain things that helped them through. Even if they aren't aware of it, they might have good parents that took care of them, they might have had money to get extra things, they might have had a quiet place to work—like me, in my house, there was always someone yelling or fighting—or they had some other kind of thing going on. What is that saying?—"violence breeds violence." Well, that's true. You want to solve the problem you can't just think you'll fix it right away or by expelling people or even by talking to them. There has to be some action that boosts up the kid so that it isn't such an impossible thing to get a degree.

Now that you've read the interview excerpt, start to develop a violence-prevention effort that would address the problem that is being articulated by this student. What else may you want to know from the student? What types of exploratory or action research would you conduct in order to develop an adequate prevention program?

2. Read the excerpt from an interview with a school social worker. Identify the problems that this social worker faces when working with students. If you were the principal of the school listening to this social worker, what changes

would you make to address the issues raised by the social worker? What may be your difficulties in implementing these changes?

I am responsible for about 150 kids who are identified as severely, seriously, emotionally disturbed. They either have internal, emotional, psychological problems like depression anxieties or they have physical, behavioral problems, aggression being the most common, or some combination [of the emotional and physical]. Most of these kids are in self-contained classrooms. Others are what we call floaters or departmentalized. They have their home base in special education, but travel throughout the building. Some are in a variant type of mainstream program but have special ed. support services. I am suppose to see each of these students for half an hour a week in some kind of combination of either group, individually, or both. But, of course, that is impossible. The only thing that saves me from being out of compliance with the letter of law is that many of these kids are not in school. So if I went right now and looked at the attendance on the computer on my 140–150 kids, probably 30% or more wouldn't be here. So on any given day I can cover most of my kids, but the problem is all the PPTs and all the reports I have to write, and all the brush fires that occur regularly that need an immediate response. Yesterday alone I had one child being arrested and interviewed by various authorities for illegal activities involving the Internet. So I was dealing with that, attorneys and police and other investigators and the family. At the same time, I was dealing with a kid who was not responsive physically. He was breathing and that was about it because he had ingested some marijuana, and he has serious asthma problems like most of the poor kids in this city, so we had to get an ambulance here because he started to vomit and was just not doing well.

3. Given what you know about school violence, what future court cases related to violence or discipline in schools do you expect to occur? Why do you think these particular cases will occur? How would you like to see these court cases conclude (with what decision)? Explain why?

4. If you were invited to provide expert testimony to a board of education that is reviewing its zero-tolerance policy, what would be the main argument of your testimony? What would be your position on the policy, and how would you support your position?

SELECTED READINGS

Burstyn, J., Bender, G., Casella, R., Gordon, H., Guerra, D., Luschen, K., Stevens, R., & Williams, K. (2001). *Preventing violence in schools: A challenge to American democracy.* Mahwah, NJ: Lawrence Erlbaum Associates.

Casella, R. (2001). *"Being down": Challenging violence in urban schools.* New York: Teachers College Press.

Devine, J. (1996). *Maximum security: The culture of violence in inner-city schools.* Chicago: University of Chicago Press.

Noguera, P. (1995). Preventing and producing violence: A critical analysis of responses to school violence. *Harvard Educational Review, 65,* 189–212.

INTERNET SOURCES

National Association of School Resource Officers, www.nasro.org.
National School Safety and Security Services, www.schoolsecurity.org.
U.S. Education Department's Emergency Preparedness Resources, www.ed.gov/emergency plan.

REFERENCES

Ayers, W., Dohrn, B., & Ayers, R. (2001). *Zero tolerance: Resisting the drive for punishment in our schools.* New York: The New Press.
General Accounting Office. (2001). *Student discipline: Individuals with Disabilities Education Act,* Report to the Committees on Appropriations, U.S. Senate and House of Representatives. Washington, DC: U.S. Government Printing Office.
Green, M. (1999). *The appropriate and effective use of security technologies in U.S. schools: A guide for schools and law enforcement agencies.* National Institute of Justice Research Report. Washington, DC: U.S. Department of Justice.
National Governors' Association and President's Education Summit. (1991). *America 2000: An education strategy.* Washington, DC: U.S. Government Printing Office.
National Institute of Education. (1977). *Violent schools—safe schools: The safe school study report to Congress.* Washington, DC: U.S. Department of Health, Education, and Welfare.

Chapter 3

Educational Warriors for Social Justice

Jaime Romo
Michael Roseman
University of San Diego

Why should teachers be involved social justice? Why now? Despite a growing body of knowledge about teachers who practice educational social justice, much more needs to be understood in order to break the following patterns (Fredrickson, 1995; Levine, Lowe, Peterson, & Tenorio, 1995; Romo, Bradfield, & Serrano, 2004). The dropout rates across the nation for Latinos, African Americans, and American Indians are particularly high (Kitchen, Velaquez, & Myers, 2000) when compared to European American students. In the United States, dropout rates for Latinos and American Indians hover between 40 and 50%, almost double that for African Americans and triple that for whites (Haycock, 1997; The Education Trust, 1998).

On one hand, we know that the quality of teaching is the most important determinant of student success (Darling-Hammond, 1998; Elmore and Burney, 1997) that leads to student success or sharecropper education (Moses, 2001). On the other hand, we need to know how teachers move the quality of their teaching to a systemic level of equity and inclusion and promote liberty and justice for all (Chávez Chávez, 1995, 1997; Delpit, 1995; Kitchen et al., 2000).

What do we mean by social justice? For clarification, we interpret social justice both as an outcome and as a process. An emphasis on justice highlights the basic rights, not just privileges, to which we are all entitled. This includes equitable access to resources, goods, opportunities, and services without arbitrary limitations based on observed or interpreted differences between us (West Virginia University, http://www.wvu.edu/~socjust/). Social justice is also an interactive social process in two senses. First, it requires the skills of inspiring, working with, and organizing others to accomplish together a work of justice. Second, it aims at the good of the city, not at the good of one agent only. Therefore, community dialogue is a significant element that differentiates between true social justice work and community service and other types of activism.

In the past decade we have seen many approaches to improving student learning. By the 1990s the Curriculum and Testing movement had reached teacher education in different ways in different states. Both movements, however, emphasized content standards, without examining the critical, adaptive practices that shape the teaching profession. In other words, the context of teacher education/certification or reform (INTASC/NCATE/NBPTS) appears to be void of a clear social justice discussion. Critical educators continued to ask whose voices were being left out and whose interests were being served by educational practice and reform policy.

The following chapter centers around the application of two frameworks related to social justice: the first identifies societal levels of institutionalized equity and inclusion; the second identifies individual classroom teaching practices related to teacher education professional development (Romo & Salerno, 2000). After a brief discussion of the study methodology, the authors present a discussion of social justice through the lives of teachers. The chapter concludes with several considerations for teachers and administrators in order to promote social justice in their classrooms and schools.

DISCUSSION OF QUADRANTS

We present two frameworks that guided our study. The first, which examines institutional or group cultures, is contextualized by the continuum from exclusive monocultural to inclusive multicultural and from informal/individual to systemic. The framework reads in a clockwise direction from systemic exclusive monocultural (quadrant I) to systemic inclusive multicultural (quadrant IV) (see Table 3.1). Quadrant I descriptors are hostile toward those perceived as outsiders; explicit exclusion and monocultural external/embedded traits, which are reinforced at individual, group, and institutional levels, yielding status quo regarding power, industrial paradigm. Quadrant II descriptors are less overtly hostile than I: exclusion via second-generation discrimination; individual representatives of "minority" groups (disconnected from group) report pioneer experience; monocultural identity/values reflected implicity via individual/group reinforcement, industrial paradigm, status quo. Quadrant III descriptors are: apparently welcoming on the surface (e.g., affirmative action may be in place); diversity practiced primarily as contributions/additive approach; symbolic difference; cultural responsiveness primarily realized as awareness and sensitivity, yielding incremental reform and symbolic inclusion of those perceived as different from dominant group. Finally, quadrant IV descriptors are: local

TABLE 3.1 Social Justice Learning & Teaching

I: NONAWARE/NAÏVE	*II: NOVICE*
Teaching to control/Learning to survive	Teaching to test/Learning to fit in
School promotes social conformity	School promotes learning stuff/facts
Pedagogy: T talk/S listen	Pedagogy: T talk "about"/S talk with
T: Tear up/disrespect student work	T: Red pen student work
Student is silent/silenced	Student answers/stays in the box
• Reading outcomes: Answers/compliance	• Reading outcomes: Information/profit
• Writing: Follow directions	• Writing: Learn how not to write badly
IV: MASTER	*III: APPRENTICE*
Teaching to create/Learning to serve	Teaching to learn/Learning to understand
School promotes learning to construct	School promotes learning to think/ask/
Pedagogy: T mentors regarding	critique
authoritative living/S becomes author of	Pedagogy: T coaching/S navigate the
own life	system
T: Coauthors	T: Models/coaches
Student construct/co-creates/shares/	Student asks questions
collaborates—asks and answers	• Reading outcomes: Understanding/
• Reading outcomes: Creation/generative	pleasure
information/enlightenment	• Writing: Learn to write with voice
• Writing: Learn to write as activist	

T = teacher; S = student

cultural pluralism/democracy exists as a result of transformational organizational change at individual, group, and institutional levels; culture reflective of postindustrial (both/and versus either/or and partnership versus power-over) values; schools that embody transformational, social action–oriented curriculum and instruction.

The second describes individual teacher pedagogy practices within the same quadrants.

The important distinctions that differentiate each quadrant in the second frameworks are concerned both with the pedagogy and orientation of the teacher. Social justice work, defined here as a transformation at the individual, group, and institutional levels, hinges on the notions of collaboration, coauthorship, and dialogue. These are fundamental to explaining the distinctions between the four teacher-based quadrants. However, although these titles directly apply to the teacher, the level of social justice work is also linked to the social climate of the community. The four quadrants also outline multicultural competency from nonaware/naïve to novice, to apprentice, and finally to the master level. In the same way that the systemic quadrant model moves from a monocultural setting that is devoid of social justice rhetoric, this model also begins with a classroom and a teacher rooted in perpetuating, either consciously or unconsciously, the status quo.

METHODOLOGY OF STUDY

Traditional research related to teacher preparation or professional development has not adequately addressed teachers as agents of social justice (Blea, 1995; Darder, 1994; Vallance, 1980). Although quantitative methodology tends to be better at prediction, control, description, confirmation, and hypothesis testing (Merriam, 1988), qualitative methodology tends to be better for generating understanding, description, discovery, and hypothesis generating. Therefore, we employed a qualitative research methodology to investigate the lives of educators who embrace social justice as a central tenet of their work.

Multiple methods might be appropriate (Seidman, 1991) to understand the lived structures of meanings (Janesick, 1994; Van Manen, 1990; Strauss & Corbin, 1994). We chose the narrative process to gain a greater cultural and professional understanding from the "inside" of transformative teachers' everyday experiences (Clifford, 1986). In other words, we sought to better understand what transformative teachers experience and the contexts surrounding their experiences, rather than to simply report what they do (Connely and Clandinin, 1988).

The study began with a selected group of educators involved with multicultural education, identified through ongoing listserve discussions by a professor not involved with the study. Participants represent geographically and demographically distinct areas of the country. The list included: four White males, three Latino males, four White females, two Latinas, one Asian female, one Pacific Islander female, one Black female, and one multiracial female. Participants represented various faith traditions, socioeconomic status experiences, and first-, second-, and third-generation U.S. residency.

The subjects met the following criteria: They were identified as a transformative teacher and/or an educator who valued social justice and they were willing to provide a narrative of their life experiences as they related to their work as educators. The educators were asked to write about "[W]hy they are where they are, do what they do and are headed where they have chosen," therefore making the study and process more meaningful (Clandinin et al., 1993, p. 15). The participants seemed confident enough to be forthright with their personal and professional experiences, even though some shared some very sad and painful memories.

The open-ended narratives allowed the participants to tell their own stories. The participants created their narratives about their experiences in cultural, social, and institutional contexts (Morse, 1994; Van Manen, 1990). As a result of a grounded theory approach, we gained "a deeper understanding of the nature or meaning of our everyday experiences," such as transformative teaching, social justice, and organizational change (Van Manen, 1990) and recognized connections among teacher development and social justice actions (Friere, 1985; Smith, 1990; Stanfield, 1994).

PRESENTATION OF DATA

The 17 case studies that we have used as the data for our study have all been identified as transformative teachers. As we began to dissect their stories, there were themes that emerged consistently as attributes or qualities of the transformative teacher. What was apparent across the board was that introspection was the initial step that prompted these individuals to make significant life changes. In other words, the authors displayed a distinctive *knowledge* base, which, when reflected upon, promoted a body of *dispositions* (attitudes, values, beliefs) related to social justice. It was through their actions or *skills*, though, that they developed as educational warriors who promoted social justice.

These 17 vignettes weave the stories of these transformative teachers' own social justice work within the context of their emerging and growing sense of self. It is this willingness to expose their own biases that acts as the catalyst for their transformative teaching. Although unlearning and deconstructing are painful processes that forced these writers to share intensely personal emotions, the extent to which they outwardly express their internal struggle is indicative of the level of their social justice work and can be intimately linked to the relative pain that self-reflection produced.

The participants ranged in terms of age, ethnicity, and gender, and because of all of these relevant factors, each case study presents a fascinating study in and of itself. This diversity represented both a challenge and a triumph. On the one hand, the variations in writing style, teaching experience, and ethnic background made isolating themes more difficult than if we had used a homogeneous selection of teachers. On the other hand, the differences that are evident are more manifestations of the cultural climate in which the individual was nurtured and where their transformative teaching experiences are than they are indicators of vast differences between teaching in heterogeneous and homogeneous settings. The principal distinction that can be drawn in terms of environment is that the systemic resistance can stymie social justice work because in a monocultural setting, the dialogue necessary to catalyze collaborative work is not in place. Therefore, quadrant IV social justice work is contingent on both the disposition and skills of the teacher, as well as a multicultural community that promotes self-respect and cultural understanding.

As a result of deconstructing and reconstructing the data, we found the discussion of educators as warriors for social justice useful to summarize the collective data set. Warriors use a developed language to teach and work proactively in order to effect change. Warriors are guided by an inner calling that guides them to do no harm. In other words, they do battle to help others, but do not seek battle or use their power or abilities to harm others. The battle or action that they promote is to take up a challenge as advocate or to protect those who are vulnerable. This challenge takes place in classrooms and within institutions.

We said that educational warriors used a developed language to teach and work proactively in order to effect change. We link this to the contemporary teacher development domains found in INTASC, NCATE, and NBPTS: *knowledge* base. We said that educational warriors are guided by an inner calling that guides them to do no harm. We described this as faith and empathy and link these to the domain *dispositions*. Finally, we said that educational warriors do battle as advocates for others or to protect those who are vulnerable. Some examples of these skills relate directly to our discussion of social justice. In the following section, we extract key ideas from the data according to contemporary professional development language.

According to the data, educational warriors' knowledge base includes:

- Understanding the theory and research behind "isms": racism, sexism, classism, and discrimination.
- Understanding key concepts, principles, and major models of diversity.
- Understanding the history of prejudice, discrimination, and racism in the United States, both personal and institutional, and the effects of prejudice, discrimination, and racism on both White and underrepresented groups (including groups based on race, gender, sexual orientation, class, and age).
- Using their understanding of "isms" to educate others and promote social justice.

When educational warriors reflect on their experiences and knowledge base, they appear to develop a strong sense of personal identity as teachers, learners, family members, and community members. In particular, they:

- Examine, reflect, and seek to understand their perspective in the role of a teacher-scholar and the role of schools in education.

- Examine, reflect, and seek to understand their own identity development (racial, cultural, gender and sexual orientation) and the impact of that identity on teaching and learning.
- Examine, reflect, and seek to understand their own identity as a member of a team or learning community.
- Examine, reflect, and seek to understand their own learning styles and ways of knowing and the impact of that knowledge on teaching and learning.

Finally, educational warriors demonstrate and develop their knowledge and dispositions that are critical to promoting equity, inclusion, and social justice. They appear to consistently:

- Apply curricular, instructional, and assessment strategies that affirm the cultural, racial, and gender identity and development theories related to students.
- Assess students' gender, cultural, and linguistic knowledge and identities to provide meaningful, challenging, cultural, and linguistic learning experiences.
- Use an understanding of individual and group motivations and behaviors to create a learning environment that encourages positive social interaction, active engagement in learning, and self-motivation.
- Demonstrate thoughtfulness and responsiveness.

EDUCATIONAL WARRIORS AND SOCIAL JUSTICE

The quadrant models have provided us with frameworks to work from in assessing the social justice work of the 17 case studies. These quadrants not only provide us with a relative gauge of each transformative teacher's identity development, they also inform us of the social conditions within which each has operated. As we have found, context is as important as disposition in determining the level of social justice work.

The environmental framework establishes the community climate. Were the teachers operating in a system that embraced multiculturalism or was their work confined to a monocultural setting where race, gender, and class distinctions were either reinforced by overt hostility or absent because of implicit biases? The model proposes a continuum for systemic change from a firmly monocultural setting to one which is infused with multiculturalism. Although this model does not imply that such a progression is always linear, we have found that each of our case studies have had to negotiate through environmental constraints in their transformative teaching. Nonetheless, in examining the social milieu of which these teachers are a product, we are simultaneously able to explain their own development across the continuum as well as determine the relative level of social justice work in which they engaged.

From the data, we devised a point system from which to assess the level of social justice work accomplished. We have concluded that the higher the resistance systemically to social change, that being when environmental conditions mirror a monocultural conception of perspective, the lower the level of social justice work. As a social justice formula emerged, we noted significant differences between quadrants II and III, as well as between III and IV. The transition from quadrant II to III represents the greatest leap, for it implies an environmental move from a monocultural setting to a multicultural one. This leap from II to III gives individual teachers the freedom to begin cultural border crossing to facilitate an open dialogue on social justice issues. At the apprentice level, the transformative teacher as the coach has exposed students to multiple perspectives, thus challenging them to think outside of the box, whereas in quadrant II, the pedagogy is still thoroughly entrenched in a homogeneous environment. The transition from II to III is the reference point for social justice work because of the introduction of voice and perspective. A quadrant III environment implies diversity of opinions and student questioning, which move students toward an awareness of self.

In the following pages, we focus on the combination of individuals who exhibit quadrant IV knowledge, dispositions, and actions (Table 3.2) and environments that relate to quadrant III and IV (Table 3.2). The point values are as follows: Q1 $= -2$, Q2 $= -1$, Q3 $= 1$, Q4 $= 2$. The formula couples the individual quadrant of the case study with the context to give us an approximation of the level of social justice work.

TABLE 3.2 Summary of Social Justice Narratives

Ed Warrior	individ	context	individ	context
BF			+2	+2
WM			+2	+2
LM			+2	+2
AF			+2	+2
APF			+2	+2
WF			+2	+2
LM	+2	+1		
WM	+2	+1		
LF	+2	+1		

In the following section, we examine the application of this formula to the individual stories themselves. We begin with the most developed social justice examples.

Social Justice (Quadrant IV)

The first case study comes from a Black female. The central theme in her narrative echoes the concept of growing and her analogy of a box; a theme helps define how perspective encloses the individual. She elaborates on the concept of a box by explaining that in her work with preservice teachers, her aim is to help "facilitate the transformation as individuals emerge from socially-constructed boxes to begin to develop independent perspectives on the world" (Romo et al., 2004, p. 148). Essentially, as the product of environment, our views if unchallenged reflect the social fabric in which we were reared. As a child she was very much a passive participant in her own life. Just as she encouraged her students to explore their own racial identity development before becoming teachers, so too did a recall of stories from her silent past force her to tear down the invisible box that she had been operating within.

The title of her chapter implies that she is growing outside of the box, but it seems to imply that one never fully escapes from it. What she appears to be saying is that the box represents a person's comfort zone and without intentional self-reflection, this box remains closed just as the mind remains closed to different perspectives. Her teaching philosophy attempts to help students identify their own boxes, which then opens up the prospect of reconstructing one's set of beliefs.

She writes that, "dialogue-the capacity of members of a team to suspend assumptions and enter into a genuine thinking together. To the Greeks *dialogos* meant a free-flowing of meaning through a group, allowing the group to discover insights not attainable individually" (Romo et al., 2004, p. 165). This passage defines the quadrant IV classroom. Through a dialogue, the individual members are able to suspend assumptions and uncover new insights that would not have been possible solely through isolated inspection. Her classroom embodies this principle of the individual constructing meaning through interaction with the group. Her job is to help facilitate their transformation by whatever means necessary including self-grading and more autonomy in material choice than usual: listerve, pair share, groupwork. Her class is student centered and in the constructivist vein, where the emphasis is on collaboration and self-reflection.

In addition to being specific about her objectives, she is explicit about how she has paired theory with practice. In her words, "thought is my talk, action is my walk," which is particularly important like she says in higher education where "theory and practice are often separated" (Romo et al., 2004, p. 152). Because of her conviction to give students authentic exposure to diversity, she brought theory out of isolation and involved the students in service learning projects in an urban Portland school. In this way, she was able to connect what they had learned and dialogued about in the class with the environmental realities that existed in an urban school. It is with this proactive element that her work steps beyond quadrant III in both arenas and can be classified as the epitome of quadrant IV work.

The next educator describes his journey as a miseducated, reeducated, and transformed White male. His transformation exposes the pain of being a member of the dominant society. He has had to intentionally unlearn, deconstruct the implicit attitudes that unconsciously poisoned his mind growing up in a homogeneous monocultural environment. "Hence, much like an alcoholic or other drug addict must first admit to his or her problem, my *transformation* began and continues when I acknowledge my psycho-social diseases" (Romo et al., 2004, p. 199). It is at the point that he intentionally began to deconstruct these views and challenge what he had always accepted that his transformation began. Like all of the other case studies, his writing echoes the theme that growth is a process, not an end. Even though he has recognized his racism and is trying to unlearn it, he knows that this is a process without an end. It is a struggle that he says, "I am grateful for having begun" (Romo et al., 2004, p. 199).

In this story, we see the critical link between theory and action. His personal development compelled him to transform his classroom from teacher centered to student driven. Because social justice concepts like equity and inclusion had been an invisible part of his education, he created an environment that allowed students to explore these issues on their own and it brought out the student voice. As the facilitator of the conversation, he used his own experiences in a quadrant II environment of learning "stuff" as the backdrop from which to launch into student-led discussions of their own perspectives. Instead of just learning the information, he scaffolded them toward individual levels of understanding by exposing them to diverse perspectives on the Civil Rights Movement. His explanation of the outcomes of this project shed light on what constitutes quadrant IV teaching and learning.

> For many World History students who all had the expectation to attend elite colleges and universities, they told me it was the first time in the school career that they were allowed to think and explore on their own. For them, the experience was transformative. They felt intellectually and emotionally liberated to authentically learn for life rather than for the next test. I observed students honestly confronting their own biases and ignorance, and seeking to

be re-educated in response to what they had discovered. For my ESL American Studies students who came from seven countries in Latin America, Asia and Europe, they gained fresh insights into U.S. culture and into their own immigrant experience from our in-depth unit on slavery and racism. Themes such as "dream to be free," "discrimination," "violent oppression," "courage" and "strong family" emerged from our viewing and discussion of *Roots*. (Romo et al., 2004, p. 210)

This unit gives us an indication of the climate that he created within his classroom. His teaching philosophy opened the lines of communication for students to make connections to their own lives. As dialogue represents the prerequisite for social justice work, the environment must support diversity at least at a cursory/additive level. Once the students became the change agents, the equity dialogue moved toward social justice. The formation of SHADES (a human relations group) at first formally established a network within the school, providing a forum for ideas to be exchanged and meaning to be constructed. Once SHADES became replicated at other schools it became quadrant IV work. It transformed the climate institutionally to the point where students could feel comfortable confronting each other and opening the lines of communication.

He asks whether multiculturalism is an additive or an intrinsic part of the school curriculum and whether school is a vehicle where meaning is predetermined, cookie cutter so to speak, or whether it is a place where journey is unique to the individual. He believes that schools should empower students to confront, contend, and interact in an environment that has social justice at its epicenter. He understands a true multicultural environment as "comprehensive, interdisciplinary, ongoing, and transformative. It is local, national, and global in perspective. It is both tragic and triumphant.... Meaningful multicultural education is a mosaic or kaleidoscope of ideas and people, not a melting pot" (Romo et al., 2004, p. 212). From this definition, which reflects our quadrant IV environment, it would seem that the transformative teaching that he has done has been systemic.

A Latino's transformative journey mirrors the last White male's journey in that rejection acts as the catalyst for the painful process of self-reflection. Though their lenses differ in terms of race and class, we see the parallel theme of painful growth in both stories. Here we find again the concept of the growth process, the continued evolution, which begins when we recognize our own biases and work to deconstruct what we have consciously or unconsciously accepted. By intentionally challenging what he had tacitly learned and silently accepted, he has been able to understand not only where he sits, but also where he has stood in the past. But as he defines it, quadrant IV advocacy is not limited to the internal reconstruction of self. This is the starting point, the origin. The awareness of self is what drives us to seek out others who are also constructing new meaning and it also gives us the ability to explicitly articulate these views. As the dialogue is opened to new people, the instability increases, but we are still bound, or compelled to grow.

> I describe high level advocates (Quadrant IV) as individuals who publicly act as allies or institutional change agents, demonstrating many multicultural competency knowledge base, attitudes/values/beliefs, and skills. A high level advocate is recognized as a mentor for others and acts as a cultural broker between groups to promote institutional cultural democracy. (Romo et al., 2004, p. 293)

Once the disposition has been established, the transformative teacher must also apply this philosophy directly to teaching. The quadrant IV teacher is intentional in his or her goals and explicit in action. He writes,

> In conclusion, my journey towards wholeness, literacy, Bly's "Black Knight" and Ignatian "Transcendence" is no less complex or difficult than my students' journeys. As a Latino, raised in poverty, violence, abuse, and shame, I identify with those who are currently seen as outsiders to our educational institutions. As a highly educated, English-speaking, middle class male, I use my privileges to influence organizational transformation through developing actively anti-racist and anti-exclusionary teachers. I believe that these teaching candidates' efforts in their particular school communities, combined with any number of external pressures related to improved character development, international economic competition, or academic performance, will till the soil and nurture the seeds of organizational transformation and cultural democracy. (Romo et al., 2004, p. 296)

His words give a theoretical framework for his teaching and in his case study we find that his teaching facilitates this growth in his students. His objectives are explicit and his approaches direct, creating an environment that gives an individual freedom to begin self-reflection and to construct a dialogue that is constantly in a state of flux and is ripe for social justice work.

A preservice teacher of Asian background exemplifies what defines the transformative teacher. Through her writing and in her work we see the commitment, the faith, and the resiliency that is characteristic of the quadrant IV individual. She is explicit, she is direct, and her writing challenges the reader to begin his or her own self-reflection. These case studies all present the individual stories of 17 transformative teachers, but her case is not simply a summary of her life experience or an account of her perspective. Her writing is active, her voice explicit and challenging. This is language of quadrant IV. The difference is in the reflective quality of the writing. Not only does it demonstrate a personal reflection on the part of the writer, but it engages the reader to construct his or her own meaning from the text. Such quadrant IV writing, as illustrated in the following passage, drives us to remove the blinders, look out from the box, and get out of our comfortable chairs.

> With our newfound conviction to end the ongoing victimization of students in schools, future teachers pledged, "Never again, not on my watch, will another child be marginalized or tormented for his/her physical appearance, culture, language, religion, sexual orientation or social class." Shedding the once-comfortable robe of the bystander, teachers armed themselves with individual and collective courage, to proactively confront school cultures, practices, structures, and policies that marginalize and disenfranchise youth. (Romo et al., 2004, p. 267)

These transformative teachers, like her, are educational warriors, crusaders for the cause of social justice. She fused critical pedagogy with authentic experience and created an environment that gave her students the freedom to apply their learning to the real world.

> Students felt compelled to seek ways to challenge forces of domination and structures that reproduce inequality. As a way of marshaling this urgency to act and as a means for students to demonstrate their understanding of critical pedagogy, students engaged in social justice projects. These projects took many forms, e.g. interviewing advertising executives about stereotypes of women and minorities in the media; writing to Hallmark executives to inform them about the non-inclusive holidays which may affect some kids adversely and making suggestions e.g. Father's Day instead of Parent/Guardian Day; organizing and raising funds for multicultural guest speakers for schools to become culturally conscious. (Romo et al., 2004, pp. 267–268)

The student ownership of the course is what is apparent from this passage and a reading of the rest of the work. Everyone had a voice, a forum to share it in, and an opportunity to grow. Simultaneously, she facilitated both individual growth and group cohesion, a pair that would seem to be a dichotomy. But through collaboration and action, these students were able to deconstruct and then begin to reconstruct their own views. The transformation that she describes is an illustration of quadrant IV from both models, demonstrating social justice work.

An Asian Pacific Islander's narrative is instructive, not only because of the powerful voice that resonates throughout, but also because of the social justice work that she has already engaged in. As we have defined quadrant IV work as dependent on knowledge, disposition, and skills, her story gives us an example of the highest level of social justice work. She paired theory with action and was able to advocate successfully for the inclusion of Tagalog as a recognized foreign language in her families' school district. Before she was able to forge alliances and open the dialogue, she had to explicitly define her own worldview, which she explains in the following passage.

> On the other hand, I don't have any intention of giving up my Filipino culture. I continue to share it with pride in every opportunity I can. However, to this day, I am reminded daily where I belong as a member of a subordinate culture. But that's based on the dominant culture's definition of how different cultures are divided. For me, there is no division, only a normal existence of different cultures, none better than the other is. The difference actually enhances what we can offer to further enrich the other culture. The more we are willing to know about and to adapt to each other's way of life, the better we can understand, appreciate and live harmoniously together. (Romo et al., 2004, p. 12)

This recognition of her status alone does not position her in quadrant IV, but her internal commitment compelled her to lobby for systemic changes. She moved into quadrant IV when she became proactive about her beliefs.

> Equally important, I got to know the administrators and some of the staff and we developed positive working relationships. Therefore, we established line of communication necessary for dialogue on different issues and concerns of the past, present, and future. I continue as an active parent volunteer, for, in doing so, I set a good example of parent involvement to my children. Also, my volunteerism and advocacy encompasses not only my children but also extends to other Filipino American students and parents who need representation, a voice, in our school district. One of the significant accomplishments or evidence of this advocacy has been the approval of Filipino as a district foreign language subject, a crucial move that can preserve the Filipino culture and build pride of being one. (Romo et al., 2004, p. 14)

Although she became the voice of change, the environment had to be multicultural for such a monumental change to occur. Her social justice work had to have parental, student, school, and administrative support to move from a dream to a reality. The inclusion of the Philippine language as a recognized foreign language gave a voice to a silenced minority and helped rekindle cultural pride in its youth. Such a maneuver indeed fits with the vision of social justice as being a reconstruction of schools toward multiculturalism. When invisible groups are given a voice, when outliers are integrated, that is the highest level of social justice work.

Many of the transformative teachers here have moved outside of the K–12 classrooms and have turned to the university setting to continue their work. Our next educator is a White female who has endeavored to make social changes through her work as a multicultural educator. Like other White men and women, she experienced the same frustration, the pain of being a member of the dominant culture and being "miseducated" to use a White male's term. Her story blends personal experience with critical pedagogy and goes beyond a mere recount of her life history. The self-reflection is ubiquitous, as is the theme of growth. Her journey is a springboard for the dialogue to begin.

> Since my role in that work impacts young children only through their teachers (my students), I strive to use MY journey to assist the preservice teachers on THEIRS. Mine is a deeply emotional, lived journey; therefore it translates meaningfully to students for whom the textbook definition of racism or the video of oppression in a different context, might not be as credible or easy to translate into an early childhood classroom... "conscientization," or the deepening of the attitude of awareness, it is a goal of mine to assist students in their ability to reflect on their own situationality, and their own historical existence in a world of incongruities and inequities. (Romo et al., 2004, p. 178)

In seeking to create an atmosphere that allows each student to construct his or her own meaning, she must "assist students in their ability to reflect on their own situationality." Through an understanding of their own experiences of being marginalized or being privileged, the students are able to see the box that has been constructed for them. The guidance she provides using her own transformative journey introduces the human element to their studies. It shows them that although she is the teacher and has already begun her self-reflection, that her growth continues as she continues to unpack her own beliefs and through her interaction with others.

> As my personal transformation continues, so also does my comfort level with allowing students more control of their learning. "Engaged pedagogy" as proposed by Bell Hooks (1994) is a philosophy and teaching strategy I attempt to instill in students. They are valued learners, respected for what they bring to the classroom, affirmed for their stories and well-intentioned attempts to broaden their perspectives. My stories are shared as well in my attempt to set an example of my own humanity. Conversations with students continue beyond the classroom as I agree with Hooks' belief that our work is not merely to share information, but to share in the intellectual and spiritual growth of our students. (Romo et al., 2004, pp. 181–182)

It is not important that people come to terms with their differences, but it is essential that we recognize that these differences exist. If we can understand our own lens and articulate it to others, we can move the dialogue beyond a mere presentation of different ideas to an exchange, where people can begin to reconstruct new views that integrate the teachings of others. This educator's teaching facilitates this growth, which we identify as a quadrant IV teacher, operating in an environment that supports this individual growth.

Social Justice (Quadrant III)

A Latino author offers an open narrative that not only gives an account of his personal development, but also explicitly defines his evolution. This intentional and overt dialogue that is present throughout his piece certainly gives him credibility at least at a quadrant III level, but his work is confined to gangs. In short, it does not fit the archetype of quadrant IV systematic social justice work.

His skills as facilitator are evident in his work in connecting the community to these kids. "The goal here is not only to get them involved with the community, but also to get the community involved with them and even employing some of these youths" (Romo et al., 2004, p. 40). The concept of reciprocal relationships is important in distinguishing social justice work, that being the work he does with at-risk kids, from community service work, which would be more quadrant III. The open dialogue, the transaction that he mentions as an outgrowth of discussion, comes when each participant learns from one another.

The proactive response, the transformation from symbolic inclusion (quadrant III) to institutional infusion (quadrant IV) is not evident. His example is isolated to a discussion of his work with gangs and he does not offer a connection or an application beyond this example. The reader might ask, "What about schools in affluent areas, aren't there kids there that are marginalized as we have seen in the upsurge in school shootings recently?" Although we recognize that this story represents the sum of his experiences, how can he as a preservice teacher hope to impart this message of justice to his students in diverse areas? Because of the limited implications of his study, the environment remains in quadrant III, even if his work and the skills that the participants gain, are at quadrant IV level. According to the formula then, his total score is 3 (+2, +1).

The next educator, a White male, presents an internal dialogue that engages the reader and impels him or her to confront his or her own perspective. He weaves in an account of where he has stood as an explanation of where he currently stands, but he does this in such a way that he is able to imply his bounded instability. This concept is central disposition of the transformative teacher. On the one hand, we have to be flexible in our opinions as he highlights in his reassessment of his earlier sexist attitudes defense. In addition, we have to be firm enough to know what it is we stand for and by the same token what we are against. This ability to be malleable yet rigid requires a high level of internal introspection and external dialogue. Hence, we see that the process of growth is as important as the actual transformation itself. He reinforces the notion of growth as a process when he writes that "my personal journey is laced with examples of how my own outlooks and beliefs have been dramatically altered, but it is the process of that alteration I believe is key to opening the path to intellectual liberation that is essential if we are going to make this a possibility to our students" (Romo et al., 2004, p. 186).

Given his strong choice of language and proactive tone, he is extremely difficult to cast into the quadrant model. His activity is designed to raise student consciousness through a dialogue on critical social issues and forces them to think and construct their own beliefs and bring their own voice, giving it elements of quadrant IV. The dialogue has begun, but the extension, its application beyond his classroom, is what would make this quadrant IV. Therefore, he is at the mastery level in teaching but the environment is still quadrant III giving him an overall score of 3 (+2, +1).

A Latina educator gives an account of her transformative teaching. With the exception of her grant-writing efforts aimed at institutionalizing bilingual education in a monocultural environment/educational system, the data suggest that her transformative teaching is theory based. She uses critical pedagogy as a means of explaining the theoretical transformation of the individual that begins with an awareness of one's own perspective. We find that critical self-reflection, an understanding of the limitations of experience, is the initial step toward a transformative worldview. At times this reflection may be uncomfortable as is the case of educators whose pain stemmed from a realization of their own privilege, but such self-examination of one's own lens is essential for the subsequent transition to an open dialogue of perspectives. This educator offers a process to understand our transformation. We have to awaken our own minds and become acutely aware of what box we are in and how this has confined us. Negotiation is the second stage, which is when multiple perspectives are shared that in turn lead again back to reflection. We see the process of change as the driving force of transformation and this idea of deconstructing as the precursor for reconstruction. Finally, the final stage is introspection, which functions as a challenge to the individual.

Her resiliency and her personal faith drove her to work beyond the limitations of her environment to eventually succeed in her grant writing. "The phases described earlier (self-examination, negotiation, reflection, and introspection) were the stages our dialogue moved through in establishing an endorsement for bilingual education, taking only 4 years to complete. It shouldn't have taken that long but the forces mentioned in Phase III (power, politics, history, culture, and language) converged to try and keep the endorsement from becoming a reality" (Romo et al., 2004, p. 134).

This example of social justice, this systemic change, was hindered by a pseudo-multicultural environment but was overcome by her disposition and her skills. Even though she indicates that there was significant opposition to her proposal, the dialogue that existed to move this issue into the public realm is evidence of a quadrant III environment. The adoption of her proposal hinged on her leadership, both her internal faith and the external manifestation. Using her example, we see how systemic resistance can stymie social justice work but with her quadrant IV perspective, she was able to overcome the opposition $(+2, +1)$.

SUMMARY

In the throes of teacher education and credentialing reform, little attention has been paid to social justice. The knowledge, dispositions, or skills related to social justice do not appear in national standards. This chapter has examined the life experiences of 17 educators who identified as transformational teachers in order to better understand the relationship between the lives of teachers and social justice.

This study suggests that teachers who worked to promote social justice, termed educational warriors, manifested identifiable knowledge base, dispositions, and skills. When educational warriors reflect on their experiences and knowledge base, they appear to develop a strong sense of personal identity as teachers, learners, family members, and community members. Finally, educational warriors demonstrate and develop their knowledge and dispositions that are critical to promoting equity, inclusion, and social justice.

These educational warriors described systemic impact, which was brought about collaboratively and which was the result of building and applying multicultural competency a well as a support base to address institutional change. They exhibited an ability to articulate their learning process as well as their social reform movements. They believed in themselves and in others, despite experiencing various painful difficulties. In fact, it appeared that their explicit work with their greatest hardships gave them the perspective to change the system and the interpersonal status quo dynamics that perpetuated patterns of inequity.

Clearly, social justice in and through education is possible. For social justice to be widely seen, increasing numbers of educators need to develop individual educational warrior knowledge base, dispositions, and skills. In addition, they must collaborate with others to institutionalize social justice practices. The questions remain as to how social justice will be fostered among educators and, if it is not, why not.

GUIDING QUESTIONS

1. Apply the social justice quadrants to an environment you are familiar with. What are the implications for you to take action in order to help create a more equitable, inclusive, and just environment?
2. Apply the classroom framework (Table 3.2) to your classroom. What are some implications for you as a teacher? What are some implications for your students regarding social justice?
3. How do you embody the key knowledge base, dispositions, and performance related to social justice/educational warriors?
4. How does the transformative teacher negotiate with external forces beyond his or her control such as a homogeneous population?

SELECTED READINGS

DeRoche, E., & Williams, M. (2001). *Character education: A Guide for School Administrators.* Lan Ham, HD: Scarecrow Press.

Freire, P. (1985). *A pedagogy of the oppressed.* New York: Continuum Press.

Levine, D., Lowe, R., Peterson, B., & Tenorio, R. (Eds.). (1995). *Rethinking schools: An agenda for change.* New York: The New Press.

Loewen, J. (1996). *Lies my teacher told me: Everything your American history textbook got wrong.* New York: Touchstone.

Kozol, J. (1991). *Savage inequalities: Children in America's schools.* New York: Harper Perennial.

McLaren, P. (1994). *Life in schools: An introduction to critical pedagogy in the foundations of education.* New York: Longman.

Romo, J., Bradfield, P., & Serrano, R. (2004). *Reclaiming democracy: Multicultural educators' journeys toward transformative teaching.* Englewood Cliffs, NJ: Prentice-Hall.

Tatum, B. (1998). *Why are all the black kids sitting in the cafeteria?* New York: Perseus Book Company.

REFERENCES

Ayers, W. (1997). *A kind and just parent: The children of juvenile court.* Boston: Beacon Press.

Blea, I. (1995). *Researching chicano communities: Social-historical, physical, psychological, and spiritual space.* New York: Praeger.

Chávez Chávez, R. (1995). *Multicultural education in the everyday: A renaisssance for the recommitted.* Washington, DC: American Association of Colleges for Teacher Education.

Chávez Chávez, R. (1997). *A curriculum discourse for achieving equity: Implications for teachers when engaged with Latina and Latino students.* Las Cruces, New Mexico State University. Unpublished manuscript.

Clandinin, D. J., Davies, A., Hogan, P., & Kennard, B. (Eds). (1993). *Learning to teach, teaching to learn: Stories of collaboration in teacher education.* New York: Teachers College Press.

Clifford, J. (1986). *Writing culture: The poetics and politics of ethnography.* Berkeley: University of California Press.

Connely, F. M., & Clandinin, D. J. (1988). *Teachers as curriculum planners: Narratives of experience.* New York: Teachers College Press.

Darder, A. (1994, Spring). Institutional research as a tool for cultural democracy. *New Directions for Institutional Research, 81,* 21–34.

Darling-Hammond, L. (1998). Teachers and teaching: Testing policy hypotheses from a national commission report. *Educational Researcher, 27*(1), 5–15.

Delpit, L. (1995). *Other people's children: Cultural conflict in the classroom.* New York: New York Press.

The Education Trust. (1998, Summer). *Thinking K-16, 3*(2), 6.

Elmore, R. E., & Burney, D. (1997). *Investing in teacher learning: Staff development and instructional improvement in community school district #2,* New York City, National Commission on Teaching and America's Future and the Consortium for Policy Research in Education.

Fredrickson, J. (Ed.). (1995). *Reclaiming our voices: Bilingual education, critical pedagogy and praxis.* Ontario: California Association for Bilingual Education.

Freire, P. (1985). *A pedagogy of the oppressed.* New York: Continuum Press.

Haycock, K. (1997). *Achievement in America.* Washington, DC: The Education Trust.

Hooks, B. (1994). Postmodern blackness. In P. Williams & L. Chrisman (Eds.), *Colonial discourse and post-colonial theory: A reader* (pp. 174–219). New York: Columbia University Press.

Janesick, V. J. (1994). The dance of qualitative research design: Metaphor, methodology, and meaning. In N. Denzin & Y. Lincoln (Eds.), *Handbook of qualitative research* (pp. 209–219). Beverly Hills, CA: Sage.

Kitchen, R. S., Velasquez, D. T., & Myers, J. (2000, April). *Dropouts in New Mexico: Native American and Hispanic students speak out.* Paper presented at the annual meeting of the American Educational Research Association, New Orleans, LA.

Levine, D., Lowe, R., Peterson, B., & Tenorio, R. (Eds.). (1995). *Rethinking schools: An agenda for change.* New York: The New Press.

Merriam, S. B. (1988). *Case study in education.* San Francisco: Jossey-Bass.

Moll, L., Gonzales, N., Floyd-Tenery, M., Rivera, A., Rendon, P., Gonzalez, R., & Amanti, C. (1993). *Teacher research on funds of knowledge: Learning from households.* No. 6. National Center for Research on Cultural Diversity and Second Language Learning. Santa Cruz, CA.

Morse, J. (1994). *Critical issues in qualitative research methods.* Thousand Oaks, CA: Sage.

Moses, R. (2001). *Radical equations: Math literacy and civil rights.* Boston: Beacon Press.

Romo, J., Bradfield, P., & Serrano, R. (2004). *Reclaiming democracy: Multicultural educators' journeys toward transformative teaching.* Englewood Cliffs, NJ: Prentice-Hall.

Romo, J., & Salerno, C. (2000). *Toward cultural democracy: The journey from knowledge to action in diverse classrooms.* Boston: Houghton Mifflin.

Seidman, I. E. (1991). *Interviewing as qualitative research: A guide for researchers in education and the social sciences.* New York: Teachers College Press.

Smith, K. (1990). Notes from the epistemological corner: The role of projection in the creation of social science. *Journal of Applied Behavioral Science, 26,* 119–127.

Stanfield, H., II. (1994). Ethnic modeling in qualitative research. In N. Denzin & Y. Lincoln (Eds.), *Handbook of qualitative research* (pp. 175–188). Beverly Hills, CA: Sage.

Strauss, A., & Corbin, J. (1994). Grounded theory methodology: An overview. In N. Denzin & Y. Lincoln (Eds.), *Handbook of Qualitative Research* (pp. 273–286). Beverly Hills, CA: Sage.

Vallance, E. (1980). The Hidden Curriculum and Qualitative Inquiry as States of Mind. *Journal of Education, 162,* 138–151.

Van Manen, M. (1990). *Researching lived experience: Human science for an action sensitive pedagogy.* Albany: State University of New York Press.

West Virginia University. http://www.wvu.edu/~socjust/.

Wiske, M. S. (Ed.). (1998). *Teaching for understanding: Linking research with practice.* San Francisco: Jossey-Bass.

Chapter 4

Comfortably Numb? Rethinking Social Studies for Social Justice

Cameron S. White
University of Houston

Tony L. Talbert
Baylor University

What really are the purposes of schooling and education in our society? What is the role of critical inquiry and problem solving in teaching and learning? What is the role of educational leadership in schooling and education? What are the roles of other institutions in society within the context of teaching and learning? Are socialization, indoctrination, and passivity the primary goals of our institutions? These and others are the questions that aren't being asked.

What of higher goals such as transforming and transgression? Is the nature of humanity such that comfort is the ultimate . . . and given the current state of society, perhaps comfortably numb? Why does it seem that reaction is the method rather than proactive engagement? Why does it take extreme events to lull us awake as to possibilities? How can we struggle to reach the potential in human endeavor?

Social studies education is part of the problem—it is guilty of developing individuals, a society, and a world that is making little progress for the betterment of humanity. Our kids are caught in a system that exists for its own sake. Status quo rules and anything "out of the box" is a threat to our comfort. Socialization and passivity are the true goals. Social studies classrooms remain text based and teacher centered with kids generally sitting in rows copying lecture notes to regurgitate on the unit "objective" test (Kincheloe, 2002). But we must think more broadly. Yes, it is a cliché to indict social studies with its Eurocentric and ethnocentric focus. The facts remain, however; social studies text books and curriculum is dominated by this focus. Loewen (1995) stated that promoting socialization and allegiance to "American ideals" are the primary goals for social studies and schooling. So, what is wrong with thinking globally and acting locally? Is blind patriotism and jingoistic verbage keeping us from meeting basic human needs? What has happened to the concept of community? Are we held captive by our desire for complacency? And . . . what is the role of administrators in all this?

Social studies should be about empowerment and efficacy; it should be about controversy; it should be about dissonance; it should be about allowing for and asking the hard questions—and ultimately having the courage to seek. An opportunity awaits: Social studies can be a tool for engaging, and it should be a tool for challenging—ourselves, others, and our world. Allowing for differing visions and enhancing a variety of stories encourages the transcendental—encourages progress beyond some market-driven media-defined conception of growth and justice.

We still focus on stories of the white male heroes of history and provide lip service to "the other" in the form of celebratory months. Many stories are missing. We are not providing the meaningful context and connections our kids deserve. Most no longer care about who did what to whom and when . . . and no wonder, as we are constantly reminded that there is one "right" answer—and this to a question no one really wants to ask anyway.

Perhaps the most accepted approach regarding social studies is transmitting essential knowledge and skills in history, government, economics, and geography. We equate more information with knowledge and learning and place this information in subject disciplines. But do we go through life moving from subject to subject in these easily compartmentalized categories; or do we integrate more holistically? We need schooling that encourages participation, critical analysis, and action (Westheimer & Kahne, 1998). How can educational leadership facilitate this?

Moving from social studies to social education would give students the opportunity to gain experience in debate, public speaking, research, and decision making by investigating controversy. Students who are given an opportunity to engage in critical analysis of issues and voice their opinion gain confidence, and with confidence they are more likely to continue to participate in society's decisions after graduation (Soley, 1996).

A major rationale for schooling is to prepare students for their future. Schools should therefore allow issues and problem-based inquiry into their classrooms because students will have to encounter controversy and social issues throughout their lives. Instead of resorting to complete withdrawal or violent rage, students would be encouraged to develop peace-making and conflict-resolution strategies. But many students will not have exposure to controversy and social issues in their classes. Social studies without controversy cannot really be social education. It does not allow for empowerment and efficacy. This is a disservice to students, teachers, and society. So what should be done to address these issues?

SOCIAL EDUCATION FOR SOCIAL JUSTICE

Social education need be about social efficacy, empowerment, and emancipation leading to social justice. What is the role of schools in promoting social justice? How do the current practices in education and the teaching and learning process impact social justice? How can educational leadership facilitate social justice in schools? The overt goal of our schools is to enhance knowledge, skills, and dispositions development for our children. Unfortunately these goals are more often than not centered around very basic components that decision makers have perceived as "essential" for being productive citizens in this country. These goals, therefore, seem to be driven by the ultimate goal of preparing our youth for the world of work. Again, traditional social studies traditionally has not been about questioning or inquiry.

Ultimately, we must prepare children for active participation as global citizens; and this means that we have a responsibility to teach for social justice and a more critical teaching and learning. The idea is to critically analyze these issues and also provide the critical efficacy children need so as to facilitate this natural desire and wonder for learning about and coping with their world. And how can this be enhanced through educational leadership?

What then is meant by an education for social justice? Social justice education moves beyond traditional essentialist practice by suggesting that students and teachers are active and equal participants in all schooling and educational endeavors. Advocates for social justice education suggest that our schools are often demeaning and disempowering places where children and their teachers are either bored into submission or where the transmission and socialization techniques destroy any hope for critical-thinking and problem-solving development. The opportunity for an education for social justice in schools is great but we must discard the traditional transmission model of social studies in favor of a transformational model leading to social education. Social education is holistic, integrative, and challenging and must allow for investigating controversy and issues rather than memorizing bland facts. Strategies such as debates, simulations, role-playing, cooperative projects, and critical-inquiry investigations facilitate a transformational model. Social studies should be a transformational process for both the individual and society (Hope, 1996). A curriculum is needed that encourages participation, critical analysis, and action.

Directly tied to teaching for social justice as stated previously is the concept of social efficacy. If one looks at the traditional goals of social studies, one can interpret these goals are at least somewhat implying some form of social efficacy. The critique here is that both social studies and efficacy mean much more than how we have traditionally applied them in the teaching and learning process. Unfortunately, or fortunately, depending on one's point of view, the truly meaningful and lifelong connections in social efficacy have been provided outside of the classroom, especially outside of the social studies classroom. And this is the real issue. Social education should be about allowing kids and teachers opportunities for choice, investigation, creativity, questioning, and debate; yes, it should allow for debate regarding the hidden curriculum. These are skills vital for a sense of self-efficacy and for promoting a meaningful democracy. These ideas suggest the development of responsible citizenship for the propensity for thinking, valuing, and acting, rather than for the promotion of particular thoughts, actions, or values (Stanley, 1992). Educational leadership must address social education and social efficacy within their schools for the benefit of all stakeholders.

ISSUES

What is the status of social studies education in our schools? Elementary social studies has increasingly become an add-on in favor of test preparation and the dominance of language arts and math. Secondary social studies remains much the same after more than 75 years, at least in regard to ensuring the transmission of essential knowledge and skills. And we are now seeing more accountability in secondary social studies in the form of end-of-course exams, state tests, and other forms of standardization. What can be expected in social studies other than teaching to these tests? Again what is the role of educational leadership in addressing these issues?

The standardization and accountability movements really contribute to this demeaning situation. What we have here is yet another example of the increased corporatization of schooling. Competition is the driving force. As mentioned briefly earlier, standardization, scripting of lessons, and teaching to the test has become the school practice. Extrinsic methods rather than intrinsic methods are the focus. The concepts of critical thinking, problem solving, and issues-centered education are antithetical to this movement as a market mentality is the driving force. If we encourage children to question and investigate themes and issues in depth, then the status quo and hegemonic powers might very well be threatened. Many may very well be threatened by a social studies that promotes a diversity of perspectives and global issues. And often we find administrators complicit in all this.

Ultimately, the goal of schooling for social studies seems to remain focused on transmission of essential knowledge, skills, and values. We seem to be attempting to "standardize" our children. Free-market capitalism replacing democracy as the governmental ideal is perpetuated by these endeavors. Examples include the increased commercialization of the Web, Channel One, and advertisement agreements between companies, which use schools for marketing their products. A social justice approach is critical of transmission, essential knowledge, and the "ideal" of free-market capitalism, thus it is antithetical to these standardization and accountability movements.

Teaching for social justice is the answer to the essentialism enveloping our schools and society. Current social studies approaches preach the joys of being a democratic society, yet democracy often cannot be found in our schools. Our classrooms are often very authoritarian with little feeling of empowerment. Our society claims to be open and just, but school praxis has all but made our schools like prisons. Kids are prisoners subjected to the whims of the prisonlike bureaucracy of the schools where teachers have become the guards. Kids are in schools to be molded into appropriately acting citizens. These citizens go along with the crowd, pleased as punch to be living in the greatest country in the world. It is time to really address power, domination, and issues with the lack of democracy in our schools (Beiner, 1995). How can we counter this through activist educational leadership?

AN ISSUES-BASED SOCIAL EDUCATION

How do we address difficult societal issues in schools? Should we allow for controversial issues in teaching and learning? What is the connection between controversy and the development of social efficacy? And how can educational leaders address these in a culture that increasingly favors standardization and essentialist accountability? Today's schools often fail to address the needs of the students because we often ignore the difficult issues and hard questions. We do not allow critical investigation of controversy because we do not want the status quo threatened in any way. School should be for cultivating the human spirit, nourishing the imagination, and promoting self-expression (Purpel & Shapiro, 1995).

Social studies has traditionally occupied a unique place in the education system. This is an area where the goal is for our youth to become well-informed active participants in a democracy (at least through lip service). A social studies classroom should be a place where students are given the opportunity to voice their opinions and pursue social topics that are relevant to them. This would motivate students to become active participants in the classroom. Students who participate actively in their education are better able to make sense of their world and in turn are better able to engage in problem solving, decision making, and peace making. Students who are given an opportunity to engage in critical analysis of issues and voice their opinion gain confidence and with confidence they are more likely to continue to participate in society's decisions after graduation. When citizenship education becomes purely socialization, many fundamental issues for facilitating democracy arise (Gutman, 1990). Couldn't our educational leaders promote a more holistic approach in our schools—schooling for active citizenship?

If you take away the controversy, you take away the depth; you take away the passion and intrinsic motivation. Social studies students will not be able to understand the ideas presented to them if the depth of their learning is shallow, and thus meaningful social efficacy will suffer. Classrooms that ignore or homogenize controversy and social issues are not conceived with student growth and development as a top priority. These classrooms produce students who, at best, can regurgitate facts and, at worst, are demeaned and disempowered. Controversy and social issues engage us in dealing with problems whose best solutions are open to disagreement and are thus ideal for application in social education, thus leading to effective social efficacy. School administrators are often hesitant regarding issues-based approaches. Why is that?

Why attempt to implement the use of controversial issues in teaching and learning when many in society are adamantly opposed to the idea? As social educators, we must look at the goals of education and decide what is the best way to attain these goals. Social education classrooms are often dominated by authoritarian models rather than democratic ones; and schools are often dominated by top-down administrative practice. Teaching and learning are bland, censored, and often offer very limited perspectives. How can we inspire our youth to be active peace makers when we preach rather than model democracy in schools? Allowing students a forum in social education classrooms to weigh diverse information, voice their opinions, debate their viewpoints, and pursue research relevant to current affairs questions can only facilitate the goals of social education in promoting lifelong social efficacy. Continuing a course where students sit in passive classrooms where the focus of the lessons are textbook chapters followed by worksheet questions does nothing but create apathy, disempowerment, and eventually rage among our youth. They feel they have no voice and can make little difference in the area of changing our society for the better. With active experience comes confidence and with confidence comes participation (Byrnes, 1997). Social educators and educational leaders must become more proactive and activist in calling for a curriculum that focuses on democracy and addresses controversy and social issues.

Differences of opinion and conflict arise from many issues. Social education suggests that we address very complicated questions such as: What is democracy? What is free speech? What causes a person to become the person that he or she is? None of these questions has an easy answer. Every person deserves the opportunity to develop his or her own answers to these hard questions as there is controversy in learning about other people and there are many interpretations in analyzing culture. Which ones are right and which ones are wrong? Teachers have to let the students go on their

own personal quest for discovery. And administrators need to encourage
schools that model democracy and empower both teachers and students.

A MILITARISTIC SOCIAL EDUCATION

Why shouldn't militaristic language and descriptions of the battles of the
American Revolution, the War of 1812, the Western Indian Campaigns, and
the Civil War serve as symbolic vocabulary of democratic prowess through
conquest for our social studies students? What's wrong with the tales of the
storming of San Juan Hill, the overpowering of Iowa Jima, the campaign
of Normandy, the battle for Pork Chop Hill, and the seizing of Panama as
the context in which our social studies students embrace the concept of
America's dominance on the world stage? Is there any inherent wrong in
depicting the bombing of Hiroshima, Nagasaki, Saigon, and Iraq as justifi-
able acts to protect American lives and promote the principles of democracy to the men, women, and children beyond the American shores? Why
shouldn't the scope and sequence of our social studies curricula and textbooks be organized around the images, descriptions, depictions, legends,
lies, and cherished myths of American military dominance and conquest of
the West and beyond? Isn't this our heritage? It's not really violence when
it is promoting democracy, is it?

Each day we lament the fact that our children are fed daily doses of violence through television, theater, video game, and music video images and
descriptions. Parents, administrators, educators, legislators, and concerned
citizens across this nation meet on a regular basis to discuss and design
ways to insulate children and teenagers from the violence that threatens the
safety of our homes, schools, and communities.

In our attempts to attach blame and seek answers to the complex questions surrounding violence, we do not hesitate to cry for censorship of violent images and content pedaled to our children and teenagers by the media
producers of the television, film, music, and video industries. We demand
that our civil and criminal courts exact justice from those who promote and
perpetrate the violence in our schools, communities, and world. With fran-
tic reaction to violence we enact zero-tolerance rules, establish safe school
zones, erect metal detectors, eliminate Internet access, and enumerate a
litany of rules that effectively censor and/or suspend the democratic principles of free expression through standardized dress and curriculum. This
is often the reaction within education leadership.

In some cases, instead of seeking to attach blame, schools and communities have responded proactively to threats and incidences of violence
by creating conflict-resolution, mediation, and violence prevention programs. These programs typically include training in empathy skills, anger

management, conflict resolution, peer mediation, cooperative games, and social skills (Cunningham, 1995). Perhaps more investigation regarding the possibilities is warranted.

Yet although we act and react to the most overt examples of violence in our schools, communities, homes and world, social studies students are exposed to violence wrapped in the victorious descriptions and glorified images of conquest, warfare and coups d'état. What is the source of these violent depictions? Who is the purveyor of this material? All one must do to find the answers to these questions is to survey the pages of print, examine the grainy and glossy photographs, and peruse the bold titles in the typical social studies textbooks, curricula, and educational media resources that occupy a prominent place in social studies classrooms across America.

Although the glorification of war is not a new phenomenon in American social studies textbooks and curricula, the irony that educators, parents, and concerned citizens continue to seek external influences for the causes of violence while ignoring the images, depictions, and glorification of violence in social studies textbooks cannot go unchallenged. Social studies curricula and textbooks are organized along a war-centric scope and sequence that provides descriptions of America's involvement in both domestic and international warfare and conflict. Militaristic imagery and language of American domestic and international conquests are organized around the three central themes: (a) land, (b) enemy, and (c) hero (Sheety, 1999). For every thousand pages published on the causes of wars, there is less than one page directly on the causes of peace (Blainey, 1988).

Although social studies textbooks, curricula, and materials are routinely filled with images and depictions of violence, warfare, armed conflict, and practices that promote the subjugation of people and nations, these examples seldom conjure the visceral reaction by educators, parents, and concerned community leaders as do films, television programs, video games, and music lyrics that fill our airwaves and children's minds. Whereas we may debate the comparative impact of television, film, and violent video game images with the seemingly benign textbook depictions of war-torn lands in times and places long forgotten, it is the constant representation of war, conflict, and violence as the pathway to our nation's rise to prowess that must certainly influence students' attitudes toward war and peace. It is the subtle and ubiquitous representation that democracy, freedom, justice, and equality are the pearls of great price that could only be achieved and can only be preserved through war.

Do social studies textbooks and curriculum promote violent acts carried out in our schools, homes, communities, and world? There is certainly not enough data to propagate such a hypothesis. However, it is incumbent on the social studies educator to begin the process of examining the impact of social studies textbooks', curricula, and media resources' continuous representation of war as the solution to conflict; armed engagement as the response to disagreement; and militaristic metaphors and symbols as the essence of security on the perceptions and attitudes of social education students toward the issues of war and peace.

Are we to eliminate the descriptions of America's past involvement in warfare, exploration, conquest, and territorial protection? There is certainly credence to Liddell Hart's memorable motto, "If you want peace, understand war" (Howard, 1983). Yet if we do not offer examples of peace, alternatives to violence, and solutions to armed conflict then the cognitive power of Liddell's notion of comparing and contrasting peace and war is lost. There must be a concerted effort on the part of social educators and administrators to seek alternative approaches to the militaristic democracy as presented by textbook authors and curriculum developers. We must provide equal representation in presenting the characters, concepts, events, and activities of persons who challenged militarism and conquest through local, state, national, and international peace movements.

Where there are stories and images of generals leading their men into harm's way on domestic battlefields and foreign shores, there must be equally prominent descriptions and depictions of the role of conscientious objectors, scientists, political leaders, and activist citizens whose collective efforts challenged the conventional wisdom of militaristic fervor during periods of war by promoting peace, social justice, democratic rights, and the responsible development and use of technology.

Social education teachers, students, parents, and community leaders must work to develop textbook and curriculum alternatives that honestly address the outcomes of war, armed conflict, and violent coups d'état. Social education content, concepts, themes, and issues that promote the advantages of peace must be incorporated by offering examples of persons, organizations, and events that worked collaboratively to ensure peaceful solutions on the local, state, national, and global arenas. The glorification of violence as the only alternative to resolving conflict must be countered by images and descriptions that identify racial similarities, celebrate cultural differences, and promote human interactions that bridge the social, political, cultural, and economic divides between nations and their people.

THE UNITY TRIANGLE—TOWARD SOCIAL JUSTICE

The Unity Triangle offers the innovative social educator an opportunity to plan and implement teaching and learning activities in a way that ensures balance in the representation of human events and characters who were primary players in peace, liberation, equal rights, and social justice movements in both the United States and around the globe. The Unity Triangle Model

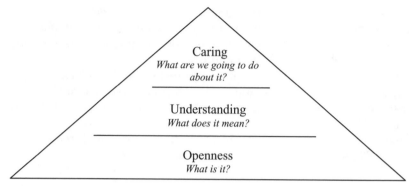

FIG. 4.1   The unity triangle model.

(Fig. 4.1) is comprised of three parts: (a) Openness, (b) Understanding, and (c) Caring.

Openness

Openness is the foundation of the triangle. It seeks diverse content and responds to the inquiry, "What is it that comprises this concept, event, issue, and/or theme?" When planning lessons with the Unity Triangle the teacher embraces the concept of openness by incorporating diverse content, perspectives, and concepts that offer alternative views to the social studies textbooks and curricula. Teaching and learning activities that foster openness of thought and expression, such as dialogue circles, discussion clusters, and open inquiry utilizing divergent questions, are planned and implemented in a way that ensure all students are free to explore and express the multiple experiences and examples of how they relate to the social studies content being studies.

Understanding

Understanding is the heart of the Unity Triangle. The social education teacher who creates an environment of openness ultimately fosters levels of understanding by allowing her or his students to elaborate on why they believe something is true or false, right or wrong, justified or unjustified. Any measure of openness fosters enhanced understanding through the pursuit of meaning found in binary opposites. The social education teacher facilitates learning activities that involve role-play, scenario, and personalized product development (e.g., diaries, essays, paintings, web pages depicting personal understanding and expression of the concept, theme and/or issue being explored) that express the students' level of understanding born from the openness of the class environment. Understanding activities empower the individual while promoting a sense of creative unity. Understanding is always supported through students being open to listening, sharing, and inquiring about others' ideas, opinions, and beliefs. Where openness asks, "What is it?" understanding asks, "What does it mean?"

Caring

The pinnacle of the Unity Triangle is caring. Caring synthesizes what we've discovered through openness and what meaning we've attached through understanding and asks, "What are we going to do about it?" Caring is an active response to the individual and collective power of a teaching and learning environment that fosters openness and promotes understanding through the cognitive and affective exploration and expression of the diverse beliefs, philosophies, principles, catalysts, and emotions that comprise the social studies.

Caring is never passive. The caring student is no longer satisfied with social studies that simply informs. The caring student is one who embraces social studies that transforms. Caring motivates the student to challenge the representation of facts in social studies textbooks, curricula, and media materials by searching for alternative viewpoints, primary documents, and ethnographic depictions. Caring bridges the gap between the abstract and the concrete by attaching personal meaning to events that take place in times, in lands, and to people far away. Caring empowers the student to write, develop, and produce posters, murals, films, pictorials, music, web pages, short stories, poetry, essays, editorials, and a litany of personalized products that juxtapose the student's contemporary world to events. Caring is the essence to the phrase, "Think globally and act locally."

The Unity Triangle, therefore, builds affective context to the cognitive information surrounding any other concept, theme, or issue by transforming the event or idea to a level that explores the broader view of peace and war by examining the catalysts to injustice and the alternatives to revenge. No longer is war the only answer or solution to the human condition of conflict. No longer is the notion of world peace unattainable.

SUMMARY

Social education should be a place where students are provided an opportunity to engage controversial social issues through inquiry and problem solving, thus leading to social justice. It should be a place that facilitates peace making rather than conflict. It should be a forum for students to find a way to voice their opinions while gaining insight into their values and an understanding and respect for others. The social studies classroom should be a place where cooperation and collaboration are celebrated as a means to achieving the goals of the majority while respecting the rights of the minority. Problem solving and decision making should be at the heart of this endeavor. Unfortunately what students are presently getting in social education is a watered down transmission of the events of mankind. Today's youth are our future and we need to help prepare them to take charge of this role by using controversial issues in our social education classrooms. Educational leadership must play a more proactive role in allowing for social education and social justice approaches in our schools—for the ultimate benefit of citizenship and democratic education.

Integrating controversy so as to facilitate social efficacy should be based on four basic principles. One, depth is more powerful and engaging than breadth. In order to facilitate any detailed understanding of a particular issue, a student needs to fully understand the issue in order to make well-organized and well-grounded arguments concerning the issue. Second, topics need to be connected through some kind of thematic, disciplinary, interdisciplinary, or historical nature. This is done to facilitate the relationships that exist between the issues. Next, content must be of a challenging nature. Last, students must experience some ownership of the learning for it to have any meaning to them personally. Taking the students interests, their prior knowledge, and their local community and showing how each is related to the issue makes it relevant to them.

Students who encounter controversy on a regular basis will emerge as more thoughtful people. They will identify and analyze their own values. The process of how we came to believe in something is an important process to understand. Students will encounter different viewpoints during discussion of controversial issues and will be able to understand why people have differing viewpoints. Students need exposure to controversial issues; this exposure will lead students to a deeper understanding of their social world. Soley says that students who are exposed to controversial issues regularly experience lower levels of cynicism, higher levels of duty, increased levels of political efficacy, social integration, trust in society, and a belief that the person can affect his or her political system (Soley, 1996). Only through these endeavors can we hope to give peace a chance.

Schooling and social studies education need not be the archaic and disempowering endeavors that they presently are. Our children, our teachers, and the future of the globe deserve more. A "powerful" social studies education that focuses on the suggested approaches by reestablishing the controversy, story, problem solving, and relevance of social studies for social efficacy is vital. These classrooms and schools can become empowering and meaningful through the model suggested. Social studies and schooling in general can be made a transformative process for individuals and society. The development and transformation of social efficacy for our kids and teachers really demands this. Administrators must recognize this and adapt to meet these needs.

A major rationale for schooling is to prepare students for their future. Schools should therefore allow controversy into their classrooms because students will have to encounter controversy and social issues throughout their lives, and administrators must support and celebrate these possibilities. Instead of resorting to complete withdrawal or violent rage, students and teachers would be encouraged to develop peace-making and conflict-resolution strategies. But many students will not have exposure to controversy and social issues in their classes.

How do we help students seek solutions to conflict? How do we promote collaboration? How do we teach tolerance? How do we equip students with the skills that lead to constructive solutions? Openness, understanding, and caring are the antithetical responses to isolation, exclusion, abandonment, apathy, and despair. Openness, understanding, and caring are also the ingredients to powerful social education. These three elements are the vehicles that inspire the citizens to initiate a letter campaign or a petition drive that calls on local, state, national, and international leaders to rebuild the homes of those who have been victims of natural or human violence and destruction; to design programs that feed the hungry and impoverished whose means of sustenance have been destroyed by domestic and international violence; to run for local, state, and national elected office on a social justice platform; to organize and lead protest movements that target political and corporate leaders whose environmentally irresponsible policies, practices, and production of goods endanger the lives of human and animal species across the globe; to seek peaceful solutions to the conflicts that arise from misunderstanding, intolerance, avarice, and prejudice at home, school, and in society.

The Unity Triangle ensures that social education and schooling not only inform, but also prepare students to reform and transform the way they think, act, and feel about themselves and the world around them. It inspires them to create movements that change the way social studies is represented in the next generation of textbooks. Thinking locally and acting globally become mantras instead of mottos. And only through these efforts can we hope to give peace a chance through social education. Educational leadership will be well served by accepting the Unity Triangle as future administrators are trained as these are vital and lifelong skills.

A transformative social justice framework needs to be the focus of social education and schools. It is high time to rethink social studies and schooling for social justice. A society not open and comfortable enough to allow for critique cannot progress and is a society in decline (Loewen, 1995). Critical teaching and learning for social justice sees the true purpose of education as the democratization of society, the highest good, not the protection of the interests of the establishment and unethical minority that dominates American political, economic, and social culture (Apple & Beane, 1995).

GUIDING QUESTIONS

1. What are the purposes of schooling and education in our society? Debate the concepts of socialization, passivity, and social justice within schooling and education.
2. How do goals such as social reconstruction, transformation, and transgression fit within schooling and education?
3. What is the role of educational leadership in addressing issues of social justice in schooling and education?

SELECTED READINGS

Apple, M., & Beane, J. (1995). *Democratic schools.* Alexandria, VA: Association for Supervision and Curriculum Development.
Kincheloe, J. (2002). *Getting beyond the facts.* New York: Peter Lang.
Loewen, J. (1995). *Lies my teacher told me.* New York: Touchtone.
Marciano, J. (1997). *Civic illiteracy and education.* New York: Peter Lang.
Zinn, H. (2003). *A people's history of the United States.* New York: Perennial.

REFERENCES

Apple, M., & Beane, J. (1995). *Democratic schools.* Alexandria, VA: Association for Supervision and Curriculum Development.
Ashford, M. W. (1996, Summer). Peace education after the cold war. *Canadian Social Studies, 30,* 178–181.
Banks, J., Beyer, B. K., Contreras, G., Craven, J., Ladsen-Billings, G., McFarland, M. S., & Parker, W. C. (1998). *Latin America and Canada: Adventures in time and place.* New York: MacMillian/McGraw-Hill School Division.
Beiner, R. (Ed.). (1995). *Theorizing citizenship.* Albany: State University of New York Press.
Blainey, G. (1988). *The causes of war* (3rd ed.). New York: The Free Press.
Bynres, R. S. (1997). Interrupting ordinary expectations in the social studies. *Journal of Curriculum and Supervision, 12*(2), 135–151.
Cohen, R. (1998). History on trial: Culture wars and the teaching of the past, by Gary Nash, Charlott Crabtree, and Ross E. Dunn. *Social Education, 62*(2), 116–118.
Cunningham, C. (1995). *Personal communication.* Hamilton, ON: Chedoke Child and Family Centere, McMaster University.
Engle, S. H., & Ochoa, A. S. (1988). *Education for democratic citizenship.* New York: Teachers College Press.

Evans, R. W., & Saxe, D. W. (Eds.). (1996). *Handbook on teaching social issues*. Washington, DC: National Council for the Social Studies.

Fleming, D. B. (1984). *The treatment of peace and security issues in social studies textbooks in the United States*. (ERIC Document Reproduction Service No. ED247163).

Gallo, M. (1996). Controversial issues in practice. *Social Education, 60*(1), C1–C4.

Gutman, A. (1990). Democratic education in difficult times. *Teachers College Record, 92*, 7–20.

Hahn, C. (1996). Investigating controversial issues at election time. *Social Education, 60*(10), 348–350.

Hope, W. (1996). It's time to transform social studies teaching. *The Social Studies, 87*(4).

Howard, M. (1983). *The causes of wars and other essays* (2nd ed.). Cambridge, MA: Harvard University Press.

Kincheloe, J. (2002). *Getting beyond the facts*. New York: Peter Lang.

Lockwood, A. (1996). Controversial issues: The teacher's crucial role. *Social Education, 60*(1), 28–31.

Loewen, J. (1995). *Lies my teacher told me*. New York: Touchtone.

McBee, R. H. (1996). Can controversial topics by taught in the early grades? *Social Education, 60*(1), 38–41.

National Council for the Social Studies (NCSS). (1994). *Expectations for excellence: Curriculum standards for social studies*. Washington, DC: NCSS.

Onosko, J. J. (1996). Exploring issues with students despite the barriers. *Social Education, 60*(1), 22–27.

Purpel, D., & Shapiro, S. (1995). *Beyond liberation and excellence*. Westport, CT: Bergin and Garvey.

Ross, E. W. (Ed.). (1997). *The social studies curriculum*. Albany: State University of New York Press.

Rossi, J. A. (1995). In-depth study in an issues-oriented social studies classroom. *Theory and Research in the Social Education, 23*(2), 88–120.

Rossi, J. A. (1996). Creating strategies and conditions for civil discourse about controversial issues. *Social Education, 60*(1), 15–21.

Sheety, A. (1999). *Curriculum and peace in the Middle East*. (ERIC Document Reproduction Service No. ED433265)

Sizer, T. R. (1992). *Horace's compromise*. New York: Houghton Mifflin.

Soley, M. (1996). If it's controversial, why teach it? *Social Education, 60*(1), 9–14.

Stanley, W. (1992). *Curriculum for utopia*. Albany: State University of New York Press.

Tibbitts, F. (1996). On human dignity. *Social Education, 60*(10), 428–431.

Westheimer, J., & Kahne, J. (1998). Education for action: Preparing youth for participatory democracy. In William Ayers, Jean Ann Hunt, & Therese Quinn (Eds.), *Teaching for social justice* (pp. 1–20). New York: The New Press.

White, C. (1999). *Transforming social studies: A critical perspective*. Springfield, IL: Charles C. Thomas Publisher.

White, C. (2000). *Issues in social studies: Voices from the classroom*. Springfield, IL: Charles C. Thomas Publisher.

Chapter 5

Religious Controversy

Suzanne Rosenblith
Clemson University

> *School is not a religion free zone.*
> —Jerry Horton, Superintendent
> Pontotoc County School District, Mississippi

> *Public Schools do not have a right to teach children a religious viewpoint.*
> —Lisa Herdahl, Parent
> Pontotoc County School District, Mississippi

From federal initiatives to lower the wall of separation through such policies as school vouchers to state and local attempts to smooth the way for more religion in our public schools through such measures as posting the Ten Commandments and redrawing our K–12 textbooks to reflect religious [read Christian] belief and doctrine, religious controversy pervades our public schools at every level. Some, like Robert Ulich, call it "The great American debate" (Freund & Ulich, 1965). In fact, religious controversy has historically permeated society at many levels, yet the manner in which we as citizens, in general, and as educators, specifically, negotiate these controversies is not something the historical record gives clear guidance on. This is the matter political philosopher John Rawls (1996) examines in the early going of his book *Political Liberalism*. He asks, "How is it possible that there may exist over time a stable and just society of free and equal citizens profoundly divided by reasonable religious, philosophical, and moral doctrines?" (1996, p. 27). In other words, how do we as a society, so profoundly separated by some of our deepest commitments, come together in order for our just and free society to exist and to thrive? Throughout his book, Rawls attempts to answer this question and in short, Rawls says we must put aside our private religious, philosophical, and moral doctrines and rely on those principles and standards of justice to which all reasonable citizens can agree. In many ways, I think Rawls is ultimately right. If we as a citizenry are so deeply divided by

73

our "private" beliefs, then we must collectively find some common ground, some common language, by which we as reasonable citizens can construct and abide by certain principles and standards of justice. Yet on another level, I think Rawls fails to appreciate the incredibly significant degree of religious difference and its impact on the public sphere, generally, and the public school, specifically. That is, Rawls makes certain assumptions, chief among them the *possibility* that one is able (or that it is desirable) to shelve his or her private beliefs for the benefit of the state. In other words, for many Americans, one's religious, philosophical, or moral doctrine guides one's outlook on public life including public education, and such compelling belief systems cannot be so easily set aside, even if for the benefit of our just and free state.

To begin to answer Rawls' very compelling question, it becomes critical to understand why religious controversy is so pervasive in the United States and, in particular, in American public schools. The question that I want to explore in this chapter, then, is not the *fact* that religious controversy exists, but rather I want to examine *why* religious controversy is so pervasive and contentious in our public schools. Historically this has been the case, and the evidence before us is quite clear: Controversies in religious matters pertaining to public education are increasing in both kind and degree. Though many might say the reason for such an increase is a direct correlation to the rise in religious fundamentalism, I think that answer is too simple. A rise in religious fundamentalism is certainly a contributing factor, but the reasons for such an increase in religious controversy is much more complicated and involved. There are in fact five identifiable groups who in their own, albeit different, ways contribute to the problem of religious controversy. The first section of this chapter introduces these five groups (or positions). The second section looks at a specific case that serves as an example of how religious controversy plays out in our public schools. The third and fourth sections examine this case from two very different perspectives. The third section explores the constitutional issues involved while section four focuses on the issue of private and public commitments. In both of these sections, readers should be able to begin to appreciate the significant problem of religious controversy by seeing the controversy through the "eyes" of each of the five groups. The final section, then, serves as both conclusions and suggestions.

FACTS, TRUTHS, AND KNOWLEDGE

Although this group remains a minority in the scheme of debates about religion and public education, this first group, the facts, truths, and knowledge group (FTK), is nevertheless worthy of mention because it presents a point of view distinct from any of the others. This group argues that religious controversy should essentially be ignored, because there should be no controversy in both principle and fact. This group argues that public schools are in the business of teaching truths, facts, and disciplinary knowledge, whereas religion is in the business of conveying faith and guiding individuals and groups personally, spiritually, and emotionally. This group does not imply that issues governing morality and values do not enter the public school, rather that these issues should only be addressed insofar as they help students become reasonable and thoughtful thinkers. A defender of the FTK view might argue that values and ethics come into school to the degree that students are taught the idea of developing ethical principles. In such a class, this group would argue, the important exercise is in enabling students to develop the ability to form principles of ethical reasoning and less so with the actual principle. Likewise, FTK advocates might suggest that discussions of values are relevant only in the context of developing in students a sense of civic pride, or for students to better understand reasons and causes of wars, for example. In both cases, the primary aim is academic, not religious or spiritual. Defenders of this point of view argue that the organization of teacher-training programs is further evidence for their view in that teachers are trained, tested, and schooled in their academic subject areas, pedagogical techniques, and age-appropriate educational psychology and not in religious matters (at least not teachers seeking certification for K–12 public education). If religion was meant to be in the schools, they argue, teacher-certification standards would reflect that. In short, supporters of the FTK view argue plainly that addressing religious matters in any reasonable sense of the phrase is not within the purview of the public schools.

STRICT SEPARATION

The second group, generally referred to as the strict separationists, argues that the Constitution, the historical record, and the framers' intentions are very clear—that the wall of separation is to be so high that the state does not interfere with religion and that religion does not enter into matters of the state. The group argues that religious controversy can be easily avoided by simply removing all vestiges of religion from the public school. And although strict separationists acknowledge that religion is important to many people, they argue that there is ample time to address religion outside of the school. In fact, this group argues that one thing we seem to do quite well in our society is religion, pointing to the fact that there is no lack of religious houses of worships, religious youth groups, and the like, and therefore it seems burdensome to add religion to the many responsibilities of the public school (Doerr, 1998, p. 228). Strict separationists are apt to remind us that our framers protected us from this issue; Thomas Jefferson made it very clear when in 1802 in a letter to the Danbury Baptists he wrote, "I contemplate with sovereign reverence that act of the whole American people which declared that their legislature should 'make no law respecting an establishment of religion, or prohibiting the free exercise thereof,' thus building a wall of separation between church and state" (Nord, 1995, p. 135). Furthermore, strict separationists assert that the Bill of Rights was put in place to protect minority points of view. They argue that even if some religion was allowed in the schools, it would be not only Christianity, but a particular version of Christianity offensive to all except those who are members of that particular denomination. Strict separationists insist that once we allow even the smallest amount of religion into our schools, the lines between church and state become blurred and the public school ceases to be a safe place for all Americans to learn—instead becoming yet another institution influenced and controlled by the religious majority in this country.

ACCOMMODATION

The third group, accomodationists, points to the constitutional record and an interpretation of establishment that differs from the strict separationist account. Accomodationists argue that the prohibition against establishment simply means that the federal government may not establish a state church— that is, the Establishment Clause of the First Amendment (Congress shall make no law establishing religion) precludes the construction of the Church of the United States. Beyond this exclusion, government may be somewhat accommodating toward religion as long as it does not prefer one religion to another. Accomodationists argue that the second clause of the First amendment also guarantees citizens the right to religious expression and that one's protected rights as a citizen do not stop at the schoolhouse door. Therefore, they point to the strict separationists as a large part of the problem of religious controversy, arguing that they have presented their ideology and point of view on the meaning of establishment as though it were absolute fact. Accomodationists argue that strict separationists do not have a special purchase on the absolute truth of things, and that an accomodationist position is far more reasonable and much more consonant with the values and tenets of a pluralistic, tolerant democracy.

NEUTRAL SEPARATION

Like the accommodationists, the fourth group, neutral separationists, argues that although it is true that the Constitution guarantees a separation of church and state, the wall of separation between these two entities need not be as high as strict separationists think. In fact, neutral separationists argue that there are many social and educational benefits to be gained by lowering the wall. They argue that there is educational value in learning about the variety of religious worldviews and that such study can contribute to a person's intellectual, social, emotional, and psychological benefit (e.g., Noddings, 1993; Nord, 1995). They also believe that schools, contrary to the FTK point of view, are in the business of much more than students' intellectual development. They caution that a society made up of citizens who are able to provide evidence and think cogently but who have no ability for empathy or to care for their fellow human beings is a frightening thought. Additionally, neutral separationists reason that because students are already thinking about religion, it makes little sense to act as though religion must be shelved in the very place where they spend the bulk of their childhood years. This group argues that one could not understand much of history, art, or literature without understanding the role religion has played in these fields. Moreover, excluding religion and maintaining a strict separationist approach disenfranchises religious adherents in much the same way as African Americans and women have been disenfranchised through omission from the formal curriculum (Nord, 1999). Finally, neutral separationists argue that the Establishment Clause of the Constitution prevents government from preferring religion to nonreligion and vice versa and that a policy of strict separation amounts to government preferring nonreligion—the secular—to religion.

NONSEPARATION

The fifth group, nonseparationists, argues that for some citizens, it is not possible to separate church and state because it is not possible to shelve religious views and belief systems. In short, everything in life is guided by and seen through the lens of their faith. Although this group asserts that it can understand the notion of separation from the perspective of the Establishment Clause (Congress shall make no law respecting an establishment of religion), it also believes that the Free Exercise Clause (or prohibiting the free exercise thereof) guaranteeing citizens the right to free expression protects its religious viewpoints. As such, liberal, secular encumbrances prevent the constitutionally guaranteed right to freedom of religious expression. The idea that one has to "check God at the door of public education" is not only anathema to this group, but also not possible given members' commitments to their faith and their obligations according to their faith. Secularists are quick to label this group "fanatical," but what secularists fail to appreciate and respect is the fact that for some religious adherents, faith enters into every aspect of their daily lives. Public schools are just that—public—and they must, according to the Free Exercise Clause, be more accommodating, at least in the sense of allowing individual citizens their rights to religious expression. Nonseparationists argue that the lack of accommodation and the lack of respect accorded them serves to disenfranchise them. Additionally, they argue that one would be foolish if he or she thought religion was not already pervasive in our schools; the religion of humanism is evinced in every class at all grade levels.

At a deeper level, however, this group differs from the accomodationists in that it thinks the notion of separating the public from the private is artificial. People identifying with this group walk through their everyday guided by their faith and find it impossible in any real sense to separate one's public commitments from one's private commitments. Nonseparationists believe that just as the African American is unable to shed his or her race, so too the deeply devout are not able to shed their commitment to their faith, which is why to even speak of separating the public from the private misses the important fact that they are guided in all that they do by their faith.

SUMMARY OF FIVE GROUPS

Although the characterizations of these five identifiably different groups should already make readers see a little clearer why religion is such a thorny issue and why our schools have such a tremendous degree of religious controversy, the issue gets even more contentious because those who identify with any of these perspectives generally takes their respective view as a primary commitment. Thus, a person in the first group is primarily committed to establishing principles, policies, and curriculum that serve to foster intellectual development. Likewise, a person identifying as a strict separationist would consider a Jeffersonian interpretation of the First amendment—strict separation—to be a primary educational commitment. For this group, when educational decisions are made, this interpretation must be given top consideration. Accomodationists are primarily concerned with striking a reasonable balance between overt proselytizing and an unnecessarily high wall of separation. The fourth group argues that public schools must be committed to the well-being of the whole child and that means including religion where relevant. Including the study of religion helps to recenter these disenfranchised students in much the same way as multicultural education has helped to recenter students affiliated with minority ethnicities, races, and cultures. The final group, perhaps the most radical of all, is primarily committed to its religious faith. As such, any notion of separation is, in any functional sense, merely semantic because religion is not simply a *part* of who they are, it *is* who they are—men and women of deep and profound faith. Whatever each group regards as a commitment is of the highest order and, as such, it becomes clear how easily religious controversy manifests itself, and how difficult some sort of agreement on religious matters becomes.

But to get an even better appreciation for religious controversy, we will now look at one issue that has dominated current debates about religion and public education; this is the matter of public school prayer. My purpose here is to show how and why religious controversy runs so deep, and how little agreement on any issue is possible. Additionally, I hope readers will begin to see how each of the five groups make relatively reasonable claims given the context and point of view from which they are primarily concerned.

LET US PRAY

The issue of school prayer is in no way a new issue facing public education. Quite the contrary; the early to mid-20th century was rife with Supreme Court cases regarding this matter. And certainly, the issue of prayer in schools dates even further back to the common school era. Nevertheless, this issue has taken on a new face in contemporary times with our courts considering a range of cases from moments of silence to prayers at graduation ceremonies and football games to organized yet "voluntary" school prayer at the start of school. The case we examine, *Herdahl v. Pontotoc County School District* (933 F. Supp. 582[1996]), is particularly interesting because the issues that emerged prior to and during the court hearings reflect the depth and complexity of religious controversy in public education. At the core of this case in particular and the debate surrounding school prayer in general are two separate, yet equally important, issues. First is the question of what happens when the Establishment and Free Exercise Clauses are at loggerheads. In other words, what happens when there is clearly government support for a religion, yet without such support, a majority of citizens' right to religious freedom is hampered? The second issue, although not a legal matter, is nonetheless equally as dicey; it pertains to the matter of private and public commitments. In other words, what happens when members of a community differ over notions of private and public commitments and the primacy of one over the other, or even the very notion of dividing these into separate kinds of concerns?

The controversy in the first instance is a battle between those who support freedom of religion and those who support freedom of religious expression. In one sense there is a semantic battle over the meaning of the term "religious freedom." Yet as we see momentarily, this battle runs deeper than mere semantics. In the second instance, we have an identity battle within a community regarding how to prioritize and best represent the highest commitments of community members.

HERDAHL V. PONTOTOC COUNTY SCHOOL DISTRICT

Pontotoc County, Mississippi, is a small, mainly rural, county in the northern part of the state. The people of Pontotoc County are quite devout, with a large majority belonging to the Southern Baptist Convention. In 1978, Lisa Gooch, then a student at the high school, initiated morning devotionals over the school intercom system. Gooch maintains that the idea for intercom prayers was "the Lord's will" (Grunberg & Crane, 1999).[1] In the fall 1994, Lisa Herdahl and her family moved from Wisconsin to Pontotoc County. Herdahl describes herself as a Christian, attending church on a weekly basis. When she took her school-aged children to register for classes, she was astounded to hear the devotional prayers broadcast over the school intercom system. She spoke with the school superintendent and voiced her concerns, which mainly focused on her belief that the public school has no right to teach her children a religious viewpoint. She also pointed out that given the nature of the prayers, such a practice might alienate those children who were not members of the Christian faith. The superintendent, Jerry Horton, responded to her that, "school is not a religion-free zone." After doing some research, Herdahl discovered that the law in fact was on her side; Mississippi law says devotional Bible reading is not allowable in public schools. When she brought this statute to the attention of Superintendent Horton, he replied, "But we've been doing it for 50 years and we're not going to stop." In addition to the intercom prayers, Herdahl discovered that the school also held Bible classes during the school day taught by the school's faculty. The nature of these classes was not academic but again devotional, culminating in a group prayer. Furthermore, in the elementary grades, teachers facilitated prelunch prayers with students acting as, "blessing-sayer helpers." Students who did not want to participate were instructed to step out into the hallway. After Herdahl and her attorneies brought suit, in February 1995 the Court ordered a preliminary injunction barring the intercom devotionals. As a result, students organized pre-school devotional activities in the school gymnasium.

RELIGIOUS FREEDOM

What is perhaps most interesting about the Herdahl case is that both the plaintiffs and defendants claimed to be fighting for religious freedom. For Herdahl and the two organizations that represented her in court, the American Civil Liberties Union (ACLU) and People for the American Way (PAW),

---

[1]All references to particular individuals come from the film *School Prayer: A Community at War.*

this was a fight to protect citizens' constitutionally guaranteed right to freedom of religion. For the defendants, the Pontotoc County School District,
this was a fight to guarantee their rights to freedom of religious expression.
Both sides asked the same question yet interpreted the question's meaning
quite differently. Both wanted to know whether government was going to
direct religious practices in the Pontotoc County School District. The plaintiffs argued that if the intercom devotionals, Bible classes, and prelunch
prayers were to continue, this would be a clear violation of the Establishment Clause. The defendants argued that if government interfered and
barred these practices, government was restricting the guarantees of the
Free Exercise Clause. Letters of support to the school district highlight the
school's position. One supporter wrote to Superintendent Horton, "Keep
standing up for your first amendment rights." Supporters for the plaintiff
considered Lisa Herdahl to be a "true patriot."

Two years after the ACLU and PAW brought suit on behalf of Lisa
Herdahl, the federal court in Oxford, Mississippi, handed down a decision.
The court was faced with deciding five matters: intercom prayer, student-
organized prayer before the start of school, Bible classes, prelunch prayers,
and religious instruction and proselytizing in classes. With the exception
of student-organized pre-school prayer, the court decided overwhelmingly
in favor of the plaintiffs. On the issue of intercom prayers, the court held
that because the law mandated students to be in their classrooms, they were
compelled to listen to the prayers, and forced prayer, also known as captive-
audience prayer, in public schools was not allowable. Student-organized
prayer prior to the start of school was upheld because, unlike the intercom
prayers, students (and their parents) could decide whether they would participate. However, the court stated that teachers could not participate in the
prayer activities and that they had to limit their involvement to a supervisory
role. On the matter of prelunch prayers, the court decided that such activity
was clearly in violation of the Establishment Clause, regardless if students or
teachers led the prayers. The issue of Bible-study classes was also found to
violate the Establishment Clause. The court used the Lemon Test, a three-
prong test used as a standard to adjudicate Establishment Clause cases, and
decided that such classes failed on all three counts.[2] The court found that
the bible classes clearly lacked a secular purpose in that they represented a
Christian biblical viewpoint. The court found that the Bible classes did not
meet the standard of the primary-effect prong either because its primary
effect was to advance not only religion in general, but a specific type of religion. And on the third prong, the court found that teaching Bible classes on

---

[2]The three prongs of the Lemon Test include: (a) The statute must have a secular purpose;
(b) its primary effect neither advances nor inhibits religion; and (c) it does not form an excessive
entanglement between government and religion.

school grounds during the school day is excessive entanglement of government and religion. The final issue of religious instruction and proselytizing in classes was also found to violate the separation of church and state, thus restricting teachers from using religious materials in the course of instruction.

That the court decided as it did is indicative of the fact that the court interpreted "religious freedom" as freedom from government support of religion rather than emphasizing, as the defendants did, freedom of expression. The court, it seems, did not think the defendants' central argument—that the majority of the community should suffer at the hands of one individual nonbeliever—was particularly compelling. Furthermore, in his decision presiding Judge Neal Biggers argued that the very purpose of the Bill of Rights is to protect the minority "from the tyranny of the majority." Additionally, Judge Biggers did not share the concerns of the defendants who worried that a judgment in Herdahl's favor would force them to do the impossible—separate their religious commitments from their public commitments. In fact as a direct response to this concern, Biggers stated, "Some of the defendants argue that this ruling will stifle all prayer in schools, but the court feels that as long as there are tests in school, there will be prayers also."[3]

The court's decision, although clearly in line with the constitutional record—the law of the land—nevertheless is a clear example of the deep-rooted nature of religious controversy. Whereas it is clear that the strict separationists were quite pleased with this decision in that the court clearly reaffirmed a strict separationist interpretation of the Establishment Clause, the other four groups likely would not see the judgment in quite the same light. The first group, FTK, likely felt that although the judge made the right decision, this case is nevertheless another example of how ideologues have taken over our public education. This group would continue to maintain that regardless of the judgment, public schools are not in the business of dispensing faith; they are in the business of teaching academic subjects and developing certain disciplinary ways of thinking in students. Therefore, school prayer (no matter the form), Bible study, and all of the other initiatives in the Pontotoc County School District were mostly problematic not because they did or did not violate one or both clauses of the First amendment, but rather because there is nothing to gain intellectually from school prayer, Bible study, or appointing students "prayer-sayer helpers."

The accommodationists would likely focus on the shared community values and argue that surely the framers could not have meant by "establishment" the Constitution trouncing on the almost entirely unanimous shared community values. This group would be very sympathetic to the defendants' argument that as a matter of fairness, one person should not have the right to dictate the cultural and religious norms of an entire community. Had

---

[3]One should note the satirical tone of the judge's statement, particularly in light of the discussion in the next section.

Herdahl and her family never moved to Pontotoc County, this community would still be intact, sharing their religious values and ideals with one another in every aspect of their lives—including public school.

From a legal perspective, neutral separationists would agree with the court's decision, pointing to the historical record and specifically to the *Abbington School District v. Schempp* (1963) decision where the court made the distinction between *practicing* religion in school and *studying* religion in public school (374 U.S. 203 [1963]). Given that each initiative put forth by the school district clearly fell on the side of practice rather than study, the neutral separationists would concur. However, it is plausible that neutral separationists would urge the school district to implement a class or a series of classes in the study of religion. This, they would argue, might be beneficial to students in the county. Yet on a deeper level, both the neutral separationists as well as the accommodationists would be deeply angry at the way this small, devout community in Northern Mississippi was portrayed. These groups would use this case as an excellent example of how religion in general is misrecognized and disrespected in this country. The defendants are made out to be religious fanatics, rather than a community with incredibly strong ties to their faith.

The final group, the nonseparationists, obviously suffered the greatest defeat. Given that this group's central position is that one's faith enters into all aspects of one's life, the court, in deciding with the plaintiff, has mandated the impossible. As a matter of fairness, this decision is very difficult to swallow, because it is clear from their point of view that Judge Biggers, holding a strict separationist interpretation of the Constitution, did not take their concerns about their religious identity seriously. By virtue of the fact that Biggers found the Establishment Clause argument more compelling, those who argued on the grounds of a violation of the Free Exercise Clause find their right to religious freedom greatly hampered. According to this group, the court failed to understand the cultural and religious values of the citizens of Pontotoc County and for them, the controversy is not over, rather it is only beginning because they have good reason to fight for their constitutionally guaranteed right to religious expression. To appreciate the depth of this point, it is necessary to examine the second issue that emerged from the case: the relationship between private and public commitments.

SEPARATION OF PRIVATE AND PUBLIC COMMITMENTS

The bigger issue in this case from all points of view is the matter under discussion in this section. What happens when a group's public commitments (the law of the land) conflict with their private commitments (religious belief)? Or, to put the question more controversially, what happens when the very possibility of separating one's private and public commitments is challenged? It is this question that lays at the crux of religious controversy; for the people of Pontotoc Country, the assumption that one's private and public commitments can be separated is one they would challenge.

To illustrate this point, consider these two comments:

"It's not prayer and religion in school; it's a part of everything we do" (Pontotoc County Prayer Advocate).

"Religion isn't something you talk about; religion is something you are in" (Lisa Gooch, Prayer Advocate).

Here it seems that both prayer advocates are trying to convey the point that it is impossible to separate religious belief from the rest of one's self. Religious belief is a part of Gooch and other prayer advocates in Pontotoc County in a way that differs from others who identify with a religious belief system. For the people of Pontotoc Country, their Christian Fundamentalism makes their religious belief an intrinsic part of their core. It is their frame of reference. It is who they are. It factors into how they see every aspect of the world and it cannot be shelved at any given time, particularly for 8 hours every day of the school year. For people like Lisa Gooch, it is not a matter of wanting to offend those who believe differently, rather it is about their relationships with their faith and how to fulfill the obligations of that relationship properly and fully. To that point, prayer advocates urged that they were not trying to force prayer or make everyone a Christian Fundamentalist, they just wanted their freedom to worship God according to the dictates of their hearts.

The Pontotoc County prayer advocates also argued that it was undemocratic for one person to tell 1,300 students that they were not permitted to pray. It seems the notion of democracy employed had more to do with local, participatory decision making and not the law of the land (the Constitution). The overwhelming majority of residents of Pontotoc County did not believe they were disregarding the Constitution outright because they genuinely believed that the Constitution guaranteed them religious freedom. What they were unable to understand were the implicit limits on their freedom. Their religious beliefs could not be fulfilled, according to the limits of the Constitution, because they were unable to separate their religious identity from the rest of their identity.

Herdahl, on the other hand, best represented by the strict separationist point of view, argues that public schools have no right to teach her children a religious viewpoint. What is interesting here is Herdahl's use of the word "right." Herdahl is making a very strong claim because her issue is not with the *content* of the religious viewpoint so much as with the basic principle of schools *conveying* a religious viewpoint. Herdahl and her representation argued that government had no business directing religious practice in the schools. Implicit in this claim is another claim that "religion" is separable from "school" and also separable from "government." This is not a claim her opponents could appreciate or understand.

The assumption that church-state or private-public are separate entities is a central issue for our five identifiable groups. This assumption gets to the heart of the matter of religious controversy in the United States.

Although many, including Herdahl, simply accept as fact the separate nature of church and state and private and public, the superintendent, principal, teachers, students, and parents of Pontotoc County cannot do the same. In fact, for them the notion that these two spheres are separate and distinct is incomprehensible. Their belief in the inseparability of public and private, of church and state, is not because of this group's wish to push their religious beliefs into the public realm, but rather it is because their "public" realm is intimately connected to and guided by their particular faith. For this reason, prayer advocates challenge not only Herdahl and other separationists, but anyone who views these two realms as separate entities acting in relation with one another. Prayer advocates do recognize the *difference* between these two realms but feel that this difference need not extend to distinctness or separateness. In other words, the very phrasing of the question as that of a *relationship* between church and state is objectionable to prayer advocates.

Why is religious controversy such a pervasive and complex issue? As we have seen in this section, it is not only a matter of individuals and groups being at odds with one another concerning a given issue such as vouchers, biological science curriculum, or faith-based initiatives, but rather, there is great contentiousness regarding the very nature of the problem. Although most people, including Rawls, see the fact of religious controversy rooted in different deep-seated views on different issues, the prayer advocates in Pontotoc County and other Fundamentalists suggest that the problem is even more basic: Are church and state separate and distinct entities or are they simply different aspects of a total worldview? From what we have seen, even this most basic question will yield a range of responses. In order to appreciate the severity and significance of religious controversy in our public schools, it is critical to remember that this is in large part because very few people remain agnostic on this issue and instead, as we have seen, whatever their view, believe in it with the highest commitment and priority.

SUMMARY

Although ultimately it seems the Mississippi federal court ruled in the way that best preserves the integrity of the First Amendment to the Constitution, Biggers, through his ruling, was not able to ease the greater problem of religious controversy. In other words, even though the judge settled the case in accordance with the Constitution (as well as the constitutional record), the deeper question pertaining to a community's identity still remains unsolved. And this is the crux of the problem when it comes to understanding religious controversy: Whose ideals and values should prevail? How does a community come together to create standards and rules by which all can agree while still safely following one's own ideals, beliefs, and values? Neither the court, the ACLU, or any individual in Pontotoc County was able to address this problem satisfactorily.

The purpose of this chapter has been to give readers a greater appreciation of why we have religious controversy. It seems to me that at bottom, religious controversy exists because of the multiple ways in which citizens understand and construct their religious identity. The residents of Pontotoc County are not necessarily religious fanatics seeking to spread religion into every aspect of everyone's lives; rather they are a group of individuals whose religious identity is part of their whole identity. For Herdahl and other separationists, there is no question that their respective religious identities may be important to their overall identities; it is one of many different commitments they share and embody. In fact, it is possible that religion may be so important to Herdahl and in fact so very private that she does not want the public schools and other adults educating her children in this matter. Nevertheless, the chief difference rests in how Herdahl, on the one hand, and prayer advocates, on the other hand, organize their highest commitments and construct their individual identities.

Oftentimes I hear people say, "When you're a teacher or principal or superintendent you have to shelve everything else that you think and believe in order to be a fair, objective teacher, principal, or superintendent." But for the teachers, principal, and superintendent in Pontotoc County, such a dichotomy is logically impossible and utterly unfair. The superintendent's religious beliefs are enmeshed in everything he is, sees, believes, and does. The lens he wears is that of a devout Christian. To ask him to separate his religious lens from the rest of his lenses is to ask him to go blind willingly. This is why he says, "School is not a religion-free zone." However, to expect the superintendent of a public school district to act in accordance with state and federal law seems to be a reasonable request.

This is why Herdahl's claim is very compelling. Her argument focuses on the belief that the only thing uniting all citizens, no matter an individual's or group's particular identity, is our shared citizenship. This, after all, is what the common school was supposed to be founded on. No matter a person's particular religious outlook, we can all join together for a civic, public education. However, a quick glance at the historical record reminds us that this view of common, public schooling has repeatedly been plagued with controversy and the case in Pontotoc County, Mississippi, reminds us that it is still true today.

And so, we return to the question Rawls attempted to answer and it seems we are no closer to a solution. How is it possible for a society to exist and to thrive when we are so very divided along doctrinal lines?

QUESTIONS FOR REFLECTION

1. Imagine yourself as a teacher, principal, or superintendent faced with a school prayer controversy in your public school. What do you think your primary role would be? What if your personal views conflicted with the law? How would you proceed? What factors go into making your decisions?

2. In a democratic society, should accommodations be made when the will of the overwhelming majority differs from that of a very small minority? Should the courts have recognized the will of the majority in *Herdahl v. Pontotoc County School District?* Does it matter that 1,300 students want devotional prayer? How would you balance community values and the law? What is your reasoning?

3. One view on the relationship between religion and public education is that when schools maintain a policy of a high degree of separation, these policies serve to disenfranchise religious believers. Do you think this is the case? If so, how do you address the problem?

SELECTED READINGS

Gutmann, A. (2003). *Identity in democracy.* Princeton: Princeton University Press.

Macedo, S. (2000). *Diversity and distrust: Civic education in a multicultural democracy.* Cambridge, MA: Harvard University Press.

Nord, W. (1995). *Religion and public education: Rethinking a national dilemma.* Chapel Hill: University of North Carolina Press.

Sears, J., & Carper, J. (1998). *Curriculum, religion, and public education: Conversations for an enlarging public square.* New York: Teachers College Press.

REFERENCES

Doerr, E. (1998). Religion and public education. *Phi Delta Kappan, 80*(3), 223.

Grunberg, S., & Crane, B. (Producers). (1999). *School prayer: A community at war* [Video production]. New York: Independent Television Service.

Herdahl v. Pontotoc County School District, 933 F. Supp. 582 (1996).

Noddings, N. (1993). *Educating for intelligent belief or unbelief.* New York: Teachers College Press.

Nord, W. (1995). *Religion and public education: Rethinking a national dilemma.* Chapel Hill: University of North Carolina Press.

Nord, W. (1999). The relevance of religion to the curriculum. *The School Administrator, 56*(1).

Rawls, J. (1996). *Political liberalism.* New York: Columbia University Press.

Freund, P. A., & Ulich, R. (1965). *Religion and the public schools.* Cambridge, MA: Harvard University Press.

Chapter 6

Censorship: Who Controls School Curriculum and Teaching Materials?

Richard Fossey
University of Houston

In 1647, when the founders of the Massachusetts Bay colony passed the nation's first school law to thwart Satan, "the ould deluder" (Alexander & Alexander, 2001, pp. 27–28), the Puritans were probably in broad agreement about what the curriculum of their schools should be. Likewise, the 18th-century Franciscan friars who established religious and vocational training programs in the missions of the American Southwest (Wright, 2002) probably spent little time debating about instructional materials. As long as America's various regional cultures were fairly homogenous, ideological disputes about what should be taught in schools were fairly rare.

However, by the early 19th century, the United States had become a much more heterogeneous society. In particular, Catholic immigrants came to this country in larger numbers, threatening the historic Protestant hegemony. By the 1840s, disputes arose among Protestants, Jews, and Catholics about the religious content of education. In New York City, Catholic families, led by Bishop John Hughes, objected to Protestant themes in the New York public school curriculum, to the reading of the King James Bible in the classroom, and to anti-Catholic bias that appeared in some school texts. Catholics attempted to use the political process to get a share of public education funds to start their own schools (Ravitch, 1988, pp. 33–57). When this effort failed, Bishop Hughes urged Catholics to abandon the public schools and create their own system of parochial education (Cremin, 1980, p. 168).

In recent years, as our society has become ever more religiously and culturally diverse, disputes about curriculum content in public schools have intensified. Often disputants have wound up in court. In general, these court cases have focused on one or more of the following questions: (a) Who has the final authority to make curriculum decisions and to choose text-books and course materials? (b) May parents insist that their children not be exposed to curriculum materials that the parents find objectionable on religious or philosophical grounds? (c) Can parents or community groups insist on the inclusion of curriculum materials that the school board elects not use? (d) Do teachers have the right to choose their own teaching mate-rials, or may the school board insist that certain texts and materials be used and prohibit teachers from introducing materials that the school board has not approved? (e) And finally, to what extent, if any, may schools introduce religious themes into the public school curriculum?

An examination of published court cases shows that the answers to some of these questions are not entirely clear. Nevertheless, the Supreme Court has given definite guidance in two areas. First, in a 1988 decision, the Court said that educators may regulate speech in the schools that is reasonably attributable to the school itself as long as they have a rational pedagogical reason for their decision (*Hazelwood School District v. Kuhlmeier*, 1988). Lower courts have interpreted the Supreme Court's decision to mean that school boards have the authority to choose the school curriculum, and courts will not overrule school officials' curricular decisions except in rare circum-stances.

Second, in a long string of cases stretching back more than 40 years, the Supreme Court has made clear that public schools may not promote prayer or religious worship in classrooms, at graduation exercises, or even at high school football games (*Santa Fe Independent School District v. Doe*, 2000; *Lee v. Weisman*, 1992; *School District of Abington Township v. Schempp* and *Murray v. Curlett*, 1963). Under the Establishment Clause of the First Amendment, the Court has determined, public schools should be secular environments in a posture of absolute neutrality regarding religious issues.

Even with this Supreme Court guidance, however, litigation continues over curriculum, textbooks, and teaching materials in the public schools. In this chapter, we examine what the courts have had to say on this contentious topic.

FIRST PRINCIPLE: SCHOOL BOARDS CONTROL
THE CURRICULUM

First of all, with few exceptions, school boards have the final say about cur-riculum content in the public schools. The Supreme Court gave support to this principle in *Hazelwood School District v. Kuhlmeier* (1988), in which stu-dents challenged a school principal's decision to delete two articles from an issue of the school newspaper. One of the articles concerned students' experience with pregnancy, and the other article discussed the impact of divorce on students. The principal believed that the article on pregnancy was inappropriate for younger students to read, and he was also concerned that some of the pregnant students might be identifiable even though the article had used false names. With regard to the article about divorce, the principal believed that parents whose behavior was described should have an opportunity to respond to remarks made about them and consent to their publication.

Students on the school newspaper staff sued the school district, claiming that the principal's censorship deprived them of their right to free speech under the First Amendment. However, the Supreme Court ruled in favor of the school district. The school newspaper was not a public forum, the Court determined, but a "supervised learning experience for journalism students" (*Hazelwood*, 1988, p. 270). As such, the newspaper was a school-sponsored publication and part of the curriculum. As long as school officials' decisions in the curricular sphere were "reasonably related to legitimate pedagogical concerns" (p. 273), the Court concluded, those decisions would not be overturned by the courts.

Hazelwood has been cited numerous times by lower courts for the proposition that school officials may regulate school-sponsored speech and the curriculum in particular. For example, in *Miles v. Denver Public Schools* (1991), a school district issued a mild sanction against a teacher who had made informal remarks in a ninth-grade government class about the alleged sexual activities of two students. The school district took the position that the teacher's casual statements were unprofessional; but the teacher sued, claiming his right to free speech had been violated. Citing *Hazelwood*, the 10th Circuit upheld the school district's sanction. The teacher had spoken in the classroom environment, where the school district had a legitimate pedagogical interest in regulating the teacher's speech.

As is discussed later, courts have occasionally come to the aid of teachers who were sanctioned for their classroom speech or for their choice of curriculum materials. Nevertheless, *Hazelwood* supports the proposition that school boards, acting through their administrative staff, have the authority to regulate the curriculum and other school-sponsored speech.

SECOND PRINCIPLE: PUBLIC SCHOOLS MAY NOT PROMOTE RELIGION

A second guiding principle regarding censorship in the schools is this: Public schools may not promote religious speech or religious exercises at any school-sponsored activity.

In a 1963 decision, the Supreme Court issued an opinion in two consolidated cases: *School District of Abington Township v. Schempp* and *Murray v. Curlett*. The first case involved a Pennsylvania statute that required that "[a]t least ten verses from the Holy Bible shall be read, without comment, at the opening of each public school on each school day." The second case challenged a school rule in Baltimore, Maryland, calling for daily reading of the Bible at the beginning of the school day "and/or the use of the Lord's Prayer." Both enactments permitted children to be excused from these religious exercises.

Rejecting arguments that these religious activities were for the secular purpose of promoting moral values, the Court struck down both provisions as being violations of the First Amendment's Establishment Clause.

> The place of religion in our society is an exalted one [the Court said], achieved through a long tradition of reliance on the home, the church and the inviolable citadel of the individual heart and mind. We have come to recognize through bitter experience that it is not within the power of government to invade that citadel, whether its purpose is to advance or retard. In the relationship between man and religion, the State is firmly committed to a position of neutrality. (p. 226)

Over the years, the Supreme Court's Establishment Clause jurisprudence has changed somewhat, but the Court has remained true to the principle that public schools should be secular learning environments. In 1992, the Court struck down prayer at a public school graduation exercise (*Lee v. Weisman*); and in 2000, the Court outlawed school-sponsored prayer at high school football games (*Santa Fe Independent School District v. Doe*). In a 1968 case (*Epperson v. Arkansas*), the Court made clear that state laws requiring schools to tailor the curriculum to comply with the views of a particular religious group are also unconstitutional. Schools may permit a formal moment of silence during the school day so long as the exercise is not promoted as a religious function (*Wallace v. Jaffree*, 1985); but school-sponsored religious activities are constitutionally prohibited.

At the same time, schools must allow religious groups to use their facilities outside school hours if they allow other civic groups to do so (*Good News Club v. Milford Central School*, 2001; *Lamb's Chapel v. Center Moriches Union Free School District*, 1993). Student-organized religious groups must also be allowed to use school facilities outside school hours if the school district allows other noncurriculum-related student groups to use its facilities (*Board of Education of Westside Community Schools v. Mergens*, 1990).

MAY PARENTS FORCE SCHOOLS TO ELIMINATE CURRICULAR MATTER THEY FIND OBJECTIONABLE?

In today's eclectic society, with its multiplicity of views, philosophies, and religions, schools are apt to find that some aspect of their curriculum is objectionable to at least one segment of the community. May parents insist that their child's school cease using curricular materials that the parents find objectionable on some religious or philosophical ground?

The answer is a clear no. Perhaps the leading case on this question is *Mozert v. Hawkins County Board of Education* (1987). In *Mozert*, a group of parents who described themselves as "born-again Christians" objected to a school district's chosen reading series. The series, published by Holt, Rinehart and Winston, emphasized "critical reading" as opposed to reading programs that just taught word and sound recognition. Critical reading required students to develop "higher order cognitive skills that enable students to evaluate the material they read, contrast the ideas presented, and to understand complex characters that appear in reading material" (*Mozert*, 1987, p. 1059).

At first, the school district attempted to accommodate the objecting parents and actually organized an alternative reading program that did not use the Holt textbook series. Ultimately, however, the district shut down the alternative program and required all students to receive instruction that utilized the Holt texts.

Fourteen parents and 17 children filed suit, arguing that the school district was violating their right to free exercise of religion by forcing children to read school books that taught values that were antithetical to their families' religious beliefs. At trial, plaintiffs testified that passages were contrary to the groups' views on evolution, secular humanism, pacifism, magic, and "futuristic supernaturalism."

On appeal, the 6th Circuit Court of Appeals rejected all the plaintiffs' arguments and found in favor of the school district. It is the purpose of public schools to teach values that are essential to a democratic society, the court noted; and those values include "tolerance of divergent political and religious views" (*Mozert*, 1987, p. 1068, internal citation omitted).

This tolerance, the 6th Circuit said, is a civil tolerance, and not a religious one. "It does not require a person to accept any other religion as the equal of the one to which that person adheres. It merely requires a recognition that in a pluralistic society we must 'live and let live'" (*Mozert*, 1987, p. 1069). In short, the plaintiffs enjoyed no constitutional right to be shielded from offensive ideas.

More recently, two cases were filed by parents objecting to the use of a reading series that contained material about witchcraft and sorcerers (*Fleischfresser v. Directors of School District 200*, 1994; *Brown v. Woodland Joint Unified School District*, 1994). Both suits were unsuccessful. In a scholarly article on these cases, two commentators (DeMitchell & Carney, 2003, p. 376) said this about the courts' holdings:

> [The] courts [are] not convinced that a grand conspiracy exists on the part of public school educators to bend the minds of our nation's young to the dark

forces of Satanism and witchcraft. . . . The courts seem to recognize that the vast
majority of educators are good people trying to do a tough complicated job in
the most professional manner that they can under very difficult circumstances.

Indeed, the courts are reluctant to substitute their judgment for that of
school administrators on curricular issues, and they realize that involving
themselves in disputes between objecting parents and school districts over
the suitability of instructional programs could lead to a morass of litigation.
One last case, *Brown v. Hot, Sexy and Safer Productions*, Inc. (1995), illustrates
just how reluctant courts are to intervene in this area.

In *Brown*, a Massachusetts school district hired an outside contractor to
present a 90-minute program to high school students on AIDS and sex education. According to the plaintiffs—two high school students and their
parents—the program presenter "used profane, lewd, and lascivious language to describe body parts and excretory functions... [and] advocated
and approved oral sex, masturbation, homosexual sexual activity, and con-
dom use during promiscuous premarital sex" (p. 529). The students argued
that this program violated several of their constitutional rights and their
legal right to be free of sexual harassment.

Affirming a lower court's dismissal, the 1st Circuit Court of Appeals rejected all of the students' arguments. Although objective observers might
agree that the program was in bad taste, the 1st Circuit found no basis for
permitting the students' to pursue a lawsuit.

MAY PARENTS FORCE SCHOOLS TO UTILIZE CURRICULAR
MATERIALS THAT SCHOOL OFFICIALS DON'T WISH TO USE?

As the earlier cases show, school districts generally have the final say regarding the choice of curriculum and the selection of textbooks. Parents are
almost always unsuccessful in lawsuits aimed at removing teaching materials from the curriculum that school officials have chosen to use. But what
about materials that school authorities have elected *not* to use? Can parents
force school authorities to adopt teaching materials that the authorities
themselves have rejected?

Here, the answer may be yes or no—depending on the school board's
motivation. An 11th Circuit decision, *Virgil v. School Board of Columbia County,
Florida* (1989), is a prominent case on the question. In *Virgil*, a school district
utilized a humanities text in an elective high school humanities class that
included these classical readings: Geoffrey Chaucer's *The Miller's Tale* and
Lysistrata, written by the Greek dramatist Aristophanes. A minister and his
wife, parents of a student who had taken the humanities course, filed a formal complaint against the use of the humanities text, objecting to sexually

explicit passages in *Lysistrata* and *The Miller's Tale*. Neither reading was assigned or required in the humanities class.

In response to this complaint, the school board appointed an advisory committee to review the text and make a recommendation about its continued use. The committee advised that the text be retained in the curriculum but that *Lysistrata* and *The Miller's Tale* not be assigned as required reading.

At a school board meeting, however, the school superintendent expressed his disagreement with the advisory committee's recommendation. He advised the school board to delete the two readings from the text or cease using the text in the curriculum. The board adopted the superintendent's second suggestion; the book was removed from the curriculum and all copies were put in locked storage.

Parents of high school students filed suit against the school district, arguing that the school board's textbook removal decision violated students' constitutional rights under the First Amendment. The parents sought an injunction that would force the school district to put the text back in the curriculum.

This suit was unsuccessful. In ruling for the school district, the 11th Circuit looked to the Supreme Court's decision in *Hazelwood*. As discussed earlier, *Hazelwood* instructed that schools have the right to regulate school-sponsored speech if they have a reasonable educational justification for doing so.

Even though the disputed readings were optional, the court ruled, they are still part of the curriculum. Moreover, the parties had stipulated that the school board had been motivated to remove the text from the curriculum by the explicit sexuality and "excessively vulgar language" in the two selections.

In ruling for the school district, the court noted that school authorities are free to take the emotional maturity of students into account when making decisions about the appropriateness of materials for an intended audience. Although the court acknowledged that *Lysistrata* and *The Miller's Tale* are literary masterpieces, the school board's decision about the readings was based on reasonable educational considerations. Therefore, the court declined to disturb the school board's decision.

In another case on this topic, a school superintendent refused a request by high school teachers to take students to a commercial theater during school hours to see the movie *Schindler's List* (*Borger v. Bisciglia*, 1995). In justifying his decision, the superintendent cited a formal school board policy that prohibited schools from using movies in its instructional program that had received an R rating by the Motion Picture Association of America (MPAA).

Ruling in favor of the school district, a federal court expressed the view of most courts when considering a legal challenge to a school district's curricular decision:

> Students do not lose their First Amendment rights when they walk through the
> schoolhouse door.... However, courts have decided that the scope of the First
> Amendment within the classroom must be tempered, and that the content of
> the curriculum is within the sound discretion of school officials, with excep-
> tions in rare cases. So strong is this concept, that the U.S. Court of Appeals
> for the Seventh Circuit has proclaimed that high school students contesting
> the curriculum decisions of local authorities must raise issues which "cross a
> relatively high threshold before entering upon the field of a constitutional
> claim suitable for federal court litigation.... Courts should not interfere with
> local educational discretion unless "local authorities begin to substitute rigid
> and exclusives indoctrination for the mere exercise of their prerogative to
> make pedagogic choices regarding matters of legitimate dispute."... Only a
> "fragrant abuse of discretion merits judicial intervention." (p. 99, internal
> citations omitted)

In the *Borger* court's opinion, the school board's reliance on the MPAA's
movie rating system was reasonable and well within constitutional bounds.

However, an 8th Circuit opinion illustrates that school districts may not
pull reading materials from the curriculum simply because they object to
the ideas that are expressed in them. In *Pratt v. Independent School District, No.
831, Forest Lake* (1982), a Minnesota school board received complaints from
parents and others about two films being shown in high school literature
classes. One film was a film version of Shirley Jackson's short story "The
Lottery," and the other film was a "trailer" that discussed "The Lottery" and
its themes. The complaining parties objected to the violence presented in
the films and their alleged impact on religious and family values.

After pursuing an administrative review process, the protesting group
brought their objections to the school board. By a 4 to 3 vote, the board
removed both films from the curriculum. A group of students then sued the
school district, arguing that the film's removal violated their constitutional
rights under the First Amendment.

A federal trial court found in favor of the plaintiffs, and the 8th Circuit
Court of Appeals affirmed. The appellate court said:

> Under the circumstances presented here, the First Amendment protects the
> right of the Forest Lake students not to have these films removed from the
> high school classrooms. The school board cannot constitutionally ban the films
> because a majority of its members object to the films' religious and ideological
> content and wish to prevent the ideas contained in the material from being
> expressed in the school. (p. 773)

In a similar vein, the Supreme Court has made clear that school boards
may not remove books from the school library simply because they do not
like the ideas contained in the books. (The Supreme Court's decision did not

address curricular materials.) The Court said the First Amendment protects not only a citizen's right to express ideas—it protects a citizen's right to receive ideas and information as well (*Board of Education, Island Trees Union Free School District No. 26 v. Pico*, 1982).

DO PUBLIC SCHOOL TEACHERS HAVE AN ACADEMIC FREEDOM RIGHT TO MAKE CURRICULAR DECISIONS?

From the discussion so far, it is clear that school boards usually have the final word on curricular decisions in disputes brought by parents and students. What have the courts said when school boards and teachers disagree on curricular matters? Do teachers have an academic freedom right that allows them to unilaterally choose their teaching materials, even when school administrators disagree?

Academic freedom has been described as "the right of teachers to speak freely about their subjects, to experiment with new ideas, and to select appropriate teaching materials and methods" (Fischer, Schimmel, & Stellman, 2003, p. 134). Academic freedom is closely connected to the First Amendment and "protects a teacher's right to evaluate and criticize existing values and practices in order to allow for political, social, economic, and scientific progress" (p. 135). Courts have recognized teachers' rights to academic freedom in some cases, but not in others. In fact, even at the higher education level, one federal court of appeals has held that public university professors have *no* constitutional right to academic freedom (although the court acknowledged that the professors have a constitutionally protected right to free speech similar to that enjoyed by other public employees) (*Urofsky v. Gilmore*, 2000).

Nevertheless, some theme can be woven from the cases involving disputes between school boards and teachers over curricular matters. In general, courts uphold school boards' decisions to choose the school curriculum, at least when their decisions seem objectively reasonable. Nevertheless, courts will come to the aid of teachers when it appears to the court that a school board has sanctioned a teacher unreasonably.

For example, in *Keefe v. Geanakos* (1969), a teacher distributed an *Atlantic Monthly* article to his high school English class as an assigned reading. The article included a word that the court delicately described as "a vulgar word for an incestuous son" and that the school board found objectionable. Called to account by the school committee, the teacher refused to give assurances that he would not use the word again, and the school district began dismissal proceedings.

In the 1st Circuit's view, the *Atlantic Monthly* article that contained the offending word was "scholarly, thoughtful, and thought-provoking" (p. 361).

Although the court acknowledged that school officials have the authority to regulate classroom speech, sanctioning the teacher for assigning an article that contains a vulgar word amounted to censorship that had the effect of chilling the teacher's First Amendment rights. The 1st Circuit court found in favor of the teacher outright.

Similarly, the 6th Circuit, in a 2000 case, ruled in favor of an adjunct community college instructor whose contract was nonrenewed after he used the words "nigger" and "bitch" while teaching a class on interpersonal communication. The court concluded that the instructor had not used the words gratuitously or for the purpose of being offensive but rather as a teaching tool that was appropriate in the context of the instructional topic (*Hardy v. Jefferson Community College*, 2000; Fossey & Roberts, 2002). In the 6th Circuit's view, the community college had violated the instructor's First Amendment rights by sanctioning him for his classroom speech.

On the other hand, several courts have upheld school boards that have punished teachers for exposing students to inappropriate materials. For example, a Kentucky school district discharged a teacher who showed the R-rated movie *Pink Floyd—The Wall* to a class of high school students (ages 14 through 17) on the last day of the school year (*Fowler v. Board of Education of Lincoln County*, 1987).

As explained by the court, the teacher showed the movie on a noninstructional day set aside for teachers to prepare their final grades. A group of students requested the teacher to allow them to watch the movie while she was completing grade cards. She was unfamiliar with the movie, and she asked a 15-year-old student to edit out any scenes that were unsuitable for viewing at school. Although testimony was conflicting, evidence was presented that students saw some nudity and violence.

Reversing the trial court, the 6th Circuit showed little sympathy for the teacher. In the court's words:

> She introduced a controversial and sexually explicit movie into a classroom of adolescents without preview, preparation or discussion. In the process, she abdicated her function as an educator. Her having the movie shown under the circumstances involved demonstrates a blatant lack of judgment. Having considered the entire record, including the viewing of the movie, which we describe as gross and bizarre and containing material completely unsuitable for viewing by a classroom of students aged fourteen to seventeen, we conclude that such conduct falls within the concept of conduct unbecoming a teacher under Kentucky law. (p. 666)

In another classroom movie case, a Louisiana court upheld a school board's decision to give a one-semester suspension without pay to a tenured teacher who showed an R-rated movie to her seventh-grade reading class. The teacher was a 32-year veteran in the district, and she had no prior disciplinary record. The movie, *Child's Play*, was described by the court as a story "about a doll named 'Chucky' which became demonically possessed by the spirit of a maniacal killer" (p. 188).

The teacher sued to overturn the school board's decision, raising procedural and evidentiary issues, not constitutional claims. In upholding the school board, the court found adequate evidence to justify the sanction.

> Roberts admitted that she showed the "R" rated movie, which contained violence and foul language, within the hearing and view of her seventh graders.... The foul language and violent scenes documented in the record provide a rational basis for the conclusion that Roberts willfully neglected her duty and was incompetent in showing the movie to seventh graders. We can perceive of no educational value of this movie to a reading class. Roberts' explanation, that she was previewing the movie, is not sufficient to exculpate her from guilt in this matter. She clearly derogated from her responsibility as a teacher. (pp. 190–191)

In a more recent decision involving a Kentucky schoolteacher, a school district terminated a teacher after she gave a class presentation on the use of industrial hemp (*Cockrel v. Shelby County School District*, 2000). Several industrial hemp farmers and actor Woody Harrelson visited the class during the presentation, and the event generated quite a bit of media attention.

After her termination, the teacher sued, claiming that the school district had violated her right to free speech by sanctioning her for including the topic of industrial hemp as part of her fifth-grade curriculum. Although the appellate court expressed no opinion about the appropriateness of the class presentation, the court was quite clear that the teacher's First Amendment rights had not been violated. "Plaintiff's presentation on industrial hemp is not a form of speech that is protected by the First Amendment," the court concluded. "Her conduct cannot be considered expressive or communicative under the circumstances alleged in her complaint, and her First Amendment rights are not even implicated. Therefore, this judicial inquiry comes to an end" (p. 776).

In addition to the cases just discussed, other court decisions have outlined other constraints that school boards can place on teachers' classroom conduct. The 7th Circuit, for example, has held that teachers do not have an academic freedom right to disregard a school's assigned text and course syllabus (*Clark v. Holmes*, 1972). And in a somewhat similar case, the 5th Circuit ruled that a teacher had no constitutional right to substitute his reading list for the one assigned by his superiors without seeking approval (*Kirkland v. Northside Independent School District*, 1989). Teachers have no constitutional right to use profanity in front of students during classes (*Martin v. Parrish*, 1986, involving a college-level instructor). Nor are they legally protected when they use novel, unapproved, and academically unsupported forms of punishment (*Celestine v. Lafayette Parish School Board,* 1973).

In short, with regard to disagreements between teachers and schools about teaching materials and curriculum, the courts usually support the school board's position. Although some courts have acknowledged a public school teacher's right to academic freedom, a teacher has no right to disregard reasonable school board decisions and administrative directives about curriculum content and textbooks. And, as one court made clear, academic freedom in a secondary school is a more restricted concept than the academic freedom rights that college-level instructors enjoy (*Mailloux v. Kiley,* 1971).

SUMMARY

Who controls the public school curriculum and teaching materials? In most instances, the school board does. As we have seen, school boards have won most of the disputes with parents, teachers, and community members with regard to what shall be taught in the public school classroom. Families do not have the right to shield their children from curriculum materials they find objectionable; nor (in most cases) may parents insist on the inclusion of particular material in the curriculum if the school board elects to exclude it.

School boards do not have unfettered discretion over what goes on in the classroom, however. They may not make curricular decisions that support a religious agenda, for example; and they may not reject texts or library materials simply because they disagree with the ideas that are contained within them. In general, however, courts recognize that curricular decisions are often controversial and that it is the job of the school board, not the courts or community dissidents, to make the final decision regarding the public school curriculum. As long as those decisions are pedagogically reasonable, the courts will uphold them.

GUIDING QUESTIONS

1. Supreme Court decisions make clear that schools may not sponsor prayer or religious exercises during the school day or any school-sponsored event. Nevertheless, media reports suggest that some school districts continue to promote prayer or other constitutionally forbidden religious activities. Why do you think this is so?

2. In the discussion earlier, we learned that the courts will sometimes support a school board that attempts to remove material from the curriculum over parental objection; but at least one court has prohibited a school

board from removing curriculum materials. What is the guiding principle the courts have articulated for deciding these cases? (See *Board of Education, Island Trees Union Free School District No. 26 v. Pico*, 1982; *Virgil v. School Board of Columbia County, Florida*, 1989; and *Pratt v. Independent School District No. 831, Forest Lake*, 1982.)

3. In the *Mozert* case, a federal court upheld the principle that students have no constitutional right to be shielded from curriculum materials that are religiously offensive to them. How did the court justify its decision?

4. According to the discussion earlier, most courts uphold the right of school boards to determine the curriculum even in cases where individual teachers disagree. Yet in *Keefe v. Geanakos* (1969), a teacher who introduced a controversial *Atlantic Monthly* article to his class was supported by the court after the school board tried to fire him. When teachers and school boards disagree on curriculum issues, what principle should determine which party should prevail?

5. In today's multicultural and multireligious society, educators may be more likely to hear objections about the school curriculum than in the past. Should educators take their communities' various political and religious views into account when making curriculum decisions?

SELECTED READINGS

Alexander, K., & Alexander M. D. (2001). *American public school law*. Belmont, CA: West/Thompson Learning.

DeMitchell, T. A., & Carney, J. J. (2003). Harry Potter, wizards, and muggles: The first amendment and the reading curriculum. *Education Law Reporter, 173*, 363–379.

Fischer, L., Schimmel, D., & Stellman, L. R. (2003). *Teachers and the law* (6th ed.). Boston: Allyn & Bacon.

Ravitch, D. (1988). *The great school wars: A history of the New York City public schools*. New York: Basic Books.

REFERENCES

Alexander, K., & Alexander M. D. (2001). *American public school law*. Belmont, CA: West/Thompson Learning.

Board of Education, Island Trees Union Free School District No. 26 v. Pico, 457 U.S. 853 (1982).

Board of Education of Westside Community Schools v. Mergens, 496 U.S. 226 (1990).

Borger v. Bisciglia, 888 F. Supp. 97 (E.D. Wis. 1995).

Brown v. Hot, Sexy, and Safer Productions, Inc., 68 F.3d 525 (1st Cir. 1995).

Brown v. Woodland Joint Unified School District, 27 F.3d 1373 (9th Cir. 1994).

Celestine v. Lafayette Parish School Board, 284 So.2d 650 (La. 1973).

Clark v. Holmes, 474 F.2d 928 (7th Cir. 1972).

Cockrel v. Shelby County School District, 81 F. Supp. 2d 771 (E.D. Ky. 2000).

Cremin, L. A. (1980). *American education: The national experience 1783–1876*. New York: Harper and Row.

DeMitchell, T. A., & Carney, J. J. (2003). Harry Potter, wizards, and muggles: The first amendment and the reading curriculum. *Education Law Reporter, 173,* 363–379.

Epperson v. Arkansas, 393 U.S. 97 (1968).

Fischer, L., Schimmel, D., & Stellman, L. R. (2003). *Teachers and the law* (6th ed.). Boston: Allyn & Bacon.

Fleischfresser v. Directors of School District 200, 15 F.3d 680 (7th Cir. 1994).

Fossey, R., & Roberts, N. (2002). Academic freedom and uncivil speech: When may a college regulate what an instructor says in the classroom? *Education Law Reporter, 168*(2), 549–564.

Fowler v. Board of Education of Lincoln County, 819 F.2d 657 (6th Cir. 1987).

Good News Club v. Milford Central School, 121 S.Ct. 2093 (2001).

Hardy v. Jefferson Community College, 360 F.3d 671 (6th Cir. 2001), *cert. denied sub. nom. Besser v. Hardy,* 122 S.Ct. 1436 (2002).

Hazelwood School District v. Kuhlmeier, 484 U.S. 260 (1988).

Keefe v. Geanakos, 418 F.2d 359 (5th Cir. 1969).

Kirkland v. Northside Independent School District, 890 F.2d 794 (5th Cir. 1989).

Lamb's Chapel v. Center Moriches Union Free School District, 508 U.S. 384 (1993).

Lee v. Weisman, 505 U.S. 577 (1992).

Mailloux v. Kiley, 3213 F. Supp. 1387 (D. Mass. 1971).

Martin v. Parrish, 805 F.2d 583 (5th Cir. 1986).

Miles v. Denver Public Schools, 944 F.2d 773 (10th Cir. 1991).

Mozert v. Hawkins County Board of Education, 827 F.2d 1058 (6th Cir. 1987).

Pratt v. Independent School District No. 831, Forest Lake, 670 F.2d 771 (8th Cir. 1982).

Ravitch, D. (1988). *The great school wars: A history of the New York City public schools.* New York: Basic Books.

Roberts v. Rapides Parish School Board, 617 So.2d 187 (La. Ct. App. 1993).

Santa Fe Independent School District v. Doe, 120 U.S. 2266 (2000).

School District of Abington Township v. Shempp and *Murray v. Curlett,* 374 U.S. 203 (1963).

Urofsky v. Gilmore, 216 F.3d 401 (4th Cir. 2000).

Virgil v. School Board of Columbia County, Florida, 862 F.2d 1517 (11th Cir. 1989).

Wallace v. Jaffree, 472 U.S. 38 (1985).

Wright, R., O.M.I. (2002). Spanish missions. *Handbook of Texas Online.* Retrieved August 16, 2003, from http://www.tsha.utexas.edu/handbook/online/articles/view/SS/its2.html.

Part II

CURRICULUM AND LEARNING ISSUES

In the second part of this book, we turn to the heart of schooling, issues that have to do with teaching and learning. Increase the size of classes, beleaguered school board members may cry. There are *better* ways and ways that are more economical! How can schools just generally be improved? How can learners be best evaluated? What's wrong with more testing? These issues are confronted in the first three chapters. And, there are surprises.

Schools exist in a multicultural environment, even schools that are in unicultural places. And, what of those students who are different, physically and emotionally? Are teachers equipped to positively affect school environments populated by children who are special? What sorts of curriculum must our schools provide that recognizes—capitalizes on—the richness of diversity that is manifest in schools?

The arts continue to be neglected when budgets get tightened and today's school budgets are constantly tightening. Are a child's needs for artistic exposure and for artistic expression to suffer? What price is a school program that values the arts? Must such a program compete with the technological advances that increasingly confront society? Must we grow so narrowly? Does something have to give?

These are the instructional and school-programming issues that the authors of part II have confronted. Are there others? Of course, but our focus has narrowed to these. Teacher development, school and student evaluation, diversity, and neglected aspects of the curriculum drive the subjects of this section.

Chapter 7

Class Size and Learning

C. M. Achilles
Seton Hall University
Eastern Michigan University

As more knowledge about class size and its effects becomes available, debates about class size reemerge. Legislators and others call for increased education "accountability." There are new demands on and alternatives to public education. Yet in its requirement that education rely on scientific-based research (SBR), the No Child Left Behind (NCLB) Act de-emphasized class size for education improvements. So much for SBR!

Many critiques and criticisms of class-size work exist, if only because the research has been around for a long time. With a history of inquiry (since just before 1900 in the United States), educators and policy makers should have learned much about class size. Ah, it would *seem* so. An old German proverb warns that "An old error is always more popular than a new truth." A concept as seemingly simple as class size would seem not to need much explanation, but recent experience contradicts common sense here.[1]

In section one of this chapter, I explore several key requirements for research and professional discourse, including the necessity for clarity. Examples are drawn from various sources to illustrate how lack of precision in using terms can confound the use of results. A second section summarizes the extent and depth of the sustained inquiry into class size since

---

[1] Some data, tables, figures, and appendices in this chapter have appeared in other materials by Achilles and Finn and in papers they have coauthored with others. I express gratitude for the assistance of many colleagues in this class-size work such as the STAR staff (H. Pate-Bain, J. Boyd-Zaharias, J. Johnston, J. Folger, N. Lintz, E. Word); the Tennessee legislators, teachers, administrators, and students who gave life to STAR; other researchers such as S. Gerber, G. Pannozzo, P. Egelson, P. Harman; persons connected with other class-size efforts that the author has been associated with, such as in Burke County and High Point, North Carolina, and class-size studies and projects in Tennessee, Michigan, Wisconsin, New York, South Carolina, Louisiana, Vancouver (British Columbia), and the like.

1900 by highlighting growth of the knowledge base. This section shows the consistency of the class-size research both for short-term and for long-term outcomes, from projects to evaluations to experiments, and explains how and why positive outcomes accrue in small classes.

Simply providing data is not sufficient for understanding of and for use of results. Section three helps potential users make sense of the class-size research and wrestle with adopting policies to support what can be expected from small classes. The move from policy to practice requires careful, thoughtful implementation, so a fourth section discusses steps to ease into class size as a cornerstone for education improvement and offers recommendations for moving ahead.

The chapter concludes with some guiding questions and activities to demonstrate points made in the chapter. There are some recommendations for further study and an extensive references section.

REQUIREMENTS FOR RESEARCH INCLUDE PRECISION AND DEFINITION

One major hurdle that keeps people from understanding "class-size" findings is *definition*. Clear, correct, compelling, and concise definition is a first step in understanding something, and a *requirement* for research. Class size (CS) might seem straightforward and simple: *The number of students in a class for whom the designated teacher is responsible and accountable* is the CS definition used here. Class size is *not* pupil-teacher ratio, or PTR. The PTR is the number of students at a site *divided* by the number of educators serving that site. The divisor may include administrators, counselors, media specialists, and so on.

In the *Digest of Education Statistics* (1999), the National Center for Education Statistics (NCES) provided separate definitions for CS ("The membership of a class at a given date") and for PTR ("The enrollment of pupils at a given time divided by the full-time equivalent number of . . ."). Data for each are presented in separate tables. The numbers are *different* because the concepts are different. Iannaccone (1975) emphasized one issue at the forefront of PTR and class-size confusion:

> [T]he clarity of the meaning of a concept turns on the precision of the relationship between the concept and its referent, the features of the world for which it is a label. One source of error in the scientific venture is lack of precision in the referent of the concepts. Lack of precision leads to lack of reliability in the concepts. (pp. 13–14)

The PTR is an administrative procedure for allocation of resources. Class size is an organizing framework for delivery of instruction. Fiscal officers,

TABLE 7.1 Some Major Differences Between Class Size (CS) or Class-Size Reduction (CSR) and Pupil-Teacher Ratio (PTR)

Variables of note in comparing PTR and CS	Pupil-teacher ratio (PTR)	Class size (CS) or (CSR)
Definition	Students (n) at a site (building, district, class) divided by: teachers, educators, adults, (etc.) serving the site.	Students (n) in a teacher's room regularly, and for whom the teacher is accountable.
Computation	DIVISION, with various divisors available depending upon the *EXACT* definition.	ADDITION. This cannot be accurately determined from large databases.
Conceptual Base	The teacher needs help; the student needs special services the teacher cannot provide.	A competent teacher can handle most education issues if given a reasonable case load.
Operation and Context	A project and "pull-out"-driven model full of commotion and "Band Aid" treatments. Loss of time on task. Difficulty in determining responsibility and accountability.	Teacher is *responsible and accountable* for the student's growth and development: Academics, Behavior, Citizenship, Development, (A, B, C, D), Small focused learning groups.
Outcomes	CONSISTENTLY MARGINAL. Education "production function" analyses (Hanushek, 1998); (Boozer & Rouse, 1995); Title I evaluations (Borman & D'Agostino, 1996; Wong & Meyer, 1998; Abt, 1997); etc.	CONSISTENTLY POSITIVE on many variables (A, B, C, D). See class-size results from many studies. There is much consensual validation, anecdotal evidence, and "commonsense" support.

budget directors, and economists are interested in PTR; teachers, instructional leaders, students, and parents focus on class size. Simply put, class size is an addition problem and PTR is a division problem. Table 7.1 outlines important class size and PTR differences in five operational dimensions: definition, computation, conceptual base, operation and context, and consistent outcomes.

THE FORCE OF SUSTAINED INQUIRY

A field advances when researchers add to it over time by exploring related questions using diverse approaches. Current knowledge about class size builds on studies that might be considered "groundbreaking" (1900–1965 or so), evaluations (1966–1979), and "refining" (1979–present). Early research emphasized "common sense." The studies were generally brief, were conducted using whatever grade levels of classes might be available, were methodologically unsophisticated, and employed rudimentary analysis procedures. The early phase of class-size studies concluded with the deservedly acclaimed meta-analyses of Glass and Smith (1978) and Smith and Glass (1979) that were part of the class-size program at the Far West Education Laboratory, which included work by Cahen and Filby (1979), Filby, Cahen, McCutcheon, and Kyle (1980), and Glass, Cahen, Smith, and Filby (1982). Indiana's Project *Prime Time* was a large-scale, statewide class-size demonstration in early grades. To expand *Prime Time* to grades K and 3, educators could use teacher assistants or aides as part of the "class-size" treatment. Although *Prime Time* was a project (demonstration), it was evaluated (Chase, Mueller, & Walden, 1986).

Texas enacted House Bill (HB) 72 (1984) that contained, among other things, class-size (and PTR) provisions for grades K–2. Small classes were extended to grades K–4 in later amendments. Gains in Texas stem from changes made by HB72.

In 1984 Tennessee legislators initiated *Project STAR* (Student Teacher Achievement Ratio), a large-scale (11,600 students), longitudinal (1985–1989) *experiment* to determine the effects of small classes (13–17 students) on the achievement and development of K–3 students (Word et al., 1990). The STAR class-size experiment has been widely publicized, so details of the study are omitted here. A summary of STAR's key features is provided in Appendix 7.A. STAR and its substantial database spawned studies and evaluations such as the Lasting Benefits Study (LBS), Challenge, reanalyses of STAR data, studies of "enduring effects" of early small-class engagement, teacher aide effects, and so on. Besides attracting critics and critiques, STAR generated renewed interest in CS leading to statewide efforts (e.g., Student Achievement Guarantee in Education or SAGE in Wisconsin, Class-Size Reduction or CSR in California), class-size legislation at state and national levels, and even a state constitutional amendment (Florida). Table 7.2 shows outcomes from various studies.

Early Small-Class Outcomes Endure, Even Longer Than 3 Years

Information presented here is excerpted from some long-term class-size studies. To the extent possible, these synopses exclude PTR efforts, and they include results from class-size work that has been sustained long enough to offer clues for success.

The Fairfax County Public Schools (FCPS) CS Evaluation. This study began with small-class pilot and planning in 1991 and implementation in 15 schools

TABLE 7.2   Some Consistent Class-Size Findings From STAR
and Other Sources*

Finding, Idea, Issue, or Question

I.	In STAR, class-size effect was found in all sites, for all participants, at all times, and for grades K–3. Small classes include tutoring and most "special" projects.
II.	Small classes work best when students start (K, 1) school in them; they are preventive, not remedial. Formal and small-class education *MUST* start no later than K, be *intense* (all day, every day), and last at least 3 years (duration).
III.	*Crowding*, not just small classes, is an issue. With small classes, school safety, environment, and student behavior are improved. (School size is important too.)
IV.	Although all pupils benefit from small (S) classes in K–3 (equality), some students (male, minority, poor) benefit more than others (equity). Small classes reduce achievement gaps among groups.
V.	A teacher aide does not improve student outcomes. This adds to crowdedness *and* causes new dynamics (Issues: training, inclusion, ESL, role description).
VI.	Teachers in small classes can use known educational-improvement processes: parent and home involvement, portfolios, alternative assessments, and the like. Small classes may not change what teachers do—just how much they do good things well.
VII.	Reduce retention in grade *especially* when student will be moving into another small class. (Retention should not be used, unless in *extreme* cases.)
VIII.	Study costs *and* benefits; use PTR and CS differences to get to small classes.
IX.	Small classes (and small schools) encourage increased student *participation* in schooling.
X.	Each pupil's learning depends on the teacher and others in the class. (Thus the class is the unit of analysis in class-size research.)
XI.	Small classes in early grades provide long-term, multiple benefits that last and increase throughout the grades and into college admissions testing (at least).

*Detailed references are available. They were omitted because of space.

in fall 1992. By 1996–1997, 48 schools were participating. Small classes began in grade 1 in schools with many low socioeconomic status (SES) pupils. Executive summary (ES) highlights of this Virginia effort are (FCPS, 1997):

> The supporting data indicated strong evidence that the Reduced-Ratio Program is more effective for students from low (SES) backgrounds. There is also evidence that *ideal program implementation* is an important factor in increasing student achievement. . . . Consider extending the program beyond first grade in the most needy schools. . . . FCPS students from low (SES) backgrounds and students in schools with *ideal implementation* showed some significant gains on a nationally norm-referenced test *three years after participating* in the program. (ES-5, emphasis added)

Differences were apparent in test-score results (1993–1994 to 1995–1996) on grade 4 ITBS (Iowa Test of Basic Skills) scores between 10 schools with ideal and 19 schools with less-than-ideal implementation. Students in ideal-implementation schools achieved significant and positive gains on six of eight subtests (the other two had positive but nonsignificant gains). In the other 19 schools there were *no* gains on six of eight, a positive gain on one, and a loss on one. This FCPS information supports the STAR finding that there are right (ideal) ways to implement class-size changes to get positive student gains. Detailed and research-based guidelines on *how* to implement small classes have been described elsewhere (e.g., Achilles & Finn, 2000). Key points are: (a) early intervention, (b) intensity—all day, each day, (c) sufficient duration, and other factors.

The Burke County, North Carolina, Class-Size Reduction (CSR) Effort. Burke County is a low-wealth western North Carolina system in the foothills of the Great Smoky Mountains. As it has grown, the school system has experienced an influx of limited english proficient (LEP), English as a second language (ESL), and low SES youngsters. To counter declining student performance, Burke County Schools (BCS) officials initiated CSR in grade 1 at four schools (1991–1992). Results were good. In 1992–1993, small classes (about 15:1) were in grade 1 of 14 schools and in grade 2 at the 4 pilot schools. By 1995–1996, CSR was in grades 1–3 at all 18 elementary schools. This small-class phase-in was done with available funds by creative reallocations and reassignments in a low-wealth district (Achilles, Harman, & Egelson, 1995; Egelson, Harman, Hood, & Achilles, 2002).

Most Burke County students who started in grade 1 in 1992 and all who started in 1993–1994 could have been in small classes, grades 1, 2, and 3. On North Carolina's end-of-grade (EOG) tests, students scoring in the top two levels are "proficient." Level 1 includes students who most need growth. A goal is to reduce the percentage of students scoring in level 1 and to increase the percentage of students scoring proficient, levels 3 and 4. By 1994–1995, about half of grade-3 students had small classes. By 1995–1996, all Burke County students could have had small classes in grades 1–3 before they took the grade-3 EOG tests. Table 7.3 shows both the decline

TABLE 7.3   Burke County, NC EOG Test Outcomes. Grade 3
(Stewart, 1998, & updated)*

	Level 1 % Not Proficient		Levels 3 & 4 % Proficient	
Year	Reading	Math	Reading	Math
1993	13.4	10.9	60.3	61.6
1995	8.6	5.6	68.6	71.4
1997	6.3	3.1	74.7	74.5
2003	3.5	1.2	84.5	91.1

*Thanks to Burke County personnel for compiling and sharing these results.

in level 1 and the increase in levels 3 and 4 (proficient) in the EOG tests, 1993 to 2003, a direct link to the small-class effort. The 2003 results show that the test-score increase was maintained despite the 18% increase in population, 55% increase in free lunch, 68.5% increase in LEP, and large Title I increase. By 2003, students from small classes in primary grades were driving improvements in high school tests, reduced dropouts, and increased college entrance test outcomes.

Initial Indicators of Class-Size Success From Texas Data. In 1984 Texas passed HB 72, which mandated small classes not to exceed 22 students in grades K–2 by 1985–1986 and in grades K–4 by 1988–1989. A Texas student who began school in 1985 could have experienced small classes in grades K–4. Academic progress in Texas has been measured several ways, including by the Texas Assessment of Academic Skills (TAAS). The first year that grade-10 students who could have had small classes in grades K–4 took the TAAS was 1995–1996. If full implementation of small classes was by 1986, the small-class effect would show up in later years of grade-10 testing (1997–1998, 1998–1999, 1999–2000) and level off about 2001–2002 unless there were other reasons, such as negative high-stakes test outcomes, identified in the analyses in Texas by Haney (2000) that show large increases in grade reten-tion, dropouts, and special education exemptions, especially for minority students in the years before testings. Yet class-size outcomes seem evident given outcomes in other states.

Table 7.4 compares the percentage of grade-10 students passing the TAAS by categories: White, Hispanic, African American, Economically Disadvan-taged, and All, from 1993 to 1994 through 1999–2000. Minority and eco-nomically disadvantaged students get larger gains than do White students. The largest gains occur *after* sophomores could have had at least 2 years in a small class (1996–1997) and increase each year. Gaps between test scores of White students and other groups reduce each year.

The Uncertainty Principle in California's CSR. California's massive class-size reduction initiated in 1996 is treated lightly not because it is unimportant (it is very important), but because there is no reliable way to determine if the CSR was actually small classes, or primarily a PTR event. The good news from California was the statewide positive test-score gains in lower grades between 1998 and 2002. Results generally follow patterns shown in closely controlled CSR efforts such as STAR and SAGE with greater benefits for poor, male, and minority youth than for others. The 2003 testings were still too early to provide evidence of long-term outcomes. Seemingly negative issues in-clude the increase of noncertified teachers, especially in schools with high incidences of low-performing and minority children (Stecher, Bohrnstedt,

TABLE 7.4   Percent of Groups of Grade-10 Students Passing All Three
Parts of TAAS by Years (Adapted from Cortez, 2000, pp. 6–7.)

Percent Passing by Groups. ( ) = Difference From White (by years).

YEAR	ALL	WHITE	HISP*	AF. AM.*	ECO. DIS.*	Possible Years (n) in Small Class (K-4)**
93–94	50	64	34 (30)	28 (36)	32 (32)	0
94–95	52	67	36 (31)	31 (36)	34 (33)	0
95–96	57	71	43 (28)	37 (34)	40 (31)	1
96–97	64	78	49 (29)	46 (32)	47 (31)	2
97–98	69	81	57 (24)	52 (29)	54 (27)	3
98–99	75	86	64 (22)	60 (26)	62 (24)	4
99–00	80	89	70 (19)	67 (22)	68 (21)	5
GAIN	30	25	36 (11)	39 (14)	36 (11)	
Diff from ALL		−5	+6	+9	+6	

*HISP = Hispanic; AF. AM. = African American; ECO. DIS. = Economically Disadvantaged
**Note. In 1993–1994, grade-10 students would have had no years of HB 72 small classes.
STAR analyses showed that 3 or more years in a small class had lasting benefits.

Kirst, McRobbie, & Williams, 2001; Bohrnstedt, Stecher, & Wiley, 2000); however, later results show that this effect was overstated in the early years.

Why and How Small Classes "Work."   Some authors argue that researchers still need to find out *why* class-size changes influence student outcomes. Stecher and colleagues (2001) offered an example of this point and wrote with imprecision: "While there is a strong perception (sic) that more learning goes on in smaller classrooms (sic), little is known about *why* smaller classes might be better learning environments" (p. 674). (STAR, a controlled, longitudinal experiment, is about cause and effect, not about perceptions. STAR was not a facility study about *classrooms*, but research about *class size*, the unit for instruction within a classroom.)

STAR researchers have explained why and how small classes produce improved outcomes and have published those results. Each of the research- and theory-based explanations of why and how small classes improve student outcomes shown in Table 7.5 happens when class size is reduced to about 13–17 students (e.g., more teacher time per student for such things as diagnosing learning problems, working with portfolios, correcting homework, reading with each child, etc.). Teachers in small classes do not employ radically different teaching approaches or methods—unless *more* is different (Achilles, Kiser-Kling, Aust, & Owen, 1995; Stecher et al., 2001; Stasz & Stecher, 2000; Filby, Cahen, McCutcheon, and Kyle 1980; Evertson & Folger, 1989; Evertson

TABLE 7.5 Small Class (K–3) Benefits Are Supported by Research and Established Theories About Groups, Teaching, Learning, and School Outcomes

I. LEARNING

A. Task Induction: Learn About School (Students' Work)

B. Participation, Engagement, Identification

C. Mastery of Basics

D. Time on Task Increases

E. Appropriate Homework

F. Child Development/Developmentally Appropriate

G. Early Intervention, Duration

II. TEACHING

A. Individual Accommodation

B. Early Diagnosis and Remediation of Learning Difficulties

C. Teach to Mastery

D. Immediate Reinforcement

E. Assessment (In Class)

F. Portfolios, Running Records

G. Effective Teaching Methods

H. Planned, Coherent Lessons (Seamless Transitions)

III. CLASSROOM and CONTEXT

A. Classroom Environment (e.g., Air Quality, Materials, Space, Crowding, Noise)

B. Personal Attention/Community

C. Inclusion, Special Needs

D. Variable Room Arrangements (e.g., Learning Centers)

E. Classroom Management

F. Less Indiscipline

G. Many Volunteers

IV. "OTHER"

A. Increased Parent Interest

B. Reduced Grade Retention

C. Increased Teacher/Student Morale/Energy

D. Teacher Accountability *and* Responsibility

E. Few Projects and "Pull Outs" (Coherence). *Intensity*

F. Student-Led Activities

G. Assessment (Outcome)

H. Field Trips Possible with Fewer Adults/Smaller Vehicles

*V. STUDENT BEHAVIOR (B)**

1. Class size and Engagement: More Engaged in Learning and Prosocial (B) and Less in Disruptive (B). Principles: (1) *"Visibility of the Individual"* (a) Time per Student, (b) Diffusion of Responsibility, and (c) Social Loafing; (2) *Sense of Belonging* (a) Group Norms (e.g., Learning [B]) Influence All Members, (b) Psychological Sense of Community (PSOC) such as Support and Inclusion. *Results are Similar to School Size Work.*

*Finn et al., 2003, pp. 348–352.

& Randolph, 1989; Achilles, 1999, esp. ch. 5). Small classes let teachers use good pedagogy *and* accommodate context changes such as diversity, inclusion, and assessment. Reasons and theories about how and why small classes "work" are shown in Table 7.5, which is divided into five categories: learning, teaching, classroom and context, other, and student behavior.

Student behavior improves in small classes. For example, students become engaged in learning and prosocial rather than disruptive behavior because of increased visibility and the force of group norms that support learning. Students and teachers develop a familylike context that behavioral scientists explain as a psychological sense of community, or PSOC, that also is found in small schools and "learning communities."

Research showing student achievement and behavior benefits of small-class involvement supports the finding of increased student participation in schools and in classes as class size and school size decrease. For example, improved student performance accompanies parent involvement and/or appropriate use of homework, conditions that are evident in small classes. Improvements for students and teachers are *reciprocal, cumulative,* and sometimes *indirect.* If you seek increased parent involvement, reduce class sizes.

DATA ARE NOT ENOUGH: SENSE MAKING IS NEEDED

There remain few questions about the power of small classes to help students and to improve schooling. Data, however, must be understood and then put to use (e.g., in policy and practice). Although specifically about class size, the STAR research was able to answer some other long-standing education questions.

An Attempt at "Sense Making"

Because of its longevity (1985–2004 and counting), size (over 11,600 students), and design (longitudinal, randomized experiment), STAR contributed much to class-size work. Not only did STAR researchers examine quantitative results such as test scores and grade retention, but they interviewed teachers and aides, collected data on teaching processes, and the like to show how and why small classes improve outcomes in grades K–3 and beyond. (Review Tables 7.2–7.5 and Appendix 7.A.) Using the original STAR database, researchers monitored later behavior and outcomes of students who had small K–3 classes (e.g., Boyd-Zaharias & Pate-Bain, 2000a, Finn & Achilles, 1999; Finn, Gerber, Achilles, & Boyd-Zaharias, 2001), even analyzing their college-entrance test-taking results (Krueger & Whitmore, 2000). Positive results for students who had small (14–18 students) K–3 classes include less grade retention, higher test scores in all grades and graduation rates, reduced achievement gaps between groups, and other long-term benefits. Evaluation results of SAGE, a K–3 class-size effort in Wisconsin, roughly mirror outcomes from STAR (Molnar et al., 1999, 2000). SAGE quantitative results have consistently been supported by qualitative and explanatory analyses of why and how small classes contribute to student achievement.

Policy Implications of Class-Size Work

Class-size information *should* be of great interest because class size is visible, administratively mutable, built on solid research, and does *not* push blame for poor performance on teachers, parents, and students. Class size is an adminstrative issue.

Since about 1965, bolstered by PL89-10 (The Elementary and Secondary Education Act, or ESEA), educators have increasingly used (a) special projects for students with all sorts of real or imagined learning differences (even low SES backgrounds), (b) teacher assistants (or aides) in classrooms, (c) "staff development" to inform teachers of all of the special services available, and so on. chapter 17 contains reasons why we should reduce staff development funds and reallocate them to class size. "Specialization" and the project mentality have changed the PTR, but research shows that PTR change has little influence on student outcomes (see Hanushek, 1998). Specialization and the project mentality have fragmented the learning community of teacher and class; they have confounded accountability (who is responsible for Pat's reading—the regular or the reading teacher?) In America, in 1995 about 45% of certified teachers actually taught *a class* of students all day, every day (Darling-Hammond, 1998, p. 11). Fragmentation increases with special-interest programs, for example, bilingual or ESL or LEP, with special education (especially LD or learning disabled), or for slow (or fast) learners, and so on. Wayson, Mitchell, Pinnell, and Landis (1988) identified stultifying effects of increasing specialization.[2] It is not so much a teacher shortage as a staffing or teacher assignment issue.

> Post-Sputnik reforms intensified the rigidities of the education system: they depersonalized the educational process; they weakened the profession by creating splits between educators; they glorified specialization by elevating teachers to positions of dominance over other teachers; they narrowed roles for teachers; and they diminished power and respect for those who work most closely with children. Rather than ameliorating problems, the post-Sputnik reforms exacerbated the endemic problems. (p. 115)

The elementary-grades PTR figures from the *Digest of Education Statistics* (NCES, 1999, p. 75, Table 65) show that PTR in the United States has changed from 30.2 (1955) to 18.6 (1998). Large PTR changes have followed education legislation. The change from 27.6 (1965) to 24.3 (1970) followed ESEA (1965) and continued as the project mentality grew in popularity (to 20.4 in 1980). Some class-size critics have claimed that special education

---

[2]One scientific-based research (SBR) alternative to the "project" mentality is to provide quality teachers with work loads that allow them to employ their professional knowledge to teach each child in a "learning community." Advantages of the context of small classes are described in Achilles (1999) and in Table 7.5 in this chapter. The proliferation of "specials" breaks up coherence of education and intrudes on the work of competent teachers. Running students in and out of the classroom and up and down the hallways may relieve stress and improve physical conditioning, but it detracts from engaged time on task.

requirements have influenced CS outcomes (e.g., Hanushek, 1998, 1999) but from 1980 (allowing 4 years for implementation of PL94-142) to 1997, the elementary PTR only changed from 20.4 to 18.6, and that would include responses to special education legislation in 1990 and 1997. In fact, stringent special education requirements and inclusion have actually brought about larger (and more challenging) classes in some cases, as administrators seek to meet special education regulations, often by adding a student or two to other classes.

Of particular interest in the growing use of full-time teacher aides is the finding of *no positive teacher-aide effects on student achievement, development, or behavior—or on a teacher's teaching* (Gerber, Finn, Achilles, & Boyd-Zaharias, 2001). Given the size and cost of the teacher-aide enterprise, these findings should raise a call to action.[3]

What Should Years of Class-Size Research Have Told Educators?

The sustained stream of research surrounding small classes with its positive findings combined with the general ineffectiveness of changing the PTR (e.g., Hanushek, 1998, 1999) and the less-than-glowing evaluations of

---

[3]Much can be said for teacher aides, especially for their help in classroom activities that *could* free the teacher to teach, or in monitoring students, and in other roles. Unfortunately, these scenarios don't seem to be the norm. Haberman (2000) noted:

A recent study of Title I (an eight-billion-dollar program focused on disadvantaged students) shows that teacher aides spend 60% of their time actually teaching (41% of this time without a teacher present). In many cases, aides are teaching in situations that call for the most sophisticated level of professional practice. They are expected to teach students the teacher cannot control or relate to and has kicked out of class or students with learning problems or students who need to be motivated. These very demanding tasks, which require the most knowledge, skill, and experience are being performed by individuals with little preparation. The more highly trained professional (i.e., the teacher) teaches those without problems or those who will follow directions. If the teacher works on keeping things under control and the aide actually teaches the most challenging students, what does that tell us about the primary purpose of "teaching" in the urban "school"? (pp. 205–206)

An analysis of the STAR kindergarten classes found that, proportionately, there were more "special education" students in small classes (13–17 students) than in regular classes with full-time teacher aides (22–25 students). Proportionately, special-education identified students were overrepresented in small classes by 5.6% and underrepresented in aide classes by 4.1%. (They were underrepresented in regular classes [22–25 students] with no full-time aide, too, but only 1.5%). Observation studies (see Haberman's quote) suggest—at least in the early grades K–2 or so—that when an aide is present a teacher is likely to send a disruptive or troubling student to the aide to "baby-sit." In a class without an aide, the teacher must determine and work on the problems. Students whose special needs are identified early (K, 1) may get services and, through early remediation, *not* end up in a spiral of high-cost special services.

Title I over the years (e.g., Abt, 1997; Borman & D'Agostino, 1996; Wong & Meyer, 1998) *should* have told educators to adopt a class-size policy as an alternative to projects, aides, and PTR changes. Long-term positive benefits of K–3 small classes reveal (a) the investment potential of small classes in early grades, and (b) that small classes need not be expensive. Work by Miles (1995), Achilles and Price (1999), Achilles and Sharp (1998), Odden and Archibald (2001), and others shows that small classes can be implemented by trade-offs, by resource reallocations, and by capitalizing on small-class benefits. But class-size benefits only accrue if CS change is implemented in accordance with the research and theory surrounding small-class use. Early small-class involvement leads to a trajectory of successful schooling outcomes.

Boyd-Zaharias and Pate-Bain (2000a) found that compared to their K–3 peers in regular classes, small-class students were more likely to graduate from high school, receive an honors diploma, and not drop out. Krueger and Whitmore (2000) showed benefits of small classes that last into a student's college-entrance test taking. Finn, Gerber, Achilles, and Boyd-Zaharias (2001) and others have shown the "enduring effects" of early small classes, to the point that students with 4 years of K–3 small classes are nearly a full year ahead of their large-class peers at the end of grade 12: Small-class benefits are sustainable, cumulative, and lasting.

WITHOUT IMPLEMENTATION, GOOD RESEARCH LANGUISHES

In spite of more than 100 years of consistently improving and highly positive class-size work, the research results are too seldom used correctly. Perhaps the ideas are so simple as to deflect interest in their use. Perhaps leaders have neither read the research nor understand it. Without use, data don't advance a field. There are correct ways to use class-size information.

What Are the Steps to Good Class-Size Initiatives?

The cumulative results are clear. From years of studying and observing small classes, researchers and scholar practitioners have developed a *research base, theories,* and *informed professional judgement (IPJ)* to guide effective class-size implementations. Small classes are not simply hiring teachers and doing business as usual. The correct steps are, really, quite direct and clear. They are presented here in summary form:

1. Early Intervention. Start when the pupil enters "schooling" in K or even pre-K.

2. Intense Treatment. The pupil spends all day, every day in the small class. Avoid pupil-teacher ratio (PTR) events, such as "pull-out" projects or team teaching. Develop a sense of "community" and close student-teacher relations.

3. Sufficient Duration. Maintain the small class for at least 3, preferably 4, years for enduring effects.

4. Use Random Assignment in early grades to facilitate peer tutoring, problem-solving groups and student-to-student cooperation (STAR).

5. Employ a Cohort Model for several years so students develop a sense of family or community. STAR results show the power of both random assignment and a cohort model. "Looping" adds teacher continuity to the cohort and may be a useful strategy for added benefits. (Research is needed here.)

6. Appropriate-sized classes in elementary grades will require policy adjustments and perhaps even legislation change.

It is time educators invest in what actually works and ease away from fads. In a quality class-size initiative, students "perform" and achieve in four key (possibly five) areas of growth (Fig. 7.1):

Recommendations for Putting Class-Size Outcomes to Work

1. Require clear *definition* of terms in any study of "class size."

2. Class size and PTR research are both useful. Research and evaluation on both should continue, separately. Treatments, variables, and processes in PTR and CS are not the same, so they should *not* be confounded and reported as the same.

3. Educate the public, parents, policy persons, researchers, education leaders, and the media on differences between PTR and CS.

ACADEMICS (E.G., TEST-SCORE PERFORMANCE ON ALL TESTS.)

BEHAVIOR/DISCIPLINE. ADJUSTMENT TO SCHOOL.

CITIZENSHIP/PARTICIPATION. RELATIONSHIPS, ENGAGEMENT.

DEVELOPMENT INTO PRODUCTIVE AND HUMANE ADULTS, WITH RESPONSIBILITY FOR ACTS: SELF-CONCEPT GROWTH.

AND

(E COULD BE ECONOMIC SUFFICIENCY.)

FIG. 7.1 The ABCDs of improvement will include positive changes in four areas.

4. Educators and policy groups must advocate for the correct use of class sizes. This advocacy can be conducted by "staff development." Department of Education and other policy information on PTR and CS should use the terms explicitly.
5. Evaluators and researchers should document carefully the contexts in which students are educated so that issues of CS and PTR are evident.
6. "Ideal" implementations of CS need to be studied and evaluated to provide a substantial base of CSR data, where the event described is really CS.

Yet as Glass (1992) noted long ago:

[T]he controversy over class size has not subsided, academic quibbling about statistics aside. As usually happens, educational research may clarify a few issues, sharpen debate or shift it slightly, and replace ordinary language with numbers, graphs, and technical/scientific jargon. But it is not likely to reduce or eliminate the conflicts of interest and political positions that are played out in the school system. (p. 165)

An obvious reason that CS languishes is that there is no "product" to sell, so there are few advocates. Less obvious reasons are teacher hesitancy to become accountable for a manageable-sized class and to part with the extra services (e.g., aides) to which they have become accustomed. Finally, few administrators have seriously studied the CS work, relying instead on secondary reports, media disinformation, and word of mouth. Controversy and inaction continue! Are *you* part of this problem? Why?

GUIDING QUESTIONS AND ACTIVITIES

1. How do educators, such as in your district or your state education agency, collect and report information on class size? Indeed, do the schools, districts, and state agency even collect, have, and report class-size data?
2. Analyze actual class sizes and pupil-teacher ratios in school settings using definitions in the text as a guide. (Studies in K–3 between 1998 and 2003 found differences of n = 8 to 10. Teachers in a setting with a PTR of 16:1 faced classes of 24–26 students daily.) What *differences* can you observe in small classes and larger classes in such things as noise, commotion, time on task, student behavior, and participation?

Activity 1: Role-play how you would respond to parents who are seeking "good schools" for their children and are considering options such as vouchers and charter schools. The parents are concerned about achievement, safety, and individual attention. Alternatives to the public schools often emphasize personalization based on "small classes." Consider the public relations power and incentive value of small classes (n = 15 or so).

Activity 2: Find and discuss examples of confusion between the terms PTR and class size in reports, texts, articles, legislation, and the like. Share and critique the examples.

APPENDIX 7.A

A Longitudinal Class-Size Experiment: Scientifically Based Research or SBR

STAR (1985–1989) and the many studies that build on STAR benefit from the experiment's tightly controlled, in-school, randomized longitudinal design. STAR was conducted by a four-university consortium with considerable external support from consultants, advisory groups, and the Tennessee State Department of Education. Basic design issues are:

1. STAR was a controlled 4-year longitudinal experiment that permitted, to the extent possible with empirical data, causal conclusions about outcomes. Pupils entering K were randomly assigned to a small class (S; 13–17), a regular class (R; 22–25), or a regular class with a full-time teacher aide (RA). Pupils entering in later years were assigned at random to classes. Teachers were assigned at random. Randomization and testing were monitored carefully.

2. Building on prior research STAR began in primary grades. Small classes had fewer than 20 students. STAR's posttest only design enabled researchers to study the effects on minority, majority, male, and female students. The design produced a "real" difference in the class sizes, from an average of 24 pupils to an average of 15.

3. The samples were large and diverse. The K year involved over 6,300 students in 329 classrooms in 79 schools in 46 districts. The first-grade sample was larger still. The large samples were maintained throughout the 4 years, producing an excellent longitudinal database. Total sample = 11,601.

4. With minor exceptions, students were kept in their class in grades K–3 (cohorts). A new grade-appropriate teacher was assigned each year.

5. The class arrangement was maintained throughout the day, all year long. There was *no intervention other than class size and teacher aides.* Teachers received no special training except for a small sample in second grade; no special curricula or materials were introduced. (Training didn't increase outcomes.)

6. Norm-referenced tests (NRT), and criterion-referenced tests (CRT) *and* measures of self concept and motivation were administered each spring. Students were aggregated to classes and classes nested into schools for analyses. Teachers and teaching were studied, as were grade retention, participation, aide use, and the like.

7. Researchers studied STAR students after STAR ended in grade 3. Most students graduated in 1998. College-entrance test results (Krueger & Whitmore, 2000) showed that being in a small class in grades K–3 increased the rate of college-entrance test taking and decreased the gap between Black and White students taking the tests.

ACKNOWLEDGMENTS

Portions of this chapter appeared in a paper by C. M. Achilles and J. D. Finn, Making Sense of Continuing and Renewed Class-Size Findings and Interest, presented to the American Association of School Administrators, February 2002, San Diego, California.

SELECTED READINGS

Achilles, C. M. (1999). *Let's put kids first finally: Getting class size right.* Thousand Oaks, CA: Corwin Press.

Achilles, C. M., & Finn, J. D. (2000). Should class size be a cornerstone for educational policy? In M. C. Wang & J. D. Finn (Eds.), *How small classes help teachers do their best* (pp. 299–324). Philadelphia, PA: Temple University Center for Research in Human Development in Education.

Achilles, C. M., & Finn, J. D. (2002, December). The varieties of small classes and their outcomes. In J. D. Finn & M. C. Wang (Eds.), *Taking small classes one step further* (Ch. 7, pp. 121–146). Philadelphia, PA: Temple University Center for Research in Human Development in Education. Greenwich, CT: Information Age Publishing.

Biddle, B. J., & Berliner, D. C. (2002, February). Small class size and its effects. *Educational Leadership, 59*(5), 12–23.

Egelson, P., Harman, P., Hood, A., & Achilles, C. M. (2002). *How class size makes a difference.* Greensboro, NC: South East Regional Vision for Education (SERVE).

Finn, J., Gerber, S. B., Achilles, C. M., & Boyd-Zaharias, J. (2001, April). The enduring effects of small classes. *Teachers College Record, 103*(2), 145–183.

Finn, J. D., & Achilles, C. M. (1999, Summer). Tennessee's class size study: Findings, implication, misconceptions. *Educational Evaluation and Policy Analysis, 21*(2), 97–107.

Gerber, S. B., Finn, J. D., Achilles, C. M., & Boyd-Zaharias, J. (2001, Summer). Teacher aides and students' academic achievement. *Educational Evaluation and Policy Analysis, 23*(2), 123–143.

Haney, W. (2000, August 19). The myth of the Texas miracle in education. *Education Policy Analysis Archives, 8*(41).

Miles, K. H. (1995, Winter). Freeing resources for improving schools: A case study of teacher allocation in Boston public schools. *Educational Evaluation and Policy Analysis* (EEPA), *17*(4), 476–493.

Molnar, A., Smith, P., Zahorik, J., Palmer, A., Halbach, A., & Ehrle, K. (1999, Summer). Evaluating the SAGE program: A pilot program in targeted pupil-teacher reduction in Wisconsin. *Educational Evaluation and Policy Analysis, 21*(2), 165–178.

Molnar, A., Smith, P., Zahorik, J., Palmer, A., Halbach, A., & Ehrle, K. (2000). Wisconsin's student achievement guarantee in education (SAGE) class size reduction program: Achievement effects, teaching, and classroom implications. In M. C. Wang & J. D. Finn (Eds.), *How small classes help teachers do their best* (pp. 227–278). Philadelphia, PA: Temple University Center for Research in Human Development in Education.

Mosteller, F. (1995). The Tennessee study of class size in the early school grades. *The Future of Children, 5*(2), 113–127.

REFERENCES

Abt Associates. (1997, April). *Prospects: Final report on student outcomes.* Cambridge, MA: Abt Associates. (Report prepared for U.S. Department of Education.)

Achilles, C. M. (1999). *Let's put kids first finally: Getting class size right.* Thousand Oaks, CA: Corwin Press.

Achilles, C. M., & Finn, J. D. (2000). Should class size be a cornerstone for educational policy? In M. C. Wang & J. D. Finn (Eds.), *How small classes help teachers do their best* (pp. 299–324). Philadelphia, PA: Temple University Center for Research in Human Development in Education.

Achilles, C. M., & Finn, J. D. (2002, December). The varieties of small classes and their outcomes. In J. D. Finn & M. C. Wang (Eds.), *Taking small classes one step further* (Ch. 7, pp. 121–146). Philadelphia, PA: Temple University Center for Research in Human Development in Education. Greenwich, CT: Information Age Publishing.

Achilles, C. M., Finn, J. D., & Pate-Bain, H. (2002, February). Measuring class size: Let me count the ways. *Educational Leadership, 59*(5), 24–26.

Achilles, C. M., Harman, P., & Egelson, P. (1995, Fall). Using research results on class size to improve pupil achievement outcomes. *Research in the Schools, 2*(2), 23–30.

Achilles, C. M., Kiser-Kling, K., Aust, A., & Owen, J. (1995, April). *A study of reduced class size in primary grades of a fully chapter-1 eligible school: Success starts small (SSS).* Paper presented at the American Educational Research Association, San Francisco. (ERIC Document Reproduction Service No. ED419-288.)

Achilles, C. M., & Price, W. J. (1999, January). Can your district afford smaller class sizes in grades K–3? *School Business Affairs, 65*(1), 10–16.

Achilles, C. M., & Sharp, M. (1998, Fall). Solve your puzzles using class size and pupil-teacher ratio (PTR) differences. *Catalyst for Change, 28*(1), 5–10.

Biddle, B. J., & Berliner, D. C. (2002, February). Small class size and its effects. *Educational Leadership, 59*(5), 12–23.

Bohrnstedt, G. W., Stecher, B. M., & Wiley, E. W. (2000). The California class size reduction evaluation: Lessons learned. In M. C. Wang & J. D. Finn (Eds.), *How small classes help teachers do their best* (pp. 201–226). Philadelphia, PA: Temple University Center for Research in Human Development in Education.

Boozer, M., & Rouse, C. (1995, May). Intraschool variations in class size: Patterns and implications. Princeton, NJ: Industrial Relations Section. ERIC Document Reproduction Service No. ED385-395.

Borman, G. D., & D'Agostino, J. V. (1996, Winter). Title I and student achievement: A meta-analysis of federal evaluation results. *Educational Evaluation and Policy Analysis, 18*(4), 309–326.

Boyd-Zaharias, J., & Pate-Bain, H. (2000a). Early and new findings from Tennessee's Project STAR. In M. C. Wang & J. D. Finn (Eds.), *How small classes help teachers do their best,* (pp. 65–98). Philadelphia, PA: Temple University Center for Research in Human Development in Education.

Boyd-Zaharias, J., & Pate-Bain, H. (2000b, April). *The continuing impact of elementary small classes.* Paper presented at the Annual Meeting of the American Educational Research Association, New Orleans, Louisiana. Lebanon, TN: HEROS, Inc.

Cahen, L. S., & Filby, N. (1979, March). The class size/achievement issue: New evidence and a research plan. *Phi Delta Kappan,* 492–495, 538.

Chase, C. I., Mueller, D. J., & Walden, J. D. (1986, December). *PRIME TIME: Its impact on instruction and achievement.* Final report. Indianapolis: Indiana Department of Education.

Cortez, A. (2000, March). Why better isn't enough: A closer look at TAAS gains. *IDRA Newsletter.* San Antonio, TX.

Darling-Hammond, L. (1998, January–February). Teachers and teaching: Testing policy hypotheses from a national commission report. *Educational Researcher, 27*(1), 5–15.

Egelson, P., Harman, P., Hood, A., & Achilles, C. M. (2002). *How class size makes a difference.* Greensboro, NC: South East Regional Vision for Education (SERVE).

Evertson, C. M., & Folger, J. K. (1989, March). *Small class, large class: What do teachers do differently?* Paper at American Educational Research Association, San Francisco, California.

Evertson, C. M., & Randolph, C. H. (1989, Fall). Teaching practices and class size: A new look at an old issue. *Peabody Journal of Education, 67*(1), 85–105.

Fairfax County (VA) Schools. (1997, July). *Evaluation of the reduced-ratio program: Final report.* Fairfax, VA: Office of Program Evaluation, Fairfax County Schools.

Filby, N., Cahen, L., McCutcheon, G., & Kyle, D. (1980). What happens in smaller classes? San Francisco. Far West Laboratory for Educational Research and Development. ERIC Document Reproduction Service ED219365.

Finn, J. D., & Achilles, C. M., (1999, Summer). Tennessee's class size study: Findings, implications, misconceptions. *Educational Evaluation and Policy Analysis, 21*(2), 97–107.

Finn, J., Gerber, S. B., Achilles, C. M., & Boyd-Zaharias, J. (2001, April). The enduring effects of small classes. *Teachers College Record, 103*(2), 145–183.

Finn, J. D., Pannozzo, G. M., & Achilles, C. M. (2003, Fall). The "whys" of class size: Student behavior in small classes. *Review of Educational Research, 73*(3), 321–368.

Finn, J. D., Gerber, S. B., & Boyd-Zaharias, J. (2004, April). Small classes in the early grades, academic achievement, and dropping out of school. Paper at American Educational Research Association, San Diego, California.

Gerber, S. B., Finn, J. D., Achilles, C. M., & Boyd-Zaharias, J. (2001, Summer). Teacher aides and students' academic achievement. *Educational Evaluation and Policy Analysis, 23*(2), 123–143.

Glass, G. V. (1992). Class size. In M. C. Akin (Ed.), *Encyclopedia of Educational Research,* Volume I (6th ed., pp. 164–166). New York: MacMillan Publishing Co.

Glass, G. V., Cahen, L. S., Smith, M. L., & Filby, N. N. (1982). *School class size. Research and policy.* Beverly Hills, CA: Sage.

Glass, G. V., & Smith, M. L. (1978). *Metaanalysis of research on the relationship of class size and achievement.* San Francisco: Far West Laboratory for Educational Research and Development.

Haberman, M. (2000, November). Urban schools: Day camps or custodial centers. *Phi Delta Kappan, 82*(3), 203–208.

Haney, W. (2000, August 19). The myth of the Texas miracle in education. *Education Policy Analysis Archives, 8*(41).

Hanushek, E. A. (1998, February). *The evidence on class size.* Rochester, NY: The University of Rochester. W. Allen Wallis Institute.

Hanushek, E. A. (1999, Summer). Some findings from an independent investigation of the Tennessee STAR experiment and from other investigations of class size effects (sic). *Educational Evaluation and Policy Analysis, 21*(2), 143–163.

Iannaccone, L. (1975). *Education policy systems: A study guide for educational administrators.* Ft. Lauderdale, FL: Nova Southeastern University (esp. pp. 11–19).

Krueger, A. B., & Whitmore, D. M. (2000, March). The effect of attending a small class in the early grades on college-test taking and middle school test results: Evidence from Project STAR. Princeton: Princeton University Industrial Relations Section.

Lindbloom, D. H. (1970). Class size as it affects instructional procedures and educational outcomes. (ERIC Document Reproduction Service No. ED059 532).

Miles, K. H. (1995, Winter). Freeing resources for improving schools: A case study of teacher allocation in Boston public schools. *Educational Evaluation and Policy Analysis* (EEPA), *17*(4), 476–493.

Molnar, A., Smith, P., Zahorik, J., Palmer, A., Halbach, A., & Ehrle, K. (1999, Summer). Evaluating the SAGE program: A pilot program in targeted pupil–teacher reduction in Wisconsin. *Educational Evaluation and Policy Analysis, 21*(2), 165–178.

Molnar, A., Smith, P., Zahorik, J., Palmer, A., Halbach, A., & Ehrle, K. (2000). Wisconsin's student achievement guarantee in education (SAGE) class size reduction program: Achievement effects, teaching, and classroom implications. In M. C. Wang & J. D. Finn (Eds.), *How small classes help teachers do their best* (pp. 227–278). Philadelphia, PA: Temple University Center for Research in Human Development in Education.

Mosteller, F. (1995). The Tennessee study of class size in the early school grades. *The Future of Children, 5*(2), 113–127.

Mosteller, F., Light, R. J., & Sachs, J. A. (1986, Winter). Sustained inquiry in education: Lessons from skill grouping and class size. *Harvard Educational Review, 66*(4), 797–828.

Odden, A., & Archibald, S. (2001, August). Committing to class-size reduction and finding the resources to implement it: A case study of resource reallocation. *Education Policy Analysis Archives, 9*(30).

Olson, M. N. (1971). Research notes-ways to achieve quality in school classrooms: Some definitive answers. *Phi Delta Kappan*, p. 65.

Smith, M. L., & Glass, G. V. (1979). Relationship of class-size to classroom processes, teacher satisfaction and pupil affect: A meta-analysis. San Francisco, CA: Far West Laboratory for Educational Research and Development.

Stasz, C., & Stecher, B. (2000, Winter). Teaching mathematics and language arts in reduced size and non-reduced size classrooms (sic). *Educational Evaluation and Policy Analysis, 22*(4), 313–329.

State of Texas. (1984). General and special laws of the State of Texas. Sixty–Eighth Legislature June 4, 1884, to July 11, 1984. Esp. Chapter 28, HB No. 72.

Stecher, B., Bohrnstedt, G., Kirst, M., McRobbie, J., & Williams, T. (2001, May). Class-size reduction in California: A story of hope, promise, and unintended consequences. *Phi Delta Kappan, 82*(9), 670–674.

Stewart, T. (1998, June 29). Reduced size classes. Data tables and narrative. Morganton, NC: Mimeo. (Updated 2000, 2003, Burke County Schools.)

Tillitski, C. (1990, Fall). The longitudinal effect size of Prime Time, Indiana's state-sponsored reduced class size program. *Contemporary Education, LXII*(1), 24–27.

U.S. Department of Education. (1999). *Digest of Education Statistics*, Office of Education Research and Improvement. Washington, DC: National Center for Education Statistics.

Voelkl, K. (1995). *Identification with school*. Unpublished PhD dissertation, Buffalo, New York, SUNY. (UMI No. 0538143)

Wayson, W. W., Mitchell, B., Pinnell, G. S., & Landis, D. (1988). *Up from excellence: The impact of the excellence movement on schools*. Bloomington, IN: The Phi Delta Kappa Educational Foundation.

Wong, K. K., & Meyer, S. J. (1998, Summer). Title I schoolwide programs: A synthesis of findings from recent evaluations. *Education Evaluation and Policy Analysis, 20*(2), 115–136.

Word, E., Johnston, J., Bain, H., Fulton, B., Zaharias, J., Lintz, N., Achilles, C. M., Folger, J., & Breda, C. (1990). *Student/teacher achievement ratio (STAR): Tennessee's K–3 class size study*. Final report and final report summary. Nashville: Tennessee State Department of Education.

Chapter 8

Evaluation of Schools: An Expanded View

Patricia E. Holland
Joy C. Phillips
University of Houston

Evaluating schools is certainly not a new phenomenon in this country. It has been an aspect of American schools since colonial days when town selectmen would visit local schools and report to the townspeople whether children were being taught "according to law" (Tanner & Tanner, 1987, p. 6). Most recently, the No Child Left Behind (NCLB) Act signed into law by President Bush in January 2002 took its place in a long-standing tradition of evaluating schools. One of the requirements of this law is that public schools be evaluated annually on the basis of standardized tests developed by each state to assess students' achievement of state standards in literacy and mathematics that prescribe the knowledge and skills expected of students in those areas.

The effort to evaluate schools as outlined in the NCLB Act is not in itself something new in the educational system of this country. Neither is the use of measures of student achievement as the basis for evaluating schools; that movement has been gaining momentum for the two decades since the publication of *A Nation at Risk* (National Commission on Excellence in Education, 1983). What is new is the attempt to use legislation prescribing the way schools are to be evaluated as leverage for a landmark overhaul of public education throughout the United States.

Given the magnitude of NCLB's aspirations, it is not surprising that the process of evaluating schools as mandated by the act has been subject to considerable scrutiny within the educational community. Nor is it surprising that heated criticism has come from scholars and educators about a process of evaluation that has become a dominant factor in America's schools. Much of that criticism has focused on the high-stakes testing that is central to the evaluation of schools under the No Child Left Behind legislation. NCLB uses testing as the means of evaluating schools and test scores as the end products by which schools are to be judged.

In this chapter, we challenge the current dominant view of school evaluation that focuses narrowly on high-stakes testing and test scores. We do not reject summarily evaluation based on testing. Rather, we argue that the range of assessment tools needs to expand beyond testing to incorporate other promising school-level approaches including both process- and product-driven strategies. To support our argument, we discuss six approaches that were used by public schools participating in a major urban school reform initiative in the southwest United States. These six strategies cause us to rethink both the means and ends of evaluating schools.

ENDS AND MEANS OF EVALUATING SCHOOLS

Underlying all the criticism of evaluating schools on the basis of student achievement on high-stakes tests are values about the purpose and process of public schooling in America. Interestingly, critics do not dispute the value of the stated purpose of NCLB to hold schools accountable for the learning of all students, including those minorities and non-English speakers who have traditionally not experienced the same levels of academic achievement as other students. Nor do they challenge the value placed on basic literacy and mathematics, or the importance of their measurable demonstration by students. After all, who could object to these being important? It is not, then, in question whether evaluation of the extent to which schools are achieving these ends or purposes is worthwhile; rather it is a matter of whether high-stakes achievement tests as the means being used to evaluate them are too limited. It is also a matter of whether there might be other important values to consider as well, values not assessed by test scores.

To frame the issue of evaluating schools in terms of this distinction between ends and means opens the box that has been created by test-driven accountability. Widening the scope of means used to evaluate schools does not disregard the value of the ends legislated by NCLB that hold schools and educators accountable for what and how much students learn. Instead, focusing on the means used to both attain and assess those ends allows an expanded range of strategies for achieving and evaluating ends, and also allows values other than those subject to testing to become part of the evaluation process.

STRATEGIES FOR EXPANDING EVALUATION OF SCHOOLS

Having made a general claim for the merit of expanding the means by which schools can be evaluated, we consider specific strategies that may be used. For this discussion, we draw data from a large research and evaluation study conducted in a major urban city in the southwestern United States between 1999 and 2002. This study examined 88 public schools—elementary, middle, and high schools—funded to engage in a unique whole-school reform initiative. The reform initiative directed dollars to individual schools willing to address three imperatives: enhance teacher learning, reduce isolation within schools and between schools and communities, and personalize the students' learning environment (Reyes & Phillips, 2003). Rather than requiring schools to adopt particular curricula programs, this reform allowed participating schools broad latitude to create their own action plans.

The overall reform evaluation was designed to be both formative and summative. The comprehensive independent evaluation study included both quantitative and qualitative analyses. Twelve schools were selected from among the 88 funded for intensive case study. A university-based research team examined each case study school. Much of what the evaluators learned about the reform came from qualitative data analysis. The study researchers looked for evidence to answer the following research questions:

- How did funded schools put the reform initiative in place?
- What did the schools do as a result of the initiative?
- What apparent impact has the initiative had on schools and teacher learning?
- What apparent impact has the initiative had on students' academic performance?

At the macrolevel of analysis, researchers compared student test data from funded schools with each school's own prior student achievement data as well as with academic performance of comparable peers from nonfunded schools. At the microlevel of analysis, researchers searched for evidence of campus changes in teaching and learning. Typically, case study researchers looked at both quantitative and qualitative data from the schools. However, the qualitative data—classroom observations, interviews, student performance, student-work products, document review—provided the deepest understanding of the reform's impact within funded schools.

We begin by providing illustrations of six effective strategies reforming schools used to implement school-based accountability systems. Because three strategies focus on process, we designate these as *people-driven* strategies; the remaining three we call *product-driven* strategies. Critical Friends Groups, Peer-Review Teams, and Constructive Partnerships illustrate the people-driven strategies. School Portfolios, School Accountability Reports, and Reflective Portraits serve as examples of product-driven strategies. Staff in the reforming schools adapted some of these strategies from national models and developed others locally through experimentation.

PEOPLE-DRIVEN STRATEGIES

Critical Friends Groups

One strategy used by many of the 88 reforming schools was the critical friends group (CFG) approach, a method of teacher-led study groups that originated in 1995 at the Annenberg Institute for School Reform at Brown University through a program entitled the National School Reform Faculty (NSRF).[1] The CFG approach consists of three interlinking components: building professional community among teachers, helping teachers engage in reflection about their practice, and using peer review and conversation to help teachers adapt their teaching practice to meet specific student needs.

CFGs provide deliberate time and structures to promote teacher professional growth that is directly linked to student learning. A CFG consists of 8 to 12 teachers who agree to work together to define and produce improved student achievement. As a group, members establish student learning goals, help each other think about better teaching practices, look closely at curriculum and student work, and identify school culture issues that affect student achievement. Each CFG chooses a peer coach who helps the group build a sense of trust, essential if they are to work together in a direct, honest, and productive way. The coach also helps the members learn and master techniques that sharpen self-insight, promote creativity, and encourage candid, usable peer feedback. Traditionally, few teachers have opportunities to develop these skills.

CFG "coaches" lead the groups, based on techniques they have obtained through CFG Coaches Training, sponsored by the National School Reform Faculty. They draw from a variety of "protocols" to structure conversations. They discuss a range of topics including shared readings, student work, lesson plans, or new ideas about teaching or school reform. CFG meetings generally begin with some informal time, refreshments, and then a more formal sharing, in which each member talks about what he or she has been doing at school or in the classroom. These conversations help create a sense of connection and community among the group. Teachers define what is important to them or what they want to share about their own work. Collectively, group members direct and define their discussions.

Teachers voluntarily participate in CFGs, and they may receive stipends for their participation. CFG groups may meet weekly, biweekly, or monthly for 1 to 2 hours per meeting. Groups may meet on the school campus or at a variety of off-campus locations. Some schools schedule annual CFG retreats, providing opportunities for members of all CFG groups at the school to interact.

---

[1]For more information about the NSRF and CFG, see http://www.nsrfharmony.org/.

Critical Friends Groups provide an important means through which teachers evaluate their own and each other's teaching practice. Teachers believe CFG participation reduces isolation by increasing trust, communication, commitment, and continuity among the faculty. Both new teachers and veteran teachers benefit from participating in CFGs. Following structured agendas and protocols created by group leaders and NSRF guidelines, group members engage in meaningful discussions about student work and instructional methods during CFG meetings. Teachers talk about gaining a new perspective from listening to their peers, about gaining confidence as they discover that their thoughts are valuable to others, and about learning how to be reflective about their teaching practices.

Peer Review Teams

Peer review and self-evaluation are at the center of the Critical Friends Group process. Based on the success of CFGs in reforming schools, the local organization charged with managing the reform initiative adapted the CFG peer-review process into an annual accountability mechanism. The annual process consisted of two components: a written report of progress—developed by faculty at each participating school—and a peer-review visit. We consider the written report a product-driven strategy; we'll discuss it in the next section. However, the peer-review process warrants attention as a people-driven process.

A peer-review team consisted typically of two classroom teachers, one school administrator, and a community/parent representative. In preparation for a site visit, the team studied the school's written report along with other documents and data about the school. After reviewing documentation, the peer-review team spent the day at the school under review listening to school representatives' reports, visiting classrooms, and touring the campus. The visit included conversations between the visiting evaluators and school representatives based on critical friends protocols. The peer evaluators concluded their visit by rating the school's progress using a scored assessment process. Approximately a month after the visit, participating schools received their assessment scores. The participating schools used this feedback to prepare continuing proposals for funding, and the local managing organization used the report along with campus student achievement data to determine subsequent funding levels.

The local managing organization trained both participants from funded schools and visiting evaluators in the peer-review process. School staff were likely to participate in both roles: once, as a host to visiting evaluators, next, as a visiting evaluator to another reforming school. The trainers introduced the reporting documents and procedures and discussed the reform initiative's

imperatives and philosophy. The managing organization believed this training was essential for participants to engage appropriately in this formative
evaluation process.

Reforming schools also prepared a summary report called *Year in Review*. From this report, peer reviewers could study the school's context and
its community. For example, the *Year in Review* report included student demographics, changing school and/or district leadership, and other pressing
community issues. This document allowed the school participants to update
the managing organization and visiting peer reviewers on critical changes
that had occurred since the last visit.

Finally, peer reviewers considered the reforming school's vision. The
managing organization required each funded school to update each year
the vision for the school/community. Formative evaluation early in the reform initiative suggested that schools with more focused efforts seemed
to make the most progress toward reform. Therefore, subsequent reporting documents required participating schools to describe how their vision
aligned with their school's focused effort. Finally, funded schools provided
evidence to support progress toward the goals declared in the previous
year's proposal. According to training documents prepared by the reform
initiative managers, allowable evidence might include, "An outward sign;
facts, qualitative and/or quantitative data, or documentation identified that
points out or points to specific conclusions or new directions." Similarly, data
were:

> Information about what goes on in schools. Some data may be presented
> in numbers, for example, promotion and retention rates, student mobility,
> teacher transfers, the number of books students read. Data may also be actual
> student work. Stories can also constitute data providing evidence of commu-
> nity involvement or documenting how teachers work together. (unpublished
> training document)

Participating schools used this written documentation to explain why
they had selected their reform goals, what their implementation plans were,
and how much progress they had achieved during the year in review. Peer
reviewers listened to school faculty give details of their reform work and
looked for evidence of progress in classrooms, on campuses, and in student
work and achievement scores. Most significantly, these reporting documents
provided a framework for the visiting peer reviewers and host school faculty
to have in-depth conversations about the reform work. The CFG-inspired
protocol process enabled the conversations to be structured in ways known
by participants to be familiar, safe, confidential, and helpful. The process
was by design intended to be a constructive partnership.

Constructive Partnerships

From the outset, this reform initiative was committed to the idea of formative evaluation. Funded school participants believed confidently that they were capable of spending reform dollars wisely to implement school change and development. However, they welcomed formative feedback. Reformers believed in Schon and McDonald's (1998) idea of evaluation based on "constructive partnerships." Building on the work of Argyris and Schon (1992), Schon and McDonald described constructive partnerships by saying:

> If the insiders are an initiative's architects and actors, and the outsiders its evaluators, then the constructive partnership implies an evaluation methodology quite unlike the common variety, in which evaluators work in a relatively "hands-off" way and seek to objectify causal connections between program interventions and their outcomes.... It does not seek to hold "treatments" stable but to subject them to continuous reflection. And its boundaries are the boundaries of the action situation it studies, leaving open the relationship between what it may discover in the situation and what might be discovered in others. Illuminating this relationship requires additional inquiry and reflection, or what we call reflective transfer. (p. 13)

This reform initiative used formative evaluation in a variety of ways. Both the critical friends groups and peer-review teams strategies previously described are examples of formative evaluation. Two additional successful mechanisms included the reform evaluators, themselves and individuals known as planning and evaluation (or P&E) consultants. Participating schools funded at the highest levels were required to select a university or community-based researcher to help them document their reform work and to guide them in their efforts. Specific job descriptions were not developed, and P&E consultants interpreted their roles in widely varying ways. However, some P&E consultants became highly valued members of the school's reform team.

All of these mechanisms reflect Schon and McDonald's notion of constructive partnerships. Funded schools developed a range of other constructive partnerships by establishing long-term relationships with other outside educational experts. For example, a high school faculty worked closely for several years with Fred Newman and Bruce King, respected authorities on authentic assessment, as they aligned their curriculum delivery with their goal of authentic instruction.

A middle school used reform dollars to hire a local university professor to work with the language arts teachers to improve instruction for "struggling readers." Study groups formed to examine research-based literature and to consider strategies for adapting theory into daily practice. Teachers reported spending more time and energy on their practice than ever before by participating in these study groups and also described feeling energized and inspired by evidence of student success. By disaggregating achievement data and targeting specific, individual student needs, these teachers and their outside partner helped students labeled at risk to improve significantly their reading and writing skills. In fact, during the 5-year reform, this school raised its official state accountability rating from Acceptable to Exemplary (Phillips, 2003).

PRODUCT-DRIVEN STRATEGIES

School Portfolios

At the outset of the reform initiative, both the reform funders and the participating schools recognized the need for establishing quickly a system for monitoring reform implementation. Because these schools were funded substantially and the reform goals were abstract rather than concrete, all involved considered this a high-stakes venture that needed close observation. Ultimately, several product-driven evaluation methods emerged. Some methods were implemented across all funded schools; others were used by sets of schools.

One set of schools decided to develop school portfolios as a method of measuring progress toward reform. Principals from 5 of the 11 schools funded at the highest level objected strongly to the idea of being given a traditional evaluation template that concentrated only on quantitative measures. These principals, who characterized themselves as having very strong personalities, argued, "We were chosen to be these top schools because we have some great ideas of what we want to do and how we want to do it. . . . We are more than just this collection of standards" (personal communication, December 13, 2001). These principals were committed to creating an evaluation process that could track their progress of putting theory into practice. Moreover, these principals wanted especially to develop richly detailed in-school records about the reform work. They viewed teacher research and teacher voice as key elements of the change process. They hoped the creation of a reflective school portfolio would bring often-neglected glimpses of teachers' practices, student learning, school context, and educational change into public view.

Therefore, early in the reform, these five schools joined forces to create a campus-level accountability process that evolved into the School Portfolio project. An outside evaluator, one of the P&E consultants, facilitated the project development. Each of these five schools had independently chosen the same local university professor to serve as their P&E consultant. This professor agreed to work with the five schools only if the schools would agree to work as a group. Each school, using teams composed of administrators and teachers, quickly formed a collective group that became known as the portfolio cohort.

Membership in this cohort was somewhat fluid with some individuals remaining active continuously, some leaving the group, some new members joining, and others participating intermittently. Several years after the group formed, a sixth school joined the cohort. Initially, principals participated actively along with a few teacher representatives. Gradually, teachers became more involved, and eventually the principals turned over primary responsibility for the work to the teachers.[2]

The portfolio cohort's facilitator, the P&E consultant, introduced the group to research literature that focused on teacher knowledge and narrative methodology. The group was particularly drawn to Lyons' (1998) book, *With Portfolio in Hand,* and Clandinin and Connelly's (1995) work, *Teachers' Professional Knowledge Landscapes.* Craig's (1997) journal article on teachers' telling stories about school context also guided them. Finally, they used White's (1981) distinction between annals, chronicles, and narratives to structure their portfolios. According to White, "annals" list major events; "chronicles" describe the events; and "narratives" discuss peoples' experiences in relationship to the major events.

Each school's portfolio was unique. Initially, these portfolios resembled coffeetable scrapbooks. Over the 5 years of their work, however, the portfolios began to capture more of the complexity of school change. The portfolios increasingly included teacher reflections, student work, and individual responses. One middle school—also deeply engaged in the New Jersey Writing Project curriculum—focused on journaling. Teachers and students in this school used journals to chronicle their experiences with learning (metacognition). They often included artifacts from their daily lives that had inspired them in their writing. Student journals frequently were created in artistic form as drawings and photos were interspersed with text. At this school, journals became a key component of each content area and are often used as warm-up activities for other lessons.

School Accountability Reports

The managing organization created an accountability process based on a reporting document that came to be known as the *School Accountability Report* (SAR). This managing organization required funded schools to

---

[2]Subsequently, principals formed study groups of their own and participated in reform-sponsored Principal Academies designed to promote in-depth professional development forums as well as to stimulate collegiality and peer support.

prepare and submit a SAR each spring. Using the SAR format, funded schools responded to a series of questions by providing evidence of progress toward implementation of reform goals.

The report format asked schools to detail their progress toward the three major reform initiatives: improving teacher learning, reducing size, and reducing isolation. Schools were also asked to chart their progress in these three areas by describing partnerships created and their impact on the school and its reform efforts, leadership development and the impact of the reform in the school and its community, and next steps or efforts made to build capacity and thus sustain emerging reform efforts.

Finally, schools were asked to rate their progress on a continuum from "beginning" work through "emerging" and "systemic" to "sustaining" efforts. In other words, faculty teams in each school were expected to explain their work to improve teacher learning by rating it as one of the four categories in the continuum. For example, beginning work may include a written mission statement along with long-term goals but may not include a comprehensive professional development plan tailored to the staff's specific pedagogical needs or the students' academic needs. On the other hand, sustaining efforts would include teacher professional development choices based on careful analysis of student achievement data disaggregated according to SES and specific student academic needs. Furthermore, sustaining efforts would typically reach outside the funded schools in their efforts to create sustainable learning relationships with other schools and other districts.

Each funded year, participating schools prepared these reports to document their progress toward both general reform goals and their specific school-based goals. These documents were not perfunctory reports destined to gather dust in an ignored filing cabinet. Rather, these reports were considered active documents to be reviewed closely by peer-review teams, a group of educational practitioners and community people from outside the school.

Reflective Portraits

In order to provide a real-time image of the school that it may not be possible to convey in the SAR format, funded schools also created reflective portraits of their campuses. School writing teams had a great deal of latitude in designing these portraits. They may have chosen to use a case study model, an analysis of common themes, an interactive experience between the school and its audience, or a longitudinal study by a student or teacher. Whatever format they chose, school teams answered these basic questions:

- Who are we? (based on our school's beliefs and values, current structures, and culture)

- What have we done? What have we accomplished in meeting our focused effort?
- What are we doing? What are our current programs? How are we sustaining our focused effort?
- How good are we at what we do? How do we know?

The intent of these reflective portraits is to allow the outside evaluators an opportunity to see how the school actually functioned on a daily basis. Because the school teams were not constrained by preimposed structures, they were able to use considerable creativity in their designs. For example, faculty from one middle school designed their school's reflective portrait as a way to document teachers' voices in the reform implementation process. This faculty believed that engaging teachers in high-quality teacher professional development would significantly impact teacher learning and would lead to increased student achievement. Therefore, teachers developed text for the portrait that included their conversational descriptions of their professional development activities and evidence of the positive outcomes for teachers and students.

WHAT THE STRATEGIES HAVE IN COMMON

When these strategies for evaluating schools are considered as a group, they have five characteristics in common. Collectively, all strategies include as key components constructive conversation, focused learning, development of narratives, consideration of ways of being, and creation of learning communities. One way to describe these characteristics is to say, as Thomas Schwandt (2002) did, that they "recast evaluation in terms of practical hermeneutics" (p. 60).[3] Although that description may not be familiar to most educators, it does point the way to a tradition of philosophical inquiry and a discourse that can be helpful in discussing in more understandable terms the salient features that cut across these evaluation strategies. What this discourse of hermeneutics offers is language for framing concepts that differ from those in the conventional depiction of evaluation as a social science. Rather than emphasizing concerns of social science about particular methods to be used to obtain the objective detachment that will provide the best and most unbiased explanations of the performance or program that is the subject of evaluation, the discourse of practical hermeneutics focuses on how individuals and groups who shape and enact circumstances and events within their

---

[3]The discussion of practical hermeneutics as an alternative perspective on evaluation in this chapter draws on the presentation of this perspective by Schwandt (2002) in his book *Evaluation Practice Reconsidered.*

social world interpret and understand their experience and themselves in relation to that experience.

In order to better understand the departure from conventional evaluation that this discourse of practical hermeneutics represents, and to prepare for discussion of characteristics that cut across evaluation strategies that were described earlier, it is helpful to consider several propositions that anchor practical hermeneutics. These propositions concern the relationship between individuals and their social world and the knowledge individuals have of that world. Shotter (1993) presented these propositions as follows:

- The social world is not simply out there waiting to be discovered but is "a continuous flux or flow of mental activity containing regions of self-producing order [and] that such activity can only be studied from a position of involvement 'within' it, instead of as an 'outsider'";
- Knowledge of that world is practical-moral knowledge and does not depend on justification or proof for its practical efficacy;
- "We are not in an 'ownership' relation to such knowledge, but we embody it as part of who and what we are" (p. 166).

Conversation

These propositions are to be kept in mind as discussion now turns to characteristics shared by the evaluation strategies described earlier. The first of these characteristics is that the strategies all depict the process of evaluation as *conversational.* This term is used to describe the way the process of evaluation occurs, the relationship between evaluators and that which is being evaluated, and also the nature of the interaction among individuals involved in the evaluation.

Conceptualizing the process of evaluation as conversational draws attention to how what is understood about a school involves an ongoing interpretation of what the information that is gathered and presented about the school means. This process is relatively easy to recognize in the critical friends, peer-review, and constructive partnership strategies that are people driven. In these strategies, the evaluation process is quite literally conversational as participants shape evaluation criteria, explore what they understand events and evidence to mean, and change their understanding based on what others say.

However, even the more product-driven strategies of reflective portraits, school accountability reports, and school portfolios can be construed as conversational in that as events occur and new evidence accumulates around the values and issues that are the focus of the evaluative process, previous assumptions and values about what is going on in the school are challenged or reshaped. The criteria for judging what information is to be included in the product and what that information means are not fixed and immutable because the school itself is constantly changing—it is "talking back" to evaluators. In other words, the relationship between evaluators and what is being evaluated is an active, two-way process. It is conversational.

Perhaps the most important aspect of the conversational characteristic of the evaluation strategies that have been described concerns the nature of the interaction among individuals involved in the evaluation. Whereas in a traditional social science approach to evaluation evaluators view others in a detached and uninvolved way as objects to be understood, in the evaluation strategies considered here, individuals within a school open themselves to the experience of coming together as participants in the evaluation process, engaging in dialogue, and "sharing in a common meaning" (Gadamer, 1989, p. 292). The philosopher Gadamer maintained that it is only in engagements of this kind, in genuine conversation, that understanding is possible (Schwandt, 2002). Such genuine conversation is risky business, however, in that it challenges individuals to be open to understanding in new ways. As Dunne (1993) put it, "the whole point of conversation is that I both allow some play to my own thinking and, in so doing, expose it to the counterweight of the other's contribution, which may confirm me in it or force me to amend or abandon it" (p. 117).

Learning

Each of the six strategies for evaluating schools can also be seen as efforts to learn more about a particular school and about how it is perceived by others. To say then that *learning* characterizes these strategies is to again differentiate them from traditional evaluation. According to Schwandt (2002), the traditional approach to evaluation is empiricist in that "it seeks to deliver objective knowledge claims (claims about the value of some human activity) that are free of the contingencies and ambiguities that mark our everyday efforts at judging the value of our actions" (p. 79). Strategies based in practical hermeneutics, on the other hand, reflect the view that social settings and the behavior of individuals within those settings are to be seen as a kind of text to be "read."[4]

Gallagher (1992) took this notion of the social world as text a step further, saying that rather than being the private act that reading is usually construed

---

[4]This view is found in the work of philosophers (Derrida, 1976; Rorty, 1979; Ricoeur, 1981; Taylor, 1985; Gadamer, 1989; Gallagher, 1992), and importantly for the evaluation strategies that are the focus of this chapter, in the work of qualitative ethnographers within the social sciences such as Denzin (1997) and Geertz (1980).

to be, the interpretation of social "texts" is a learning process that "is interwoven with explication and application" (p. 330). In other words, it reflects the kind of conversation already discussed as a characteristic of the evaluation strategies.

Characterizing the evaluation strategies as learning also implies that they serve a different purpose from traditional evaluations that seek to provide empirical evidence and explanations about the value of programs and practices. Such evidence and explanations are seen as products or things to be used as tools to shape and control the social contexts that have been evaluated. Evaluation characterized as learning emphasizes the importance of the *process* of interpreting events and experiences in an interactive conversation with them and with others who are part of the social world in which those events and experiences take place. Although products may result from such evaluation strategies—for example, school accountability reports or portfolios—these products are artifacts of an evaluation that sees its greater purpose to be the shaping and reshaping of participants' understanding of their lived experience within the evaluated setting. Furthermore, participants in this kind of evaluative process view the products of evaluation as tentative and provisional accounts of their knowledge and understanding at particular points in time. Evaluation as learning is never finished.

Narratives

Narratives as a form for rendering the judgments made in the evaluation of schools are found in each of the evaluation strategies. Such narratives employ a kind of communication that is familiar to educators within school settings. As such, the use of narrative is consistent with what was described earlier as the conversation among those within the school community to construct and convey their understanding of how their school is working.

Schwandt (2002) contrasted these narratives with traditional evaluation. He noted that in traditional evaluations the evaluator attempts to manage dialogue and deliberation within the parameters of what the evaluator has predetermined as the evaluation's design and purpose. On the other hand, evaluations in which narratives are used promote genuine dialogue about the different perceptions that may exist among those within the evaluation setting about the value of practices that are being evaluated. He also noted that narratives are well-suited to provide complex and possibly conflicting evidence, and to convey the often tacit interpretations and values that stakeholders derive from this evidence.

Helpful insight into the working of narrative in the evaluation strategies also comes from a famous essay of Walter Benjamin's (1968), "The Storyteller." In that piece, Benjamin noted that stories, or narratives, are good ways to convey and exchange experiences. He also pointed out that the communal aspect of this sharing of experience through stories has been devalued in modern society, replaced by more private forms that privilege "information" over what he described as the "counsel" and "intelligence" that stories provide.

Benjamin's point that stories offer intelligence and counsel rather than just information is important in thinking about narrative as a characteristic of evaluation strategies. Stories leave it to a reader or listener to interpret their meaning. According to Benjamin, stories invite interpretation because of their power to arouse astonishment and thoughtfulness by their slow piling on of thin, transparent layers. Through stories, "The most extraordinary things, marvelous things are related with the greatest accuracy, but the psychological connection of the events is not forced on the reader. It is left up to him to interpret things the way he understands them, and thus the narrative achieves an amplitude that information lacks" (Benjamin, 1968, p. 89).

In the context of evaluation, stories are a vehicle for conveying details that inform the evaluation. Stories also present a particular way of interpreting and understanding the meaning of those details. Because this information is provided in a narrative form that is familiar and comfortable, it is easier to determine whatever implications the stories contain for the process or program that is being evaluated. For the particular school evaluation strategies that have been described here, stories are an important form for communicating both internally and externally. Within the school setting, educators who are participants in the evaluation process use stories to economically express their understanding of the complex conditions of their school. Because stories serve as a kind of proposal about the importance and meaning of evidence, they invite others within the school community to enter into conversation about the value of particular stories and about alternative explanations of the experience contained in them. So also, stories are used to communicate what educators have come to understand about their school to audiences outside of the school. Again, stories serve to focus on key elements of the school environment while at the same time revealing its complexity.

Way of Being

To say that the six evaluation strategies all reflect a particular *way of Being* uses the language of practical hermeneutics to describe the way that educators who are involved in a process of evaluation think about themselves and about the process of evaluation in which they are engaged. In these strategies for evaluating schools, all teachers and administrators recognize that they have an active role in both the evaluation's design and its implementation.

Rather than objects to be studied as in traditional evaluation, educators using the six strategies are agents who construct and interpret what goes on in their school. In so doing, they are operating out of a sense of themselves as empowered to influence and make judgments about what occurs in their schools. Such a mind-set favors the use of the narrative form discussed earlier to communicate information and the development of qualitative case studies of schools as a product of evaluation. Not only are educators empowered to construct the narratives and qualitative cases that indicate their own values and judgments about their experience within the school, they are also empowered to use these values and judgments as evidence to direct their ongoing practice.

The way that educators think about themselves and their role in these evaluation strategies also suggests how they think about evaluation itself. In the first place, the strategies point toward an internal audience of educators as the primary beneficiaries of the evaluation process. The value of the strategies, and of evaluation generally, is to support educators' understanding of their school. Second, evaluation is not thought of as a methodology but rather as an ongoing process that assists teachers and administrators in their efforts to improve their school. Although the process may produce a product such as a portfolio, that principal value of such a product is to portray current understanding of the school in ways that make that understanding available for study as formative information that informs the ongoing process of school evaluation.

Thinking about the evaluation of schools as a way of being rather than what traditional evaluation frames as a way of doing is consistent with theories used in education to describe how people think about their work. One such theory, Donald Schon's (1987) elegant conceptualization of reflective practice, explained the decision making required of professionals when they encounter situations for which best practice solutions are not readily identifiable. Schon said that a professional must be able to respond in such situations by reshaping her understanding of the situation so that she "invents on-the-spot experiments to put her new understandings to the test" (1987, p. 35). Schon said that such a process is based in a "*constructionist* view of the reality with which the practitioner deals—a view that leads us to see the practitioner as constructing situations of his practice" (p. 36).

Learning Community

Finally, the six evaluation strategies all help to develop and sustain schools as *learning communities*. This view of schools is based on the belief that all of the members of a school community should consciously focus on creating a culture that supports learning for everyone within the community. Such a view of schooling has come to be seen as crucial to the reform and improvement of schools, because rather than demands for improvement being imposed on the school from the outside, the agency for change comes from within the school itself. In schools that strive to be learning communities, administrators and teachers see themselves as empowered and capable of making their schools better places (Barth, 1990; Reyes, Scribner, & Paredes-Scribner, 1999; Sergiovanni, 1994). Roland Barth (1990) contrasted this attitude with that of schools where improvement efforts are based on "monitoring adult behavior, on controlling students, on the assurance of student achievement, and on the visible attainment of prescribed skills" (p. 45).

SUMMARY

According to Barth, in schools that are learning communities, the central question is "Under what conditions will principal and student and teacher become serious, committed, sustained, lifelong cooperative learners?" (1990, p. 45). It is a question that is consistent with the mind-set of the six evaluation strategies described in this chapter. That mind-set was described earlier as the *way of Being* rather than a methodology for doing school reform. It is also a question that connects the means for evaluating schools described in each of the strategies with the ends of school evaluation. In each of these strategies means and ends are the same. The means of critical friends protocols, peer reviews, and partnerships with university or community researchers, and the development of school portfolios, accountability reports, and reflective portraits are all means of examining and interpreting evidence about schools. At the same time, they are ends in themselves in that they engage educators in evaluation as part of their daily practice as they use these evaluation strategies to help them make decisions about how to have their schools become better learning communities.

GUIDING QUESTIONS

1. How might the strategies for evaluating schools discussed in this chapter serve to

   - promote teachers' professional development,
   - reduce isolation in school settings,
   - enhance students' learning?

2. Explain why the evaluation strategies described in this chapter help schools develop as professional learning communities in ways that test-based school accountability cannot.

3. Which of the evaluation strategies discussed in this chapter would be well suited to your school? Why?

SELECTED READINGS

Newman, F. M., Secada, W. G., & Wehlage, G. G. (1995). *A guide to authentic instruction and assessment: Vision, standards, and scoring.* Madison: Wisconsin Center for Education Research.

Newman, F. M., & Wehlage, G. G. (1997). *Successful school restructuring: A report to the public and educators by the Center on Organization and Restructuring of Schools.* Madison: Wisconsin Center for Education Research.

Popham, J. (2001). *The truth about testing: An educator's call to action.* Alexandria, VA: Association for Supervision and Curriculum Development.

Schwandt, T. (2002). *Evaluation practice reconsidered.* New York: Peter Lang.

REFERENCES

Argyris, C., & Schon, D. (1992). *Theory in practice: Increasing professional effectiveness.* San Francisco: Jossey-Bass.

Barth, R. (1990). *Improving schools from within.* San Francisco: Jossey-Bass.

Benjamin, W. (1968). The storyteller (H. Zohn, Trans.). In H. Arendt (Ed.), *Walter Benjamin, illuminations* (pp. 83–109). New York: Schocken Books.

Clandinin, D. J., & Connelly, F. M. (1995). *Teachers' professional knowledge landscapes.* New York: Teachers College Press.

Craig, C. J. (1997). Telling stories: A way to access beginning teachers' knowledge. *Teaching Education, 9*(1), 61–68.

Denzin, N. (1997). *Interpretative ethnography: Ethnographic practices for the 21st century.* Thousand Oaks, CA: Sage.

Derrida, J. (1976). *Of grammatology* (G. Spivak, Trans.). Baltimore: Johns Hopkins University Press.

Dunne, J. (1993). *Back to the rough ground: "Pronesis" and "techne" in modern philosophy and Aristotle.* Notre Dame, IN: University of Notre Dame Press.

Gadamer, H. (1989). *Truth and method* (2nd Rev. ed.) (J. Weinsheimer & D. Marhall, Trans.). New York: Crossroad.

Gallagher, S. (1992). *Hermeneutics and education.* Albany, NY: SUNY Press.

Geertz, C. (1980). Blurred genres: The refiguration of social thought. *American Scholar, 49,* 165–179.

Lyons, N. (1998). *With portfolio in hand: Validating the new teacher professionalism.* New York: Teachers College Press.

National Commission on Excellence in Education. (1983). *A nation at risk: The imperative of educational reform.* Washington, DC: Government Printing Office.

No Child Left Behind Act of 2001, PL 107-110.

Phillips, J. C. (2003). Powerful learning: Creating learning communities in urban school reform. *Journal of Curriculum and Supervision, 18*(3), 240–258.

Reyes, P., & Phillips, J. C. (2003). Transforming public schools: Evaluation report, year three. Retrieved October, 10, 2003, from The University of Texas at Austin http://www.utexas.edu/projects/annenberg/index.html.

Reyes, P., Scribner, J., & Paredes-Scribner, A. (Eds.). (1999). *Lessons from high-performing Hispanic schools: Creating learning communities.* New York: Teachers College Press.

Ricoeur, P. (1981). *Hermeneutics and the human sciences* (J. Thomson, Ed.). Cambridge, UK: Cambridge University Press.

Rorty, R. (1979). *Philosophy and the mirror of nature.* Princeton, NJ: Princeton. University Press.

Schon, D. (1987). *Educating the reflective practitioner: Toward a new design for teaching and learning in the professions.* San Francisco: Jossey-Bass.

Schon, D., & McDonald, J. P. (1998). *Doing what you mean to do in school reform: Theory of action in the Annenberg Challenge.* Providence, RI: Brown University, Annenberg Institute for School Reform.

Schwandt, T. (2002). *Evaluation practice reconsidered.* New York: Peter Lang.

Sergiovanni, T. (1994). *Building community in schools.* San Francisco: Jossey-Bass.

Shotter, J. (1993). *Conversational realities: Constructing life through language.* Thousand Oaks, CA: Sage.

Tanner, D., & Tanner, L. (1987). *Supervision in education: Problems and practices.* New York: Macmillan.

Taylor, C. (1985). Philosophy and the human sciences: Philosophical Papers. Vol. 2. Cambridge, UK: Cambridge University Press.

White, H. (1981). The value of narrativity in the representation of reality. In W. J. T. Mitchell (Ed.), *On narrative* (pp. 1–23). Chicago: University of Chicago Press.

Chapter 9

Evaluating Students: Nightmares and Dreams

Richard J. Meyer
University of New Mexico

> *It is not the people who must be judged but the circumstances that made them that way.*
>
> —Alinsky (1969, p. 90)

This chapter juxtaposes the literacy evaluation lives of two teachers. Rather than focus on broad issues of high-stakes testing (see Kohn, 2000), the main purpose of this chapter is to demonstrate what is at stake by looking closely at and comparing two settings. Children's learning occurs in both settings, but the substantive nature of that learning is qualitatively different. The first is in a school that has been forced to adopt a phonics program that takes huge amounts of teacher and student time and offers limited evaluation possibilities. In this classroom, teacher reflection and the use of teacher knowledge has been appropriated by the district and the school. It is quite clear that she and I find her position an insult to her professionalism. In the second classroom, a reflective teacher engages students based on what they know and continually demonstrates what she knows about the complexity of the reading process. Looking closely at the second teacher's interactions with one child provides insights into the teacher's expertise and the freedom she has to exercise that expertise. The benefits to the student include curriculum that addresses the student's needs; linguistic, cultural, and social relevance and appropriateness; and the availability of the teacher's full repertoire of teaching possibilities. Such a close look in the first teacher's classroom is no longer possible when the teacher uses the highly scripted program because it homogenizes all the children through constant and regimented whole-class instruction. Of course, such a view is available during other parts of that teacher's day.

KAREN'S EVALUATION NIGHTMARE

One way that we capture children's learning and development is by kid-watching (Goodman, 1985). Kid-watchers know that teaching, learning, development, and language are complicated by their own and their students' social, political, psychological, linguistic, cultural and spiritual contexts. Kid-watchers are knowledgeable about these and, thus, are informed decision makers. But, to paraphrase Langston Hughes (1967), what happens to a kid-watcher deferred? In this section, readers meet Karen, a veteran and smart teacher and kid-watcher who relinquishes her knowledge, sacrifices valuable class time, and follows district mandates.

At that cusp, at that gentle, vulnerable, and amazingly resilient place where the child and the curriculum unfold and engage, something quite ordinary, typical, and sad has happened in Karen's primary classroom. Her use of evaluation for informed decision making was confiscated after the local newspaper painted a picture of classrooms of children not being taught to read. The only hope, the paper touted, would be the initiation of a direct systematic intense phonics instruction program; the district adopted one before the school year was out. Newspaper articles rejoiced, the community heaved a sigh of relief, and thoughtful teachers panicked as the district sent the message that developmentally appropriate practice (Bredekamp, 1987) was cast aside.

Karen's classroom was restructured for a daily hour- (sometimes up to 90 minutes) long session, during which her students were all seated for the phonics program. The block of time previously devoted to literacy was disrupted as Karen relinquished her decision making about teaching to an almighty publisher that did not know her children. She had a choice in this decision to relinquish: give up the time to the program or lose for being insubordinate. For the sake of the rest of the school day, during which she made decisions based on state standards, her students' interests, and her expertise, she succumbed.

Kid-Watchers Consider the Data

"Ms. L, what is a 'schoolbun'?" one of her students demands when Karen changes "schoolbus" to "schoolbun" on the markerboard during the scripted phonics lesson.

Before she can respond, "It's not a word," as she had when other nonwords were made during phonics, one of her students says, "Like, when you're at school, if they have hot dogs for lunch, they give it to you on a schoolbun." The lesson continues as Karen reads from the script. Some children participate (those who know the answers), others echo what their classmates say (as a way of participating), and others remain silent and uninvolved. They begin with "recess" and "baboon," but the script demands the changing of their final sounds as a way of teaching phonological awareness. The children struggle to say "reced" and "baboot," nonwords.

Teachers around the district pointed out that the new program had no assessment built into it. One was added. It required students to write dictated sentences consisting of the "regular" words of the program (cat, sat, and, sat, pad, etc.). Teachers were also to listen to students' responses as a way of assessing. But Karen sees the patterns of her children's responses (the echoing and the silences tell her much). Karen knows how to assess much more accurately than this; she brackets her assessment skills in order to comply with district mandates.

The lesson moves swiftly from one activity to the next, but Karen can never complete a lesson in the 20 minutes the guide says it will take. Next, Karen reads a short story on an overhead and the children say the sound of the letter /d/ twice after each line of the story. The script tells them they are making sound effects for the walking dinosaur in the story. Of course, saying the sound of the letter "d" is virtually impossible without adding a vowel sound, so children say "duh."

Next, the children are given five cards with one letter on each card. One of the letters is a vowel. They are told to make words and call them out. Karen sees some children engage, some follow their neighbors, and others move the cards around aimlessly. Karen is a demanding teacher, but she tells me she can't force the children to pay attention. "I know this [program] is not for everybody," she says. As an act of conscience, she cannot make them do what is not supportive of their learning. She knows her students too well to demand they behave when behavior means compliance but not genuine engagement.

Karen is articulate about the ways in which the program is undermining some of her children's learning to read by beginning with and remaining committed to reading as sound making. There is little or no connection between the program and real reading. The *vulnerable* learners suffer most because they are unsure of what reading is and their minds are open to defining the process. The students from homes in which stories have not been read, at which nightly reading is not a ritual (and perhaps weren't exposed to books much in other contexts prior to attending school), are the children most open to learning during the school day the very essence of what reading is. This program is teaching them that quite often reading is not about anything that is meaning-rich or meaning-full. Fortunate students, from richly literate homes, probably arrive at school with a strong idea about what reading is all about. Those children are not as vulnerable.

Before the adoption, Karen's children wrote in journals every day. They read books and wrote as a whole class, in small groups, and alone. They had whole-group experiences that provided broad opportunities for children to think, like when Karen asked, "What did you notice?" or "What do you wonder?" as she read a book. Now, the children read stories about a *cat* at a *pad* (a mouse *pad*, but children can't read "mouse," can they?) that *sat* on a *cap*. Now the curriculum seems to be one size fits all but is really "one size fits few" (Ohanian, 1999). Now there is no time for questions about a story. Who'd want to ask them about these stories anyway? Now Karen's assessing strengths are deferred because, as the consultant for the program told the teachers at a district inservice, the program is "good for all kids" just the way it's written. But it's not.

Historically, assessment in Karen's classroom was never limited to a test or worksheet. One facet of her kid-watching still includes interpreting children's behaviors as important indicators of their engagement as learners. During phonics lessons, Karen typically sees behaviors she does not see at other times in her classroom:

- One child has carefully rolled up one leg of his jeans and works at unraveling his sock.
- A few of the children are rocking back and forth.
- One child is quietly making the sounds of bombs dropping ("eeeeyowwwwwww plichhhh").
- One of the children picks his nose; eventually others do this, too.
- A child plays with her ears.
- A child is rubbing her hands up and down her braids (later she'll undo and redo them).
- One child is poking another (in a friendly manner).
- One child is pulling at the rug.
- Children chat with friends.
- A child sucks his bracelet.
- A child is styling her cuticles with her thumbnail (Meyer, 2001).

One could argue that these are frustration behaviors, but naming the actions as frustration may deny their complexity. The more recent research on children's behaviors acknowledges their social nature. Durand (1990) explained that such actions suggest the children want social attention, want to escape, want a consequence, or want sensory stimulation from another person. Snell and Brown (2000) posited that, "Many problem behaviors are attributed to specific pragmatic intents; that is, the behavior serves a specific function for the individual and is a form of communicating for the individual" (p. 101). The children's actions during phonics may be viewed almost metaphorically as a response to the lesson. They are communicating that they want their minds massaged and stimulated. They want their ideas considered. They want to be interactional with each other and transactional (Rosenblatt, 1978) with texts. If they don't get their needs addressed by the formal curriculum, they respond with behaviors that are more stimulating than the undemanding and uninteresting cognitive stuff at hand. Their behaviors demonstrate their nonengagement with that formal curriculum. Karen is worried because no one at the policy level seems concerned about these behaviors. The classroom is imbalanced during the phonics lesson because rather than having four broad areas of assessment (Anthony, Johnson, Mickelson, & Preece, 1991) to inform curriculum (process, product, classroom-based measures, and decontextualized measures [like standardized tests]), the curriculum is being driven by decontextualized measures.

Kid-Watching Deferred

Part of Karen's kid-watching skills are deferred during phonics because kid-watching is not passive note taking. It is actively taking notes (Power Miller, 1996) and systemically using what she sees and what she knows in order to teach. Kid-watching is informed responding to the lives, needs, interests, and passions of children. Karen, as a captive of the script (Meyer, 2002), cannot act; she cannot respond. She and her students are being held hostage of the curriculum and the curriculum cops—the phonics patrol—administrators who systematically circulate in the building to ensure every teacher is on the same page.

A crucial question in good teaching is this: What are the children learning?

Here are some answers that Karen concludes from kid-watching during phonics lessons, answers that are an assessment of the program and its consequences:

- They are learning that reading is unpredictable and not necessarily meaningful. Reading is operationally defined as gluing together sounds, regardless of the meaning.
- They are learning to be compliant to a curriculum even when it may be too easy, too difficult, or meaningless.
- They are learning that school is a place where sense is deferred for the sake of the stuff that one does there.
- They are learning that their identities and culture are dismissed during a part of their day because culturally relevant pedagogy (Ladson-Billings, 1994) is bracketed during phonics.
- They are learning that curriculum comes from places far from their own realities.

- They are learning teachers read from scripts, so perhaps they're not all that smart.

They learn more, too, during science, math, social studies, and other discipline-based curricular areas that have not yet been mandated for change. During these times, Karen engages children with hands-on and minds-on activities that support their curious and reflective natures. Unfortunately, time for these has been reduced since the phonics mandate. And, because no children are allowed to leave the classroom for special areas (ESL, reading recovery, and special education) during phonics, some children are gone during the discipline-based experiences. The conflicts between what and *how* they learn at different parts of the day is confusing at best. We still don't know what it is at worst.

Daily, Karen collects data that documents what her students are learning. Karen, like all good teachers, has learned, too. She's learned that she is not valued as a professional, her knowledge of her students does not matter, her knowledge of reading process and strategies does not matter, and her district does not value her decision making.

Kid-Watching and Consequences of Curriculum

Karen's data about what she and her students are learning points to the bigger issue of "consequential validity" (Johnston, 1998, p. 90). Consequential validity "refers to *the value of the consequences* of the particular assessment practices and interpretations" (p. 90, emphasis added). I suggest that we consider the consequential validity of *curriculum* as an integral facet of kid-watching. This means that we question "the value of the consequences of" the phonics curriculum. We evaluate the curriculum's educative (Dewey, 1938) usefulness in the short term (the teaching of reading) and in the long term (what it teachers about reading, schooling, learning, language, culture, and more).

Karen's data suggests a new responsibility for her as a teacher. Rather than assessing children's progress and needs, she is now also collecting data to report the consequences of curriculum. She is assessing an imposed curriculum so that she might report to parents, administrators, and other stakeholders in children's learning. She could report about children's behavior, their emerging definition of what it means to be a reader as influenced by the phonics program, and the impact of the program on her use of time for more authentic literacy instruction as compared to years past. She could present the portfolios of students from previous years of her teaching and compare them to the work of students in her present class. Viewers of this data would see how little her students have accomplished as substantive readers and writers during the year that phonics "saved" the readers in the district. They'd see fewer books read, fewer pieces of writing, fewer genres explored, fewer authors studied, fewer responses to literature, fewer child-as-author books, and less evidence of inquiry projects. In place of child-authored books, they'd see sets of one-page photocopied books with bizarre language in them (that fat cat sat); they'd see identical sentences students wrote for assessments.

Moving Toward Action

Karen is like many good teachers. She didn't become a teacher to be po-litical and didn't view teaching as political work. Increasingly she sees and understands the political nature of her teaching. Her kid-watching has taken on new meaning as she sees a new facet of it that involves building a case that she may eventually make public. At present, Karen has not committed to presenting her data. She feels too vulnerable to talk publicly about her concerns. Instead, she is meeting privately with colleagues, making plans to move through the prescribed lessons more quickly, and trying to salvage the remnants of her former teacher-designed literacy program that met the needs of all of her students by centering on their learning. Her journey is a cautious one because of the oppressive climate of the district.

In Karen's classroom and in her professional life, there is hope and the beginnings of activism. It's not earth-shattering but it is clear and moving. It is strong and rooted in data collected by a kid-watcher in her classroom. Karen is a reflective and sensitive teacher who understands the dynamics of power and control in which she teaches. I hope it is clear that she will take risks that may come close to endangering her job, but will not do so to the extent of being forced out of her classroom and away from her work with children. If Karen taught under different circumstances, as she was doing just a few months prior to the phonics adoption, all of her talent could be realized to her students' benefit.

Now let's look at Lisa's classroom in a school in which a strong principal told the district office that his teachers would continue to teach as thoughtful decision makers.

LISA'S EVALUATION DREAM

Lisa learned about kid-watching during an assessment course. Two parts of that course focused on the Reading Miscue Inventory (RMI) (Goodman, Watson, & Burke, 1987) and Retrospective Miscue Analysis (RMA) (Goodman & Marek, 1996). Miscue analysis leads to in-depth discussions of what readers are doing and why they might be doing it. Teachers learn about the cueing systems and they learn to think about how readers think, process, make decisions about their oral reading (such as when to regress and when not to regress), and construct meaning. RMA involves the teacher or researcher in making decisions about which miscues to ask the reader about. The reader is asked if the miscue makes sense, if it sounds like language is supposed to sound, whether they corrected it, and whether they needed to correct it to construct meaning. This discursive process (Paulson, 2001) supports the reader in becoming metalinguistic as a way of monitoring strategy use and meaning construction. Watson and Hoge (1996) engaged readers in selecting their own miscues for discussion.

Lisa is a first-grade teacher in a diverse school in which 75% of the children receive free or reduced lunch and 17 different language groups are represented. During and after the assessment course, her goal as a teacher was to integrate into her classroom her learning about miscue and retrospective miscue analysis. Let's look at parts of a typical morning and, within that timeframe, focus on Maria as an exemplar of how Lisa assess and teaches reading as a kid-watcher informed by miscue analysis and retrospective miscue analysis.

It's almost 8:15 AM and children are entering the school building. After they hang up their backpacks and jackets in the hallway, they enter the classroom. Lisa is waiting in a chair near the door to greet the children. Prior to her students' arrival, she posted the daily quote on a markerboard near her. Children must read the phrase, title, short poem, or other text on the markerboard before they enter. Lisa selected the text because it's interesting and to generate teachable moments based on what she knows and notices about her students. One day she has "And in that dark dark house there is a dark dark room" on the markerboard. Most of the children recognize this from *In a Dark, Dark Room* (Schwartz, 1988), a book the class heard at literacy circle the previous day. Lisa asks different children different questions once they've read the sentence. "Where's a period?" she asks one child. "Find the word 'dark' and . . . tell me another word that has a /d/ in it" she asks others. Some do as she asks and move into the room, others linger to hear what their colleagues are asked and sometimes to help them respond.

Maria enters the room with her typically broad smile displayed. Maria is bilingual; her home language is Spanish and she is part of the school's ESL program. Maria says good morning to Lisa, and Lisa asks her to read the markerboard. Maria says, "I don't know."

Lisa reminds her, "It's from the book we read yesterday." Lisa points to the book on a table near the markerboard. Maria is silent. Lisa picks up the book and reads the title to Maria. Lisa opens the book and begins reading the first page aloud. She hesitates, waiting for Maria to join in the reading. Maria joins in and they read a few pages, with the children around them joining in. When Lisa reaches the lines that are on the markerboard, she says, "Look, I took these same words, didn't I?"

"Yes," Maria answers. Lisa and Maria both smile because they know that she can read it.

Maria reads the markerboard, smiles, and goes to one of the centers that is not yet filled to capacity with other children. Lisa's commitment to teaching that reading is meaning making is always at the forefront of literacy activity in her classroom. She recontextualized the text for Maria by providing the source text and reminding Maria of what they'd read the day before. This single teachable moment in the classroom is one of many in which Lisa will value and revalue readers. She gently supports them, reminding them that they know a lot by demonstrating that very fact. As Maria leaves the markerboard, Lisa says to her, "I thought you could read that."

Over her shoulder, Maria responds, "Oh yeah, I thought so too. I like reading it out of the book better."

Lisa has a class list on her lap as the children enter each morning. She makes notes about what she learns from each child as they read from the markerboard. These notes will eventually find their way to a three-ring binder in which each child has a section where Lisa notes their progress in reading. She writes about Maria's use of text to learn text. Lisa notes that Maria read the sentence in the text without making a miscue. She also notes that Maria's attitude is one of growing confidence in terms of text and in the teacher-student relationship. After the last child enters the room and reads and discusses the markerboard with her, Lisa circulates to get a sense of the children's engagements at the centers.

Jumping ahead for just a moment to the next morning, Lisa has another excerpt on the markerboard from the same book. Maria bounds into the room, clearly excited. Lisa asks her to read the markerboard, but before Maria focuses on the board, she says to Lisa, "Read this!" Maria has a shoebox wrapped in aluminum foil and held closed by layers of duct tape. There are holes punched in the top of the box and all the children around her are excited. On a piece of paper that she taped to the box, Maria wrote in marker, "in that dark dark box there was." She had a second piece of paper taped over the end of the sentence so that no one could see the last word. Lisa read the box sign and asked, "Ohhh, Maria, is there something alive in there?"

"You have to guess," was her reply.

More children gathered around and one said, "I know what it is." Maria had apparently revealed the contents to this child and Maria admonished her, "Don't tell." Then she announced, "I will tell you all at group time."

Later, at group time, Lisa helped Maria cut through the layers of duct tape, peel back the foil, and before opening the lid Lisa asked Maria once more, "Is it alive?"

"Noooo," Maria almost howled with laughter, loving the attention from everyone.

"Wait," Lisa said. "Before we open the lid, let's have people guess."

When Lisa asks if they think it's an elephant, she is playing with predictions and possibilities. The children analyze what might be in the box and eventually ask for clues but Maria can no longer contain herself. She holds up the paper with her sentence on it, peels back the piece of the paper covering her sentence, and reveals the word "klay" to her classmates. Some read it, a few mention that it really begins with /c/, and Maria triumphantly holds up a big blob of green clay.

Lisa knows that she has just witnessed an evaluation moment. Maria understood the "dark dark" part of the book, the mystery of not knowing how something will end, and then she made a connection to her world at home. She constructed a dark dark *something* to bring to school. This was a remarkable example of transactional (Rosenblatt, 1978) relationships with texts and across contexts and shows that Maria thinks about school at home. Her emerging understanding of reading as positioning her in the world is evidenced by her use of a note—written text—as a way of gaining prestige in her classroom. Although the green blob of clay passed quickly into the collective memories of the children in the class, that blob was a moment when a young reader demonstrated how she embraced an experience with a text and made powerful personal and social connections on returning to school with a text she built.

Centers

After all the children have arrived, Lisa circulates in the room to note what children are doing at the centers they selected. She also stops to teach and interact with students. Centers last for about 20 minutes. This is a social learning time when children interact with each other and transact with texts as they work with: computers, blocks, literacy games, math materials, and more. Today at the Discovery Center, there are sets of rubber stamps and stamp pads. Some of the rubber stamps have animals on them and the name of each animal is written on the wooden handle of the stamp. Maria gets writing paper from the writing center and stamps three insects on her paper. Then she builds sentences around what she stamped by writing "I love" before each stamp. Her paper then says "I love" followed by a picture of a butterfly. The next sentence says "I love" followed by a ladybug and the last one says "I love" followed by the grasshopper stamp. She goes back to each stamp and carefully copies the words from the stamps so that her sentences read "I love," followed by the stamped picture, followed by the words "butterfly," "ladybug," "grasshopper." She rereads the three sentences and then goes back to each and adds an /s/ onto each insect word.

At this point, Lisa comes over and asks Maria to read what she wrote. Quickly, Maria says, "I love butterflies. I love ladybugs. I love grasshoppers."

"How do you know that isn't 'silkworm'?" Lisa asks Maria.

She laughs and says, "It looks like a grasshopper."

"That makes sense," Lisa says. "How else would you know, if there wasn't a picture?"

Maria says the sound of the letter /g/ three times, "guh, guh, guh," and looks up at Lisa.

"Oh, the sound of /g/ helps you know, too, doesn't it?"

"Yes," Maria says.

"So it looks like a grasshopper and the letters tell you that you're right, too, huh?"

"Yes," Maria affirms.

Lisa uses many such teachable moments to address what she knows Maria is struggling with as a reader. Maria is demonstrating her emerging understanding of the reading process and the cueing systems. Lisa's questions are rooted in RMA questions: *Does it make sense? Does it sound the way you think it should? Does it sound "right"? Does it look right for the way it sounds?* These are questions Lisa asks constantly during the day, particularly of readers like Maria who are struggling somewhat. The questions are part of the literacy discourse in the room, the ways that language is used here to talk about reading. Lisa plays music as a signal that it is time to clean the centers and gather for a whole-group experience.

Group Time

The first part of group time typically involves the presentation or review of a whole text. That text might be a book, a poem, a story, a song, or just about any other text you might imagine appropriate for first graders. One day Lisa reads *Peanut Butter and Jelly* (Westcott, n.d.) to the class. It's a "play rhyme" (according to the cover of the book) that explains and shows the making of bread, jelly, and peanut butter, and then the putting of all those together to make a sandwich. It also repeats "peanut butter, peanut butter, jelly, jelly" on every page. The loaf of bread is huge and all the helpers (bakers, elephants that smashed the peanuts to make the peanut butter, and others) are shown sharing the huge sandwich at the end of the book. Lisa reads it, discusses it with the children, encourages them to make predictions and connections and tell what they notice, rereads it, and eventually moves to very specific parts of the illustrations and verbal text in order to make some points and push the children's understanding of reading and themselves as readers. Taking words out of the text to discuss onsets and rimes (Moustafa, 1997), looking for patterns in the text, asking how children might figure out challenging words, asking what to do if part of the story doesn't make sense, and discussing the joys of rereading a text that you love are all parts of Lisa's teaching of strategies for proficient reading.

Personal Reading

This 15-minute period of time prior to recess will extend as the year progresses and children can sustain their reading of longer and more complex texts. Maria grabs a book and starts to read. During personal reading, Lisa notes that Maria is appropriating some of the strategies from RMA that Lisa has taught. Maria is reading *The Hungry Giant* (Cowley, 1990) about a grouchy giant that intimidates people in the village. Maria reads the giant's words, "Get me some butter," and then she stops. "I thought it was bread, but it's butter," she says to me.

"Oh, how come?"

"Well, it would make sense you know. And it has the /b/."

"Wow, you know a lot. So why did you say *butter* because *bread* has a /b/, too?" I ask.

"Because it's *butter!*" she says. It's her way of saying only this word really makes sense here when a reader knows that the giant already has bread.

On another day, Maria chooses *I Like Me* (Carlson, 1988) to read during her personal reading time. Lisa meets with children individually during this time to assess their comprehension and their use of reading strategies and to teach. She offers strategies and chooses one or two miscues to discuss with Maria in a fashion modeled after RMA. One line in the book reads: I eat good food. Maria reads, "I eat good fish," and regresses to correct. Lisa asks Maria, "How come when you read this you said *fish* and then went back and read *food?*"

"Because it's food," Maria responds.

"How'd you know?" Lisa asks.

Maria makes the sound of /d/ a few times.

"Ohhh," Lisa says, "so you knew because of the letter /d/."

"Yes."

Lisa suggests, "But fish makes sense. It's a good guess."

Maria points out that fish are in the picture, but that food is the best word to use because, "that's the word *food.*"

Lisa talks about one or two miscues and also engages in a retelling discussing. The conference takes 6 minutes and then Lisa moves on to the next child on her list for this day. She is gathering data specific to individuals and also ideas that will inform her teaching for the whole-group sessions. Lisa will design whole-group lessons that are broad spectrum, meaning they will serve many needs. The text, the nature of Lisa's question, and the discussions that ensue contribute to each child's appropriation of strategies that will support their efficient making of meaning.

Teacher Read Aloud

Lisa reads to the children throughout the day; the morning time lasts between 5 and 15 minutes depending on the text she's chosen and time available. Often, when she makes a miscue, it is named and discussed. They engage in lofty discussions about texts, including graphophonic elements of text, its syntax (including vocabulary and grammar) and meaning. She reads texts that many of the children will be able to pick up and read on their own and she reads complex texts that they might not be able to read independently for a few years. She reads novels, newspaper articles, encyclopedia entries, and more depending on their interests, the balance of those interests with state and district curriculum standards, and her knowledge of their needs.

Children as Record Keepers

The children keep track of their reading and writing using literacy portfolios. Aside from collecting their various written work, they note books they've read and keep literacy projects they've completed (making bookmarks about story characters, puppets, etc.) in them. The portfolios also serve as evidence of the connections between reading and writing, as Lisa uses their writing miscues to teach reading and writing strategies. The children re-view their portfolios monthly, writing captions for different pieces. They present their portfolios to their families throughout the year.

Conferences and other communication with families are political work. They let parents know that their children are learning, competent, and challenged. Visitors to Lisa's classroom see stark contrasts between what goes on there and what occurs in Karen's classroom during phonics lessons. Observers do not see the aberrant, nonengaging behaviors in which Karen's students engaged. They do see collaborative efforts as children work together doing what they know is important work. The children in Lisa's class know that culture is a critical facet of their lives in school because of the literature they hear and read and the events that they plan or attend. They know that curriculum is a local event and emerges from their interests. They learn every day that reading is about making meaning and that text is supposed to make sense. This certainly is not meant to imply that Lisa does not have management problems in her classroom. Of course she does, but they are not typically rooted in inappropriate curriculum. And if Lisa decides that the curriculum (standards) is presenting problems, she adjusts her teaching so that children's curricular experiences are more appropriate.

HIGH STAKES AND STARK CONTRASTS

Most of the differences between Karen's and Lisa's classrooms were discussed in the sections earlier. Teacher agency—the freedom of teachers to exercise assessment and teaching options—was one constant theme in both classrooms. Lisa maintained her freedom because of a strong principal; Karen gave up some freedoms in order to remain in the classroom at her school and engage her students during the other times of the day. There is one aspect of the two classrooms that demands further explication and that is the social nature of the learning environments. The two very similar teachers have very different social settings for students' learning because of the circumstances in which they are teaching. The high stakes have precipitated high contrasts.

During the phonics portion of Karen's morning, the students have little space to learn from each other. There is the subgroup of children that echoes and mimics their first-grade colleagues, but that is a very limited social interaction. The children in Karen's classroom wait for her instructions and follow her lead. There is rarely time for them to bring literacy issues or things they notice into the phonics lesson. The program has low expectations for some of her students, has high expectations for others, and completely ignores others.

Lisa's classroom is a highly social environment in which all the children contribute their understanding, questions, concerns, and curiosity. Maria's presentation of the box of "klay" is one such example. There was time (made by Lisa) to use Maria's composition as a way of teaching about predicting, confirming, and spelling. And there was the larger lesson that in this classroom texts matter, they are important, and their composers play an integral role in the presentation of their texts. The social nature of learning is subtle and no test will see it or use it (as Lisa does) to cultivate subsequent learning experiences.

SUMMARY

This chapter is not about a good teacher and a bad teacher. It is, as Alinsky says at the top of the chapter, about circumstances. The circumstances in this chapter are the contexts of the schools in which Lisa and Karen work. Lisa is lucky to be in a place where her voice is heard and her professional decision making is accepted and honored. Karen is in a setting where she is not, at present, honored or heard. Threats about her job security are constant as teachers are reminded that they must comply with the district's curriculum demands or leave.

The stakes in evaluation are high and the sanctions are painful when a teacher and her students must endure curriculum that is not appropriate. When we start to stand back from individual classrooms, and consider schools, districts, states, and the national scene, the picture is increasingly eerie. The stakes become student and teacher individuality, their very identities seem to be at risk. Many have pointed out that the crisis in education is manufactured (Berliner & Biddle, 1995), but the attacks continue to come. Expert teachers are leaving the field or fleeing to schools that perform well enough to be left alone. As Coles (2003) pointed out, the most accurate predictor of performance on standardized tests continues to be zip code. If we know that socioeconomic conditions correlate so highly with performance, why do we continue to place such high stakes on tests rather than work to improve social conditions? Street (1995) eloquently presented the holes in the argument that literacy will raise socioeconomic levels; in fact, quite the opposite is true: Raising socioeconomic levels enhances test performance.

I offer no simple solutions to the complex problems associated with high-stakes testing. Perhaps the crucial question that each of us must answer is this: Whose classroom would you want your child, niece, nephew, or grandchild in, Karen's or Lisa's? Once we honestly face the answer to that question, we can decide what actions we may take collectively to ensure that no child and no teacher is held hostage by a test or a curricular program.

GUIDING QUESTIONS

1. What larger issues of assessment facing teachers across the country are represented in these two cases?
2. One way Karen may use her assessment knowledge is by collecting data to present to her principal, school board, families of her students, and colleagues. How might she do that? What dangers are inherent in such action? What other options does she have for using her knowledge about literacy and evaluation?
3. In the context of her literacy program, what does Lisa know about her students (perhaps using Maria as a focal point for discussion)?
4. In the context of the phonics program, what does Karen know about her students?

5. How are each teacher's skills and knowledge about assessment and teaching displaced and/or enacted?

6. Compare and contrast your understanding of the school contexts in which the two teachers work. You might consider: the view of the teacher, the leaner, the reading program, individuality, individual differences, teaching as a profession, culture, language differences, teacher agency, and more.

7. Observe in a classroom and take substantial notes about how the teacher and children spend time, what the teacher does to learn about children's literacy (or other target area) as that area is being taught, and how the teacher uses what is learned to structure future teaching or other interactions.

8. Interview teachers in various types of reading (or other area) programs. Develop interview questions that will provide insights into teacher agency, teacher decision making, uses of assessment, choices, and knowledge.

SELECTED READINGS

Allington, R. (2002). *Big brother and the national reading curriculum: How ideology trumped evidence.* Portsmouth, NH: Heinemann.

Coles, G. (2003). *Reading the naked truth: Literacy, legislation, and lies.* Portsmouth, NH: Heinemann.

Goodman, Y. (1985). Kidwatching: Observing children in the classroom. In A. Jaggar & M. T. Smith-Burke (Eds.), *Observing the language learner.* Newark, DE: NCTE, IRA.

Meyer, R. (2001). *Phonics exposed: Understanding and resisting systematic direct intense phonics instruction.* Mahwah, NJ: Lawrence Erlbaum Associates.

Murphy S., with Shannon, P., Johnston, P., & Hansen, J. (Eds.) (1998). *Fragile evidence: A critique of reading assessment.* Mahwah, NJ: Lawrence Erlbaum Associates.

REFERENCES

Alinsky, S. (1969). *Reveille for radicals.* New York: Vintage Books, Random House.

Anthony, R., Johnson, T., Mickelson, N., & Preece, A. (1991). *Evaluating literacy: A perspective for change.* Portsmouth, NH: Heinemann.

Berliner, D. C., & Biddle, B. J. (1995). *The manufactured crisis: Myths, fraud, and the attack on America's public schools.* Reading, MA: Addison-Wesley.

Bredekamp, S. (Ed.). (1987). *Developmentally appropriate practice in early childhood programs serving children from birth through age 8.* Washington, DC: National Association for the Education of Young Children.

Carlson, N. (1988). *I like me.* New York: Trumpet.

Cowley, J. (1990). *The hungry giant.* Bothell, WA: The Wright Group.

Dewey, J. (1938). *Experience and education.* New York: Collier Books, Macmillan.

Durand, V. M. (1990). *Severe behavior problems: A functional communication training approach.* New York: Guilford.

Goodman, Y. (1985). Kidwatching: Observing children in the classroom. In A. Jaggar & M. T. Smith-Burke (Eds.), *Observing the language learner.* Newark, DE: NCTE, IRA.

Goodman, Y., & Marek, A. (Eds.). (1996). *Retrospective miscue analysis: Revaluing readers and reading.* Katonah, NY: Richard C. Owen.

Goodman, Y., Watson, D., & Burke, C. (1987). *Reading miscue inventory: Alternative procedures.* Katonah, NY: Richard C. Owen.

Hughes, L. (1967). *The panther and the lash: Poems of our times.* New York: Knopf.

Johnston, P. (1998). The consequences of the use of standardized testing. In S. Murphy with P. Shannon, P. Johnston, & J. Hansen (Eds.), *Fragile evidence: A critique of reading assessment.* Mahwah, NJ: Lawrence Erlbaum Associates.

Kohn, A. (2000). *The case against standardized testing: Raising the scores, ruining the schools.* Portsmouth, NH: Heinemann.

Ladson-Billings, G. (1994). *The dreamkeepers: Successful teachers of African American children.* San Francisco: Jossey-Bass.

Meyer, R. (2001). *Phonics exposed: Understanding and resisting systematic direct intense phonics instruction.* Mahwah, NJ: Lawrence Erlbaum Associates.

Meyer, R. (2002). Captives of the script: Killing us softly with phonics. *Language Arts, 79*(6), 452–461.

Moustafa, M. (1997). *Beyond traditional phonics: Research discoveries and reading instruction.* Portsmouth, NH: Heinemann.

Ohanian, S. (1999). *One size fits few: The folly of educational standards.* Portsmouth, NH: Heinemann.

Paulson, E. (2001). The discourse of retrospective miscue analysis: Links with adult learning theory. *Journal of College Reading and Learning, 32*(1), 112–127.

Power Miller, B. (1996). *Taking note: Improving your observational notetaking.* Portland, ME: Stenhouse.

Rosenblatt, L. (1978). *The reader, the text, and the poem: The transactional theory of the literary work.* Carbondale: Southern Illinois University Press.

Schwartz, A. (1988). *In a dark, dark room and other scary stories.* New York: Scholastic.

Snell, M., & Brown, F. (2000). *Instruction of students with severe disabilities* (5th ed.). Upper Saddle River, NJ: Merrill/Prentice Hall.

Street, B. (1995). *Social literacies: Critical approaches to literacy in development, ethnography and education.* New York: Longman.

Watson, D., & Hoge, S. (1996). Reader-selected miscues. In Y. Goodman & A. Marek (Eds.), *Retrospective miscue analysis: Revaluing readers and reading* (pp. 157–164). Katonah, NY: Richard C. Owen.

Westcott, N. B. (Illustrator, no author cited). (n.d.). *Peanut butter and jelly: A play rhyme.* New York: Dutton Children's Books.

Chapter 10

The Challenges of Diversity: Moving Toward Cultural Proficiency

Reyes Quezada
University of San Diego

Keith Osajima
University of Redlands

Demographic shifts are bringing increasing numbers of students from diverse racial, ethnic, religious, class, and linguistic backgrounds into the public schools. The goal of this chapter is not to debate whether it is important to address diversity in the public schools. We see this as an inescapable reality in public education. Instead, the goals are to help educators think about diversity in a broad and integrative manner by providing what we find to be important and valuable perspectives and strategies. We begin with a discussion of cultural proficiency and argue that an important first step is to think reflectively about one's own and the school's position in relation to cultural proficiency. Cultivating a willingness, openness, and commitment to meet the challenge of diversity is a vital foundation for the development of effective educational practices.

The remainder of the chapter is organized to provide an overview of three key areas: multicultural curricular reform and teaching, teaching English-language learners, and building home-community-school partnerships. In each section, we discuss the important theoretical and research work that informs approaches to educational practices. We argue that it is important to take a comprehensive approach to diversity, one that sees relations among classroom learning, school environments, and home/community influences.

SETTING THE SCENE—THE DEMOGRAPHY OF THE DIVERSITY CHALLENGE

The demographics of public schooling present 21st century educators with a critical challenge. On the one hand, the population is becoming increasingly diverse, along racial, ethnic, cultural, and linguistic lines. Between 1990 and 2000, for example, the Hispanic and Asian populations grew by 61% and 69% respectively (Zhou, 2003). In the next 20 years, California will add 12 million Hispanics and 6 million Asians. Texas and Florida will add 8 million Hispanics (Hodgkinson, 2002). These general demographic shifts promise to have a significant impact in public school classrooms. It is predicted that by 2025, nearly half of all students will be students of color (McFalls & Cobb-Roberts, 2001, p. 164). Already, in major metropolitan areas, the public school population is majority "minority." In Los Angeles Unified School District, 70% of the 700,000 students are Hispanic. About half of these are from poor families and more than a third are limited English proficient (Zhou, 2003, p. 216). In Miami, nearly 80% of the under-18 child population is Hispanic and Black (p. 216). In New York, 70% of the under-18 population is Hispanic, Black, and Asian (p. 216).

On the other hand, the demographic profile of teachers and administrators contrasts sharply with the student population. Hodgkinson (2002) reported that nationally 86% of the teachers are White and 84% of the principals are White. Glazier (2003) observed that those entering the teaching profession continue to be White, monolingual, and middle class. A widening cultural gap exists. The relative homogeneity of the teaching and administrative populations, when compared to the demographics of the student body, means that most educators are, to borrow from Lisa Delpit, serving "other people's children" (Delpit, 1995). That is, they are working with children whose cultural, linguistic, class, and racial backgrounds are different from their own. Christine Sleeter described these educational staffing patterns as "the overwhelming presence of whiteness" (2001, p. 94).

Until the racial and ethnic composition of the teacher and administrator population moves closer to that of the student population, the effectiveness of public education rests largely on how well predominantly White, middle-class, monolingual educators can serve the needs of a diverse student body. The immediate challenge, then, is to prepare the relatively homogenous teacher and administrator population to work effectively with students who are culturally, racially, and linguistically different.

CULTIVATING CONDITIONS FOR EDUCATIONAL SUCCESS

As is shown in subsequent sections, there is no shortage of information available on multicultural educational theory and practice that can help

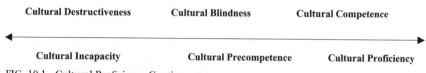

FIG. 10.1 Cultural Proficiency Continuum.

educators meet the needs of their diverse student population. But, amount and availability of information does not, in itself, guarantee that teachers and administrators will work effectively with students from diverse backgrounds. It is equally important that educators and institutions match cognitive knowledge with a strong commitment to learn about and implement practices suited for their multicultural and multilingual students. Bridging the widening gap requires that teachers and administrators be willing and able to learn about student cultural and linguistic backgrounds that may differ significantly from their own and transform that knowledge into effective multicultural educational practices. This is not an easy task. School personnel and schools may hold widely varying positions in relation to multicultural education. Thus, before moving to a discussion of strategies and approaches to multicultural education, it is important to first think about how to cultivate a school environment that would support and encourage the implementation of those practices.

The cultural proficiency model presented by Lindsey, Robins, and Terrell (1999) is extremely useful in this area. The model provides theoretical frameworks and suggestions for practices that will help individuals and organizations to "interact effectively in a culturally diverse environment" (p. 21). A central component of the model is an emphasis on an "inside-out" approach to assessing individuals and institution's ability to work with difference. This means focusing "on those of us who are insiders to the schools, encouraging us to reflect on our own individual understandings and values" (p. 25) and thinking about the school's culture in relation to difference. By taking a self-reflective approach, the cultural proficiency model relieves those "outsiders" from "the responsibility of doing all the adapting" (p. 25).

The inside-out approach encourages educators to assess where they and their institution are "at" with respect to dealing with cultural differences. The cultural proficiency model provides a useful framework to guide that reflective assessment. The cultural proficiency continuum represented in Fig. 10.1 defines six "unique ways of seeing and responding to difference" (Lindsey et al., 1999, p. 31).

The lowest, most negative point is "cultural destructiveness," which refers to attitudes, policies, and practices destructive to cultures and individuals within a culture (Lindsey et al., 1999, p. 32). Examples of cultural destructiveness are English-only policies and the elimination of bilingual education programs that essentially prohibit students from using their native language at school (p. 33). Such policies, enacted at a statewide level, can reverberate at the school level and fuel resistance to working flexibly with non-English-proficient students.

The middle point, cultural blindness, "is the belief that color and culture make no difference and that all people are the same" (Lindsey et al., 1999, p. 35). As Lindsey and colleagues noted, this is the most vexing point on the continuum, for culturally blind educators' well-intentioned beliefs make it difficult to recognize the persistence of problems linked to cultural and racial differences. Moreover, as Eduardo Bonilla-Silva (2003) pointed out in his excellent book *Racism without racists*, color-blindness is an ideological position that is quite dominant among Whites, leading them to deflect, often in a defensive manner, attention away from structural racism. For these reasons, it is likely that a significant portion of a school's staff will find themselves at this point in the continuum.

As one moves closer toward cultural competence, the level of acceptances and respect for differences rises. People "carefully attend to the dynamics of difference, continually assess their own cultural knowledge and beliefs, continuously expand their cultural knowledge and resources, and make various adaptations of their own belief systems, policies and practices" (Lindsey et al., 1999, p. 37).

Culturally proficient educators unabashedly support culturally proficient practices in all facets of the learning environment. They function effectively in different cultural contexts and, when presented with new groups and situations, know how to gather research and resources to help them learn about cultures (Lindsey et al., 1999, p. 37). Culturally proficient educators seek to institutionalize cultural knowledge and attendant practices into the fabric of the school. They possess cross-cultural communication skills needed to articulate their vision to students, parents, community members, and other school personnel. They take proactive steps to involve a wide variety of people in educational decisions.

Educators can use the inside-out, reflective approach and the cultural proficiency continuum to assess the readiness and willingness of individuals and the school to move toward cultural proficiency. Lindsey and colleagues (1999) offered a number of practical, well-designed activities. For example, activities like self-identity portraits, exploring your cultural roots, circle of stereotypes, and assessing your school's culture (pp. 139–159) promote self-reflection about one's cultural background and how it differs from others. They also create safe spaces where important open dialogues can take place. An activity like the "great egg drop" (p. 170), in which groups compete to package an egg for an 8-foot drop, helps in team building and collaborative work. To help select appropriate activities for where participants are at on the continuum, the authors designated whether the activity is best for beginning, intermediate, or advanced participants. They also indicated how much experience the facilitator needs to run each activity.

We believe that attention paid to assessing the levels of cultural proficiency at a school site and then engaging in activities that increase knowledge, team building, and open dialogue supports the effective education of multicultural and multilingual students. It also increases an educator's willingness and commitment to work with students from diverse backgrounds. As the school culture moves toward cultural proficiency, teachers will find more support and reinforcement, and resistance will diminish. In these circumstances, the students from diverse backgrounds will stand greater chances for educational success because the educators are positioned to tailor suitable pedagogies from the widest range of options. In the next section, we examine some of the options in the area of curricular reform.

APPROACHES TO MULTICULTURAL CURRICULAR REFORM AND TEACHING

There is a range of approaches available to educators interested in reshaping their teaching practices to infuse multiculturalism. The availability of choices makes it possible for educators, from a variety of points on the cultural proficiency continuum, to find strategies suitable to their needs and levels of commitment. James Banks (2001) has long been a leader in the field of multicultural curricular reform. He offered a number of multicultural curricular options, each with its own advantages and disadvantages.

The contributions approach is characterized "by the insertion of ethnic heroes/heroines and discrete cultural artifacts into the curriculum" (Banks, 2001, p. 229). Individuals like Crispus Attucks and Cesar Chavez are added to augment discussion of other historical figures like George Washington and Betsy Ross. In the cultural sphere, lessons on the foods and customs of various ethnic groups are inserted into the curriculum, often around holidays like Cinco de Mayo or Martin Luther King Day.

In a curriculum that has largely ignored or excluded significant individuals and cultures of different groups, the contributions approach represents a step forward. It is an unobtrusive way to integrate new material into the curriculum. It can also be implemented by teachers who have relatively little knowledge about or commitment to multiculturalism, and thus is suited for teachers and schools that are at the early points of the cultural proficiency continuum.

As Banks (2001) noted, however, the educational impact of this approach has several severe limitations. The approach often results "in the trivialization of ethnic cultures" and can portray different people and cultures as strange and exotic (p. 213). It makes cultural difference an appendage to the mainstream curriculum. It also glosses over relations of oppression by focusing on success stories that validate Horatio Alger mythology (p. 231).

Overall, students may learn about important contributions, but they do not develop a broader understanding of social and political forces that place cultural groups at odds.

An "additive approach" inserts "content, concepts, themes and perspectives to the curriculum without changing its basic structure, purposes, and characteristics" (Banks, 2001, p. 232). This approach moves beyond the contributions approach and infuses more cross-cultural material into the curriculum. Books, videos, and units may be inserted. But this approach is still limited because it continues to view ethnic and racial minority experiences through the dominant, mainstream curricular perspectives. For example, a teacher might add content on the Oglala Sioux Indians in a unit on "The Westward Movement," but it remains a mainstream unit because its focus remains on European Americans as they move from East to West.

The "transformation approach" differs from the first two in that it seeks to transform the "fundamental goals, structure, and perspectives of the curriculum" (Banks, 2001, p. 233). Challenging the mainstream, Eurocentric curriculum, a key goal is to enable students to "view concepts, issues, themes and problems from several ethnic perspectives and points of view" (p. 233). This approach infuses "various perspectives, frames of reference and content from different groups" so that students will develop a more complex understanding of U.S. society (p. 234). The main limitation is that it requires a critical view of the underlying assumptions about the development of U.S. society and the construction of knowledge. It would take considerable in-service training to transform existing curriculum and this approach is best suited for teachers who are culturally proficient.

The "social action approach" includes all of the elements of the transformative approach, "but adds components that require students to make decisions and take actions related to the concept, issue, or problem studied in the unit" (Banks, 2001, p. 236). The goal is not simply to comprehend the nature of society but to empower students to take political action to bring about social change. As with the transformative approach, implementation of the social action approach requires a high commitment to social change and culturally proficient educators.

In addition to outlining strategies to reform curriculum, scholars like Carl Grant and Christine Sleeter (1998) offered teaching approaches that can help students from diverse backgrounds to succeed. In the "human relations approach," the primary objective is not to transform the content of the curriculum but rather to infuse activities that build respect and cooperation in the classroom. An underlying assumption is that students from diverse backgrounds will learn better in classrooms where they respect themselves, are respected by others, feel supported, and have strong self-concepts (p. 57). Moving toward this approach may simply require a teacher to take an existing lesson plan and "re"-teach it using procedures and activities that bring in principles of cooperative learning. Or, it may involve lesson plans that specifically address issues of stereotyping, cultural misunderstanding, and discrimination.

In the "teaching the exceptional and culturally different approach," the goal is "changing one's instructional patterns and classroom procedures to fit the students and facilitate their academic success" within the existing curriculum (Grant & Sleeter, 1998, p. 12). Grant and Sleeter recognized that students bring into class tremendous diversity of learning styles, skill levels, language backgrounds, and abilities. Teaching all of these children the same way is likely to be unsuccessful because of these differences. Thus, it is incumbent on teachers to be able to identify the particular strengths and weaknesses of each student and to have at hand a range of teaching strategies that match the needs of students and build bridges between students and the curriculum (p. 12).

These two approaches remind us that a significant component of working effectively with multicultural and multilingual students lies in a teacher's understanding of the students and their ability to tailor curriculum and teaching to build on the strengths and experiences of those students. Gloria Ladson-Billing (1994) further defined characteristics of teachers who work effectively with culturally diverse student populations. She argued that racial minority students, particularly African Americans, do best when taught by "culturally relevant teachers" (p. 34). Culturally relevant teachers see themselves and colleagues as highly regarded professionals and see teaching as an art, requiring flexible, innovative, and creative thought (p. 34).

Culturally relevant teachers recognize and take advantage of community resources and firmly believe that all their students can succeed (Ladson-Billings, 1994, p. 38). Although one would think this to be the assumption of all teachers, many teachers are susceptible to the powerful negative stereotypical views circulating about students from poor and predominantly racial minority neighborhoods.

Finally, teachers with culturally relevant practices "help students make connections between their community, national and global identities" (Ladson-Billings, 1994, p. 49). Education, then, is not simply the acquisition of skills, but the development of interest in and commitment to the use of those academic skills to understand the world and communities in which students live.

The foregoing discussion suggests that there is a wide range of approaches to multicultural curriculum and teaching that educators can draw on as they work with students. As in any profession, the more skills and tools one possesses, the better the chance that a suitable and effective practice can be tailored and implemented. Expanding the tools and skills gives educators more choices to work with, opening up possibilities of blending or combining strategies in creative ways. In the next section, we examine theoretical foundations, teaching strategies, and curricular approaches to work with English language learners (ELLs).

THINKING ABOUT ENGLISH LANGUAGE LEARNERS

To this point, the chapter has focused on diversity and multiculturalism, in fairly general terms, presenting broad approaches to curriculum change and teaching that can be adapted to meet the needs of a student population that diverges along race, ethnic, national origin, religious, class, and gender lines. Although this general approach to multiculturalism is sufficient to address a majority of public school students, there is a subset of this increasingly diverse student population that deserves special consideration and attention—students from immigrant backgrounds who are English language learners. The enrollment of ELLs in U.S. schools has surged in recent years. The 2000 language census reported that ELLs make up 9% of the total K–12 student enrollment, totaling 4,584,946 (U.S. Census Bureau [USCB], 2000). In California alone, the ELL enrollment for 2001 was reported at over 1.5 million, representing 40% of the total student enrollment (California Department of Education [CDOE], 2002).

Given this growing number, it is vital that educators strengthen their cultural proficiency knowledge and skills needed to work effectively with ELLs. Certainly, reaffirming basic principles of effective multicultural and culturally relevant teaching outlined in previous sections is an important foundation for work with these students. Incorporating the cultural experiences of ELL students into the curriculum is vital to creating an inclusive classroom. Believing all ELL students can learn is critical to moving beyond negative stereotypes.

In addition to basic multicultural education strategies, it is important that educators understand the particular teaching and learning challenges faced by ELL students. Here, an understanding of second-language acquisition theory by noted researchers Stephen Krashen and Jim Cummins (1980, 1994, 2003) is extremely valuable. Underscoring their work is a key assumption—supporting a student's primary language development is beneficial to his or her learning a second language.

Krashen's (2003) language-acquisition hypotheses help to demonstrate how people come to learn a second language. He argued that second-language fluency is not learned but acquired in much the same way that a first language is "picked-up." Moreover, the parts of a language are acquired in a predictable order and the order of acquisition for first and second languages is similar but not identical (p. 1). Once the primary language is learned, one can then apply the rules of the primary language to assist in the learning of a second language. That is, a learner can "monitor" or "edit" the proper written and oral use of the second language by applying the rules of the first language.

A second language is acquired when one not only knows the rules and words, but also can understand messages in that language. Krashen wrote, "We acquire language in only one way: when we understand messages; that is, when we obtain 'comprehensible input.' We acquire language, in other words when we understand what we hear or what we read, when we understand the message" (Krashen, 2003, p. 4). Language teaching must be comprehensible and the quality of exposure to the language is what counts not the quantity. Therefore when ELLs receive instruction in their primary language, the transfer skills in learning a second language are much more comprehensible.

Finally, Krashen noted that the process of second-language acquisition has a strong affective dimension. Negative feelings arising from unsupportive classroom and school environments can extend the time it takes to learn a second language. These affective variables do not impact language-acquisition ability but can prevent comprehensible input from reaching the part of the brain responsible for language acquisition (Krashen, 2003, p. 6). Negative factors that ELL students may encounter are a lack of self-confidence, anxiety, lack of motivation, and inappropriate instructional strategies used by teachers, and the attitude of the school toward them and their families can affect comprehensible input by not "allowing it through." Teachers need to lower the "affective filter" of ELLs if they are to successfully teach them a second language (Crawford, 1999).

Jim Cummins (1994) supports and extends Krashen's work. Like Krashen, Cummins claimed that there is a close interrelationship between learning the first and second language. Here, Cummins is critical of a commonly held view that the process of learning second languages is distinct and independent from first-language learning. This view, which Cummins calls Separate Underlying Proficiency (SUP), says that instruction in one's primary language can hinder second-language learning.

Cummins (1980) argued the opposite of SUP. He claimed that first- and second-language learning develop interdependently in the brain. The skills learned in one language are transferable to the other language being learned. He referred to this as the Common Underlying Proficiency (CUP) hypothesis, where different languages build on common underlying principles and processes. Cummins predicted that ELLs who have strong literacy skills in their first language will learn a second language much sooner and with greater ease. The "affective filter" is lowered and the common underlying proficiency will then transfer the academic skills. Those ELL students who do not reach a "threshold level" in their primary language will then most likely have a tendency to fail in both languages and in school (Crawford, 1999).

Ideally, the design of educational programs for ELLs will build on the lessons learned by researchers like Krashen and Cummins. In fact, there are several models of bilingual education that have been developed that incorporate second-language learning theory. The primary aim of these models is "additive" by nature, where the goal is to promote bilingualism and biliteracy in two languages, as opposed to subtracting or transitioning an ELL student out of their primary language into English. Additive programs build on students' primary language knowledge and promote further development of primary language skills as a way to enhance the learning of a second language. Successful bilingual education programs that have survived are those that articulate language benefits, cognitive benefits, and sociocultural benefits available to everyone (Quezada & White, 2000). Those that take an additive view to language learning and that emphasize maintenance of primary language include Dual-Language, Two-Way Bilingual Education, Two-Way Bilingual Education Immersion, and Maintenance Bilingual Education programs.

1. **Dual-Language Schools**. These programs offer schooling in two languages. The amount of both languages offered is usually 50%, or half a day in one language and half a day in another. Many of these programs are offered through private schools or for international children living abroad. This type of setting does not accommodate language-minority students in many cases.

2. **Two-Way Bilingual Education**. The model is similar to dual-language programs except that in this situation the program seeks to integrate both language minority students and English speakers. The main goal is both to develop fluency in two languages and to learn each other's cultural background, therefore having an appreciation for both cultures' language, traditions, and customs.

3. **Two-Way Bilingual Education Immersion**. This program is designed to serve both English-only speakers and other primary language speakers. The difference is that native primary language speakers are immersed in their own language while the English speakers are immersed in the second language. It provides content instruction and literacy to all students in both languages. When well implemented, these programs have proved to be among the most effective in the United States, graduating students with both grade-level academic ability and proficiency in two languages (CREDE, 2003).

4. **Maintenance Bilingual Education**. This program aims to maintain the child's primary language and to promote the child's appreciation for his or her cultural background. Both the primary language and the second language are developed simultaneously.

CONSTRAINING REALITIES

Although there are multiple bilingual programs available, the realities of educational life can often constrain and limit choices. In the United States, the attitude toward speaking and being educated in two languages has been primarily negative. Many times policies and program models of education and research have been dictated on political moods rather than on sound linguistic and educational research (Brisk, 1998). Current changes in societal attitudes toward ELLs, particularly in states where English only is the norm or in states that have passed legislative propositions (such as California's Proposition 227 that has restructured bilingual education) have created many challenges and constraints for schools, educators, and ELL students.

As student diversity and language diversity have increased, so has the student academic achievement gap between majority and minority students, particularly children in poverty. Unfortunately, ELLs are receiving less primary language instruction and support services in classrooms. In some cases, instruction is limited to 1 year of primary language support. Teachers are faced teaching to new standards to students who may or may not understand the language and school districts are being held accountable to meet new federal regulations under the No Child Left Behind (NCLB) legislation. The results are that more ELLs are left to "sink" rather than swim or even stay afloat. Many times ELLs are tracked into less rigorous courses that will lead to educational failure. In California, primary language instruction dropped from 29% of students in 1999 to less than 10% in 2001–2002 (UCLMRI, 2002).

In addition to the political constraints, other circumstances work to limit options for ELL students. Dual-way, two-way, and maintenance bilingual programs are more costly and difficult to support in times of tight budgets. Bilingual programs are logistically simpler to implement when there is only one main second-language population within a district. But as language diversity expands, and school districts have 10–60 language groups, limited resources and logistical constraints make it difficult to establish bilingual programs for each group.

Finally, misconceptions about how long it takes to learn a second language can be problematic. Research consistently indicates that it takes English language learners 3–5 years to develop oral proficiency and 4–7 years to gain academic English proficiency (Hakuta, Butler, & Witt, 1999; Cummins, 1994). English communication experiences vary from having a playground conversation where there are many clues that may be provided (context embedded) to the use of more higher order thinking language skills where there are fewer clues (context reduced). ELLs perform best in academic subjects when they have reached an advanced level of English fluency.

Unfortunately, many educators believe that it only takes 1 to 2 years to learn English and be academically proficient to compete with English-only-speaking students. They make the mistake of assessing ELLs at an early stage, when they appear to be proficient in English. But these students may only have developed their basic interpersonal communication skills (BICS). Students with BICS can communicate and understand at basic levels, relying on clues, visuals, gestures, physical interactions, and conversational responses. They do not, however, have the cognitive and academic language proficiency (CALP) skills required to successfully transition into an English-only classroom. It can take 5 to 7 years to develop CALP (Cummins, 1994). Based primarily on BICS, ELLs are too often transitioned early from second-language programs, making it difficult for them to keep up with their English-only peers. Many subsequently fail, and older students drop out of high school.

Ironically and unfortunately, constraining realities contribute to the widespread adoption of weak forms of second-language learning programs. These programs generally do not support the development of students' primary language. They promote monolingualism and assimilation into the mainstream English-language society. The language of the classroom is usually that of the majority language, with "pull-out" second language and at times beginning with the minority language but moving quickly to the majority language. The three most common second language programs in use today are:

1. **Transitional Bilingual Education**. This program utilizes the native language of minority students as they acquire English. The objective is to help students learn English as quickly as possible, and the program is not concerned with maintaining primary language. The use of primary language can take up to 4 years as they transition into English-only instruction. According to Ramirez, Yuen, and Ramey (1991), two types of programs are in place: "Early Exit" or "Late Exit." In an early-exit program, children receive instruction in their primary language usually until second or third grade in literacy and language arts. In a late-exit program, children transition into English-only instruction after fifth or sixth grade.

2. **English as a Second Language**. This type of program is utilized when there are not enough language-minority students in one grade level to form a bilingual classroom. Language-minority students are taught in mainstream classrooms and pulled out for English language instruction either in small groups in the teacher's own classroom or integrated with other children in other grades in a special setting. Instruction in ESL in middle school and high school is usually set up according to ability levels (beginning, intermediate, and advanced ESL).

3. **Structured Immersion**. In this type of program students who are usually in the same language proficiency level are placed together in the same classroom. Students receive English language development (ELD) and specially designed academic instruction in English (SDAIE). Teachers should have been trained in the methodology and apply specific strategies such as activating prior knowledge, utilizing visuals, and using simplified speech, context clues, and hands-on and cooperative groups to develop both language and content instruction in English. Teachers may utilize the child's primary language for support or clarification if needed (Ramirez, 1992).

Ultimately, programs for ELLs should be designed to help immigrant students succeed in this country while maintaining their cultural identity. To succeed academically without losing cultural and linguistic ties is the basis of effective bilingual education programs. Research has shown that early-exit bilingual programs and ESL fared the worst in instructing ELLs (Ramirez et al., 1991). Further, research indicates that bilingual programs can only be successful if the support of families and of the community is existent and apparent (Quezada & White, 2000).

Even with constraining forces, educational leaders need to determine which programs are the most effective for the type of language population their school districts and schools are serving. The number of English language learners, number of different languages spoken in a school, language proficiency levels, age levels of students, and prior education in the home country and availability of bilingual certified personnel, time, costs, available funds, materials, and curriculum to provide instructional services are some of the many factors that need to be examined and evaluated. We know that children need to acquire English skills to be able to compete successfully in this society, but this should not be at the expense of their education, or their cultural and language heritage. Programs need to consider the use of qualified certificated teachers as a priority, but when not available, the use of bilingual paraprofessionals is also a model to consider. All programs can benefit through the use of volunteers, peer tutors, translators and other professionals to support the instruction and education of English language learners.

EFFECTIVE INSTRUCTIONAL PRACTICES FOR ENGLISH LANGUAGE LEARNERS

We know from the research on effective schools that regardless of students' sociocultural background, they can attain high achieving standards when effective instructional practices are implemented. Further, we know that when a child's language and culture is taken into consideration, it facilitates the learning of English and in the process maintains the native language as well as the culture. So what can educators do or take into consideration when planning and instructing English language learners and other ethnically diverse students in order to close the achievement gap? What factors should they consider?

As in general multicultural education models, it is important for educators to respect a child's language and culture and take them into account when designing program and course goals. It is useful to draw on a variety of instructional strategies, such as cooperative learning groups, to assist ELLs. It is vital to hold high expectations out for all ELLs.

Beyond these general prescriptions, it is important for educators to be knowledgeable of second-language acquisition theory and the implications such a theory can have on teaching practices. Teachers, for example, should be able to draw on language-sensitive and special instructional strategies ground in English language development. This means having classrooms that are rich in aural comprehensible input, through the use of realia and lessons that involve action and movement. Teachers modify their speech by talking naturally but using less-complex sentences (Krashen, 2003, p. 7). The total physical response method is very effective for beginning-level students learning a second language.

Students at intermediate levels of acquiring English are best taught through SDAIE. This method of instruction focuses on subject matter not language. It should be engaging, hands-on, relevant, academically demanding, and comprehensible. It should include visuals and use of graphic organizers, real objects, and construction of prior background knowledge, having cooperative structures to allow for interaction, and it should negotiate for meaning to promote language facility. The use of pictures is very important, including paraphrasing and repeating and focusing on key vocabulary in order to make lessons more comprehensible and to elevate the use of language to higher cognitive level with the focus on grade-level instruction (Colon, 2000).

Strategies such as these can support educational leaders in the planning and training of teachers on how to best work with our ethnically and linguistically diverse student population. A team effort is the most appropriate in order to develop a community of learners and a community of practice by involving all of the stakeholders, students, teachers, other education personnel, and parents in order to foster mutual respect and collegiality. Last is believing that all students have the potential to succeed under the right circumstances in an appropriate and nurturing school setting with the most qualified teaching staff and educational personnel.

SUPPORT OF LANGUAGE AND CULTURAL HOME-SCHOOL, FAMILY INVOLVEMENT

To this point, our focus has been on the school and classroom, on what teachers and administrators can do to enhance the educational performance of students from diverse racial, cultural, linguistic, religious, and class backgrounds. Whereas what happens inside schools is clearly important, so too is the role families can play in a student's education. Families have also long been considered a central factor in promoting student academic achievement (Abey, Manning, Theyer, & Abey-Carpenter 1999; Greenwald, Hedges, & Laine, 1996; Hoover–Dempsey, 1987). Research indicates that when families, schools, and communities develop partnerships student academic achievement increases and greater participation by parents is evident, including language-minority populations (Epstein, 1992; Goldenberg, 1993; Lezotte, 1997). Parental involvement can improve student behavior, improve parent and student attitudes toward school, help parents improve their self-confidence and expertise, improve home-school relations, and increase student's cognitive growth (Bermúdez & Márquez, 1996). For these reasons, it is important to examine how schools can foster effective school-home relationships.

Developing those relationships can be a challenging task. It is well documented that barriers exist regarding parent involvement in schools (Mattingly, Prislin, Mckenzie, Rodriguez, & Kayzar, 2002). School personnel tend to view parents as agents of service for the school rather than as equal partners in the educational endeavor. In many instances families representing different language and cultural groups are the ones who least participate or are ignored in the educational process of their children. Traditional family involvement in schools needs to be redefined in order to have full participation of families who least participate in schools but participate in the education of their children. How can schools take advantage of the potential synergy found in diverse school and community involvement, and enhance home, school, and community relationships and partnerships? How can schools ensure that all families are involved? How do you reach "hard-to-reach families," particularly ethnic and language diverse families, and include them as part of the partnership? Multifaceted partnerships with families and communities cannot be developed by taking one course or by providing an inservice once per year (Epstein, 1992). They need to be fostered, nurtured, and developed over time.

Research indicates that strong parent-community-school relationships are formed when school personnel have knowledge of community needs, view parents and community members as equal partners, and open lines of communication. Many times schools are not in touch with the needs of the community. School personnel do all the planning and provide a "description and prescription" of what's best for them instead of working together with parents and community members to diagnose and design preventive programs and actions. Such relations reduce the incentive for parents and community members to "buy-in" into the school's agenda.

Jacobs (2002) described three actions that can enhance community partnerships and create alliances with parents and the community. The first, limitations, helps to establish realistic parameters and expectations for school-home-community relations. The goal here is to clearly outline the possibilities and limitations for all partners. Teachers and schools should invite parents and community members to be part of the instructional team to define and communicate these limitations. Action two, announcements, addresses the manner by which schools communicate with parents and community members. Jacobs encouraged school personnel to move beyond the relative passive and ineffective school flyer approach and to establish more active and creative forms of communication. This might mean teachers speaking to community groups at church gatherings. It could mean going to community functions if schools are serious about reaching the hard-to-reach families. A wealth of instructional support can be found in community organizations where one can solicit both speakers and materials. Finally, action three involves finding common ground by identifying views and issues that both the community and the school share. Issues of curriculum, discipline, and community resources can better be discussed by informing each other.

Quezada's (2003) research findings of six parent involvement programs recognized as exemplary by the California School Board Association in 2001 when working with ethnic and language diverse families support the literature on effective home-school-family, community partnership programs. These programs developed innovative activities that demonstrated a commitment to families and communities that extended well beyond the cursory service model most schools use. Schools provided free transportation and translation services for families and free daycare for their children, and the programs were widely publicized in various languages. At many venues, college tutors were utilized frequently, and program activities varied from family math, geography, literacy, camp-outs, weekend service projects, English-language courses, home visits, and a community read-aloud. An evaluation component for students, parents, and teachers was also conducted annually.

These efforts produced significant positive results. The schools showed an increase in academic performance index scores on state standardized tests. There were fewer student behavior problems reported. A connection between program activities and the schools' curriculum was evident, as was more involvement by parents in Parent Teacher Association organizations from those who traditionally do not participate. Teachers felt a stronger connection to parents and students, and business and service organizations were in partnerships with the schools.

In summary, home-school-community partnerships are effective when they use all available resources, are grounded in mutual respect, and are connected to teaching and learning. Establishing strong home-school-community partnerships requires an active and ongoing commitment that carries school personnel beyond passive outreach. The payoff is evident. Effective home-school-community partnerships help all youngsters succeed in school and later in life. They make schools an exciting place to be, a place where ethnicly, linguistically, and culturally diverse communities care about their schools and schools care about their communities.

SUMMARY

As demographic shifts bring increasing numbers of students from diverse racial, ethnic, religious, class, and linguistic backgrounds into the public schools, there is no escaping the challenge of diversity. The issue is not whether diversity should be addressed, but rather in what ways educators can meet the needs of students from diverse backgrounds.

The chapter is organized to help educators think about diversity in a broad and integrative manner. To prepare school personnel to meet the challenge of diversity, a first and critically important step is think reflectively about where one is situated in relation to cultural proficiency. Assessing and cultivating willingness, openness, and commitment to meet the challenge of diversity is a vital foundation for the development of effective educational practices. Without such willingness and commitment, educators will lack sufficient motivation to venture beyond comfort zones to learn about and employ the resources available to help students from diverse backgrounds. The discussion of cultural proficiency (see Fig. 10.1) is intended to help educators locate themselves, their peers, and their schools on the continuum, via an inside-out reflective assessment, in hopes of moving educators toward cultural competence.

Armed with an interest and commitment to cultural proficiency, the remainder of the chapter provides educators with an overview of perspectives, strategies, and practices designed to address the needs of the diverse student populations. The overview ranges from general approaches to multicultural curricular reform and teaching strategies to more specific discussion of how to work with English language learners. It also emphasizes the need to move beyond the school borders and into communities and homes to develop collaborative partnerships. We hope the discussion serves as an introduction to key issues in the various areas and provides a base from which further understanding and actions can be developed.

GUIDING QUESTIONS

1. Where on the cultural proficiency continuum would you locate yourself? Your peers? The school you work in?
2. What attitudes, circumstances, and/or conditions help or hinder your movement (and the movement of your peers and your school) toward cultural proficiency?
3. In thinking about the diverse student population in your class/school, what multicultural curricular and teaching approaches would be most suitable to meet their needs? What support do you need to bring those approaches into your work?
4. In what ways can you better support and address the needs of English language learners? What additional information, resource, and support are critical to help you meet those needs?
5. In assessing your own, your peers', and your school's relationship with students' families and communities, what is working well and, what areas need improvement?

SELECTED READINGS

Crawford, J. (1999). Bilingual education: History, politics, theory, and practice (4th ed.). Los Angeles: Bilingual Education Resources, Inc.

Lindsey, R. B., Robins, K. N., & Terrell, R. D. (1999). *Cultural proficiency—A manual for school leaders.* Thousand Oaks, CA: Corwin Press.

Quezada, R. (2003, Fall/Winter). Reports from the field: Effective parent involvement practices. *The School Community Journal, 13*(2), 137–156.

Ramirez, J. D., Yuen, S. D., & Ramey, D. R. (1991). Final report: Longitudinal study of structured Immersion strategy, early-exit and late-exit programs for language-minority children. Report submitted to the U.S. Department of Education. San Mateo, CA: Aguirre International.

REFERENCES

Abey, G. V., Manning, H. B., Theyer, A. B., & Abey-Carpenter, T. (1999). Comparing outcomes of an alternative school program offered with and without parent involvement. *The School Community Journal, 9*(1), 17–32.

Banks, J. (2001). Multicultural education: Characteristics and goals. In J. Banks & C. McGee Banks (Eds.), *Multicultural education—Issues and perspectives* (4th ed., pp. 3–30). New York: Wiley.

Bermúdez, A. B., & Márquez, J. A. (1996, Summer). An examination of a four-way collaborative to Increase parental involvement in the schools. *The Journal of Educational Issues of Language Minority Students, 16*, 1–16.

Bonilla-Silva, E. (2003). *Racism without racists—Color-blind racism and the persistence of racial inequality in the United States.* Lanham, MD: Rowman & Littlefield.

Brisk, E. M. (1998). *Bilingual education: From compensatory to quality schooling.* Mahwah, NJ: Lawrence Erlbaum Associates.

California Department of Education (CDOE). (2002). DataQuest: Educational demographics unit. Retrieved July 21, 2004, from http://www.data1.cde.ca.gov/dataquest/.

Center for Research in Education, Diversity and Excellence. (2003). A practical guide to understanding and implementing two-way immersion programs. UCSC. *6*(2), 1, 9, & 10. Santa Cruz, CA.

Colon, A. M. (2000, Spring). Keeping languages alive through maintenance bilingual education programs. *The Multilingual Educator, 2*(1), pp. 14–15.

Crawford, J. (1999). Bilingual education: History, politics, theory, and practice (4th ed.). Los Angeles: Bilingual Education Resources, Inc.

Cummins, J. (1980). The entry and exit fallacy in bilingual education. *NABE Journal, 4*(3), 25–29.

Cummins, J. (1994). The role of primary language development in promoting educational success for language minority students. In California State Department of Education (Ed.), *Schooling language minority students: A theoretical framework* (2nd ed., pp. 3–46). Los Angeles: California State Department of Education.

Delpit, L. (1995). *Other people's children—Cultural conflict in the classroom.* New York: The Free Press.

Epstein, J. L. (1992). School and family partnerships. In M. Alkin (Ed.), *Encyclopedia of educational research* (6th ed., pp. 1139–1151). New York: Macmillan.

Glazier, J. A. (2003). Moving closer to speaking the unspeakable: White teachers talking about race. *Teacher Education Quarterly, 30*, 73–94.

Goldenberg, C. (1993). The home-school connection in bilingual education. In M. B. Arias & U. Casanova (Eds.), *Bilingual education: Politics, practice, and research* (pp. 225–250). Chicago: University of Chicago Press.

Grant, C. A., & Sleeter, C. E. (1998). *Turning on learning—Five approaches for multicultural teaching plans for race, class, gender and disability* (2nd ed.). Columbus, OH: Merrill.

Greenwald, R., Hedges, L. V., & Laine, R. D. (1996). The effect of school resources on student achievement. *Review of Educational Research, 66*(3), 361–396.

Hakuta, K., Butler, Y. G., & Witt, D. (2000). *How long does it take English learners to attain proficiency?* UC Linguistic Minority Research Institute, *9*(1). Retrieved July 21, 2004, from http://mri.ucsb.edu/resdiss/2/pdf_files/hakuta.pdf

Hodgkinson, H. L. (2002). The demographics of diversity. *Principal, 82*, 14–18.

Hoover-Dempsey, K. V. (1987). Parent involvement: Contributions of teacher efficacy, school socioeconomic status, and other school characteristics. *American Educational Research Journal, 24*, 417–435.

Jacobs, T. (2002). Teacher-parent partnerships: Making community education real for indigenous families. *NABE NEWS, 75*(5), 24–25.

Krashen, D. S. (2003). *Explorations in language acquisition and use.* Portsmouth, NH: Heinemann.

Ladson-Billing, G. (1994). *The dreamkeepers—Successful teachers of African-American children.* San Francisco: Jossey-Bass.

Lezotte, L. (1997). *Learning for all.* Effective School Products. Michigan: Okemos.

Lindsey, R. B., Robins, K. N., & Terrell, R. D. (1999). *Cultural proficiency—A manual for school leaders.* Thousand Oaks, CA: Corwin Press.

Mattingly, D., Prislin, R., Mckenzie, T., Rodriguez, J., & Kayzar, B. (2002). Evaluating evaluations: The case of parent involvement programs. *Review of Educational Research, 72*(4), 549–576.

McFalls, E. L., & Cobb-Roberts, D. (2001). Reducing resistance to diversity through cognitive dissonance instruction—Implications for teacher education. *Journal of Teacher Education, 52*, 164–172

Quezada, R. (2003, Fall/Winter). Reports from the field: Effective parent involvement practices. *The School Community Journal, 13*(2), 137–156.

Quezada, R., & White, J. (2000). It takes a village to raise a bilingual child: Forming collaborative partnerships among schools and bilingual communities. *The School Community Journal, 10*(2), 99–109.

Ramirez, J. D. (1992). Executive summary. *Bilingual Research Journal, 16*(1 & 2), 1–62.

Ramirez, J. D., Yuen, S. D., & Ramey, D. R. (1991). Final report: Longitudinal study of structured immersion strategy, early-exit and late-exit programs for language-minority children. Report submitted to the U.S. Department of Education. San Mateo, CA: Aguirre International.

Sleeter, C. E. (2001). Preparing teachers for culturally diverse schools—Research and the overwhelming presence of whiteness. *Journal of Teacher Education, 52,* 94–106.

University of California Linguistic Minority Research Institute (UCLMRI). (2002, Fall). Language minority students account for most of California's enrollment growth in past decade. *UCLMI Newsletter,* University of California, Santa Barbara.

U.S. Census Bureau. (2000). *Census 2000.* Retrieved July 21, 2004, from http://www.census.gov.

Zhou, M. (2003). Urban education: Challenges in educating culturally diverse children. *Teachers College Record, 105,* 208–225.

Chapter 11

Navigating Special Education Tensions and Controversies

Judy A. Mantle
University of San Diego

Areas of potential tension and controversy in special education are numerous and can be evidenced particularly in processes focused on important target areas for decision making. In their discussion of the Individuals with Disabilities Education Act (IDEA), Drake and Roe (2003) stated that perhaps the most challenging regulations pertain to the full due process rights for children and parents as they apply to referral, evaluation, and placement procedures. Involved parties may also debate issues such as the types and frequency of services that will be provided and the proportion of time a given child will receive general education services compared to the proportion of time they will receive special education services. The plethora of issues sometimes appears to be endless and often results in conflicts of varying intensity that require skillful leaders and negotiators to resolve. Some of the issues may escalate to the degree that they require resolution through formal mediation, through due process hearings, or in worst-case scenarios, through litigation.

Assuming that the environment within which the school conducts its mission is the most complex of all our social inventions (Hanson, 1979), one can deduct that school leaders have long been faced with a multitude of issues, concerns, and problems that emerge from among vested stakeholders. For a host of reasons, the contemporary complex special education arena can add to the difficult challenges faced by even the best school leaders and administrators. Yell (1998) explained that special education is governed by an elaborate and extensive body of statutes, regulations, and court decisions. It is not surprising that many become fearful and apprehensive of special education. However, by acquiring knowledge and skills in several focus areas, it is possible to significantly increase one's competency and confidence to lead special education programs in spite of the challenges and complexities that can arise. In a discussion of the nature of leadership in complex organizations, Hughes (1999) stated that good leaders know how to work the system.

BASIC ASSUMPTIONS

At the outset, I am making three basic assumptions about leaders of special education programs in contemporary schools. The school leader:

- values persons with disabilities and their families and the array of contributions they make to society,
- is committed to helping each person with disabilities achieve the highest desired level of success and maximum degree of independence and the highest possible quality of life,
- is dedicated to their own ongoing personal and professional growth relative to the ultimate purpose of maximizing the achievement of positive student outcomes for all students.

It is important to realize the important differences that one in a leadership capacity potentially can make in the lives of persons who manifest various types of special needs. It seems only logical that the more school leaders learn about the characteristics and needs of students with disabilities, effective teaching strategies, and available services and resources, the more likely they are to organize instruction to positively impact student outcomes. Those leaders who possess positive attitudes and who demonstrate a genuine and pervasive commitment to embrace all students have a healthy foundation on which to further build creative and exemplary special education practice. In their discussion of the role of school principals and vice principals, Lewis and Doorlag (2003) explained that as educational leaders of their schools, their activities, the attitudes they convey, and the support they provide can help to establish the necessary school climate for successfully serving students with special needs.

This chapter begins with an explanation of the need for informed and competent leadership in special education and the role of the leader in this area, especially that of the principal. Most of the discussion is organized around three key topics that are often fraught with issues, tension, and controversy: (a) multiple and conflicting demands on the school leader, (b) diverse constituencies and multiple perspectives, and (c) the general education/special education interface. Recommendations and practical suggestions are made relative to navigating and negotiating the tensions and controversies surrounding each topic. Next, a summary emphasizing major points is provided. Last, there are questions for reflection followed by a case study. There is also a section of selected readings.

INFORMED AND COMPETENT LEADERSHIP

There is an array of school personnel concerned with providing many forms of service and leadership to the area of special education. No matter what leadership role one plays in program delivery to students with exceptional needs—whether principal, vice principal, director of special education, instructional or program manager, general or special education teacher, mentor, or others—it is vital that those responsible for special education programs provide informed and competent leadership at all levels. By subscribing to a shared-leadership approach that originates at top levels, it is possible to access a multitude of talents and resources and then orchestrate services in a manner that truly enhances program administration. A comprehensive service-delivery model has many tentacles, and all aspects of the model require careful management in order to assure that effective and high-quality services are consistently delivered. Because there are multiple dimensions to special education programming, it is imperative that thoughtful facilitation and direction be given in a consistent and coherent manner to the many teachers and support personnel who deliver services, and especially to those who do so at the grassroots level where students with disabilities are directly impacted.

Key decision makers must determine who should lead specific aspects of special education programs, which students need services and why, what programs and services will be provided, and how and where they will be delivered. In any case, the principal, in particular, must set a positive and constructive tone. Further, principals can assist in providing for children's needs and be a facilitator of resources for its achievement (Hughes & Ubben, 1994; Ubben, Hughes, & Norris, 2001). According to Walther-Thomas and DiPaola (2003), principal leadership is critical to assuring that disabled students have effective learning programs. Further, the authors stated:

> To help special needs students learn, principals can do the following: create a positive school culture that supports their academic success, use knowledge of special education laws that protect students' rights, understand how teachers and specialists can better assist disabled students, and work continuously and collaboratively with their key stakeholders to address all students' learning needs. Principals must also provide high-quality professional development for all personnel to enhance disabled students' outcomes. (p. 125)

Roles and functions of principals and program administrators may vary considerably between schools depending on the size of the school, needs of the students, and the manner in which instruction is organized. Whatever their role, their actions directly impact special education students and programs. Among other functions, principals must demonstrate competence in the areas of planning, staffing, budgeting, and communicating to a wide array of audiences in order to be effective in the role of special education leader. They also make decisions regarding curriculum and instruction, scheduling, support services, program assessment, transportation, parent meetings, and communication systems required for facilitating all programs operations. Additionally, they may also chair or participate in Individual Educational Program (IEP) meetings. In a discussion of the role of the program administrator relative to interactive teaming and special needs students, Chase Thomas, Correa, and Voelker Morsink (2001) explained that the role of the administrator is that of overall management of the schools and its programs but not necessarily as a leader of an interactive team. Additionally, the administrator's priority is the welfare of the entire unit. Further, the authors stated:

> For the team to function effectively, however, it is particularly important for the administrator to understand and convey to the public that she values this team and has delegated to it decision- making authority for special needs students. It is equally important for the administrator to provide the members of the team with information about the legal policies and procedure within which they are authorized to operate, and to provide them with information about the fiscal and instructional resources available to them in program implementation. After having established the team, however, the administrator steps down from the direct leadership role and delegates responsibility for the team's functioning to the team itself. (p. 132)

Unquestionably, effective contemporary leadership for special needs school-aged populations requires considerable knowledge and skills in numerous areas.

Last, school leaders must be able to implement policies and procedures resulting from perpetual changes that originate at national, state, and local levels. In recent years, an active and dynamic advocacy focused on enhancing the rights of persons with disabilities and their families has given tremendous impetus to movements that have resulted in far-reaching changes relative to special education practices in the schools. As a result, lawmakers have passed key pieces of legislation that have resulted in a number of changes in our nation's schools. For example, PL 94-142, the Education for All Handicapped Children Act, was a landmark piece of legislation that was passed in 1975 (Lewis & Doorlag, 2003; Turnbull & Turnbull, 1997). That law required that students with disabilities be educated with general education peers to the maximum extent appropriate. The practice of "mainstreaming" students with disabilities into general education classrooms and programs commenced on a large scale. The movement gained significant attention as the momentum to support it increased in subsequent years. This law resulted in sweeping changes that continue to significantly impact school leader decisions about how students with disabilities are integrated into general education and special education learning environments. At the time PL 94-142 was passed, the movement toward integrating special education students into the general education arena boldly contrasted with the common practice of segregating students with disabilities from the general education population in the school environment. In many instances, school leaders found themselves reeling from an imposed "culture shock" in their schools; yet they were charged with the task of implementing that mandate, often against the wishes of teachers, parents, and students. Then, in 1990, PL 94-142 was renamed the Individuals with Disabilities Education Act (IDEA) and was reauthorized with significant amendments in 1997 (Turnbull & Turnbull, 2001). Great impetus was given to the inclusion movement with the passage of IDEA, and school leaders found themselves implementing yet another wave of significant changes that impacted both general education and special education.

Due in great part to the strength and persistence of the collective advocacy that supports the needs of individuals who manifest various types of disabilities, there is continuous activity in the political and legislative arenas relative to special education. Consequently, the political wheel of change seems to always be turning, and new trends in education are constantly evolving. At the time of this writing, school leaders are determining how they will fully implement all provisions of the reauthorization of the Elementary and Secondary Education Act, known widely as the No Child Left Behind (NCLB) legislation. Also, the next reauthorization of the IDEA legislation is on the near horizon. These two pieces of legislation collectively will again significantly impact current school-based practices. At the same time, the accountability movement has increased in intensity, and school leaders and teachers of general and special education students are wrestling with how best to respond to requirements that apply to their students in a manner that is appropriate, reasonable, and fair. In the *Quality Counts 2004: "Count Me In: Special Education in an Era of Standards"* special report published in *Education Week* magazine, authors explain that states are confronting how to help a diverse population meet the same standards expected of all. School leaders must become adept at anticipating forthcoming changes, and they must then be responsive to all federal and state mandates once they are passed.

Recommendations

Many *layers of leadership* are required to provide comprehensive special education services; subsequently, there are corresponding multiple *layers of knowledge* that must be cultivated in the various stakeholders who serve special education programs. Knowledge clearly leads to empowerment in this area. At a minimum, it is imperative that all school leaders are well versed in the basic provisions of special education law. In their study of administrators' knowledge of expected special education practices, Davidson and Algozzine (2002) reported in their recent study that the majority of principal fellows in their study were able to provide the application of special education law to only three of the IDEA provisions (i.e., IEP, zero reject, and related services). In that same study, principal fellows demonstrated difficulty with their applications of the law to the provisions of least restrictive environment, parent participation, procedural safeguard, and appropriate evaluation. These researchers also reported that incompetent leadership in the area of special education law could lead to the continuance of formal complaints and due process proceedings. Further, they emphasized that the principal's lack of knowledge about special education law could be detrimental to students with disabilities who are already at a disadvantage. Unquestionably, knowledge of special education law is vitally important and cannot be overemphasized.

It is also important for school leaders to keep abreast of key determinations that result from special education litigation. Knowledge of activity in this area can greatly assist leaders in avoiding dangerous pitfalls. Further, lessons learned from court decisions can help to inform program policies and procedures. Litigation is an area of prolific and complex activity that often requires top school officials to seek legal consultation and advisement. Acquiring knowledge in the areas of law and litigation relative to disability and school-aged children and youth can greatly enhance one's ability to become a truly effective leader of special education programs. Mastery of fundamental concepts in both of these areas is vital, and knowledge of these areas will serve as important points of reference when it is necessary to make determinations about the legality and legitimacy of special education program practices.

MULTIPLE AND CONFLICTING DEMANDS

Leaders of special education programs may frequently be caught in cross fires between stakeholders. Perhaps no other action they take draws more "lightening" than that of allocating resources. For example, when scrutinizing funding practices, those in general education might claim encroachment by special education personnel on the school or district budget while special educators may claim that they need even more resources so that they can respond to the pressures of improving student outcomes and meet increased accountability expectations. At the same time, parents and families naturally want the best education program possible for their children.

However, some request, or even demand, resources and support beyond what school leaders believe is "reasonable" or even affordable. Especially in times of fiscal restraint, there is heated competition for scarce resources. Financial gatekeepers may feel as though they are walking a tightrope as they attempt to balance passionate program requests with limited available funds.

Some parents engage the assistance of an advocate, sometimes at their own expense, who can place even more pressure on school personnel for resources. Because certain rights of parents are so clearly defined, the school system becomes very vulnerable to complaint procedures if they feel that rights have been violated (Drake & Roe, 2003). On a more positive note, the authors indicated that the overwhelming majority of differences of opinion among parents and school officials are resolved at the local level.

Another topic fraught with tension is that of exactly what should constitute an "appropriate" education program for students with disabilities as required by the IDEA. There can be a significant mismatch of opinions among interdisciplinary team members, including parents, about what comprises an appropriate education program for a given student. Discussions and debate are sometimes prolific about issues such as the types and frequency of services that should be provided, the proportion of time a given student will receive general education services, compared to the time they will receive special education services, and the types of personnel required to deliver the program. Leaders, program providers at all levels, and parents each bring their own philosophies, beliefs, and opinions to discussions about how to serve the wide array of students with disabilities. Disagreements can easily arise, making it difficult to reach consensus on important decisions that must be made, and therefore adding to the leadership challenge.

Controversy can also easily erupt over the determination of fair and appropriate discipline policies and procedures that are utilized in general education as compared to those utilized in special education. In the case of children with disabilities, intricate federal and state regulations govern the administration of punishment with these students (Ubben, Hughes, & Norris, 2001). The school leader must be especially thoughtful when applying discipline, particularly for those students who are identified as having behavior disorders and who are receiving special education services for such. Leaders can find themselves facilitating what may appear to be a dual behavior management system where there is one system that applies to general education students and a different one that applies to students with disabilities. For example, it may be particularly confusing and angering for parents who cannot see why two students (one who manifests behavior disorders, and one with no disabilities) who exhibited the same inappropriate behavior in the same episode might receive different consequences.

When a behavior incident is serious, school leaders typically must notify the student's parents. Perspectives about what happened in a certain situation can be quite varied, and intense debates involving many parties can result from decisions made about how a single incident was handled. Of course, navigating through complex and emotionally charged situations can be quite frustrating and uncomfortable at times. Positive parent and professional relationships that have taken years to build can become instantly and seriously jeopardized when parents make a determinations that their children have been treated unfairly by school personnel.

Recommendations

School leaders need to carefully listen to the positions presented by all involved parties on various issues, particularly those that are relevant to the budget. This is especially important when there are competing priorities for limited resources. They also need to use good judgment when deliberating on the multitude of factors that ultimately comprise a free and appropriate public education for specific students. Showing respect, carefully weighing all factors, and consistently exercising fairness in decision-making practices are also vital for negotiating across the many constituencies who place multiple and conflicting demands on school leaders. When finding themselves in intense situations where differing opinions are articulated by various parties, it is essential that leaders carefully listen to all perspectives, requests, and demands, and then act with prudence.

Leaders may also need to help others reexamine the "big picture" on occasion. In doing so, it may be useful to frequently restate the district mission, philosophy, beliefs, values, and commitments relative to special education in order to remind others of the school's genuine commitment to serve all students, including those with disabilities. Further, it may be necessary to explain specific provisions of special education law and policy, along with primary considerations that are used for decision making at the local level, so that others can gain a better understanding of the rationale for why certain determinations are made in particular situations relative to students who manifest exceptional needs. Explaining why and how difficult or unpopular decisions are arrived at may not reduce all conflicts; however, this practice can sometimes assist in diffusing at least some of the tensions.

Conflict resolution is an area that deserves particular attention. Traditionally, school professionals have been uncomfortable addressing conflict. Professionals often avoid conflict when school culture has emphasized isolation (Friend & Cook, 2000). Contemporary participatory governance approaches engage more individuals in decision making, and this approach can also result in more conflicts. It is very important that school leaders consistently model desirable conflict-resolution practices. School leaders can also facilitate learning about conflict-resolution approaches by organizing forums where various real-world scenarios are shared by team members, along with corresponding strategies for resolving specific types of problems. Further, it is important to articulate the goal of arriving at "win-win" solutions whenever possible.

On occasion, school leaders may need to access consultants who can provide them with sound advice and technical assistance relative to difficult special education issues or concerns. A multitude of negative and potentially embarrassing situations might be avoided if the school leader is wise enough to seek appropriate consultation when the situation warrants. It can be challenging, time consuming, and costly to keep abreast of all the critical information that one must know regarding special education legislation, litigation, funding, service-delivery options, and effective instructional practices. However, it ultimately may be more time consuming and costly not to do so. School leaders should exercise scrutiny when determining if and when they need assistance, and which individuals they might consult for advisement on important matters.

Formally convened mediations and fair hearings may be employed in more challenging cases that cannot be resolved through the usual channels of parent-professional conferencing and Individualized Education Program (IEP) meetings. Legal action may result when amenable solutions between aggrieved parties cannot be reached after all prior avenues of due process are exhausted. Of course, school leaders should negotiate in good faith to reach reasonable solutions whenever possible. In their discussion of teachers and the law, Fisher, Schimmel, and Stellman (2003) emphasized that going to court is expensive, both emotionally and financially. Further, the authors indicated that litigation tends to intensify conflict and polarize participants. For obvious reasons, investments into efforts toward conflict prevention are likely to lead to the most desirable outcomes.

Very importantly, after thoughtful deliberation, special education leaders must have the courage to take strong stances on difficult issues amidst demanding circumstances and then defend their positions on those issues, even when the decisions may be unpopular. Finally, leaders at all levels must learn to contain their own personal tensions and frustrations when they realize that on occasion, the outcome of a dispute may not result in what is desired as the optimal solution. Sometimes it seems that all one can do is accept the bold realities, learn everything possible from the situation, and move on.

DIVERSE CONSTITUENCIES AND MULTIPLE PERSPECTIVES

Recognizing that numerous stakeholders play integral roles in the development, delivery, and evaluation of special education programs, it is common to find that a wide range of perspectives surfaces in discussions about students with disabilities. There can be tremendous disparity in concerns, interests, and recommendations for desired practice from among internal school and district constituencies as well as from among external stakeholders. Concerns at all levels must be given the attention they deserve. However, it can sometimes be extremely difficult to achieve consensus on how to satisfactorily address various issues, especially when there are tremendous discrepancies in opinions about proposed solutions to specific problems. Just as tremendous diversity is evident among student bodies, tremendous diversity also exists among the families and community members who actively participate in decision-making processes regarding students who manifest exceptional needs to the degree that they require special education services.

Many factors can positively or negatively influence the beliefs and opinions that one holds about students with disabilities as well as the nature of the programs and services that should be provided to address their special needs. Some of those factors may be emotionally based and therefore "invisible." For example, some individuals are more comfortable than others in their engagements with persons with disabilities. To illustrate, individuals who are fearful of those who manifest disabilities may be somewhat apprehensive in their interactions and therefore very reticent to engage with persons whose physical, mental, and/or behavioral characteristics are quite obvious and perhaps draw a significant amount of attention. They might even avoid interactions altogether, except on a very superficial level. Yet some who have had firsthand experience with students who manifest disabilities may exude tremendous confidence in their interactions. Consequently, it is not surprising to discover that differences in perspectives are evident among special education leaders, various stakeholders, including parents, and persons with disabilities themselves.

Those who receive special education services represent an incredibly heterogeneous population in that they possess a very wide range of abilities and disabilities. It is unrealistic to expect that everyone would have the same, or even similar, attitudes, beliefs, philosophies, and opinions about matters such as these that have the capacity to stir deep emotions and can often inspire great passion at a very personal level in each individual.

Recommendations

Given the reality that multiple perspectives predictably exist among diverse groups of stakeholders, I propose that all involved parties stay keenly focused on *student needs* and consider them the *central driving force for making decisions* about how to organize curriculum, instruction, and support services for those students who manifest disabilities. At the outset, it is recommended that school leaders make a genuine effort to learn about the characteristics and needs of students with disabilities who are served in their programs. At a minimum, it is recommended that they form personal relationships with a representative sample of students who manifest exceptional needs as well as with their families. By learning from firsthand experiences, leaders can enhance their knowledge and skills considerably. Subsequently, they can make determinations and judgments with more confidence and with greater conviction about meaningful ways to allocate resources and to orchestrate services for specific students with disabilities and then realize the ultimate goal of producing positive learning outcomes for all students.

School leaders must assure that student performance and achievement are continually assessed for all students, and they must subsequently assure that teachers respond to changes in student learning and growth by routinely making the appropriate instructional adaptations. Keeping abreast of the wide range of needs that students across the spectrum of disabilities possess can pose daunting challenges. At the same time, if school leaders are to genuinely serve all students effectively, they must fine-tune their instructional focus so that they can zero in on the learning needs of all. They must also be able to speak with authority to the many audiences who hold keen interest in the learning needs of students with disabilities. At all levels, school leaders must exercise creativity and flexibility when crafting service-delivery models, curriculum, instructional methodologies, and assessment practices if they are to facilitate optimal student learning environments for students with disabilities.

In contrast to this style of programming is that of organizing and delivering instructional services in modes that facilitate administrative convenience, but not necessarily in ways that enhance student learning. Within this framework, programs may be easy to manage; however, the needs of the system are given greater priority than the special learning needs of individual students. Consequently, children and youth are forced to fit into delivery models that are not necessarily responsive to their particular needs.

Leaders of special education programs should insist on the utilization of positive practices among all team members and assure that everyone recognizes how their constructive interaction patterns ultimately enhance the team dynamic. Effective leaders of special education services also need to help everyone know the roles and responsibilities of team members, and they need to diplomatically and firmly enforce boundary issues among various members of the interdisciplinary team.

It is extremely desirable that those who serve as leaders of special education programs possess and model effective interpersonal communication skills, especially in the area of listening. In particular, the principal's ability to cultivate relationships, build teams, and implement shared leadership practices is especially important to their ultimate success as leaders of interdisciplinary and interagency collaboration initiatives. Additionally, they must be able to effectively collaborate with interagency audiences so that they can obtain resources required for addressing student needs that are more involved and technical in nature. Among the types of agencies that might be consulted to provide expert consultation and specialty programs are those concerned with health, social services, and law enforcement. Public schools may also contract with nonpublic and private schools because they provide viable services and program alternatives for many students.

Because their needs are central to team discussions, persons with disabilities and their parents are important members of the interdisciplinary team. Therefore, it is vital that leaders are especially sensitive and responsive to their concerns and questions. In their discussion of communications between parents and professionals, Ulrich and Bauer (2003) proposed a "levels of awareness" framework for working with families that is grounded in transformation experiences as presented by Senge (1990). This approach offers a potentially useful method for understanding the family's construction of disability as well as one's own method of understanding the same.

Leaders should also maintain personal integrity by delivering on their promises to parents and families. Further, they should insist that all others uphold the same standards relative to integrity. Regular communications and timely follow-through can serve to greatly enhance relations with parents and families of students with exceptional needs.

THE GENERAL EDUCATION/SPECIAL EDUCATION INTERFACE

According Gartner and Kerzner Lipsky (2002), the essential feature of the 1997 amendments to the IDEA legislation is the requirement that a student with disabilities be involved and progress in the general curriculum. The general curriculum is defined as that which is required by each state for students in general education. A major implication is that those who presently provide instruction in either general or special education settings must know the general curriculum, and they must be masterful at paving the roads of access to that curriculum for students with disabilities. The IDEA legislation further increased the momentum of the inclusion movement that was already in motion for several years at the time the IDEA amendments were passed in the 1990s.

Clearly, the contemporary trend is to implement inclusive practices; however, there is not consensus among the education community or the general public about the exact meaning of inclusion and what effective inclusive practices should look like in various settings. In a recent publication about reform in special education, the following statement relative to inclusion was made:

The present inclusion movement tells a tale of ambivalent goals and muddied outcomes, a tale of confusion between the philosophic and the pragmatic as well as between intention and implementation. So far, the debate on inclusion has been largely at the university level rather than at the level of teacher and parent participation, on the highly visible dimension of placement rather than on the level of curriculum, and about conceptual needs rather than about practical needs. (Winzer, 2002, p. 7)

In spite of this confusion, a major implication of this law is that all leaders of special education programs must come together to grapple with their best determinations about how to define and implement inclusive practices appropriate to their educational settings. In doing so, they must give consideration to arguments that can be made in favor of inclusive practices as well as those that are made against them.

Arguments in favor of inclusion are plentiful. For example, Lewis and Doorlag (2003) explained that many benefits accrue when students with special needs are members of general education classrooms, including the fact that they remain with their peers, they are not segregated from normal activities of the day, and labeling is deemphasized. The authors further explained that general education students also benefit from association with their peers with special needs, as do general and special education teachers and specialists as a result of their collaborations on given students. Bray Stainback (2000) stated that every day that a student remains in a segregated setting, he or she is being denied opportunities to learn with and from their peers. Further, she explained that a lack of self-confidence, lack of motivation, and lack of positive expectations for achievement result from segregated learning environments. Another argument in favor of inclusion is that academic success and achievement result from appropriate instruction. Wood (1993) supported this argument and stated that improved social and emotional growth are also benefits that accrue from inclusion. Last, many parents are passionately in favor of inclusion and want their children educated in the regular classroom environment with nondisabled peers.

On the other hand, parents may become fearful for the physical, psychological, and emotional safety of their children when they are placed in a general education environment that is not well supported. Also, they may fear that their children will not receive the same levels of individualized instruction that they receive in segregated special education settings with special education teachers. Another argument against inclusion is that some general education teachers do not have the knowledge, skills, or perhaps the desire or disposition to serve students with special needs and are therefore reluctant to serve those students. A dark side presented by Wood (1998) is that often people with the least knowledge are making educational delivery and curriculum decisions. Considering a bigger picture, Wood further explained that state mandates are sometimes not only inappropriate but also unreasonable for developing programs at the local level. Further, the author commented on how those who establish certification requirements for teacher training programs sometimes lack current knowledge of education.

Issues and concerns can also arise for school leaders around practices pertaining to strategic delivery mechanisms. In larger programs especially there is considerable potential for possible "breakdowns" in the efficient and effective delivery of services for special needs students. Because special education programs must be individualized, and because numerous types of services might be required for a given student, discrepancies in communications can easily occur between any of the involved parties, including school administrators, general and special education teachers, support personnel, and parents. Further, there can be miscommunications among team members that impact efficient transitions to and from required services at a given school site. Special attention is also required when students must move between locations to receive services, whether at the school site or to other locations. Similarly, grade level transitions are sometimes not smooth between the sending and receiving teachers. Communications between administrative offices can also add to the chaos and confusion in some instances. The lack of communications between home and school poses yet another area where significant communication breakdowns can occur.

Frequently adding to the tensions is a lack of full or even partial funding required for implementing important initiatives. Additional stress factors result from increased performance expectations for everyone in the education arena as a result of the accountability movement. One potential threat for those in general education is that achievement and performance data gleaned from those students in special education might lower overall school performance data, depending on how that data is factored into school performance results. Finally, adding to an already aggravated situation are the conflicting views resulting from a dual behavior management system.

Unquestionably, the many challenges are great for the school leader in the area of inclusion. The principal plays an especially crucial role in assuring that all students have access to the general education curriculum. A recent study by Praisner (2003) provided important insights about the attitudes of elementary school principals. In a survey of 408 elementary school principals, relationships regarding attitudes toward inclusion and variables such as training and experience and placement perceptions were examined. Results from this study indicated that about one in five principals' attitudes toward inclusion are positive whereas most are uncertain. Importantly, positive experiences with students with disabilities and exposure to special education concepts were associated with a more positive attitude toward inclusion. Further, findings indicated that principals with more positive attitudes and/or experiences were more likely to place students in less restrictive settings. Finally, Praisner (2003) concluded from her results the importance of inclusionary practices that give principals positive experiences with students of all types of disabilities as well as provide principals with more specific training.

Recommendations

Because those who oversee special education programs must navigate so many critical tension points at all levels in the general education/special education interface, several recommendations centered on a variety of themes are presented to assist school leaders with effective implementation of inclusive practices. They are: (a) personal qualities, (b) positive professional practice, (c) providing support, (d) communications, (e) professional development, (f) networking, and (g) cultivating leadership. First, it is important that school leaders at all levels become proactive by investing into planning so that they can cast a collective vision relative to their values and beliefs about what inclusive practices should look like and how they should be manifest in specific school environments. Extensive discussions are required at all levels if one seeks to change the school culture and climate in meaningful ways. Leaders should also help to bring focus to desired practices and then provide a plan for bringing those ideas into fruition. As stated previously, it is imperative that the leaders at all levels know the law and the rights of students with disabilities and their parents, especially as they pertain to their job role. At the same time, it is recommended that leaders learn all they can about student characteristics, interests, and needs of those with disabilities, in part by forming meaningful personal relationships with these students and their families.

Discussions about the need for school leaders to know special education law are much more plentiful in the professional literature than are discussions about the fundamental need for the leader to possess an appropriate disposition and a set of desirable core beliefs that enable him or her to effectively engage with all students, and especially with those who manifest disabilities. Goleman, Boyatzis, and McKee (2002) spoke to the emotional task of the leader:

> This emotional task of the leader is primal—that is, first—in two senses: It is both the original and the most important act of leadership. Throughout history, and in cultures everywhere, the leader in any human group has been one to whom others look for assurance and clarity when facing uncertainty or threat, or when there's a job to be done. The leader acts as the group's

emotional guide. . . . In the modern organization, this primordial emotional
task—though now largely invisible—remains foremost among the many jobs of
leadership: driving the collective emotions in a positive direction and clearing
the smog created by toxic emotions. This task applies to leadership everywhere,
from the boardroom to the shop floor. (p. 5)

Vital personal attributes and professional dispositions that should be possessed by all school leaders include the leader's ability to demonstrate genuine acceptance, caring, concern, respect, and compassion for *all* students.
So many critical actions and decisions about the education and general
welfare of students with disabilities can stem from personal attributes, dispositions, and core beliefs. These factors and core beliefs tend to reflect
one's attitudes, values, and philosophies about a multitude of issues, and
in this case, about students with exceptional needs. If the leader is to embrace Goleman and colleagues' (2002) hypothesis and act as the group's
emotional guide, and if he or she is to drive the collective emotions in a
positive direction, it seems only logical that demonstration of highly desirable personal attributes, professional dispositions, and core beliefs in the
leader must be clearly evident. Further, it is important that the leader is sensitive to fears communicated by others, including fears expressed by general
and special education teachers. The leader should be especially sensitive to
student and parent fears. Responsiveness to all parties and a sincere commitment to serve every student in a quality manner should be obvious to all
stakeholders, resulting in a climate where everyone who is embraced within
the school community is valued.

A related area that should be given attention by the leader is that of positive professional practice. By modeling desired behavior and skills and by
providing encouragement to all, the leader helps to set the tone and further establish the preferred culture he or she wishes to achieve. When the
leader can look for potential in everyone, set high expectations, and build
on the strengths of each individual in his or her sphere of influence, the
leader's actions can make an important statement. Taking the extra time
to recognize and reward effective practice and good efforts can go a long
way in helping to inspire everyone on the interdisciplinary team. It is also
important that school leaders at all levels proactively enforce a policy of zero
tolerance regarding bullying or teasing of any student. If one does not act
on these inappropriate behaviors, they are inadvertently reinforcing those
behaviors in others, and they are communicating a powerful endorsement
of such behavior from someone who holds a position of authority. Last, it
is vitally important to stay apprised of empirically validated models of inclusive practices that have application for students with disabilities. Whenever
possible, changes to existing practice should be argued based on findings
from research-based practices.

The school leader's skill and willingness to provide support to all team members is vitally important to the success of the general education/special education interface. Among the areas to be considered is time for all team members, especially general and special education teachers, to genuinely communicate so that they can plan and carefully deliberate on student needs, instructional strategies, student progress, and recognition that is given for achieving milestones in all program settings. The efforts of all team members should be carefully coordinated. Leaders need to keep abreast of key findings from these conversations, and they need to assure that all aspects of the IEP are being delivered, including provisions regarding equipment, materials, supplies, and transportation. School leaders can also provide support by organizing forums for sharing solutions to problems that have produced conflict among team members. All team members can gain a great deal of knowledge by learning from strategies that have worked in a given situation. They can also benefit by learning about those strategies that failed.

Communication is another area requiring attention for an effective interface between general and special education. Those who lead special education programs would be wise to devote significant time, talent, and resources to the design of clearly articulated, comprehensive, integrated communication systems that are genuinely responsive to the diverse needs of students with disabilities and their families. A functional and well-coordinated communication structure that effectively serves all personnel who manage or administer any aspect of the special education program should be incorporated into the communication system.

Ongoing professional development and training is an absolute must for those who lead or serve the area of special education in any way. This is a perpetually changing field, as are all areas of education at this time. School leaders must instill in themselves and in others a philosophy of continuous learning about all aspects of special education, including student characteristics, behavior management, student and program assessment, effective instructional practices, law, litigation, and discoveries from research in education, administration, psychology, and education. The audience for professional development is wide. At a minimum, top school officials should assure that support for these activities is made available to leaders at all levels, and especially to teachers, related service personnel, and to parents and family members as appropriate. To help guide others, leaders may choose to share their own journeys in professional growth relative to special education. Professional development is an area that requires thoughtful planning and coordination. Priorities will need to be clearly established, and activities will need to be carefully coordinated in order to maximize funding for these activities.

Learning how to network effectively can be a lifesaver for leaders of special education programs. Whether one needs to network internally with other school leaders, professionals members of the interdisciplinary team, and parents and families, or among key members of the community, these types of connections are vitally important if one is to know the extent of available resources and to utilize them to the utmost of their ability. By exercising help-seeking behaviors and employing effective networking strategies, one can become greatly empowered as a leader of special education programs. Most importantly, students with disabilities can greatly capitalize on information and resources that are utilized to enhance their educational experiences.

Finally, school leaders are advised to identify potential special education leaders and to cultivate knowledge, skills, abilities, and dispositions in those who demonstrate the potential to lead, including those individuals who manifest disabilities. According to Goad (1996), an administrator of special education programs faces difficult challenges because of job complexity, lack of adequate training, isolation from other administrators, role ambiguity, and frequent turnover in positions. Therefore, mentoring new special education leaders can be crucially important to their continued success.

Maxwell (1995) provided a number of reasons for why leaders need to develop leaders. He argued that those closest to the leader will determine the success level of that leader, and that those leaders who mentor potential leaders multiply their effectiveness. He also stated that developed leaders expand and enhance the future of the organization (pp. 3–12). Because the delivery of quality special education programs requires the engagement of so many individuals at so many different levels, it seems only logical that those in top leadership positions would invite and reward good leadership from among all ranks at the school or district level. One's effectiveness can be increased greatly by wisely choosing and cultivating those leaders who can serve to extend one's agenda. Given the challenging nature of the field of special education, it would be wise for leaders at all levels to give careful thought to their investments in those who can serve to advance their special education initiatives.

SUMMARY

This chapter serves to explore several key issues that frequently generate tensions and controversies in the field of special education. After presenting three basic assumptions about leaders in this area, I provide information about the need for informed and competent leadership and then explore the role of the special education leader. Most of the chapter is centered on discussions of three special education issues often fraught with tensions and controversies. Varying perspectives portraying the areas of potential conflict are presented along with suggestions and recommendations to help reduce the tensions and controversies surrounding these issues. A summary of key ideas and concepts is presented.

GUIDING QUESTIONS

1. Given what you have learned about the multiple and conflicting demands placed on school leaders, what key personal attributes, professional dispositions, and core beliefs must one possess in order to effectively lead special education programs, and why?

2. As a school leader, you wish to consider expanding inclusive practices for children and youth with disabilities at your school. What are the arguments you might anticipate from general education teachers in favor of more inclusive practices? What arguments might you hear against inclusive practices?

3. What are the arguments for and against expanding practices of inclusion that you might anticipate from among special education teachers?

4. How would you explain and justify the need for a dual behavior management system to your general education teachers, to their parents, and to other students?

5. What are the pros and cons of the current accountability movement relative to the field of special education? Can you provide an argument that parents of children with disabilities might pose in favor of the accountability movement? What arguments might they make against the accountability movement?

CASE STUDY

Two students engage in a fight in the cafeteria during the lunch period. As witnessed by their teacher, the one who initiated the skirmish was a special education student whose IEP indicates that he has a primary disability of "behavior disorders" and that he should be served in a self-contained class with others who have similar needs for most of the school day. The other boy is in general education and manifests no known disabilities. It was necessary for the boy in general education to be medically treated for a fractured wrist as a result of the fight. Parents of the boy in special education are furious and are claiming that the boy in general education provoked their child into this action by making fun of him and calling him names. They want him suspended immediately. Parents of the boy in general education are very angry and insist that the boy with behavior disorders has a reputation of bullying others and getting into fights at school. They are furious that their son was injured at school. Also, they want both boys to receive the same discipline. The principal must take action.

1. Identify the valid facts, issues, and problems to be solved in this scenario.
2. Prioritize those issues and problems that need to be solved and provide your rationale.
3. Identify any apprehensions or concerns that you might have in a school leadership role as you consider key aspects of the situation.
4. Consider if there are any other individuals you would employ to help resolve the problem. If so, what role(s) would they play in doing so?
5. What are the specific strategies and timelines that you would include in your action plan to bring closure to this problem?
6. Consider whether your approach to addressing this issue in an elementary school setting would be different from how it might be in a middle school or high school setting. If so, why and how would it be different?

SELECTED READINGS

Hammeken, P. A. (2000). *Inclusion: 450 strategies for success: A practical guide for all educators who teach students with disabilities*. Minnetonka, MN: Peytral Publications, Inc.

Hepworth Berger, E. (2000). *Parents as partners in education*. Columbus, OH: Merrill.

Heward, W. L. (2003). *Exceptional children: An introduction to special education*. Columbus, OH: Merrill/Prentice-Hall.

McLean Benner, S. (1998). *Special education issues within the context of American society*. Belmont, CA: Wadsworth.

Obiakor, F. E., Utley, C. A., & Rotatori, A. F. (Eds.). (2003). *Effective education for learners with exceptionalities*. Oxford: Elsevier.

Woolfolk Hoy, A., & Kolter Hoy, W. (2003). *Instructional leadership: A learning-centered guide*. Boston: Allyn & Bacon.

Ysseldyke, J., Algozzine, B., & Thurlow, M. (2000). *Critical issues in special education*. Boston: Houghton Mifflin.

REFERENCES

Bray Stainback, S. (2000). The inclusion movement: A goal for restructuring special education. In M. A. Winzer & K. Mazurek (Eds.), *Special education in the 21st century: Issues of inclusion and reform* (pp. 27–40). Washington, DC: Gallaudet University Press.

Chase Thomas, C., Correa, V. I., & Voelker Morsink, C. (2001). *Interactive teaming: Enhancing programs for students with special needs*. Columbus, OH: Merrill/Prentice-Hall.

Davidson, D. N., & Algozzine, B. (2002). Administrators' knowledge of expected special education practice. *Educational Leadership and Administration, 14*, 135–147.

Drake, T. L., & Roe, W. H. (2003). *The principalship.* Columbus, OH: Merrill/Prentice Hall.

Fisher, L., Schimmel, D., & Stellman, L. R. (2003). *Teachers and the law.* Boston: Allyn & Bacon.

Friend, M., & Cook, L. (2000). *Interactions: Collaboration skills for school professionals.* New York: Longman.

Gartner, A., & Kerzner Lipsky, D. (2002). *Inclusion: A service, not a place, a whole school approach.* Port Chester, NY: Dude Publishing.

Goad, L. C. (1996). *Descriptive study of assigned and unassigned relationships of first year special education administrators in Virginia.* PhD dissertation, Virginia Polytechnic Institute and State University.

Goleman, D., Boyatzis, R., & McKee, A. (2002). *Primal leadership: Realizing the power of emotional intelligence.* Boston: Harvard Business School Press.

Hanson, E. M. (1979). *Educational administration and organizational behavior.* Boston: Allyn & Bacon.

Hughes, L. W. (1999). *The principal as leader.* Columbus, OH: Merrill.

Hughes, L. W., & Ubben, G. C. (1994). *The elementary principal's handbook: A guide to effective action.* Boston: Allyn & Bacon.

Lewis, R. B., & Doorlag, D. H. (2003). *Teaching special students in general education classrooms.* Columbus, OH: Merrill/Prentice-Hall.

Maxwell, J. C. (1995). *The leaders around you: How to help others reach their full potential.* Nashville, TN: Thomas Nelson Publishers.

Praisner, C. L. (2003). Attitudes of elementary school principals toward the inclusion of students with disabilities. *Exceptional Children, 69,* 135–145.

Quality counts: "Count me in: Special education in an era of standards." (2004, January). *Education Week, 23*(17). (With support from the Pew Charitable Trusts).

Senge, P. (1990). *The 5th dimension: The art and practice of the learning organization.* New York: Doubleday.

Turnbull, A. P., & Turnbull, H. R. (1997). *Families, professionals, and exceptionality: A special partnership.* Columbus, OH: Merrill/Prentice Hall.

Turnbull, A., & Turnbull, R. (2001). *Families, professionals, and exceptionality: Collaborating for empowerment.* Columbus, OH: Merrill/Prentice Hall.

Ubben, G. C., Hughes, L. W., & Norris, C. J. (2001). *The principal: Creative leadership for effective schools.* Boston: Allyn & Bacon.

Ulrich, M. E., & Bauer, A. M. (2003). Levels of awareness: A closer look at communication between parents and professionals. *Exceptional Children, 35*(6), 20–24.

Walther-Thomas, C., & DiPaola, M. F. (2003). What instructional leaders need to know about special education. In W. A. Owings & L. S. Kaplan (Eds.), *Best practices, best thinking, and emerging issues in school leadership* (pp. 125–136). Thousand Oaks, CA: Corwin Press.

Winzer, M. A. (2002). The inclusion movement: Review and reflections on reform in special education. In M. A. Winzer & K. Mazurek (Eds.), *Special education in the 21st century: Issues of inclusion and reform* (p. 7). Washington, DC: Galludet University Press.

Wood, J. W. (1993). *Mainstreaming: A practical approach for teachers.* Columbus, OH: Merrill/Prentice-Hall.

Wood, J. W. (1998). *Adapting instruction to accommodate students in inclusive settings.* Columbus, OH: Merrill.

Yell, M. L. (1998). *The law and special education.* Upper Saddle River, NJ: Prentice-Hall.

Chapter 12

What's at Stake for High-Quality Art Education in a High-Stakes Testing Era? The Importance of Escaping a View-Master® Conception of Education

Sara Wilson McKay
Texas Tech University

While You Were Sleeping. Copyright 2003 by Haden Garrett. Reprinted with permission.

> *As long as art is the beauty parlor of civilization,*
> *neither art nor civilization is secure.*
>
> —Dewey (1934, p. 344)

In watching my daughter, a toddler, explore for the first time my childhood View-Master® complete with a souvenir slide set of Elvis at Graceland, I noted how she engaged with the toy. She explored at length its lever that changed the picture on display; she looked through the lenses on both ends, noticing the differences of each. But ultimately, after she had learned how it worked, she settled on the conventional way of using the toy, content to click through the alternate fixed scenes and was happy to sit through the cycle of 12 pictures more than once—eyes fixed on the static pictures before her.

Much teaching today, even in some poorly conceptualized art education classrooms, is akin to the clicking through of fixed scenes on a View-Master®—educating students how to conquer (or master) whatever is before them. The "what" might be math equations or a descriptive paragraph, or whatever is the current test topic d'jeur. In many classrooms today, there is very little time (and in some cases, interest) to consider anything beyond the test objectives, and the result is often a lack of interest in actually knowing if there might indeed be anything else to know or learn. In short, students are taught to accept that the only things that matter are the fixed views of the View-Master®. Creative exploration shuts down and wondering of what is in between the captured moments is lost, as students learn to focus only on the information presented.

Although many educational researchers have assessed the impact of high-stakes testing on learning (Hargreaves, 2003; Thompson, 2001; Kohn, 2001; Sheldon & Biddle, 1998), in their comprehensive review of the Texas State standardized test (TAAS), McNeil and Valenzuela (2000) invoked a similar View-Master® conception of the unavoidable impact standardized tests have on learning:

> The TAAS mode of learning is to "master" brief, discreet, randomly selected pieces of information. The reading comprehension and grammatical sections of the writing TAAS, for example, cover isolated skills through very brief written passages. These written passages are not intended to build a cumulative knowledge base; they are not meant to connect with children's understanding. (p. 14)

McNeil and Valenzuela go on to suggest that when test-prep takes the place of substantive curriculum, as it frequently does in many underresourced schools, all that remains are the isolated bits of information meant to pass for education; in short, a View-Master® conception of education.

In an educational environment where statistics, teacher pay, administrator job security, and school district reputation all depend on students getting the right answer, the outcome of such a system is a graduate (or very likely a drop-out) whose natural curiosity and passion for learning has been squelched. The strategies schools choose to employ to meet numbers and quotas for test results generally leave little time for the complexity of learning. Students are trained to simplify all information to arrive at the right answer.

High-quality art education is an antidote, of sorts, to the scenario described earlier. High-quality art education requires that students and teachers safeguard and utilize their curiosity. Most importantly, high-quality art education requires and values a variety of answers to questions, and particularly that we cultivate an interest in viewing things from more than one point of view, to truly investigate the complexity of the realities we are exploring.

In this chapter, we thus consider the following question: How does high-quality art education interrupt static pictures of education and draw out multiple perspectives that are connective visions between the static frames that standardized tests are designed to measure? Asked another way in terms of school leadership, the question reads: How can school leaders expand their understanding of the role of art education in a high-stakes testing climate?

The chapter is organized as a piece of what Elliot Eisner (1998) called educational criticism, including: (a) a description of the scenarios of what is at stake for high-quality art education in a high-stakes testing climate; (b) interpretation of the high-stakes testing educational climate using various theoretical lenses; (c) evaluation of four different field-based examples; and (d) an assessment of the thematics, or generalized ideas, that have evolved through this investigation. The chapter concludes with a summary of the major ideas about this issue and presents a scenario to test understanding of the complexities of this issue after reading the chapter.

DEFINITION OF THE ISSUE

This book is designed to address current issues in education, issues having been defined as those ideas that derive from tension or, as Hughes states in the introduction to this text, cognitive dissonance. Certainly the many perspectives about what the role of art education should be in schools in a high-stakes testing era is just such an issue. In describing a few of those perspectives of art education, I work toward what Eisner (1998) considered a "thick description" of any scenario one is choosing to look at critically: A "thick description is an effort aimed at interpretation, at getting below the surface ... to the construction of meaning" (p. 15). Thus, consider the following four scenarios.

1. **Skill, drill, and kill.** In this version of art education, school leaders dedicate all resources to ensure students can pass each test, jump through each hoop, achieve every static view of what counts as education that is imagined in a high-stakes testing era. In this scenario, no time or energy will be devoted to anything not directly assessed on the test; therefore, instruction in the art classroom should be entirely devoted to helping students read better, solve math problems, and so on, discontinuing all art instruction while preparing for the test. Art is not tested and should therefore not be taught during test time or at all.

2. **Art as the helpmate to testing.** Attitudes toward art education in this version suggest that resources should be devoted to art education because students who win art contests and have a little downtime during the day make better, happier test takers. Whenever possible, basic academic concepts should be taught in the art classroom through art. It is another way to reach those students who understand concepts in a different way. Thus, art teachers should teach writing and problem solving in concrete ways, like by writing descriptive paragraphs about artworks and using ratio to enlarge a work of art. The students will not even know they are learning test skills because art is so much fun.

3. **Art as therapy and a source of enrichment.** This common attitude toward art education is related to the previous one but has a crucial attitudinal distinction: a belief that art is separate from "real" knowledge. In this version of art education, resources should be allocated to art education because the arts are the only place for emotional outlet and cultural development within the school system. Students need to learn the language of art in order to understand the cultural enhancement the arts provide and so that they can freely express themselves as an alternative to and refuge from the academic pressures of high-stakes tests. The major belief here is that indulging this kind of art has nothing to do with the learning or academic skills needed for a complete life; rather, art education in this respect is the proverbial "frill" subject that performs important psychological functions on occasion, but most generally it is separate from anything important in school or life.

4. **Art as complex and critical experience.** A fourth attitude toward art education suggests that resources should be devoted to high-quality art education because it promotes critical thinking that indirectly impacts students' performance on tests, but more valuably, it promotes an idea of education that goes beyond fixed visions of discreet information to be learned and regurgitated. High-quality art education considers aesthetic dimensions of art that are difficult—unsettled ideas that can be pursued for a lifetime. It involves educating students to critically perceive art and their environment, deliberately looking for more than one viewpoint or interpretation of an idea. This form of art education cultivates the skills and roles that are

inherently democratic and necessary as a component of critical American education.

Given at least these four possible views of the role of art in the schools, the issue can clearly be stated that the importance of art education in a high-stakes testing era is a matter of wide debate. This question follows: What impacts various audiences' perceptions of the importance of art education? A place to begin thinking about this question is to ask "who is being educated?"

DESCRIPTION: WHO IS BEING EDUCATED?

In *The Development Dictionary* (Sachs, 1992), several authors take aim at the discourse of development, which generally employs Western notions of progress as justification for colonialist behavior. The text problematizes a naïve view of "progress" by identifying flawed and short-sighted buzzwords that are frequently touted by policy makers. One such notion that is frequently mobilized in the name of "progress" is the concept of schooling, an idea that Ivan Illich challenged in his *Deschooling Society* in 1973: "the pupil is thereby 'schooled' to confuse teaching with learning, grade advancement with education, a diploma with competence, and fluency with the ability to say something new" (p. 9). Illich's (1992) later entry in *The Development Dictionary* overtly addresses schooling as the antidote for the concept of manufactured needs. Illich (1992) argued that the institution of education, and more specifically of schooling, is a direct response to a growing discourse of needs. He differentiated between schooling and learning, claiming a falsity of education in the name of "needs." This idea is very similar to social theorist Thomas Docherty's (1996) discussion of education narrowly conceived of as a process of correction.

Illich goes on to suggest that much institutionalized schooling really serves a definition of humans that is akin to *homo economicus,* by meeting only the minimum defined needs for efficiency; ultimately such a form of education creates a type of person that is better described as *homo systematicus*: "Thus, the human phenomenon is no longer defined by what we *are,* what we face, what we can take, what we dream . . . but by the measure of what we lack and, therefore, need" (1992, p. 99). The results of such a needs-oriented approach to life (which is a windfall to niche markets) can be witnessed in parents' desperation to meet the "needs" of their infants with the latest multilingual gadget for the nursery and Baby Einstein tapes and videos for their 3-month-olds. Is *homo systematicus,* the institutionalized product of needs discourse, really who we want to be educating? The costs of such a narrow,

market-driven definition of education are far grander for political and
social policies. The definition of who we are educating begs investigation
if we are to think through what substantively constitutes education.

Social theorist Ellen Dissanayake (1995) named an alternate conception
of person to be educated in her book *Homo Aestheticus: Where Art Comes from
and Why*. This species-centric view of art creates a demand to educate *homo
aestheticus*—the necessarily aesthetic and artistic human: "Once we recognize
that art is intrinsic to our specieshood (our *humanity*)—each of us should
feel permission and justification for taking the trouble to live our life with
care and thought for its quality rather than being helplessly caught up in the
reductive and alienating pragmatic imperatives of consumer and efficiency-
oriented and 'entertain-me' society" (p. 225). Dissanayake (1995) cited examples from preliterate societies in which the necessary face to face for
communication resulted in shared meanings at least between two individuals
(p. 202). According to Dissanayake, the emphasis in such societies on interpersonal meaning has been diminished by increasing modern reliance
on literacy to establish meaning. This is not to say that literacy de facto
creates a less meaningful society, but rather that more work must be done
in addition to learning to read and write to preserve the social context of
meaning.

The efficient and economical education of *homo systematicus* provides no
room for and assigns no value to social variability. Such an approach to
education (reflected in high-stakes testing) reduces "meaningful" learning
to mechanistic needs-driven information acquisition by extracting meaning
making from the social process of learning.

THE FUNCTION OF SCHOOLING

Undoubtedly who we conceptualize that we are educating is important to
shaping attitudes toward the role of art in schools, but additionally the subsequent structuring of the school as an institution has an equally strong impact
on attitudes toward art education. There are as many models for schools as
there are apt metaphors, but I discuss two such structures to demonstrate
further the institutional factors that shape school leaders' perspectives about
art education.

School as Factory

With the invention of the assembly line in the early 1900s, imagining education in a similar vein where individual teachers do their part to the product,
schooling becomes only about outcomes. Measurable outcomes are the basis

for what counts as fully preparing students for jobs and roles in society. The school-to-work notion of education is supported by industry because better workers create better products, which in turn create a more prosperous society. Typically the mode of creating such workers is, following the assembly line metaphor, to deposit the same fixed body of knowledge into students (akin to the banking system of education that was Freire's target). Students, in this system, are all thus able to do the same basic skills that are necessary for the workforce. Variation is not planned for and in fact is viewed as an anomaly or failure in the system.

In this mode of schooling, high-stakes testing is exactly the prescribed model to assess product development. Additionally, in pure business mode, products that do not meet expectations or the standard set by someone at the top become part of a profit and loss statement—profit meaning those students who measure the same as everyone else, and loss meaning those who don't. This is not dissimilar to economic bottom-dollar incentives modeled for us by the likes of Enron and other large corporations. But to follow the Enron model to its unfortunate demise, in the case of drop-out reporting, particularly in Texas, products (students) that do not meet the expected levels of achievement are reported in off-shore accounts. In other words, as Dr. Linda McNeil from Rice University recently commented, high-stakes testing has led to an Enron accounting of results (personal communication, November 2002).

In the school as factory model, teachers become automated with scripts to follow, students become receptacles that are disposed of if they do not meet the standard, and learning is driven and measured by the bottom line. It dictates resource allocation and most importantly disallows any room for creativity, variation, or criticality. Most educators want to believe that this one-size-fits-all system of education is far behind us, but in the era of high-stakes testing when scores are the litmus test for success, uniformity and standardization of teaching practices and student performance gives schools the market advantage.

School as Studio

Another metaphor for examining schooling is much more open. Stevens (2002) suggested conceptualizing schools as an artist's studio: "In schools where works of art and the artistic process provide models for learning and knowing, the school becomes a studio. The student is seen as an artist, having joy in interpreting, presenting, performing and influencing his or her own medium—the quintessential learner" (p. 20). The artist's studio is marked by creativity, experimentation, and critical judgment in the process of accumulating knowledge.

One pervasive characteristic of the school-as-studio approach is that of the "negotiated stakes" students create when engaged with an art critique process. During critique sessions, peers set up the stakes of engaging with new ideas. The critique process is a constant process of valuing choices by "highlighting the consequences of creative choices" (Soep, 2002, p. 15). Through negotiated stakes, students maximize the stakes by actively making work matter, modulating the stakes in ways that invigorate participation. On the opposite end of the spectrum, students minimize stakes in ways that promote creativity and experimentation (Soep, 2002). The concept of negotiated stakes in the school-as-studio model acknowledges the reality of high-pressure moments in learning and life, while also preserving the safe space of creative experimentation necessary for authentic, personalized learning.

Susan Neuman, former assistant secretary of elementary and secondary education and major official responsible for implementing No Child Left Behind (NCLB), was quoted as saying that a goal of the NCLB legislation was the eradication of creative teaching (Balta, V., Stockton Record [California], Friday, October 25, 2002). Clearly the high-stakes accountability model advocated by the Bush administration is contrary to the ideas conceptualized in the school-as-studio model. NCLB not only promotes ideas of standardized input and outcomes, it has punitive repercussions for schools that don't embrace the stakes. How our legislatures define school and then how our school leaders structure those environments both have tremendous impact on the perceived value of art education in schools—as far reaching as an end to all creative teaching in schools and as immediate as no individualized, personalized outcomes in the wake of standardized learning.

INTERPRETATION: THEORETICAL PERSPECTIVES ON THE ISSUE

The descriptions earlier of who is being educated and how schooling is structured lead us to attend to various theoretical perspectives that inform the debate about the role art education should play in schooling. Focusing primarily on what constitutes an experience, this section attends to two related yet distinct philosophies that inform an idea of art education playing a crucial role in achieving a concept of education that goes beyond the View-Master® model of static, discreet bits of knowledge that is reinforced by high-stakes testing. First, philosopher John Dewey's pragmatic writings consider in depth the structure of meaningful experiences and the relationship of art to experience. Second, critical theorists Gilles Deleuze and Felix Guattari posit a rhizomic view of experience, complete with connective grasslike growth in spots that are most fertile and growing around areas that are inhospitable. A discussion of what counts as meaningful experience and how art figures into such experience brings us closer to thinking about the way art figures into meaningful educational experiences more generally.

John Dewey

Dewey's *Art as Experience* (1934) and *Experience and Education* (1997/1938) both focus on experience being demarcated by full awareness, an aesthetic experience. These aesthetic experiences hinge on the distinction between easy recognition (often a process of habitual identification) and perception through which detail and attention to newness or conflict occur. Dewey (1934) described the vast gulf between these two forms of reception. Recognition for Dewey is "perception arrested before it has had a chance to develop freely" (p. 52). He characterized recognition by pointing out the habitual reliance on a stereotype or some other previously formed scheme of recognition that allows us to greet a person on the street without really seeing the person.

Conversely, Dewey (1934) explicated perception as seeing in a pregnant sense, which is to say that it is "an act of reconstructive doing" (p. 53) that makes one fully conscious. For Dewey, an act of perception is therefore a lived body experience through which an entire organism is affected. If we live in a state of easy recognition, we no longer experience a fully embodied life. In short, we are anaesthetized. However, embodied perception uses conflicts between old and new information to slow down our judgment, interrupting easy recognition, in favor of being fully aware of our lived experience. This perceptual moment for Dewey indicates the moment when tension creates reflection, turning an otherwise exercise in recognition into an aesthetic experience. If something beyond the easily recognizable is not sought, our experience of the world is limited.

Deleuze & Guattari

The rhizome and the *and* in educational discourse call for a never-ending vision of what counts as and what informs education. According to Deleuze and Guattari (1983):

> a rhizome doesn't begin and doesn't end, but is always in the middle, between things, inter-being, *intermezzo*. The tree is filiation, but the rhizome is alliance, exclusively alliance. The tree imposes the verb "to be," but the rhizome is woven together with conjunctions: "and ... and ... and ...." (p. 57)

The defining feature of a rhizome is its connection and heterogeneity: Any point on a rhizome can be connected with any other, and must be. There are ruptures in rhizomes but these become part of the rhizome. For example, "we can never get rid of ants, because they form an animal rhizome that never ceases to reconstitute itself, even when almost completely destroyed" (p. 18). Additionally, a wasp and an orchid make a rhizome insofar as they are heterogeneous (p. 19).[1] Music, too (jazz especially), can be rhizomic by "altering codes that structure it or render it arborescent...in its ruptures and proliferations [it] is comparable to a rhizome" (p. 24). The rhizome enacts difference and seeks multiplicity.

PERCEPTION AND THE *AND* IN EDUCATIONAL EXPERIENCE

These two theoretical positions that share a foundation of pragmatics behoove us to ask: What is education if not a series (or a rhizome) of punctuated aesthetic experiences? Dewey (1934) demerited mere recognition in favor of fully experienced perception wherein experience is a fully embodied demarcated aesthetic moment, a moment fully self-aware of how an organism is acting on its environment and how the environment is acting on the organism (p. 53). This kind of experience is punctuated by disruption. Incongruence among our expectations and our experiences constitute disruptions that create more fully aware experiences. This kind of disrupted experience is imperative in order to engender a sense of constant critical change in the status quo. Although often understood in a negative sense, disruption is a marked rejection of fixation and staidness; it marks a distinct propensity for change and novelty, all characteristics that are precluded in the current education systems of "soulless standardization" (Hargreaves, 2003).

With regard to the rhizome and its need to *and*, educational experiences that are always differing and connecting also stand in stark contrast to the system that has evolved to a definition of education marked by that which is on the test. Art, falling outside of that which is tested, is the kind of educational experience that is best described by the rhizome. Looking at art, talking about art, making art, understanding its connections to societies past and present—all of these aspects that are taught and explored in the art classroom require a connective sense of learning and a rejection of finality. The never-ending rhizome mirrors the never finished artwork. For example, when I look at a work of art in my home, I am never done looking at it. It will be different when I look at it tomorrow, next week, and in 10 years. This

---

[1]John Dewey (1934) also spoke of an example in experience wherein organism and environment simultaneously differ yet form a unity: "The epidermis is only the most superficial way an indication of where an organism ends and its environment begins" (p. 58). It is this sense of interconnectedness that the rhizome describes.

variability of art and its processes requires an open concept of experience, one that allows for change and provides space for newness and extensions of new ideas.

So it is with high-quality art education. Beginning in pre-K–12 formal schooling, education systems that are open to such real, meaningful versions of lifelong learning (versus mere lip service to a buzzword) value the role art plays in learning. But various audiences' perceptions of art experiences, including those of school leaders and their beliefs in either fixed or connected visions of what makes education, ultimately determine the value that is assigned to art education in schools. School leaders, through their beliefs and the power to act on their beliefs, end up choosing (often by lack of action) between providing aesthetic experiences for students or, by not valuing art education, effectively administering doses of *anaesthesia* (an-aesthetic education) to their students.

EVALUATION: LOOKING AT SOME EXAMPLES FROM THE FIELD

In this section, we look at a variety of field experiences surrounding the value of art in schooling. Each situation is presented through at least two different views, hopefully to encourage a dialogue among the many views. Presenting a variety of voices on the topic creates an opportunity for readers also to enter into dialogue with the various viewpoints. The range of examples include principal views of how to allocate money for art; parent views of a school dropping an art program from the curriculum; teacher views of how the arts count as education; and student comments during an arts intervention program at various school sites. By looking at each of these real-world examples, the issue of what's at stake for high-quality art education in a high-stakes testing era should become more apparent.

Principal Views of How to Allocate Money for Art

When it comes to allocating funds to art at the school budgetary level, principals, and all their past experiences and beliefs about art, have tremendous power. In general, principals allocate money for art according to their belief in the role of art in education as discussed previously. Those who approach education in a drill-and-kill kind of way generally do not budget for art.

In another scenario common in these budget-tight years when large portions of budgets have to be carved out for test-prep materials, testing coordinators, and the like, principals—even those typically in favor of having an art program in their school—often find themselves deciding whether the art program at their school is a go or not at the very last minute. Each August, as the coordinator of a university art education program, I get calls from principals who have decided they can keep art in the budget. Frequently the format for the art teacher they seek is some kind of part-time appointment, such as a position that is three-fourths of the time art and one-fourth of the time reading lab (for low test performers), or an absurd schedule with the art teacher being scheduled to serve two full classes simultaneously in order to provide classroom teachers their required planning time. This kind of budget allocation is driven by other needs and would fall into the attitude that art can be a helpmate to testing as discussed earlier.

Occasionally, the art teacher who was perhaps at that type of school previously (if in fact there was some degree of art continuity in the school) has sensed a lack of firm commitment from the principal and has already moved on, seeking a more secure, more art-supportive school. Sometimes these teachers find security with principals who believe in art as therapy and a source of enrichment for students. These principals budget for and value their art teacher for the awards and blue ribbons they earn with the students. Time and again, principals I meet with talk about the contest awards and pretty hallways that the art teacher creates, effectively encouraging art teachers in these types of schools to curtail art learning in favor of continuing to please this school's limited expectation of art in schools. In these kinds of schools, there is also frequently a concomitant belief from other teachers or school personnel that the art teacher exists to provide the beauty of the school; art teachers are asked to create banners for spring festivals, centerpieces for back-to-school nights, and birthday cake sculptures for the school's anniversary. Caught between jeopardizing their colleagues' support in general and compromising their rich discipline-based curriculum,[2] many art teachers do much of this kind of work after school hours until they finally give in and forfeit their art curriculum. In short, art experiences in these types of schools do not consider art to have a rich curriculum, but rather it is a place of production and self-esteem building. In such schools, principals allocate money to art contingent, it appears, on winning awards and supporting school activities, not for the value of art itself.

The fourth view of art discussed at the beginning of this chapter considers art as complex and critical experience. Unfortunately, most principals are hardly ever able to act on this level of belief because one of the three previously discussed beliefs has already interfered. A principal leading a school that is in danger of being deemed low performing may chuck art due to a need to drill and kill for test-prep, despite their beliefs in what art can

---

[2]Discipline-Based Art Education (DBAE) requires art teachers to teach all the disciplines of art: (a) art production, (b) art history, (c) art criticism, and (d) aesthetics, the philosophy of art. Such a comprehensive curriculum in art is supported by the National Visual Arts Standards and the National Art Education Association (Wilson, 1997).

provide students. A principal who values art for the complexity and critical experiences it provides may have to abandon this ship because test-prep has defined most of the approach and expectation of what goes on in schools from 8 AM to 3 PM. The third intervening belief would be that if schools do have art, at the very least students should enter contests and contribute positively to the school's record in another way.

A general lack of action not only by school leaders but also by society as a whole as to how education is really more of a complex process than a standardized one-size-fits-all process creates an inhospitable environment for art education to operate at the level of aesthetic experience advocated by Dewey. If administrators cannot put their faith in the nonstandard messiness of meaningfulness, how can we expect them to invest their limited monies for high-quality art education?

Parent Views of a School Dropping an Art Program from the Curriculum

In 2000, I was approached by a principal to do an inservice for her teachers because she wanted art integrated across her K–5 school's curriculum. As an advocate of art integration, I agreed, not knowing that this was a move on the principal's part to save money by cutting the art position and then "integrating" art into the regular classrooms. A year later, a parent of two students in that school asked me to participate on an arts advisory board for the school because of the principal's lack of dedicated budget and support for art in the school. The parent, an exhibiting artist, was astounded that a school that is progressive in so many ways would continue to be short-sighted as to the necessity of art as a formal part of any school curriculum.

This constructivist school leader focused on cultivating meaningful experiences for students, stating the value of the whole child. To her credit, this administrator recognized that classroom integration of art was not effective, in her eyes, because there was a lack of accountability for art, and subsequently made one-fourth of an "art-interested" teacher's job to teach art in small timeframes while serving as the school's special education teacher for the other three-fourths of the time. The next year this teacher's art commitment increased to half her responsibility, allowing her more time to work with older students on classroom "projects" perhaps having carryover into the consciousness of the classroom teachers. The administrator observed that this occurred only partly in one faculty member.

However, because of funding difficulties (as is often the case), and the priorities of what gets funded, art at this school has slipped continually down the priority list. A most recent rendition of the art program at the school can be summarized by an advertisement I received from the principal wanting to recruit my art preservice teachers that stated that the school was looking for an art teacher to come into the school to teach 50+ art classes for a per class fee. In this new attempt at providing art for the school, it appears that it is not necessary that this drop-in teacher be connected with school personnel, much less the children—a seemingly strange move for a school espousing a constructivist philosophy.

So what is happening here? Why does parent advocacy to walk the 50 yards to the nearby art museum fall on deaf ears for this principal who fervently talks about the education of the whole child? Why is it that the art opportunity now at this school has been diminished to a disconnected afterschool art program essentially functioning during the school day? My supposition is that this is happening only because there is a parent group requiring some exposure to art, and from the administrator point of view, this is "something." It serves the basic purpose of "art" in a conventional sense without asking that it be as meaningful and innovative as the rest of her program. It is likely that this is the administrator's attitude despite her constructivist philosophy, because her current arrangement does not provide entrée for the drop-in art teacher to actually contribute to the overall school climate. The parent, an artist, has decided that the energy necessary to change this administrator's efforts for art in the school is too much and has thus settled for her own peace of mind that at least her own children are exposed to the arts on a regular basis through their family activities. She believes that is not enough, but it will have to do.

Teacher Views of How the Arts Count as Education

During the three operating years of an innovative traveling art experience, through which over 20,000 elementary students were served in an urban area, teacher comments of the student art experience they witnessed were overwhelmingly enthusiastic. But one response in particular stood out. Responding to the question What about this experience is valuable for your group?, this teacher wrote:

> Children today in the Texas public school system RARELY have the chance to be truly creative on a large scale. They walk in line, mouths closed, preparing for tests to make administrators look knowledgeable to the media. For children to be able to break out of the "test rut," even for an hour, is WONDERFUL. How intelligent are we REALLY as a society if we educate the mind while killing or stifling the soul and spirit? Are we truly going to see creative problem solving in future generations?

This indictment of test-driven education by a 25-year veteran of the school system completely articulates how art experiences can positively intervene in the era of soulless standardization. Also, her questions parallel the questions explored previously in this chapter: Who are we educating? What is the function of schooling? The answers to these questions are crucial if we are to minimize the negative impact on the human stakes of high-stakes testing.

Student Comments During an Arts Intervention Program at Various School Sites

In the same innovative art intervention program in schools, students shared their excitement and impressions of their art experience. Through the guidance of facilitators of the intervention program, elementary students engaged with art ideas, created digital art in small groups, and discussed impressions of art, in a climate that values the input of the student. Sometimes students were shocked to be asked for their participation and opinions throughout the art experience. At disturbingly early ages, they have become accustomed to schooling (not learning) as a one-way exchange. Interrupting that expectation by asking for participation and dialogue, the facilitators created the environment for transformative aesthetic experiences, opportunities for perception, not simply recognition.

Students' words describing the dialogic impact of the art experience were often simply expressed and yet, in quickly written replies on an evaluation form, young students were able to articulate what made this experience so notably important and different from their usual classroom interaction. One fourth grader wrote that the reason he or she would want to visit the interactive art exhibition again was "because you get to share your thoughts without raising your hand." This comment could be taken as expressing the student's desire to not have rules to follow and dismissed as nothing more, but I'd like to draw attention to the beautiful expression of "you get to share your thoughts." A fourth grader noted that this art experience was a space for developing shared meaning, in a way very similar, yet far less academic, than Dissanayake's idea of shared social meaning in preliterate societies as discussed earlier. This student was excited about the chance to make such meaning, versus just participate in rote, unshared "learning" experiences.

When asked about why he or she liked the interactive art experience, another fourth grader in the same school, a school incidentally that does not have a regular art teacher, wrote, "We got to tell why. Some of the reasons were funny." The context of the telling of why was in terms of explaining their choices in the small-group digital artmaking activity. Students were frequently asked to suggest why they made the artistic choices they made. Just the simple sentence "we got to tell why" speaks volumes. The value for this student was in getting to speak, having his or her voice valued, and not just talking to talk but to tell "why"—something certainly more profound than simple regurgitation, a sharing, rather, of perceptions in Dewey's sense instead of recognition. And it is nice to note that such deep conversations about choices can also be fun!

THEMATICS: DISCUSSION/IMPLICATIONS

Thematizing is a way of generalizing ideas from specific situations to get at a larger issue (Eisner, 1998). What emerges from the previous discussion is a clearer picture of the complexity and qualities of meaningful experiences. Additionally, it seems apparent that there is very little room afforded in the current high-stakes testing climate for such experiences. It is difficult to test and measure complexity. Art experiences, real ones that emphasize the value of looking and exploring from more than one point of view (not colorful hand-turkeys, and the like, that so often are expected merely to beautify the school), epitomize the processes of working toward shared meanings and the realities of the unlikelihood that any two people will ever see the same event or experience exactly the same way—and that's a good thing! Multiple interpretations, varieties of expression, and the critical choices that are involved throughout aesthetic experiences are integral to the meaning of what it means to engage in the human activities of teaching and learning.

One school leader described his efforts to stimulate these very ideas in school environments in an article entitled "Art and Human Potential" (Hurley, 2002). Advocating a culture-building program where school employees are asked to share aesthetic experiences with the whole faculty—experiences such as the description of a beautiful double play, a video of Martin Luther King's "I Have a Dream" speech, or a stirring moment in an art museum. Hurley suggested that the activity of sharing and reflecting on the different aesthetic moments within a group refocuses the attention in education to human potential as opposed to statistical compliance:

> The aesthetic perspective on leadership is that managers confront human vice and leaders cultivate human virtue. Leadership involves asking people to reach for their human potential. It is about helping people develop nobility, generosity, compassion, love, and caring for others. One way to do this is to experience and explore human creativity. We reach our potential as we develop our aesthetic sensibilities and share them with others. (p. 24)

Hurley went on to suggest that aesthetic experiences may also raise to the fore what Roland Barth (2002) called the "nondiscussables" of the school climate that are inversely proportional to the health of the school. The sometimes difficult, unfamiliar, or even potentially uncomfortable qualities of different aesthetic experiences, which by our very natures and previous experiences are going to vary tremendously, mirror exactly the idea of moving from a Deweyan space of easy recognition to a space of meaningful perception. Appreciating a diversity of ideas, changing attitudes toward change, and interrupting the status quo move education back into a human arena. Hurley went on to write: "I hope the aesthetic experiences are so rich that they cause us to reach into the depths of our humanity. And when we do this, we will see more clearly why we have chosen to be educators. Unless we have an appreciation for our human potential, we cannot help others reach theirs, which is what education is all about" (p. 25).

SUMMARY

This chapter explores in depth the role of art education in a high-stakes testing climate. Four different perspectives on art education are discussed: skill, drill, and kill; art as the helpmate to testing; art as therapy and a source of enrichment; and art as a complex and critical experience. As a means for discovering how these perspectives play out in schools and contribute to school leaders' attitudinal predispositions, definitions of who is being educated and the structure of schools are explored. Out of the progress-driven needs-discourse, *homo economicus* has evolved into *homo systematicus*, the systematized and standardized product of education. A different take on who the client of the school system is explores the idea of *homo aestheticus*, the inherently artful human. These differences in clientele are further delineated in terms of school structure. This chapter explores two apt schooling metaphors—the school-as-factory model and the school-as-studio model.

The chapter also explores John Dewey's theoretical lens of *Art as Experience*, advocating critical perception over easy recognition as the makings of an aesthetic experience. The rhizomic interconnections of meaningful experience are also considered, epitomized by Deleuze and Guattari's discussion of the value of the *and* as a marker of the continuity of experience versus the division of learning into discreet measurable standard bits. These theoretical lenses showed that school leaders, through their beliefs and the power to act on their (or ignore others') beliefs, can choose to value art education and its role in cultivating continuous meaningful experiences, or they can choose effectively to administer a form of anaesthesia to their students, by limiting (or eliminating) art education in the school.

The chapter then discusses the perceived role of art education in the schools as expressed by principals, parents, teachers, and students. This portion of the chapter considers issues influencing principals, the ineffectiveness of parental concern for art, the witnessed evidence of learning in and through meaningful art experiences by teachers, and the welcoming of opportunities to share and think critically by young students. Ultimately, the chapter concludes with a call to remember schooling as a human endeavor requiring the cultivation of aesthetic experience to maximize human potential, as should be the goal of education.

McNeil and Valenzuela (2000) indicted the high-stakes testing climate and all its by-products because of what it is doing particularly to minority school children. But for all schools, the implications of short-sighted definitions of education that exclude the complexity of what happens between the View-Master® scenes is much grander, especially in schools where school leaders are poorly informed about the role of art in education. By promoting creativity and critical thinking through art education in schools, school leaders can endorse, support, and make real change in the meaningful qualities of teaching and learning. The question remains, will they cultivate aesthetic experience in the school culture or continue to prescribe doses of anaesthesia at every turn?

GUIDING QUESTIONS

Provide a rationale for initiating a strong school art program.
    OR
Develop a defense for not abandoning a strong school art program.
    OR
Provide suggestions for strengthening a school's art program that is functioning at a most basic level. Be sure to describe some of the factors that may be inhibiting the art program and suggest ways to overcome such obstacles.

In developing responses to these test cases, be sure to consider the following points:

1. What are the underlying beliefs in who is being educated that have to be articulated in this project?
2. What beliefs about the goals of education are evident?
3. In what ways does this case present an opportunity to incorporate an aesthetic lens in the making of curriculum?
4. How might the various stake holders of the school regard art teaching and its benefits for students?
5. How might aesthetic experiences be cultivated in the school climate?

SELECTED READINGS

Dewey, J. (1934). *Art as experience.* New York: Perigee Trade.
Dewey, J. (1938/1997). *Experience and education.* New York: The Free Press.

Dissanayake, E. (1995). *Homo aestheticus: Where art comes from and why.* Seatle: University of Washington Press.
Eisner, E. (2000). *The kind of schools we need: Personal essays.* Portsmouth, NH: Heinemann.
Eisner, E. (2002). *The arts and the creation of mind.* New Haven, CT: Yale University Press.

REFERENCES

Barth, R. S. (2002). The culture builder. *Educational Leadership, 58*(8), 611.
Deleuze, G., & Guattari, F. (1983). *On the line* (J. Johnston, Trans.). New York: Semiotext(e).
Dewey, J. (1934). *Art as experience.* New York: Perigee Trade.
Dewey, J. (1938/1997). *Experience and education.* New York: The Free Press.
Dissanayake, E. (1995). *Homo aestheticus: Where art comes from and why.* Seatle: University of Washington Press.
Docherty, T. (1996). *Alterities: Criticism, history, representation.* Oxford: Clarendon Press.
Eisner, E. W. (1998). *The enlightened eye: Qualitative inquiry and the enhancement of educational practice.* Upper Saddle River, NJ: Prentice-Hall.
Eisner, E. W. (2000). *The kind of schools we need: Personal essays.* Portsmouth, NH: Heinemann.
Eisner, E. W. (2002). *The arts and the creation of mind.* New Haven, CT: Yale University Press.
Gunzenhauser, M. G. (2003). High-stakes testing and the default philosophy of education. *Theory into Practice, 42*(1), 51–58.
Hargreaves, A. (2003). *Teaching in the knowledge society: Education in the age of insecurity.* New York: Teachers College Press.
Herman, J. (2000). *Making high-stakes assessment systems work for kids and you.* Paper presented at the AASA Suburban School Superintendents Conference, July 18, 2000.
Hurley, J. C. (2002). Art and human potential. *Principal Leadership, 3*(4), 24–28.
Illich, I. (1973). *Deschooling society.* New York: Penguin.
Illich, I. (1992). Needs. In W. Sachs (Ed.), *The development dictionary: A guide to knowledge as power.* Atlantic Highlands, NJ: Zed Books Ltd.
Kohn, A. (2001). Fighting the test: A practical guide to rescuing our schools. *Kappan, 82*(5), 349–357.
McNeil, L., & Valenzuela, A. (2000). The harmful impact of the TAAS system of testing in Texas: Beneath the accountability rhetoric. In G. Orfield & M. Kornhaber (Eds.), *Raising standards or raising barriers? Inequality and high stakes testing in public education.* Cambridge, MA: Harvard Civil Rights Project.
Protheroe, N. (2001). *Meeting the challenges of high stakes testing: Essentials for principals.* Alexandria, VA: National Association of Elementary School Principals.
Sachs, W. (Ed.). (1992). *The development dictionary: A guide to knowledge as power.* Atlantic Highlands, New Jersey: Zed Books Ltd.
Sheldon, K. M., & Biddle, B. J. (1998). Standards, accountability, and school reform: Perils and pitfalls. *Teachers College Record, 100,* 164–180.
Soep, E. (2002). Arts in the city. *Kappa Delta Pi Record, 30*(1), 12–16.
Stevens, K. (2002). School as studio: Learning through the arts. *Kappa Delta Pi Record, 30*(1), 20–23.
Thompson, S. (2001). The authentic standards movement and its evil twin. *Kappan, 82*(5), 358–362.
Wilson, B. (1997). *The quiet evolution: Changing the face of arts education.* Los Angeles: The J. Paul Getty Museum.

Chapter 13

Technology in the Classroom: Thinking Beyond the Machines

Melissa E. Pierson
University of Houston

What does integrating technology in 21st-century classrooms look like? The field of educational technology has matured beyond simple questions of purchase and basic skills to the more complex contemplations of intelligent and effective use. Thanks to a variety of national and state programs aimed at equipping schools with computers and installing the wiring necessary to connect those computers to the Internet, access to technology is reasonably prolific. According to the National Center for Educational Statistics (2001a), 98% of schools in this country were connected to the Internet in 2000, including 77% of the computers used for instructional purposes. Now that issues of procurement have been quelled, parents and communities want to see demonstrated growth from the early financial support for technology initiatives. Expectations are shifting from using technology simply for technology's sake to using technology to meet specific learning, teaching, and management goals.

Consideration of some of the most prominent current issues in this area will serve to inform dialogue at the state, district, school, and classroom levels. School leaders play a pivotal gate-keeping role, and thus regulate to a great degree the availability of technology. The chapter is organized by key questions that educators should ask about the use of technology in education. It first confronts criticisms of the use of technology, arming school leaders who believe in the power of technology with information to answer the challenging questions that may arise. It continues by defining technology integration and then reviews the particular role of technology in learning, teaching, assessment, and school leadership. The discussion concludes with a consideration of the overarching ethical, legal, and social issues about which educators must be aware in order to ensure meaningful and fair use of technology.

WHY ISN'T THERE UNIVERSAL SUPPORT FOR THE USE OF TECHNOLOGY IN SCHOOLS?

The charm of technology is lost on those critics who cite reasons why computers either are not performing as promised or do not belong in classrooms at all. School leaders who believe in the overall promise of technology when used meaningfully to achieve learning goals must recognize that technology is not a panacea. Being alert to these caveats will prepare school leaders to respond to these critics.

Those who see computers as detrimental to learning in general recommend a careful consideration of the costs and benefits of technology before schools decide to make computer purchases (Learning in the real world, n.d.). Such supporters of the ban on computers in classrooms believe that literacy is not developed through technology but rather through good teachers. They say that computers limit creativity and connection to the real world and present concepts in inflexible and superficial ways rather than through developmentally appropriate strategies. Other more specific concerns raised by technology critics include students becoming so focused on learning how to use the technology itself that they miss the content learning opportunities (Oppenheimer, 1997); students working in groups (common when there is not a 1:1 ratio) not fully participating in the learning experience; and some students experiencing increased attention challenges in classrooms filled with the noises, activity, and distractions found in technology-enhanced rooms (Sandholtz, Ringstaff, & Dwyer, 1995). Still others have expressed concerns about using computers with young children. A prominent voice in this argument is Jane Healy (1999), who believes that the physiological shifts occurring in the young child's brain that allow for the mental and abstract learning required to use computers do not happen until a child is 7 years of age. Until then, children benefit more from physical activities and social interaction than from sitting mindlessly in front of computers.

Finally, although taxpayers have invested billions of dollars in purchasing hardware and software, wiring schools, and generally embracing the presence of technology in schools, research on the effectiveness of computers in teaching and learning has yielded mixed results. In light of sometimes conflicting findings, it falls to school leaders to interpret the research so that they can make wise technology choices for their students. The bulk of existing research on technology integration has focused on incorporating computers into traditional teaching practices (Berson, 1996) so that teachers can do what they normally do, but faster. However, it is not the machines themselves that will impact learning; it is the ways in which computers are used that matter (Proctor & Burnett, 1996). When technology is used to assist students to arrive at predetermined correct answers, learning outcomes will be markedly different than when technology tools are used by students to investigate, problem solve, and analyze data to come to their own understandings.

One crucial argument that school leaders need to use is that reliable results cannot be expected when teachers are not prepared to use computers. Whereas 66% of technology expenditures is spent on hardware, only 15% is targeted for teacher professional development (*Technology in Education 2002*, 2002). The presence of computers has not transformed classrooms, from preschools to high schools, in either positive or negative ways. On the contrary, computers have been used by teachers as a "benign addition" to traditional programs, used in part to maintain teacher-centered instructional approaches (Cuban, 2001). When teachers do not know how to use computers for meaningful ways with students, machines sit unused, students waste valuable learning time using computers for low-level learning activities, or computers become simply a tool to prepare showy electronic reports.

School leaders must consider these caveats as part of a complete and ongoing decision-making process regarding technology integration. Any use of technology should be seen as enrichment to a range of tactile, experiential, and literacy activities. So, rather than dwelling on the question of whether computers are good or bad, educators must work to recognize the unique ways technology can be used to improve what teachers and students do, and at the same time resist the pressure to "plug in" students with no real instructional purpose in mind. Changed educational practices as a result of the use of technology can only be expected to occur over time, so those hoping for a quick fix will be disappointed. It is not the technology alone that will revolutionize education; instead, it is the potential for innovative thinking, unique access to information, and the ability to engage students in multiple ways that show promise for schools in the 21st century.

WHAT DO WE MEAN BY *TECHNOLOGY INTEGRATION?*

Most proponents of technology advise that educators cannot hope that technology itself will cause good things to follow (Means, 1994), nor can they conceive of technology as a vitamin which energizes schools to academic outcomes (Dede, 1998). Regardless of the rhetoric, the debate remains centered around the reality of how computers are actually being used in classrooms. Clearly, one teacher's idea of integrating technology by having students sit in front of a drill-and-practice game once a week will yield different learning results than another's practice of integrating technology by having students compose electronically, consult online resources, and author multimedia products. Can both of these two scenarios be termed *technology integration*? Coming to an understanding of what it means to effectively integrate technology impacts decisions in the areas of policy, purchasing, hiring, staff development, scheduling, planning, assessment, classroom management, and even to the arrangement of classroom furniture. Incomplete operating definitions produce inconsistencies in the vision of what is possible, or what should be possible, with technology. Technology is just one tool among many that teachers have at their disposal to be used when most appropriate. Unless the teacher views technology use as an integral part of the learning process, it will remain a peripheral supplement.

Where computers and other technology tools are used determines in many ways *how* they will be used. An ongoing debate pits advocates of placing computers into common labs, a cost-effective solution that gives all students in all grade levels a chance to use the machines, against those who recommend distributing computers out into classrooms, an option that provides learners on-demand access required for technology to be an integral part of the learning process. Most actual school computer distributions fall somewhere in between these two extremes. The issue of "to lab or not to lab" is best tackled with plenty of information about a particular school's needs, including student skills, teacher preferences, and technology resources.

HOW CAN TECHNOLOGY BE EFFECTIVELY USED FOR STUDENT LEARNING?

Arguably the most notable issue in the field of educational technology is its impact on student learning. Using technology for learning results in modest but positive gains in learning outcomes (Waxman, Connell, & Gray, 2002); provides environments where students develop improved attitudes about themselves and about their learning (Sandholtz et al., 1995); encourages interaction and problem solving (Tierney et al., 1995); and allows learner control of progress through learning relevant to the real world (Valdez et al., 1999). Overall, children from high- rather than low-socioeconomic-status homes, boys more than girls, and White students more than ethnic minorities show the highest academic gains from using home computers (Attewell & Battle, 1999). So, how are teachers to know how and when to integrate technology? A look at subject-specific effects of technology will help to shape the discussion of technology integration.

Receptive and productive language can be improved by the use of technology. Electronic story books have been used to improve comprehension over reading printed texts (Matthew, 1997) and motivate students to want to read the stories over and over. Word processing, one of the most common uses of technology, can serve not only a productivity function but also as a powerful way to impact the way that students learn to write. In general, word processing allows students to produce higher quality, longer written pieces with more words and more sentences (Barrera, Rule, & Diemart, 2001; Reed, 1996), revise written work more quickly and easily than students using paper and pencil, and be assisted by powerful features and tools specific to word processing software (Barrera et al., 2001). Demonstrating the mixed research findings on the effects of technology, other studies did not show improved language abilities in reading with computer-assisted instruction versus with traditional basal reading preparation (Hamilton, 1995), or in quality, complexity, or accuracy of writing on word processors versus by hand (Dybdahl, Shaw, & Blahous, 1997; Nichols, 1996).

Computer programming draws on early ties to mathematics. Students using educational software have been shown to outperform other students when working with fractions, problem solving, estimation, algebra, geometry, and calculus (McCoy, 1996). Mathematics-specific software leads to increased motivation and self-confidence and allows students to attempt more complex problems (Rochowicz, 1996). Math becomes enjoyable for many students when using the computer, motivating more effort (Funkhouser, 1993). Regardless of increased motivation and confidence levels, though, results showing no significant difference between the achievement levels of computer-using students versus their traditional learning peers counter the positive results (McCoy, 1996).

Research findings on computers in science and social studies learning are as diverse as those with other disciplines: Computers can allow students to learn more than they would working solely in experimental settings; technology is effective as a supplement to traditional instruction; secondary students have consistently been shown to benefit from computer-assisted instruction, such as simulations and tutorials (Ardac & Sezen, 2002; Chang, 2001); and finally, computer software is not as effective as other more traditional learning methods (Weller, 1996). Students of history have used drill-and-practice software to make modest gains in recall-type skills and motivation (Berson, 1996). However, more sophisticated simulation software brings distant locales right into the classroom, refines students' skills to locate and analyze vast amounts of historical data, and leads to increased fact recall, enhanced problem solving, curiosity, and personal initiative.

HOW CAN TECHNOLOGY FACILITATE STUDENT ASSESSMENT?

Technology can play a central role in measuring the effectiveness of instruction, a vital step in the learning cycle that yields data to inform continuous school improvement. The greatest issue for school leaders regarding technology and assessment is understanding the interplay of the technology with assessment functions. Technology itself is the focus of assessment at the national, state, and district levels when educators attempt to determine the value of years of technology expenditures. Educational stakeholders count the numbers of computers in schools and the "contact hours" teachers and students have with computers, measure how teachers and students feel about using technology, and chart teacher and student computer proficiency. Vital to understanding the assessment of technology is that possessing technology hardware, or even being proficient in basic technology skills, does not in and of itself indicate a quality technology-enhanced learning environment as it does not give an indication of how technology is being used.

Ideally, the focus of assessment should be on student mastery of content rather than on the technology. If students learn through technology-assisted processes and technology-produced products, learning can be measured with the same strategies teachers use to measure other nontechnology-enhanced learning. Frequently the use of technology leads to more student-centered, problem-based, interdisciplinary, constructivist learning environments; therefore, assessment strategies should likewise be designed to account for these types of learning in a format that most closely matches how the information was learned (e.g., conferences with students, anecdotal records, observation) (Kumar & Bristor, 1999).

The power of technology can make for organized and accurate test-based assessment, from more sophisticated college entrance exams to teacher-made tests and quizzes for all ages of students. Technology is most effective when automating the collection of objective data, such as right or wrong answers, although the capability for assessing essays is improving. Scoring and reporting of results is fast and accurate, teachers can use information to immediately adjust instruction, and test questions can be edited and updated as needed to reflect changes in instruction (Bushweller, 2000). *Computer-based tests* are exact electronic versions of the paper-and-pencil instruments, whereas the more sophisticated *computer adaptive tests* draw test questions from large banks of items and customize the testing experience to a test taker's responses. Teachers can create their own informal electronic exams and quizzes with various productivity tools or online test-creation sites, some of which actually score the tests automatically and e-mail the results directly to the teacher.

Data on student learning is collected informally almost continuously by teachers and more formally at set times during the year in the form of exams. The simplicity and functionality of grade book software makes it an easy adoption for teachers. Class lists can be modified, grades can be adjusted, computational functions from simple averages to more complicated calculations like weighting scores can be performed, and student scores can easily be graphed and charted. Web-based grade book systems provide teachers with tools to manage grades from any computer connected to the Internet and provide students and parents with up-to-date reports on progress, grades, and attendance. Classroom technology can also provide a means to record student progress in words rather than numbers. Creating or modifying an existing database or word-processed record for each child allows teachers to collect observations in one organized place and search through a student's record to track patterns or make predictions, functions not easily possible with paper-and-pencil notes.

Learning portfolios are collections of student work over time. Portfolios have traditionally been collected in paper form in notebooks and boxes; however, with the ever-increasing amount of student work produced in digital form, electronic portfolios have become the accepted solution to representing student progress. Electronic portfolios can be compiled of word-processed writing examples, scientific data stored in spreadsheets, scanned mathematic problem-solving examples or drawings, digital photos, videos of actions or unique performances, audio files of oral reading, or integrated multimedia projects.

School, district, and even classroom planning is being transformed by the recognition of the power of technology-managed and analyzed data. These *data-driven decisions* are made with the support of multiple forms of data, including achievement scores, teacher qualification statistics, and enrollment figures. Analyzing this data gives educators clues as to what methods and practices are working and where they need to focus additional attention. Teachers can use student data from previous years to inform the instruction in the present year, rather than beginning the year as if with a blank slate. Data-informed thinking also helps school and district leaders to demonstrate accountability needed to meet federal regulations on reporting demanded by the No Child Left Behind (NCLB) Act of 2001 (see http://www.nclb.gov/). NCLB requires districts to measure student success on an annual basis. Most districts and schools already collect great amounts of data; however, the tricky part of this new federal requirement is compiling these disparate and often incompatible data sources into one organized location and format so that they can be analyzed in meaningful ways. Clearly technology can impact the learning and assessment of students although success hinges on school leaders understanding the factors associated with teachers' use of technology.

WHY IS IT VITAL TO PREPARE TEACHERS TO EFFECTIVELY USE TECHNOLOGY?

Teachers are the most influential figures in the education of their students. Thus, issues of technology integration and its effects on student achievement must begin with an understanding of the role of technology in the teaching profession. A mere third of teachers felt either "well prepared" or "very well prepared" to use computers or the Internet in their teaching in 1999 (National Center for Educational Statistics, 2001b). The issue related to technology that weighs heavy on the minds of teachers is a perceived desire by society to have them become fast-and-regular technology users, thus enabling students to benefit from the tools to a greater extent. The tendency to blame teachers when this unrealistic vision is not immediately fulfilled should be tempered by findings into the types of teachers who use technology and the ways that technology encourages teachers to reexamine their own roles as teachers and those of their learners.

School leaders know who among their staff are technology users. These teachers are more experienced not only at using technology but also in general teaching; they have had more computer training, education, and experience teaching their current subject; and they are, more often than not, male. These educators invest significant personal time using computers (Pflaum, 2001), and they view computers as integral components in the learning process (Higgins, Moseley, & Tse, 2001).

Exemplary computer-using teachers work in technology-friendly environments. School leaders should aim to design school climates in which: (a) using computers is the norm; (b) computers are used for authentic, meaningful purposes; and (c) financial and technical support exists for technology at both school and district levels (Tiene & Luft, 2001). Technology has proven to be a uniting power, with teachers using technology communication tools to commiserate, to share ideas, and to support each other. Despite the importance of a supportive environment to a teacher's ability to teach with technology, funding for professional development of teachers is minimal; whereas 66% of school spending for technology is allocated to hardware, a mere 15% is budgeted for professional development for teachers (*Technology in Education 2002*, 2002), and lower SES schools spend even less (Anderson & Becker, 2001). When teachers do have a supportive, rich environment and adequate time and training in which to develop their skill and confidence, they progress in their use of technology for teaching through predictable stages, from novice to advanced proficiency (Sandholtz, Ringstaff, & Dwyer, 1997). Recognizing that essential conditions exist and ensuring the conditions are established leads to effective technology use by teachers for learners.

Finally, school leaders must consider how technology can strengthen new teaching and learning roles. Used in a traditional, teacher-centered classroom, technology tools might only serve to perpetuate outdated learning models. Allowed to empower students to identify, research, and solve authentic problems, with teachers playing the roles of skilled learning guides, technology tools can truly spur meaningful learning. The understanding that environment and support play significant roles in teacher technology use should prompt a wider consideration of the requirements of effective technology school climates.

HOW CAN SCHOOL LEADERS CREATE TECHNOLOGY-RICH LEARNING ENVIRONMENTS?

The hierarchical school system often works against inspired technology-using teachers who are not supported, or who are supported only half-heartedly, by their administrators. It is true that innovative educational practices can be spearheaded by teachers at the grassroots level; however, when the ideas venture outside the classroom door and require parallel changes in the practices of others, additional funding, or revised scheduling, the innovation is doomed unless it receives the passionate backing of an administrator who has the purse strings and the clout to see it through. When the innovative practice involves the use of technology, another interesting dynamic enters the mix. It vital for an administrator not only to be an advocate, but that person must also be a regular user of technology for real purposes central to both professional and personal activities. Leaders in any profession, but especially in education, who read e-mail only once it is printed by a secretary, or are fearful of online information, will simply not buy into the argument that technology can create changed information-rich contexts for their learners.

Too often, once computer purchases are made and equipment distributed, school leaders consider their schools technologically fit. Procuring the visible components is just one step, though, in the process of envisioning the ways technology will be used; school leaders at all levels must be key participants in creating environments conducive for technology use (Solomon, 2002; Stolarchuk & Fisher, 2001). Those in leadership have the power to allocate the needed resources, teacher release time, and vital support necessary for teacher success with technology (Higgins et al., 2001). The vision needs to go beyond informal work sessions among school staff and should be articulated in a way that the entire school community, including parents, staff, and students, understand it and are encouraged to play a role in its manifestation. In short, the vision should express clearly the importance a school places on the use of technology and the ways the school intends all stakeholders to help make the vision a reality.

The important work educators and students do within the walls of a classroom cannot occur without coordinated technical, curricular, financial, and organizational support, and these components are meshed most effectively by a passionate school leader convinced of the power of technology for the learning of children. Using technology requires more than just technical support. Gone are the days when a teacher who showed interest in using computers could be asked to take over the training, technical support, and curricular visioning in the spare time after school. Each of these areas requires unique sets of knowledge and significant, undivided time investments. Hiring competent personnel in these areas is key, and questions about a variety of technology skills, preferences, and ideas should be part of interviews for most school personnel.

As districts and states adopt standards for teacher technology proficiency, principals will be called into the service of evaluating this particular proficiency. In this capacity, principals must understand the relation of technology use to teaching. If principals are unduly impressed that all the computers are turned on or that students can create flashy web pages, they may overlook less obvious signs of inadequate teaching. Conversely, an absence of overt technology use at any one snapshot in time may not necessarily mean a teacher is resisting adopting new learning tools, but instead may demonstrate a particular teacher's judicious use of technology only when it is appropriate to meet a particular learning goal.

WHAT LARGER ISSUES ARE RAISED BY TECHNOLOGY USE IN SCHOOLS?

Understanding the use of technology in schools demands a broader look, past computer purchases, quality curricular integration, and teacher training. The overarching issues that provide the context in which technology is used in schools involve keeping students safe, information secure, opportunities to use technology equal, and student work original.

Security

Just as students have a right to be safe at school, they have a right to have their academic information kept safe. The vast amounts of student personal and assessment data that is stored on computers makes security a high priority. Security measures include something a person has (a key or badge), something a person knows (a password), or something about a person (a fingerprint or a facial feature). Although no system is completely foolproof, logical security choices include knowing who has access to what information and thinking through security as a systemwide issue. Malicious programs called viruses and worms damage or purposely violate confidential computer data, and the incidence of these programs is on the rise with society's preeminent reliance on e-mail. Educators and students must be vigilant about using virus detection software, updating the definitions of new viruses, questioning e-mailed attachments that appear suspicious, and even limiting the transfer of electronic files from school to home back to school.

Individual Privacy

Identity theft or harm caused by misusing private information has the potential to cause even greater harm than loss of data. The Children's Online Privacy Protection Act (COPPA) of 1998 is legislation passed to protect the privacy of children using the Internet (see the Electronic Privacy Information Center at http://www.epic.org for more information). Web sites must now obtain parental consent before collecting, using, or sharing personal information from children under the age of 13 and must display a prominent link to a Privacy Policy disclosing how personal information is collected, used, and disclosed.

Ethical and Legal Concerns

A great number of the issues presented in this section could be lessened by educating computer users about ethical technology practices, a job that falls to teachers, administrators, and parents. In order for their children to use the Internet, parents must sign An Acceptable Use Policy (AUP), a key component of a school's technology plan, which states the rules governing computer and Internet use and the consequences for violations. As part of this larger policy, schools frequently install filtering software to monitor and block access to questionable online materials. However, filtering software is only a limited prevention measure, and there is no substitute for proper supervision of students when they are working online.

Plagiarism has received some ominous assistance from the Internet, and school leaders must stay a step ahead of cheating students. "Paper mill" Web sites offer for free entire essays on hundreds of topics that can be passed off as original work, and for a charge, some sites even allow students to request custom-written essays. Even more of a challenge for educators is the ease with which students can copy text from the Internet and paste it verbatim into their papers. Even young students can be caught in this trap when they are not taught acceptable information usage; when given an assignment to research a certain topic on the Internet, the text they find often sounds so complete that they do not see a need to change it.

To detect electronic plagiarism, educators can look for clues that a piece of writing might not be written by the student, can paste a phrase of text into a search engine in quotation marks to see if the text was copied from an online source, or can even make use of more advanced plagiarism-detection Web sites. Even better than catching students at cheating is discouraging the practice in the first place. Educators can structure their assignments so that students are encouraged to take the honest route with their work, such as assigning in-class writing or requiring smaller parts of assignments at regular intervals, rather than requiring a complete product at the end. Modeling appropriate citation strategies and use of existing text to form original arguments develops information-management skills required of learners in the 21st century. Most importantly, teachers can be open with students about plagiarism, not only so that students recognize it is an issue, but also so that students know their teachers recognize it is an issue.

Health Issues

Recent concerns about the health of computer-using children have caught the attention of school leaders. In some schools, it is now common for children to use computers for a few hours a day at school and then go home and sit in front of a computer monitor for another several hours. Depending on the seating options, equipment placement, and body posture, this schedule of computer operation could place significant strain on children's physical well-being. In the best case, furniture that can be adjusted to fit various-sized children would be available in multiple-use labs; more typical, though, is the classroom computer station with a random compilation of mismatched tables and chairs. Ergonomic guidelines such as having students look down slightly at the monitor; encouraging them to change positions frequently while they are at the computer rather than sitting still; and resting their feet on a footrest or stack of books should be followed so that students develop lifelong positive computer-use habits (Northwest Regional Educational Laboratory, n.d.).

There is a growing question about the short- and long-term effects on children of the radiofrequency energy (RF) that runs wireless technologies, like cell phones and mobile computers. Children have the potential to be exposed to RF possibly several hours a day over the course of several years as schools are increasingly opting for wireless computer technologies. Research into this potential risk has yielded conflicting results. The few studies on potential cancer effects on humans have shown no adverse effects; however, these studies did not address any long-term effects (U.S. Food and Drug Administration, 2003). The special concern for children may be their particularly incomplete physical development and the real potential for years of wireless usage. School leaders should use ongoing research findings to inform school wireless policy.

Equity

Schools must lead the effort in ensuring that every student, regardless of gender, ethnicity, socioeconomic background, or disability, has adequate access to computers and the Internet. The term *digital divide* means to educators the gap between students who are able to use various technology tools and those who are not (National Institute for Community Innovations, 2001). It is acknowledged that those who do not have regular access to endless information sources and technology tools will be at a disadvantage for future learning. Ensuring that all students have equal access to and knowledge to use technology tools is referred to as *digital equity*. The job of ensuring that students can reap the benefits provided by regular computer access often falls to educators, especially when students come from homes with limited computer access (Wilhelm, Carmen, & Reynolds, 2002). Of importance to school leaders is that even in schools that appear to provide adequate access to technology tools, computers may sit unused or be used for low-level activities. This misuse of technology may also characterize an inequitable situation. Technology can place students from low-income homes on an even playing field with their more affluent peers for whom technology is common (Department of Education, n.d.). Yau (1999) suggested framing a discussion of school technology equity issues with these considerations:

1. whether traditionally underserved students are receiving a fair or adequate share of technological resources;
2. whether teachers of these students are receiving adequate training on the effective uses of educational technology;
3. whether specific uses of educational technology are particularly effective for teaching traditionally underserved populations; and
4. whether students have sufficient access to computers at home.

An equity issue that technology tools frequently can be used to alleviate is that which involves students with a variety of disabilities. Recent advances in assistive technology have sought to meet the specific needs of disabilities in the areas of (a) hearing loss and deafness; (b) vision impairment; (c) speech disorders; and (d) cognitive delay and learning impairment. Any peripheral, software or system of components that is used to increase, maintain, or improve functional capabilities of individuals with disabilities is considered to be an assistive technology device, according to the Individuals with Disabilities Education Act (see http://www.ed.gov/offices/OSERS/Policy/IDEA/).

Finally, there are gender issues specifically related to technology use. Research has consistently shown that boys are more interested and involved with technology than are girls, and many software programs emphasize activities of interest to males, like competition and violence. School leaders need to pay special attention to ensuring equal access and equivalent learning opportunities aimed at a variety of interests and needs to be effective for all students. Involvement and vision from all stakeholders, including teachers, administrators, parents, and community members, will help to ensure there is the funding and support to provide equitable technology access for all students.

SUMMARY

As the issue of integrating technology into teaching and learning has matured past simple questions of numbers of machines and connectivity, educators are faced with increasing pressure to produce measurable results of student learning. This challenge has proven difficult to meet, however, as the research on the effectiveness of technology is mixed and the argument about the right ways to integrate technology is ongoing. What it means to effectively integrate technology into teaching and learning is an understanding that impacts planning, teaching, assessment, and administration. The larger issues of keeping students safe, information secure, opportunities to use technology equal, and work original provide the context in which technology is used in schools.

GUIDING QUESTIONS

John Pera's sophomore literature class is studying selected works of Shakespeare. He is excited that today is the technology day for this unit. He has chosen and carefully reviewed three exemplary Web sites that specifically target the plays and characters on which his students are focusing.

When his first-period students enter the classroom, he reminds them that they will be using some online resources today and asks them to get out their notebooks to take notes. One of the three classroom computers is connected to a television monitor hanging in the corner of the classroom. Mr. Pera has already turned on the computer and the television, and has pulled up the first site. He turns off the lights so students can see the monitor and proceeds with the lesson.

Mr. Pera animatedly summarizes for students the key points of the first site as he scrolls through long paragraphs of text analyzing the character development of Macbeth and Othello. Moving right into the next Web site, he clicks through the homepage of a theatre company specializing in Shakespeare, showing photos of a recent performance. He is disappointed to have the bell ring just as he is pulling up the third site that shows detailed diagrams of Shakespeare-era costumes and stage sets. He calls out to students as they gather their books to leave the classroom that there will be a quiz tomorrow over this information, so they should review their notes.

Thinking back over the lesson as students from the next period shuffle into class, Mr. Pera hopes that students learned something from using these authentic online resources. He realizes that his normally inattentive students were just as inattentive today, passing notes in the back of the darkened classroom. And he regrets that students did not ask more questions during the lesson, but maybe they just were not sure what to ask. He feels confident, however, that the use of technology has brought a new dimension to his Shakespeare unit.

Refer to the case scenario to consider these guiding questions.

1. Mr. Pera researched Web sites, connected online resources to his content, and ensured that the technology was functioning. If all of these elements were present, why was he unable to engage students in this lesson?
2. How could the lesson be restructured to allow for new teacher and learner roles?
3. In what ways does technology impact assessment in this lesson?
4. What evidence of administrative support for technology is apparent?
5. How might Mr. Pera have addressed diversity in this lesson?

SELECTED READINGS

Center for Applied Research in Educational Technology (CARET). Retrieved August 21, 2003, from http://caret.iste.org/.

FromNowOn.org: The Educational Technology Journal. Retrieved August 21, 2003, from http://www.fno.org/.

Milken Family Foundation Education Technology. Retrieved August 21, 2003, from http://www.mff.org/edtech/.

Technology and Learning's "The Educator's Guide to Copyright and Fair Use." Retrieved August 10, 2003, from http://www.techlearning.com/db_area/archives/TL/2002/10/copyright.html.

REFERENCES

Anderson, R. E., & Becker, H. J. (2001). *School investments in instructional technology.* Retrieved April 9, 2003, from http://www.crito.uci.edu/tlc/findings/report_8/startpage.htm.

Anderson, R. E., & Dexter, S. L. (2001). *School technology leadership: Incidence and impact.* Retrieved August 21, 2003, from http://www.crito.uci.edu/tlc/findings/report_6/.

Ardac, D., & Sezen, A. H. (2002). Effectiveness of computer-based chemistry instruction in enhancing the learning of content and variable control under guided versus unguided conditions. *Journal of Science Education and Technology, 11*(1), 39–48.

Attewell, P., & Battle, J. (1999). Home computers and school performance. *Information Society, 15*(1), 1–10.

Barrera, M. T., Rule, A. C., & Diemart, A. (2001). The effect of writing with computers versus handwriting on the writing achievement of first-graders. *Information Technology in Childhood Education Annual,* 215–228.

Berson, M. J. (1996). Effectiveness of computer technology in the social studies: A review of the literature. *Journal of Research on Computing in Education, 28*(4), 486–501.

Bushweller, K. (2000). Electronic exams. Electronic School [Online]. Retrieved June 20, 2000, from http://www.electonic-school.com.

Chang, C.-Y. (2001). Comparing the impacts of a problem-based computer-assisted instruction and the direct-interactive teaching method on student science achievement. *Journal of Science Education and Technology, 10*(2), 147–153.

Cuban, L. (2001). *Oversold and underused: Computers in the classroom.* Cambridge, MA: Harvard University Press.

Dede, C. (Ed.). (1998). *Learning with technology.* Alexandria, VA: Association for Supervision and Curriculum Development.

Department of Education. (n.d.). Reasons for bringing technology into schools. Retrieved February 20, 2004, from http://www.ed.gov/pubs/EdReformStudies/EdTech/reasons.html.

Dybdahl, C. S., Shaw, D. G., & Blahous, E. (1997). The impact of the computer on writing: No simple answers. *Computers in the Schools, 13*(3/4), 41–53.

Funkhouser, C. (1993). The influence of problem-solving software on student attitudes about mathematics. *Journal of Research on Computing in Education, 25*(3), 339–346.

Hamilton, V. (1995). Computers and reading achievement (ERIC Document Reproduction Service No. ED 382 923).

Healy, J. M. (1999). *Failure to connect—How computers affect our children's minds—for better or worse.* New York: Touchstone.

Higgins, S., Moseley, D., & Tse, H. (2001). Computers and effective teaching. *Education Canada, 41*(3), 44–47.

Kumar, D., & Bristor, V. J. (1999). Integrating science and language arts through technology-based macrocontexts. *Educational Review, 51*(1), 41–53.

Learning in the real world. (n.d.). Retrieved February 17, 2004, from http://www.realworld.org/

Matthew, K. (1997). A comparison of the influence of interactive CD-ROM storybooks and traditional print storybooks on reading comprehension. *Journal of Research on Computing in Education, 29*(3), 263–275.

McCoy, L. P. (1996). Computer-based mathematics learning. *Journal of Research on Computing in Education, 28*(4), 438–460.

Means, B. (Ed.). (1994). *Technology and education reform: The reality behind the promise.* San Francisco: Jossey-Bass.

National Center for Educational Statistics. (2001a). *Digest of education statistics, 2001.* Retrieved August 8, 2003, from http://nces.ed.gov/pubs2002/digest2001/tables/dt421.asp.

National Center for Educational Statistics. (2001b). *The condition of education, 2001.* Retrieved August 8, 2003 from http://nces.ed.gov//programs/coe/2001/section4/indicator39.asp.

National Institute for Community Innovations. (2001). The digital equity toolkit. Retrieved February 19, 2004, from http://www.nici-mc2.org/de_toolkit/.

Nichols, L. M. (1996). Pencil and paper versus word processing: A comparative study of creative writing in the elementary school. *Journal of Reasearch on Computing in Education, 29*(2), 159–166.

Northwest Regional Educational Laboratory. (n.d.). Early connections: Technology in early childhood education. Retrieved August 1, 2003, from http://www.netc.org/earlyconnections/kindergarten/health.html.

Oppenheimer, T. (1997, July). The computer delusion. *The Atlantic Monthly, 280,* 45–62.

Pflaum, B. (2001). How is technology impacting student performance? *School Planning and Management, 40*(12), 41–43.

Proctor, R. M., & Burnett, R. C. (1996). Computer attitude and classroom computers. *Computers in the Schools, 12*(3), 33–41.

Reed, W. M. (1996). Assessing the impact of computer-based writing instruction. *Journal of Research on Computing in Education, 28*(4), 418–437.

Rochowicz, J. A. Jr. (1996). The impact of using computers and calculators on calculus instruction: Various perceptions. *Journal of Computers in Mathematics and Science Teaching, 15*(4), 423–435.

Sandholtz, J. H., Ringstaff, C., & Dwyer, D. C. (1995). Student engagement revisited: Views from technology-rich classrooms. In *Apple education research reports* (pp. 29–30). Eugene, OR: International Society for Technology in Education.

Sandholtz, J. H., Ringstaff, C., & Dwyer, D. C. (1997). *Teaching with technology: Creating student-centered classrooms.* New York: Teachers College Press.

Solomon, G. (2002). Digital equity: It's not just about access anymore. *Technology and Learning, 22*(9), 18–20, 22–24, 26.

Stolarchuk, E., & Fisher, D. (2001). An investigation of teacher-student interpersonal behavior in science classrooms using laptop computers. *Journal of Educational Computing Research, 24*(1), 41–55.

Technology in Education 2002. (2002). Retrieved April 9, 2003, from www.schooldata.com.

Tiene, D., & Luft, P. (2001). Teaching in a technology-rich classroom. *Educational Technology, 41*(4), 23–31.

Tierney, R. J., Kieffer, R., Stowell, L., Desai, L. E., Whalin, K., & Moss, A. G. (1995). Computer acquisition: A longitudinal study of the influence of high computer access on students' thinking, learning, and interactions. In *Apple education research reports* (pp. 31–32). Eugene, OR: International Society for Technology in Education.

U.S. Food and Drug Administration. (2003). Cell phone facts. Retrieved August 7, 2003, from http://www.fda.gov/cellphones/qa.html#25.

Valdez, G., McNabb, M., Foertsch, M., Anderson, M., Hawkes, M., & Raack, L. (1999). *Computer-based technology and learning: Evolving uses and expectations.* Oak Brook, IL: North Central Regional Educational Laboratory.

Waxman, H., Connell, M., & Gray, J. (2002). *A quantitative synthesis of recent research on the effects of teaching and learning with technology on student outcomes.* Retrieved June 11, 2003, from http://www.ncrel.org/tech/effects/.

Weller, H. G. (1996). Assessing the impact of computer-based learning in science. *Journal of Research on Computing in Education, 28*(4), 461–485.

Wilhelm, T., Carmen, D., & Reynolds, M. (2002). Connecting kids to technology: Challenges and opportunities. The Digital Divide Network. Retrieved February 17, 2004, from http://www.digitaldividenetwork.org/content/stories/index.cfm?key=244.

Yau, R. (1999). Technology in K–12 public schools: What are the equity issues? A review of issues related to equity in education. Retrieved February 17, 2004, from http://www.maec.org/techrev.html.

Part III

ORGANIZATION AND MANAGEMENT ISSUES

How do leaders manage a productive school? That is the subject of the final part of this book. We move on several fronts in this final part.

How can leaders work most effectively with teachers? What do good leaders do? We devote four chapters to this important subject and answer some questions. Are staff development programs successful? The reader may be surprised. How do leaders in downtown schools behave to get things done? How does any leader behave to improve teacher work groups? And, how does all of this relate to the culture and climate of the schools?

The operation of the schools in many communities is the most expensive thing the community engages in. Throughout the land, ways of supporting the school enterprise continue under study. And does anyone believe the schools are adequately financed to perform the function for which they were created? Has anyone ever thought of school finance programming as having the elements of a Russian novel? Two of our authors have.

Finally, are there options to the way schools are organized? What part do alternative schools play in the scheme of schooling? The final chapter of this book examines modes of organizing charter schools and the problems with which charter schools are confronted.

Chapter 14

Leading the Teacher Work Group

William D. Greenfield Jr.
Portland State University

Discussions of school leadership generally focus on advice about how to lead effectively, differences in leadership style, and the personal qualities of effective leaders. These are important concerns, but they fail to focus attention on the teacher—the one to be influenced through leadership by a principal or by teacher leaders themselves. The approach taken here is to focus on the daily milieu within which the teacher is situated and to discuss critical aspects of that milieu that must become part of one's leadership strategy if a school leader is to succeed.

Every teacher is a member of one or more groups at work, and the groups to which a teacher belongs have a major influence on a teacher's day-to-day behavior at work. Although there are groups to which teachers belong that are not associated directly with their daily work in a professional sense (family, volunteer and recreational groups, etc.), the teacher work group at the school is of great significance for most teachers.

Most discussions of the principalship and school leadership pay little attention to the nature of the teacher work group in schools and its implications for the principal and other school leaders who aspire to success-fully lead and improve a school.[1] Without any doubt, the recurring call for *leadership* by the principal is a reflection of the complex problems that a school faces in providing adequate, much less excellent, instruction to the youngsters it serves. What is too often missing from such admonitions is

---

[1]The author assumes that leadership is an organizational process and that teachers as well as school administrators may participate as leaders. Although school principals have a formal responsibility to lead as well as manage school affairs, teachers often contribute in critical ways as school leaders. The ideas discussed in this chapter are therefore as relevant to teacher leaders as to principals.

concrete guidance as to what it is that a school principal or a teacher leader actually does to provide the leadership so desperately needed.

The chapter answers four questions: (a) What is *value leadership* and why is it important; (b) Why is it important for school leaders to understand the sociocultural dynamics of the *teacher work group*; (c) What key ideas can guide school leaders as they seek to understand the *norms* of teachers in a particular school; (d) In being a value leader, what can one do to influence the attitudes and beliefs (the norms) of teachers in ways that foster and sustain the development of a *school-based professional community*?

The discussion to follow offers a framework for understanding one of the biggest challenges that successful leadership in schools entails: to encourage and support collaboration among teachers that results in improved teaching practices and desired learning outcomes for children, that is, to develop the school as a community of professionals working together to serve children well. This challenge is summed up in a straightforward question grounded in Louis, Kruse, and Associates' (1995) concept of a school-based professional community.

How can we develop and sustain a school-based professional community that is characterized by:

- reflective dialogue committed to improving teaching and learning,
- deprivatization of practice,
- a collective focus on student learning and not simply on teaching strategies and techniques,
- collaboration among staff that results in development of the work group itself, and
- shared norms supporting the foregoing practices and a commitment to on-going study and improvement of teaching and learning in one's school? (Adapted from Louis et al., 1995, pp. 28–34)

Too often, principals proceed along traditional lines of action to lead and manage the school as if the efforts of individual teachers, acting in isolation from one another, can add up to an effective school. Although this is possible under certain conditions of student and community homogeneity and teacher excellence, commitment, and responsiveness to student differences and capabilities (and often not even then), today's student bodies and communities are complicated and increasingly diverse in terms of many variables, including social class, race, ethnicity, English-language proficiency, home stability and support, readiness for school, the adequacy of earlier schooling, parental support and involvement, and so on. All of these differences complicate the challenges faced by a school as it seeks to support learning for all children.

It is easy to say what schools should be like in order to be more effective. There is a tremendous amount of research to guide us as to what needs to be done (Cotton, 1995; Hoachlander, Alt, & Beltranena, 2001). This research suggests that a professional learning community characterized by the five features noted earlier can succeed in responding to this increasing student diversity. However, a supportive, vibrant, and effective climate for teaching and learning does not just happen. The development of the school as a professional community requires sustained and focused effort by school leaders and teacher colleagues.

The problem is not that we do not understand what teachers should do or how they need to work together. These answers are clear. The biggest challenge is getting teachers and schools (and school leaders) to change their practices, to work differently. This is easy to say and difficult to accomplish. The reason this is difficult to accomplish is that the changes needed are changes in teachers' and administrators' *beliefs* about how they should be working with one another. Most importantly, the *norms of the school and the teacher work group need to change* in ways that enable the school to realize its potential as a school-based professional community (Louis, Kruse et al., 1995). This is one major leadership challenge faced by contemporary school leaders.

A related challenge is to develop a norm of continuous improvement to replace the traditional idea held by many teachers that one is an "expert" by virtue of one's veteran status, and therefore exempt from needing to consider "new" research about best practice. A major obstacle in this arena is how to help teachers become good consumers of "research" and to move beyond the erroneous and simplistic belief held by many teachers that research results can be made to say whatever one wants them to say. Principals can be very critical in cultivating among teachers an informed understanding of how to assess the validity and usefulness of research results.

LEADERSHIP

Leadership is a reciprocal influence relationship between leader(s) and led, and in schools it generally involves efforts intended to improve the school's ability to accomplish its goals effectively. Greenfield (1995) argued that there is in every school a constellation of situational imperatives to which school administrators and others striving to lead schools must respond. These include five different sources or types of demands on school leaders:

- Managerial (keep things running smoothly),
- Instructional (provide the supports teachers and students require to succeed),

- Political (influence the allocation of scarce resources),
- Interpersonal (work effectively with and through teachers and others to get things done),
- Moral (fostering deliberate dialogue and influencing decisions regarding judgments about and choices to be made among competing standards of "good" practice).

These pressures vary in terms of their demand for attention from school to school, depending on the mix of teachers, students, and various district and community factors. Which of these deserves or receives the most attention by a principal or other school leader will change with the school situation, and hence they are not listed in any particular order of importance.

Although these all are interrelated and interactive in day-to-day life in schools, the two that are most critical for this discussion of leading the teacher work group are the moral and the interpersonal dimensions of being a school leader. The *interpersonal* dimension is critical because not much that is important happens in schools except that which occurs as a result of the interpersonal relations among people (students, teachers, the principal, and others on the scene). This *is* how the work in schools gets done.

The *moral* dimension is critical because the terrain being navigated by teachers as well as school leaders is full of value dilemmas. Teachers as well as the principal and other school leaders regularly find themselves having to choose between *competing standards of good practice.* It is not simply a choice between a good alternative and a poor one. This is not a dilemma. A dilemma exists when the preferred choice or course of action is not clear and two or more options are desirable. These competing standards are normal in schools and are reflected in the discussions educators have about the goals of schools, lesson objectives, curriculum content, teaching processes and strategies, and myriad other aspects of daily life in the school. These "value issues" are central and warrant being addressed deliberately through what I term *value leadership* (Greenfield, 1982).

VALUE LEADERSHIP

This idea is a reflection of the relationship between the moral and the interpersonal dimensions discussed previously. When one confronts a value dilemma, a choice must be made as to which decision or action to take (and even a decision to not act or decide counts as a choice). The critical idea is that any time one makes a choice or a decision, doing so reflects a *valuing* of one alternative over one or more others. That is, a *judgment* has been made as to which is the most valued alternative. One can gather and consider the relevant facts and the opinions of others, but every active decision or action fundamentally requires a *value judgment* on the part of the actor.

Thus, a great deal of one's ability to be effective as a school leader is related to one's ability to be a value leader. That is, the key focus of value leadership in schools is to influence teaching practices and learning outcomes in a manner that reflects what is understood about effective practices and cultivates learning outcomes that serve the best interests of a school's children and its broader community.

Beyond the resolution of particular value dilemmas associated with specific actions and decisions, being a value leader also entails working with and through teachers to gain their valuing of and commitment to particular means and ends associated with teaching, learning, and other affairs of school life. That is, value leadership not only involves making judgments about particular actions and decisions for oneself, it also includes efforts to influence the valuing (value preferences) by others. A *value dialogue* occurs between school leaders and others. The purpose of this dialogue is to develop an understanding of and a commitment to particular shared processes and purposes, particular means and ends related to one's work as a schoolteacher or administrator.

A school leader or the principal may have a great idea about preferred practice, and it may even be a practice supported by extensive empirical evidence. However, unless others come to voluntarily share the valuing of that practice, it is not likely to be adopted by them. Value leadership thus entails an informed, sustained, and continuing dialogue among teachers and school leaders about preferred practice. Such dialogue is the mark of a school-based professional community. It is not typical of most schools and usually results only from a deliberate effort to cultivate and develop authentic, open, and trusting relationships with and among teachers, and between leaders (formal and informal) and teacher work groups.

The challenge for a school leader is to spark and sustain such a dialogue and to work with and through teachers to develop a shared commitment to implementing the desired practices effectively. This dialogue also is critical to facilitating individual and collective reflection on possible gaps between intentions and actual practices, and must be part of the discussion of changes being considered. Only with such discussions can embedded models of poor practice be exposed and collaboratively massaged into new beliefs and agreements about effective practices. Value leadership can be a critical stimulus to the teacher work group in its efforts to develop such a school-based professional community.

THE TEACHER WORK GROUP

What do we mean by the phrase "teacher work group"? For our purposes we can distinguish two basic types of groupings of teachers in a school: formal and informal. These types can be further categorized as either temporary or continuing groups. Formal groups would include grade-level teams or departments, while informal groups would include groups of teachers who voluntarily come together on a regular basis to have lunch or to pursue some other social or friendship need. Other formal groups might come together on a more temporary basis, as in the case of a special task group created to address a specific issue or problem, and do so within a specified time period. When the work of the temporary group is finished, the group typically disbands and stops functioning as a group.

What is the significance of these ideas about the different types of groups of teachers in a school? Although there are other points that can be discussed, the most important concept for school leaders to understand is that a critical consequence of these various groups is that *attitudes* are shaped in part as a result of teachers coming together in these various groups. Of special interest to school leaders is a particularly powerful type of attitude, referred to as a *group norm.*

A *norm* is a shared belief held by most members of a group about what behavior is appropriate and expected of the group's members in order for a member to remain in good standing with the group (Homans, 1950; Cohen, Fink, Gadon, & Willits, 1995).[2] A critical variable that distinguishes more effective from less effective schools are the work group norms or rules influencing teachers' day-to-day orientations in their classrooms and as group members. Group norms are the accepted ways of doing things—the taken-for-granted rules of the road by which teachers guide their daily affairs, in relation to one another, in their interactions with students and others, and in terms of the expectations they hold for themselves and for one another.

A typical norm in many schools is that teaching is a private affair. That is, teachers generally are reluctant to openly share with others the problems they encounter in their teaching. A teacher might consult a trusted friend about a difficulty he or she is encountering in his or her teaching, but it is unusual for teachers to openly discuss such matters with colleagues. The norm is that what goes on in one's classroom is that teacher's business and nobody elses. Most teachers believe that this is an acceptable and appropriate practice. It is the norm.

Norms are not formally written down, and frequently the way a newcomer to a group learns about a norm is by violating it. Norms operate such that members of the group reinforce one another's conformance to the norm.

---

[2]The concepts and the discussion to follow draw heavily on the work of these two scholars.

Norms can have positive as well as negative effects vis-à-vis a given criterion or standard of good practice. For example, if the norm in a school is that teachers basically refrain from being involved in one another's classrooms or from openly sharing and discussing the problems one is encountering in his or her classroom or in achieving a particular teaching objective, the individual teacher who deviates from this informal rule likely will be subtly or not so subtly discouraged by other members of the teacher group from initiating such involvement or discussion. It might be a rookie, eager to learn from more experienced colleagues, who is politely rebuffed after unwittingly asking to visit and observe a colleague's classroom. It as easily could be an old-timer who attempts to engage colleagues in a substantive discussion of teaching strategy, having just returned from participating in a Critical Friends (2003) training orientation and becoming excited at the prospect of engaging colleagues in authentic dialogue about instructional practices and how to improve them.[3] If the existing norm or unwritten rule is that "teaching is a private matter," or that "we stay out of each other's classrooms," initiatives such as those mentioned previously will be discouraged. On the other hand, if the unwritten rule or norm is that "we have a lot to learn from each other," or that "we talk with one another about the teaching challenges we're facing," then both the rookie teacher wanting some guidance and the old-timer excited about exchanging substantive ideas about teaching with colleagues would be more likely to have their needs met.

The important thing to remember about a *group norm* is that it is in effect an unwritten rule that reflects the group members' beliefs about how group members are supposed to behave in order to be considered a member in good standing. For example, some common group norms among teachers are that:

- teaching is a private affair, not to be shared with others,
- teachers have rights to pursue individual goals in their classrooms,
- teachers feel a responsibility to support their colleagues' rights to pursue individual goals and strategies in their respective classrooms,
- noninterference in each others' work and classrooms is expected,
- teachers have a right to exercise discretion as autonomous artisans such that each classroom in a school is functionally independent,
- the curriculum in one teacher's classroom need not be related to the curriculum in other teachers' classrooms in a given school.

---

[3]Critical Friends Groups is a professional development strategy initiated by the Annenberg Institute for School Reform at Brown University. An excellent description of the strategy may be found at http://www.cic.uiuc.edu/groups/DEOLiaisons/archive/BestPractice/Critical_Friends_descipt.pdf.

The foregoing are group norms common to many schools, and they result in a school community where teachers rarely discuss substantive matters of practice with each other, don't coordinate their instructional efforts, more or less agree to disagree on instructional approaches, and serve to permit a broad range of differences in individual goals, beliefs, and instructional practices across classrooms. The operating assumption is that the individual teacher, as an autonomous professional, is the best judge of what specific practices will be most effective in *his or her* classroom. Indeed, clients or the curriculum, not teachers' practices, too often are cited as the reasons for a failure to achieve desired learning outcomes.

By contrast, norms that support a more interdependent, interactive, and professionally collegial and collaborative teacher work group are found in more effective schools. Examples of these norms include:

- frequent discussions among teachers about substantive and serious problems they are encountering in their teaching, or which students encounter as learners,
- invitations by teachers for colleagues to observe their classrooms and their teaching in order to help them improve their practices,
- frequent and critical discussions of what children are learning,
- a commitment to get beyond superficial conversations,
- regularly sharing with group members one's efforts to identify and solve problems interfering with one's effective classroom instruction.

There are two aspects about group norms that make them significant for a school leader. One aspect about a norm is that it reflects group members' *shared beliefs* about how to behave if one wants others in the group to continue to perceive one as a member in good standing. Contrasting the two sets of norms described earlier, it is clear that the daily pressures and expectations of teachers for one another would be quite different in two schools reflecting these two different sets of norms.

With a norm, one is dealing with a *belief* about the right or correct way to behave. It is not only a belief about how one is supposed to behave, it is a belief that is shared by others in one's group. This makes it a very powerful force in shaping a teacher's day-to-day behavior. This feature also makes norms very difficult to change.[4]

---

[4]Some school districts employ a policy that requires the transfer of school principals every 3 years. A policy such as this makes it very difficult for a principal to establish the level of trust, rapport, and credibility needed to provide normative leadership. Although normative change takes time, the advantage is that the resulting change will be reinforced by teachers (because it is a group norm) and therefore will be more likely of being sustained by the teacher group when a transfer of principals occurs.

Additionally, norms are very subtle and are not explicit or written down. Group norms are assumed to be understood by members of the group. In fact, it would not be unusual for a norm to not be noticed by a newcomer to the group, until it is violated—and then the informal rule (the norm) that has been broken becomes visible through seeing how others in the group react to the fact that a group member is violating the group's expectations for how members are supposed to behave.

Something that complicates this a bit further in the case of the teacher work group is that the most central and pervasive group norms typically do not vary much from school to school. This is because these norms not only are a product of the interactions of group members, but are influenced as well by the broader occupational norms and ideology of the profession of teaching and organizational characteristics of the school itself. Among the most comprehensive discussions of the interplay among these factors are the works of Louis, Kruse, and associates (1995) in their study of professionalism and community in high schools, Little and McLaughlin (1993) in their edited volume focusing on individuality and community in the school workplace, and Westheimer's (1998) comparison of community autonomy and ideology in teachers' work in two middle schools.

Thus, what we have here, with group norms, is a very subtle yet powerful influence on teachers' beliefs about what is valued, about what practices are acceptable and preferred. An important implication is that school leaders would be wise to consider group norms as they reflect on their school's effectiveness in achieving its goals, and as they consider issues and strategies intended to improve practices in a school. Key questions for a school leader to answer include:

- What are the formal and informal groups in the school?
- What are the norms influencing group members' teaching practices and interactions related to improving learning outcomes?
- Do the norms reinforce behaviors that the school leader believes will facilitate effective teaching and learning?
- Are norms at work that impede the accomplishment of effective instruction or that otherwise have a negative impact on what it is that school leaders believe should be occurring to improve learning outcomes?

For example, let's say that one of the school leader's goals is for teachers to collaborate and work as a team in the delivery of instruction. In what ways do existing group norms foster such cooperation among teachers—and how might these be reinforced and perhaps strengthened? Equally, how might existing norms work against meaningful teacher collaboration—and what might a school leader do to diminish the effects of these "negative" norms?

Who are the informal teacher leaders in each of these normative arenas? Who stands to lose power when norms are changed? There are important power dynamics at work within every teacher work group, and questions such as these are critical for a school leader to ask before embarking on a change strategy.

Now, remembering that group norms reflect the *shared beliefs* of group members about the right way to behave, what can a school leader do to influence and change teachers' *beliefs*, particularly when those beliefs are shared by all or a large number of the group's members? This, in a nutshell, represents one of the major challenges of school leadership, and it is a major reason why schools are so difficult to change. The leadership challenge is to change teachers' *beliefs* about effective teaching practices and about working together to improve learning outcomes in the school. That is, to change their beliefs about what it means to be a member in good standing in the eyes of the other members of the group.

Successfully influencing teacher beliefs and practices thus involves *normative change*. Such changes in teacher behavior occur because teachers, as a group, have come to hold a different set of shared beliefs about how one is supposed to behave as a "good" teacher, as a member of the work group who is in conformance with the expectations of other members. Normative change includes introducing new norms and eliminating or reducing the potential negative effects of existing norms.

Said somewhat differently, norms are the group's guides to individual member behavior, and an important goal for school leaders is to cultivate the development of new (positive) group norms and/or mitigate the effects of existing norms that are negatively influencing teaching practices and school learning outcomes. The idea of negative and positive norms, as used here, is intended to differentiate between norms viewed as favorable to accomplishing what is desired and norms viewed as unhelpful to accomplishing what is desired. Accomplishing normative change is a the central value leadership challenge.

KEY FEATURES OF THE TEACHER WORK GROUP

In considering the teacher work group, and in anticipation of engaging in value leadership intended to influence group norms, two key questions arise for school leaders: (a) Where do group norms come from? and (b) What can school leaders do to influence, shape, and develop a group's norms? School leaders who understand the answers to these two questions are well on their way to being effective as value leaders.

The discussion now turns to an exploration of three basic ideas about groups and how they work. Understanding these three ideas will enable

one to describe how key characteristics of groups come together to produce group norms. Knowing these basic ideas provides the school leader
with a framework for understanding how to influence and shape group
norms. This is the information one needs in order to be an effective school
leader and change agent. Indeed, as Seymour Sarason (1990) observed,
the predictable failure of so many school reform efforts is rooted precisely
in their failure to address the *normative* dimensions of the school. That is
to say, ignoring teachers' beliefs about effective practice and about what it
means to be a member in good standing in the eye's of one's colleagues is
a major reason why so many reform initiatives fail. What teachers believe is
important!

Understanding how norms develop is necessary if one is to successfully
change a norm, introduce a norm, or sustain an existing but perhaps fragile
norm. Norms, the informal and unwritten beliefs of the group that provide
such an important frame of reference for members, emerge from the activities, interactions, and sentiments of the group as a social system (Homans,
1950). Once we understand how norms develop, we can explore strategies
for developing or changing norms. Let us take each idea separately.

Interactions refer to the exchanges and interchanges of two or more members of the group. We can distinguish these interaction behaviors in terms
of whom they include, their duration, frequency, intensity, substance, the
time of day and conditions under which they occur, and their location.
Teachers interact with other teachers in formal and informal ways in the
course of their daily work. A formal interaction might be a planned collaboration in the delivery of a lesson, or it could include the task-oriented
exchanges among teachers during a school site council meeting or a faculty, grade-level, or department meeting. Informal interactions also occur
in these contexts and can be characterized by informal exchanges and interactions at a more expressive or social level, as during breaks between classes,
in the faculty lounge, and in the halls before, during, and after students are
in session. How often teachers interact with each other, and under what conditions and for what purposes, are important determinants of how teachers
feel about each other, their levels of trust toward one another, and other
feelings and attitudes. These patterns of interaction among teachers have
important consequences related to introducing, changing, and sustaining
the group's norms.

A second group behavior that is important is the *activities* of teachers.
Activities refer to what teachers do in the course of their work as a member
of the group, in addition to their interactions with one another. Activities of
teachers include formal and informal as well as work-related and nonwork-
related things that teachers do. Teaching, disciplining students, having a
cup of coffee, meeting with a parent, eating lunch with friends or alone,
visiting the media center, doing a Web search to locate needed resources,

and reviewing students' papers or previewing a lesson plan are all examples of activities. What teachers spend their time doing has important consequences related to introducing, changing, and maintaining the group's norms.

A third idea that is needed to understand the work group and the evolution of group norms deals with group members' *sentiments*. Attitudes, feelings, perceptions, and values of group members, toward one another, toward outsiders (nonmembers, including students, teachers, parents, and [frequently] school administrators), and toward their work and themselves as individuals and as a group are the group's *sentiments*. Although teachers may bring certain perceptions, feelings, and attitudes with them to the group, sentiments also arise as a result of group member activities and interactions. It is this last point that is critical: Sentiments emerge from group member activities and interactions. These shared attitudes, feelings, and values have important consequences related to introducing, changing, and sustaining the group's norms.

A *norm*, as mentioned earlier, is a special type of group attitude that can develop as a result of the activities, interactions, and sentiments of the group members. It is important to note that a norm can either be changed or reinforced and sustained by the activities, interactions, and sentiments of the group's members.

A group norm is, in effect, an unwritten rule that reflects the group members' *beliefs* about what is expected as appropriate behavior for the group's members. Any effort to introduce change into a school that does not take into account the *norms* of the teacher group thus is at risk of failure. If a change agent is not cognizant of teacher group norms, he or she is in effect "flying blind." To use another metaphor, this is akin to trying to pin the tail on the donkey while blindfolded. It is often not a successful venture. This may be great fun at a child's birthday party, but the stakes are higher when it comes to school leadership and change.

One may be fortunate in a school reform effort to encounter work group norms that are supportive of the desired change. However, such efforts frequently fail because the existing norms of the teacher work group do not support the change. Many of the effective practices that school leaders seek to implement involve fundamental changes in the ways teachers interact, in their attitudes and feelings, and in what they do. Accomplishing such change is very difficult and the amount of time required to change norms frequently is underestimated. A school change is inevitably going to impact some aspect of the teacher group.

If the change runs counter to what teachers believe is appropriate behavior for group members, if it runs contrary to the group's norms, their core values and beliefs, then members will resist the change. To succeed requires leadership that can successfully foster normative change.

School leaders who are able to move their school toward being the kind of professional community described by Louis and colleagues (1995) may be said to have been successful in their efforts at normative change. Some of the norms identified by Louis and colleagues include:

- putting client needs before personal interests and treating all clients as equally deserving of professional respect,
- feeling a sense of responsibility for the collective good,
- a high willingness to work hard for the goals of the *school,*
- conversations about serious educational issues or problems that involve the application of new knowledge in a sustained manner,
- deprivatization of practice, including frequent examination of each others' individual teaching behaviors, rooted in a desire to improve,
- collaborating with other teachers in professional development activities that have consequences for the group, not just the individual,
- a shared commitment to the outcomes and the principles of professional community. (Adapted from Louis et al., 1995, 232–234).

Even after successfully negotiating all of the building-level beliefs held by teachers, a school leader must weigh as well the impact of district, professional association, and community norms and related influences. For example, when a teacher group changes norms and practice within one school in a district, there may continue to be very strong external pressures to return to or maintain the status quo. A school leader needs to anticipate that changes within one's school may necessitate managing external resistance to the change from district leaders, from professional associations, and perhaps from teachers and principals in other schools.

Normative change is extremely difficult. To accomplish such change means that teachers themselves have changed their beliefs about what sorts of behaviors and orientations (activities, interactions, and sentiments) are desired of group members. Key group norms must change and new ones must be introduced if such a school-based professional community is to evolve. How a school leader might accomplish this is addressed next.

VALUE LEADERSHIP TO INFLUENCE GROUP NORMS

How does one change teacher work group norms? This is the biggest leadership challenge facing educator leaders today. Value leadership, discussed previously, is a particular leadership emphasis that is specifically concerned with influencing norms by striving to change teachers' activities, interactions, and sentiments. Value leadership assumes, of course, that one has a clear idea about the valued learning outcomes and/or desired teaching, classroom, and school practices.[5]

Value leadership entails first and foremost an understanding of and a commitment to valued outcomes and practices. The reference point for the author, as to what is desired in terms of teaching practices and learning outcomes, are the standards of good practice associated with the research on effective schooling practices (Cotton, 1995) and the normative ideal of the professional school community as reflected in the growing body of empirical work about teacher professionalism and community (Little & McLaughlin, 1993; Louis et al., 1995).

If value leadership is important to facilitating normative change, how does it occur? Edgar Schein (1985) described several strategies as means to articulate, embed, and transmit culture. The two sets of ideas listed here can be adapted as value leadership strategies by school administrators and other school leaders:

1. Primary Mechanisms

   • What leaders pay attention to, measure, and control,
   • Leaders' reactions to critical incidents and crises,
   • Deliberate role modeling, teaching, and coaching,
   • Criteria for allocating rewards and status,
   • Criteria for recruitment, selection, promotion, retirement, and ex-communication.

2. Secondary Mechanisms

   • Organizational design and structures,
   • Organizational systems and procedures,
   • Design of physical space, facades, buildings,
   • Stories, legends, myths, parables about important people and events,
   • Formal statements of organizational philosophy, creeds, charters.
   (Adapted from Schein, 1985, 224–242)

By being deliberate and strategic in terms of what the school leader pays attention to, celebrates, and reinforces, one can in effect send important signals to group members about what behaviors, activities, ways of working together (interactions), and beliefs and attitudes are desired and to be re-warded. It is being deliberate and strategic in relation to the leader's core values around teaching practices and learning outcomes that constitutes value leadership. In this manner one can begin to influence the activities, interactions, and sentiments of members of the teacher group. Introducing key values and related ideas about teaching practices and learning outcomes

---

[5]See Hoachlander, Alt, and Beltranena (2001) or Cotton (1995) for examples of such practices and outcomes.

can make a difference. Providing teachers with opportunities to visit other schools where the desired practices and outcomes are being achieved, and encouraging them to discuss with one another what they observed and learned as a result of talking with teachers in the "model" school, can stimulate changes in teachers' views about what is possible and desirable.

As Dewey (1957) reminded us, educators have a special responsibility to the broader community and the children to be served by the school to be deliberately moral in their conduct. That is, to be purposeful and intentional in selecting and promulgating the means and ends of public schooling such that the best interests of students and the broader community are well served. Thus an important responsibility of school administrators, and other school leaders, is to provide value leadership that results in shaping school and work-group norms so that desired learning outcomes for children and effective teaching practices occur.

A key to successfully leading in today's schools is to understand that normative change is not only possible, if undertaken with adequate knowledge of what is required in order for such change to be accomplished, but most importantly, such change is necessary if reforms are to be successfully implemented. Improvement efforts in schools typically attempt to get teachers to change their practices in some manner. Such efforts invariably involve change at the normative level. For teachers to voluntarily adopt a change in practice, they must believe it is the right thing to do and that it will be beneficial for children and for themselves as teachers. Individual teachers are more likely to change their practices if others in their work group share a belief in and a commitment to that practice. Achieving this end is the goal of value leadership in schools.

CASE STUDY

Using your school as a source of information, describe some of the key norms that influence teachers and have consequences for teaching practices in classrooms and student learning outcomes. Talk to teacher colleagues to learn from them about what it *means* to them to be a member in good standing.

Ask teachers to tell you what sorts of things a new teacher (a true rookie or perhaps an experienced teacher newly assigned to the school) might do that would be frowned on by current staff; what might be expected of the newcomers; what might earn applause (or at least some positive feedback from current members)? The answers to these questions will provide hints about key group norms in your school.

Make a list of the norms that you feel are positive in their consequences (define what you mean by "positive") and the norms that you feel are "negative" in their consequences for teachers and/or students. Defining what you mean by positive and negative will require you to stake out a position about valued and desired practices and learning outcomes. Consult the Hoachlander, Alt, and Beltranena (2001) and the Cotton (1995) Web sites (listed in the reference section of this chapter) to help you with this decision making.

After you've made a list of the different norms and their consequences, work on developing your value leadership strategy—that is, your normative change strategy. To help you do this, answer the following questions and try to connect these ideas to the various norms you've identified:

- What are the activities of teachers in relation to the norm?
- What are teachers' interactions (with other teachers, with students, administrators, and others) in relation to the norm?
- What are teachers' feelings and attitudes (about themselves, other teachers, their work, students, others) in relation to the norm?

Once this information is available to you, work to develop some strategies that you believe might be effective in helping to influence (change, sustain, or reduce the power of) the norms you've identified. Which norms would be your initial focus; why? Make a list of the different strategies you believe might help you influence this norm in a way that achieves your goal as a school leader. One strategy to consider is the potential of introducing and developing one or several new norms within the teacher work group. How would you do this?

Develop a value leadership action plan to review and discuss with your classmates or colleagues:

- What is the norm about which you are concerned?
- What are the effects of the norm on teaching practices, learning outcomes, or other consequences; how do/will you know this?
- What teacher activities, interactions, and/or sentiments are associated with the identified norm?
- What strategies can you employ that you believe will foster the normative change(s) you desire?
- What might be some negative consequences associated with your change strategy, and how will you address those?

SUMMARY

Contemporary school improvement efforts inevitably assume some sort of change in teaching practice (what they do, how they do it, with whom they do it, how often they do it, etc.). Current work-group norms either will support and facilitate this reform effort or will serve to blunt, negate, or undermine the intended change.

A key leadership challenge is to understand the connections between desired reforms and teacher group norms. What are the key norms that will either facilitate or impede the desired change? More specifically, what teacher activities, interactions, and sentiments are (or might be instrumental in) shaping these norms?

The value leadership challenge is to design and implement strategies that will help shape teacher work-group norms in a manner that facilitates desired change. Critical to being an effective value leader in a school is the necessity to develop one's understanding of and commitment to preferred teaching practices and student learning outcomes. Finally, one cannot be an effective value leader without the ability to understand and influence teacher work group norms.

GUIDING QUESTIONS

1. What are my core beliefs about teaching practices and student learning outcomes, and why are these so important to me?
2. What is important to me about my school community, and how would I describe its key features and characteristics?
3. What are the primary activities, interactions, and sentiments of the teacher work group in my school? Why are these noteworthy and how do they impact teachers' practices, children's learning, me?
4. What kind of school community do I advocate; why? How can I as a school leader mobilize the teacher work group toward this vision?
5. What are the consequences or effects (positive as well as negative) of my school's sense of community as it currently functions: for teachers, for students, for the principal, for overall school effectiveness?
6. How do the work-group norms in my school influence teaching and learning (for better or for worse)?
7. What are the particular activities, interactions, and sentiments that I believe can help teachers work effectively as a collaborative team?
8. What key norms do I feel would be helpful in supporting teacher collaboration, and how might I cultivate their development?
9. What do I anticipate would be the consequences of such norms for my school, individual teachers, and for teaching and learning?
10. As a school leader, what can I do to influence, change, or otherwise shape my school's sense of community?

11. What are the key values I'd like others to adopt as standards for their work as classroom teachers and as colleagues? Why are these important to me as a school leader?

ACKNOWLEDGMENTS

Many of the ideas expressed in this chapter build on an earlier paper, "Connecting Value Leadership, Normative Change, and School Improvement," presented at the 8th annual Values and Leadership Conference held at Pennsylvania State University, State College, Pennsylvania, October 16–18, 2003.

SELECTED READINGS

Sources the interested student or professor may find useful in more fully understanding the issues include:

Johnson, S. M. (1990). *Teachers at work: Achieving success in our schools.* New York: Basic Books.

Johnson's work is a highly readable account of the daily lives of teachers at work in schools. She captures teachers' classroom lives as well as the broader picture of what it means to work in a school.

Little, J. W., & McLaughlin, M. W. (Eds.). (1993). *Teachers' work: Individuals, colleagues, and contexts.* New York: Teachers College Press.

Little and McLaughlin's edited volume explores the tensions between the teacher as an autonomous professional and pressures for teachers to work together as colleagues. The idea of community and its multiple meanings is explored, and the importance of teachers' work contexts is examined.

Lortie, D. C. (1975). *Schoolteacher: A sociological study.* Chicago: University of Chicago Press.

This study of teachers' work and their school work world offers a basic grounding in the social dynamics of daily life in schools and the anxieties and rewards of life as a classroom teacher.

Louis, K. S., Kruse, S. D., & Associates. (1995). *Professionalism and community: Perspectives on reforming urban schools.* Thousand Oaks, CA: Corwin Press, Inc.

This edited volume includes an in-depth examination of the idea of a school-based professional community, what it is, and why it is important. It includes five cases illustrating the struggles and successes of schools striving to develop their capacity as a professional community.

Waller, W. W. (1932). *The sociology of teaching.* London: Chapman and Hall.

This early study of teachers and their work world is as relevant today as it was over 70 years ago. The tensions between students and teachers in the classroom, between teachers and the principal, and between the school and community are richly reflected in Waller's observations of the school and teachers and their world of work.

Westheimer, J. (1998). *Among school teachers: Community, autonomy, and ideology in teachers' work.* New York: Teachers College Press.

This study compares two middle schools and the different versions they represent of the idea of professional community. It offers very practical insights about the challenges of building a school-based professional community, reminding the reader of the importance of school structures, teachers' beliefs, and their interplay in the development of community.

REFERENCES

Cotton, K. (1995). Effective schooling practices: A research synthesis 1995 update. Northwest Regional Educational Laboratory. Retrieved August 24, 2004, from http://www.nwrel.org/scpd/esp/esp95.html.

Cohen, A. R., Fink, S. L., Gadon, H., & Willits, R. D. (1995). *Effective behavior in organizations: Cases, concepts, and student experiences.* Boston: Richard D. Irwin, Inc.

Cromwell, S. (2004). Critical Friends Groups: Catalysts for Change. Retrieved August 24, 2004, from http://www.education-world.com/a_admin/admin136.shtml.

Dewey, J. (1957). *Human nature and conduct.* New York: Random House.

Greenfield, W. D. Jr. (1982). Value leadership as it relates to the principal's role in school improvement. In J. D. Kise (Ed.), *Effective schools.* OATE-OACTE Monograph Series No. 5. Ohio Confederation of Teacher Educators. Kent, OH, 20–28.

Greenfield, W. D. Jr. (1985). Instructional leadership: Muddles, puzzles, and promises. Athens: The Doyne M. Smith Lecture, University of Georgia.

Greenfield, W. D. Jr. (1986). *Values and actions: The principal's role in leading school improvement.* Nashville, TN: Center for Excellence, Tennessee State University.

Greenfield, W. D. Jr. (1995). Toward a theory of school administration: The centrality of leadership. *Educational Administration Quarterly, 31*(1), 61–85.

Greenfield, W. D. Jr. (1999). *Moral leadership in schools: Fact or fancy?* Paper presented at the annual meeting of the American Educational Research Association, Montreal, Canada, April 19–23, 1999.

Hoachlander, G., Alt, M., & Beltranena. (2001). *Leading school improvement: What research says.* Southern Regional Education Board. Berkeley, CA: MPR Associates, Inc. Retrieved August 24, 2004, from http://www.sreb.org/main/Leadership/pubs/LeadingSchool_Improvement.pdf.

Homans, G. C. (1950). *The human group.* New York: Harcourt Brace.

Louis, K. S., & Kruse, S. D. (1995). *Professionalism and community: Perspectives on reforming urban schools.* Thousand Oaks, CA: Corwin Press, Inc.

Sarason, S. B. (1990). *The predictable failure of school reform.* San Francisco: Jossey-Bass.

Schein, E. H. (1985). *Organizational culture and leadership.* San Francisco: Jossey-Bass.

Chapter 15

Principal Behaviors and School Outcomes: A Look Inside Urban Schools

Joseph J. Flessa
St. Mary's College of California

For the past several years, I have been asking various groups of people in various settings—prospective principals in the credentialing courses I teach; professors of education at the national conferences I attend; colleagues from graduate school; teachers, principals, and school board members in local urban districts—if they think that there is anything particularly *urban* about being a principal in a big-city school district, or if in fact being a principal is being a principal is being a principal. Without exception, the people I talk to are quick to say that there is something different about the principalship in an urban school. By way of explanation, people summon a variety of "urban" characteristics that, they say, make the job of being principal in an urban district more difficult than doing that work in other settings.

For example, some observers point to high rates of family poverty in urban areas and the corresponding student mobility that challenge traditional curricular planning; many link poverty and "low achievement." Others note that the number of teachers prepared to teach effectively in settings of racial, ethnic, and linguistic diversity is small while the needs in urban schools are large, so finding qualified teachers for every vacancy is a challenge. Funding concerns are also raised. In particular many students of school finance lament the way that urban school principals by necessity fund even basic educational programs in their schools via deft management of a patchwork of grants and of categorical funding; coherent planning often collapses when budgets drive instructional programming and not the other way around.[1] In short, the responses indicate, there is something urban about being an

---

[1] Thanks to Norton Grubb in particular for this observation. See Grubb and Huerta (2001).

urban school principal: The urban part is what makes an already difficult job almost impossible to do well.

Yet being a public school principal in *any* setting is hard work, by design. Part of the challenge derives from the way that schools are governed: As middle managers, school principals are the hierarchical heads of their sites, yet they are subordinate to and dependent on a central district office for the budgets and supports they need to make schools run more effectively. Part of the challenge of the job is found in the contradictory mandates principals face: Cuban (1988) suggested that principals cope daily and simultaneously with the instructional, political, and managerial imperatives of school administration. These frameworks, although generically accurate, cannot explain why many observers of educational leadership are so quick to identify the urban school principalship as a special case. Nor do generic frameworks illuminate the particular challenges of being principal in an urban school.

To begin to answer that question and to illuminate those challenges, I interviewed and observed a set of principals in one large-city school district in California. What follows are vignettes of four principals working in Springfield Unified School District (SUSD).[2] A few words about this sample of principals are in order here. First, I focused on principals at the middle school level. As a former urban middle school teacher, I am interested in the particular challenges facing that level of schooling. In addition, my review of previous research into the principalship indicated that most principal ethnographies have focused on the elementary school level, something that I did not seek to replicate. I avoided studying high schools both because of their organizational complexity and, frankly, because of personal preference.

In selecting my principals from the set of all middle school principals within the same district, I deliberately decided to diverge from the sampling decisions found in the Effective Schools literature, which typically focuses on exceptional schools. That literature is currently enjoying renewed attention (see, originally, Edmonds, 1979; Carter, 1999; Haycock, 1999) and making contributions regarding the characteristics of successful urban high-poverty schools. However, the Effective Schools work focuses on "outliers"—the handful of excellent schools for poor children in any given region that are the exceptions proving the rule. I wanted to study the rule. In other words, I studied principals whose reputation was neither exceptionally positive nor negative, working in schools whose racial and economic demographics as well as standardized test scores were typical of the district at large. All four principals work in one of the wealthiest metropolitan areas in the United States but their schools are majority poor, majority ethnic minority, and are among the lowest-ranked schools in the state. Three of the principals are

---

[2]All names are pseudonyms.

women; one is a man. None of the principals has been at his or her site for more than 4 years. Two of the principals are experienced yet new to their sites; the other two principals are new to the profession.

In some senses the cases are incomparable: The principals differ in age, sex, race, and experience, and their schools vary in size and racial breakdown. And although the principals face similar inputs—they share a level of schooling, a district, and an urban context—each principal has adapted differently to the work at hand. Part of the point of this chapter, then, is that the portraits that follow show how a combination of work context and circumstances as well as personal skills and actions led to both frustrations and successes on the job. Hopefully the variety of experiences described in the following pages provide readers with a variety of different entry points for studying and questioning their own school leadership practices.

PRINCIPAL #1: CARLA MARTIN AT CRUZ MIDDLE SCHOOL: "I AM REALLY ON THE RUN"

Carla Martin is an African American woman in her mid-40s. She carried a handheld (palm) organizer and referred to it often. Her compact frame, good posture, strong voice, and energetic walk projected self-confidence, even when she was harried. She made it clear that she was in charge, which sometimes worked against her among staff at the school. "When she got here," the veteran female security guard told me, "she told us she was the Queen Bee of the campus. And she keeps reminding us who she is. She wants us to know who she is."

Ms. Martin is a career Springfield educator (and, in fact, a Springfield public schools graduate) who came to Cruz after two years as an assistant principal at another, even more challenging middle school in the district. The conditions of her arrival were not exactly smooth: with her appointment to the position, she replaced an 18-year veteran with a career's worth of connections to the school and its community and numerous downtown connections that ensured at least a smooth daily operation. Ms. Martin has never met her predecessor; he was demoted to the classroom at another middle school across town and did not return her phone calls. When I met her, Ms. Martin was in her second year as principal.

Ms. Martin was friendly and always rushed. She often used words like "frenzy" to describe her day and characterized her approach as "very hands-on . . . it's exhausting." Each of the dozen or so e-mails that we exchanged included at least one line about feeling pressured for time, something like "this is a really difficult week for me" or "I'm sorry I have to postpone, but I'm really on the run." On the other days that I shadowed Ms. Martin, she usually greeted me with a smile and a version of "give me a minute" while she brought some sort of student disciplinary issue to a conclusion. In other words, although Ms. Martin regularly used her handheld computer scheduler, the reality of her work meant that she couldn't live by it. As she put it, "I don't get a chance to reflect and think about things because things tend to happen to me rather than me being able to manage my day." Ms. Martin was motivated by her love for "the kids" but, as a principal, she admitted that she was still learning the ropes. During my weeks of visits to the school, I got to know the visitor's-side counter in the office very well as I waited to shadow Ms. Martin and thus add another layer of complication to her already frenzied day.

Martin described her approach to the job as "child centered." What this meant in practice at Cruz Middle School was that Martin spent large portions of her day in lengthy conversations and interventions with individual students. So, although she had two assistant principals to help her with supervision of student discipline in her relatively small school with an enrollment of fewer than 500, she took a "hands-on" and "exhausting" approach to site management—with students. Her decision to shape her job in this way corresponds to the way that she talks about the purpose of schooling at Cruz.

> What keeps me coming back? The kids. Even though the kids may not be reading on grade level, or they may not be doing math on grade level and they may not all be ready for algebra, there are other needs I believe that we are meeting, and I think we have to meet those first. The social/emotional piece.

Martin also explained that she addressed the social and emotional needs of her students with this individualized focus on, especially, crises because that's what she's good at.

> I think it is definitely easier for me being African American to deal with the issues of the African American family.... I usually invite people to visit or to walk through the campus with me or something along those lines so they can get a better view of what it is that actually goes on here. So they can understand. I don't take it personally when a parent comes in here and is angry. I try to see it from their perspective and what it is. And then really just listen. And agree sometimes. Just really trying to bend over backward to help.

Ironically, Martin's individual conferencing with students was seen negatively by both the security officer (who said, "She fusses too much.") and the school secretary (who told me that when Martin's not around, "It's better here. Much happier. The kids are calmer."). Student-centeredness, then, enacted in this way and in this context, seemed to be a weakness, not a strength. It also happened to be what Martin was good at, as I saw during my shadowing. Her lunchtime conversations with students, several of whom she bought lunch for or hugged, and her availability via cell phone to her special Cruz Middle School "mentees" (the only interruptions she allowed once our taped interviews started were to talk with her mentees) were clearly at the heart of her work as principal. This work of one-by-one mentoring was also decoupled from systematic school improvement efforts.

Cruz Middle School was last remodeled in the mid-1970s, and the subsequent decades of deferred maintenance are obvious. For example, there appear to be more broken lockers than functioning ones on the campus; an ancient, car-sized, brown and yellow Kodak photocopier stands marooned, broken, in the middle of the teacher workroom; the one-story school has what appear to be bags of garbage on its roof. The classrooms in this school open directly to the outside; covered walkways designed to protect students from rain during the winter are overgrown with moss and plants and are full of holes. Unlike other schools in Springfield, Cruz has a large grass playing field in addition to the blacktop behind the school. It seems a remarkably large campus for fewer than 500 students.

According to the California Academic Performance Index (API) Cruz is ranked a 1-3. In other words, the school is in the bottom tenth of schools in the state—and at the bottom third of comparable schools. Ms. Martin described the school as serving a "very diverse group of people—we have some people who do not work at all . . . all the way to people who are professionals who own their own businesses and are entrepreneurs," but the largest proportion of the students (57%) qualify for free and reduced lunch. This statistic is most often used as a measure of family poverty. With 480 students, the population of the school is small and relatively racially homogenous; 88% of the students are African American, a small number of Asian and Latino students make up the remainder. The students do not come from the streets directly surrounding the school, where small bungalows sell for more than half a million dollars; most students arrive on the bus, are dropped off by relatives who work nearby, or cross a busy four-lane road a few blocks away to come to Cruz.

At Cruz Middle School, 58% teachers are fully credentialed. (Compare this to 78% districtwide and 86% county- and state-wide.) A significant number of Cruz teachers, 17%, are working on emergency credentials. In the 2001–2002 school year, Cruz had a total of 24 teachers, equally divided between men and women. Eleven teachers were African American; ten were White. There were two Latino teachers and one Asian American teacher. More than one-third of the students who finished the 2001–2002 school year at Cruz started the year at a different school. Ms. Martin identified this high student-transfer rate, the result of transfers both into and out of Cruz, most often prompted by a Disciplinary Hearing Panel (which is a district intervention reserved for the most severe disciplinary cases), as one of the largest challenges facing her school. "When you're talking about less than 500 kids, that's a lot of movement, in terms of really being able to make a difference in what kids are getting out of the [instructional] program."

A Management Vignette

Carla Martin at Cruz prioritized lunchtime supervision. Of the four principals in this chapter, she spent the greatest amount of time at it, supervising lunch from 11:25 AM to 1:00 PM daily, or about 7 hours per week. For Martin, this investment of time helped her to get to know students personally. By working the student lunches, she was able to take a more individualized, personalized approach to the principal's work. She was also able to catch her breath; recall that for Martin the principalship feels like a "frenzy."

> It's somewhat relaxing. If the kids were mellow that day, and they're getting along, I just kind of patrol. Sometimes I get a chance to sit and even converse with kids. And I always tell them when they're in their classes when I come through that they can see me at lunch. And so kids will be waiting; it's a chance that they know that they can catch me. I try to give everybody a few minutes. But I'm out there and that's my way of getting to know their names, getting to know that these are sixth graders and these are seventh and eighth graders. It really helps me. At first, people said to me, "You do lunch duty every day?" I think some principals don't, especially if they have two APs. But I find it helpful to me in terms of my interactions with the kids. That's a huge chunk of my day.

In this quote, Martin acknowledges that other principals in her position might not supervise both lunches. Recall that her school has an enrolment of just under 500 students. She clearly finds this lunchtime supervision satisfying ("it's relaxing"), as well as something aligned with her statement to me that "the kids" keep her committed to doing this difficult job ("sometimes I get a chance to sit there and even converse with kids"). By spending this "huge chunk" of time with students eating lunch, she has given herself a way in her daily work to interact with students in something other than punishment mode.

Principals' time is a limited resource; someone evaluating Martin's job performance would want to know whether her dedication of so much time to student supervision provided a payoff proportionate to that investment or whether in fact it might have contributed to the "frenzy" she felt on the job and was therefore counterproductive. It is not my purpose to provide that assessment in this chapter. From Martin's perspective, the personalization that she is able to provide by systematically getting to know students does have a payoff; it provides more of the "social/emotional" scaffolding that she stated was the heart of Cruz's mission. "When ninth graders come back to visit," Martin told me, "they say 'We thought you guys were mean, but now we realize you were there for us.' What I hear them saying is that [the high school] has 1,800 kids. They don't get the one-on-oneness that they're getting here with us."

PRINCIPAL #2: CAROL CARTER AT WEBSTER MIDDLE SCHOOL: WORKAHOLIC "OMBUDSMAN"

The principal of Webster Middle School is Carol Carter, a White woman in her 50s. Although this is her first principalship, Ms. Carter has held a series of schoolwide leadership positions in two districts in the Springfield area. A self-described workaholic with self-diagnosed Attention Deficit Hyperactivity Disorder (ADHD) and great management skills, Ms. Carter was in her third year as Webster's principal when I met her.

Both the head custodian and the veteran security officer attested that the school felt different under Carol Carter's principalship. "Things have changed 100%," the security guard told me. "And 100% of that change is due to her. She's very strict with everyone, she's not hidden in her office doing paperwork, and she's making the adults do their job and making sure that the kids see her in the halls." The school nurse told me at our first meeting that, "This woman moves mountains," and the in-school suspension teacher told me, "If we had a principal that didn't care here, things would go to shit overnight." The sense every interviewee gave me was that at Webster, Ms. Carter was very much in charge. She is, according to one teacher, the "alpha dog" of the school. Other teachers regularly referred to it as "Carol's school," and the after-school coordinator reflected that, more than at other schools she'd worked with, Carter was the "head honcho."

Carter called herself the "ombudsman" and saw her job as facilitating school operations and handling complaints. I came to understand her and her repeated references to being ADHD and overachieving as reflections of how much value she placed on visible, constant effort at Webster. "The school is effective," she said, "because somehow I had a knack of finding and hiring really appropriate people who fit the category of probably ADHD and are workaholics. And so that I really choose people that aren't going to be what I call clockers—they're 8:00–4:00." Her school-improvement strategy, as she explained it, was to clean things up first, to get rid of clockers, and to hire new and better people—it was with these new people that she built a new school culture. As she put it, Year One was "Mop-and-bucket," whereas Year Two was "Bulldozer," when she evaluated people out. Carter noted, "We've been very successful with grant writing, [and] the more adult humans you can have in a building that individually touch kids and help move them forward, I think the better the things that happen with respect to anything." These grants funded a variety of extra programs, including several that took place after school, such as a homework club and a Chinese orchestra, and Carter was quick to note that she was not aware of every single thing happening on Webster's campus at any one time. "One of the things I'm proudest of is that I don't know a lot of what's going on here. I feel like my knack for hiring good people means that good things are happening."

"Carter is a real starter. She's the kind of person that could go some-where and start something, but I don't know that she's a real developer," according to one of the Webster Middle School assistant principals. And one consequence of Carter's use of a hiring strategy (as opposed to a profes-sional development strategy) as the focus of her school-improvement efforts is that she has dramatically changed the racial makeup of the teaching staff at Webster. In 1999, her first year on the job, there were 14 African Amer-ican teachers and 17 White teachers. By the 2001–2002 school year, the number of African American teachers had fallen to 8 and the number of White teachers increased to 20. In 1999 there were 19 female and 21 male teachers at Webster. By 2001–2002, there were 23 female teachers and 14 male teachers. In short, Carter had a reputation among some at Webster as having overseen a transformation of a racially integrated urban school faculty into a "White woman's school." I learned that this dynamic was quite visible to Webster veterans, many of whom were proud of the changes that were taking place but also concerned about the shrinking numbers of non-White teachers. A veteran instructional aide said this about the changes she'd seen:

> Well, I'm not necessarily saying that it's bad. But I think that to be, to get, to really get some diversity, some energy and some differences of opinion, there needs to be some male and there needs to be some color. Black, Hispanic, Asian, anything but just White.

During interviews, as Carter described the changes she had instituted at Web-ster, she made statements such as "Every person I've replaced I've traded up for a better human," or, "You know, the accident that most of the people that are hired are not people of color." In that context, it is not a surprise that racial tensions between the remaining Black faculty members and Carter increased year to year during her tenure. These tensions were made most obvious to Carter herself when the remaining Black faculty and staff or-ganized a retirement party for one of Carter's assistant principals (whom Carter, by her own admission, simply ignored), a 30-year veteran of SUSD. Carter was not invited.

Webster Middle School is a building surrounded by concrete. The front of the school, with its semiopaque plexiglass windows from a late 1960s re-model, faces a busy freeway access road. Behind the school an expanse of crumbling blacktop provides the fenced-in physical education and lunchtime recess area. Although larger in size than a football field over-all, some of the play areas feel cramped. Portable buildings, brought in to address overcrowding, were placed directly in the center of the back lot, not along the perimeter, and interrupt what could otherwise have been a large open recreational space. Webster does not sit in the middle of a residential neighborhood and its feeder pattern is therefore quite large. Students travel relatively long distances from different parts of town to attend Webster. The result is that this school contains an ethnic diversity of students that their residentially segregated neighborhood elementary schools lack. During my observations, the school was always clean and orderly; student work adorned bulletin boards in the hallways and laminated signs, uniform in appearance and including the school slogan, "Tigers Triumph!" indicated the teachers and staff members at work behind every door. The halls were empty during class except for students with hall passes, custodians, security officers, and teachers on their planning periods.

During 2001–2002, Webster served approximately 720 students, of whom 39% are classified as English language learners. This statistic is used to in-dicate the number of students requiring additional support in reading and language arts because they speak a language other than English at home. At Webster, 67% of students self-identified as qualifying for free and reduced lunch. The racial breakdown of the student body was 44% African Ameri-can; 35% Asian/Asian American; 15% Latino. There were Bosnian, Filipino, Ethiopian, and Pacific Islander students at Webster also.

The point to take from this description is that Carter defined her job in such a way that it highlighted her significant technical managerial skills and downplayed the human relations work that, by her own admission, held less importance for her. For example, of the four principals in this chapter, Carter was the most effective money manager; she was skilled at knowing when and how to utilize "pots" of money to support Webster's instructional program. Alone among this set of principals, she knew how to use the district's budgeting software. She was also committed to and successful at ongoing grant writing to support auxiliary programs at the school. She chose not to put this technical disposition or overachieving ethos to work on issues that she described as peripheral to her mission such as the racial complexion and dynamics within her staff or relationships with families and community groups. Her within-school expertise did not lead to making connections beyond the schoolhouse door. Although she obviously had blind spots, Carter earned the reputation as an exceptionally capable manager of the school budget. She also put in long hours—regularly

7:30 AM to 6:00 PM, daily, more when meetings required her attendance, and she often sent e-mails or worked on drafts of grants or school plans from home, at night.

A Management Vignette

Carter indicated that she spent more time on management than instruction in her day-to-day work. In the following vignette, she describes a situation in which she focused on making immediate, visible improvements in the school facility, although she concludes that work like this "gets in the way" of more academically oriented tasks.

> CC: Here's the carpet story. So, we scraped together our $4,000 out of [General Fund] money to get a carpet for the library because I think it's really important. We've been really pushing to make the library a user-friendly place. And having carpeting that doesn't look like crap was important. So we got the money together, and interviewed all kinds of companies, and got somebody to lay it. And they came to, they pulled up the old carpet, and they went to lay the new carpet, and they started like on a Saturday at 10 o'clock or you know, and they're laying it. And we're kind of peering in. And finally at 2 o'clock the evening custodian and I kind of look in, and I realize that the carpet has what looks like tire tracks down it, very consistently. So of course I say to them, "Did you see this?" And these are the installers, they are only hired by the carpet company. They say, "Yeah, we saw it." "Did you check with anybody about it?" " No." I said, "It looks defective to me." So then, I call the carpet company and get the guy from the carpet company out, and he comes and he says, "Oh, it'll go away in a month."

> Author: Go away?!

> CC: I say, "Screw you. This is not going to happen." And so I say, "This is defective. It's through all the runs of it. It's there. Why didn't somebody stop a long time ago?" Now this conflict is going to cost me another hour or 2 of my time. More than that too because we've already interviewed four carpet companies. Got bids. Had a team of people to select carpet, and now we're finding that this carpet is unacceptable. So we will now, one, have to deal with the hassle of getting the money back. And two, there'll be the hassle of getting a new carpet company to come and do something close to what we want. So again, this is going to be that very kind of thing that we were talking about. Time away from educational processes. Is it really important to have quality stuff, and should I be the keeper of the gate with respect to accepting or not accepting? Of course I should. And will it be nice to have instead of a really old, dirty, spotted carpet a nice carpet? And you know, the inclusion of more furniture that will make it look like a nice place for kids to study and be? Yeah. But it's just one of those levels of involvement as the principal that just gets in your way.

I observed Carter devote hours on several different days to arguments and negotiations, in meetings and during phone calls, with the private contractor hired to install the new carpet in Webster's library. She was supervising the installation herself in the facility she had closed 6 months earlier for cosmetic renovations, of which the carpet was to be the most visible component. Carter acknowledges in her retelling of "the carpet story" that her hands-on approach to this issue took "time away from educational processes." When I asked her why she didn't take the more academically oriented stance in dealing with the library, focusing on the librarian, for example, whom she had previously described to me as "someone I'm trying to get rid of," she told me two things. First, she said that the librarian had tenure. Next, she told me that replacing carpet was easier and quicker than replacing a teacher. In this way, Carter made a calculation to pursue the more visibly rewarding path, and the one over which she had more direct control. That Carter's decision to spend time on this problem would, in the end, have some sort of visible and lasting benefit to the school site is accurate. It is also accurate, as she acknowledges, that her devotion of time and energy was not directed at teaching and learning and in fact "got in the way."

That said, Webster Middle School has made dramatic academic gains during Carol Carter's tenure.[3] Furthermore, she reports that she finds her distance from the classroom frustrating.

> I do believe that a lot of the work that I do has nothing to do with what I thought being the educational leader of the school would be. And I think a lot of time is spent doing things like fighting with the carpet people about carpet that should have been laid fairly expeditiously. Why do I need to worry about the bushes that are outside? Why do I need to worry about a variety of things that fall into that category? Modernization, you know, as older schools have become upgraded. Why isn't there enough money for wiring to have a computer in every classroom that's connected with the Internet? I mean, although these [managerial tasks] are related to an educational and a safe environment for kids, I would much rather spend most of my day sitting in a teacher's classroom saying, "Here's what I saw you do. This looked good. Here's a way that you can improve." Because I think that ultimately, that's the most important job of a [principal] because if I can touch you as a teacher to do a better job, then you can touch kids to do a better job.

In this quote Carter communicates her vision for instructional leadership: She wishes that she could spend "most of my day in a teacher's classroom because if I can touch you as a teacher to do a better job, then you can

---

[3]Webster is no longer on the California "Immediate Intervention Underperforming Schools Program" list, and the leadership team was invited in 2003 to present to a statewide audience about how they made such progress so fast.

touch kids to do a better job." She chooses not to do that, though, because the managerial tasks facing Webster are important and demand on her time. Although Carter found her work on "things in the bushes that are outside"[4] category frustrating, she nonetheless continued to do that work. Carter says in the quote above, "A lot of the work that I do has nothing to do with what I thought being the educational leader of the school would be." In making this statement, Carter highlights the fact that the expectations and conditions that principals work under sometimes function at crossed purposes; she wants to focus on teaching, but instead she works on bushes and carpets.

PRINCIPAL #3: CLARK CAMPBELL AT FRANKLIN MIDDLE SCHOOL: THE CAMPBELL SYSTEM IS WORKING

Clark Campbell is principal of Franklin Middle School, and he carries a bullhorn. Although only in his second year as principal at Franklin, Mr. Campbell has more than 20 years' administrative experience in Springfield, many of them as principal and assistant principal at some of the district's most challenging schools. He is a tall African American man in his early 50s and has earned a reputation for establishing discipline and routines in out-of-control schools accustomed to daily fights and chronic student truancy. Although I had been warned that Mr. Campbell wouldn't have time for me—"He's got his system *down*, and he isn't interested in interruptions" is how one assistant principal put it—Campbell in fact welcomed me with very little preamble and was a lively and open participant in my investigation.

Campbell's reputation was very good among everyone I spoke with at Franklin. The head of the cafeteria told me that I was "shadowing one of the best." One of Campbell's two assistant principals told me:

> because he knows the community so well and he has been at this school [previously, as assistant principal] for so long, he has a big advantage of being a known quantity and being here a lot. He's here early and people know the school is taken care of. And I don't know how he really does it besides his presence, but he knows about everything going on here.

In part, the assistant principal's quote acknowledges that Campbell's presence as an African American principal of what had been until recently an African American school in a predominantly African American neighborhood made school/community interactions, at least for some parents, more

---

[4]The worry about the bushes was not a cosmetic landscaping issue. She was concerned because they provided "shelter," during the night, for homeless people to sleep, individuals who were sometimes still on campus when students started to arrive.

familiar and comfortable. During my visits, Campbell seemed to remember parents' names, ask after their other, already-graduated children, and communicate an interest in those graduates' continued well-being. Franklin's other assistant principal stated that Campbell's just a natural at the work of being principal and is charismatic enough to accomplish serious things there. This assistant principal said,

> This particular school is very fortunate because it has a principal who, how can I put this, who has an exceptional understanding of the community and the community understands him, relates to him, and the school. It definitely comes from his own background. And his appreciation of the culture. Just, how can I put this, it's an intuitive appreciation, too. It's not a put-on appreciation or like he's faking it. It's instinctive for him.

Campbell was often blunt, even with parents, some of whom interpreted that bluntness as disrespect and rudeness. Although the positive changes he'd made at Franklin protected him from too much fallout, the district office got its share of complaints from families about Campbell's rudeness.

> CC: I'm too direct with some parents, and they don't like it. Just like I'm direct to students and stuff, sometimes I'm direct to parents when I think that they're out of bounds, too. They say, "Well, you don't talk to me like that!" And I say, "Ma'am, you asked me a question and I gave you an answer. You didn't like the way I said it, then that's on you." And then, "Oh! I'm going to go tell the superintendent." And I say , "I don't care who you're going to tell. Go tell him!" "You think I'm not?" I say, "You just said you was! What you waiting for?" You know, then they go down and they tell [the superintendent] that I'm rude and that I'm abrasive and I'm disrespectful to the parents and all this kind of stuff. But you know, all you got to do is talk to my [School Site Committee], all you got to do is talk to my PTA, all you got to do is talk to my [English Language Advisory Committee], my bilingual parents, they'll march down there and they'll tell them, "No, no, no, that's not true." So I don't worry about those isolated parents who are trying to get something for nothing.

> Author: So, the superintendent calls you and he wags his finger at you, and that's it?

> CC: [The superintendent] don't call me no more. He used to call me saying stuff, but he just calls and says, "I hear you had a conflict with such and such." And I'll say, "Yep, I sure did." "Okay, well, have a good day." Yeah, he don't mess with me no more.

Campbell's contact with parents, then, is in some ways more comfortable and routine than is Carter's. His "abrasive" style, however, caused him some problems downtown.

Campbell saw his responsibility at Franklin as first and foremost maintaining discipline and order among the students and hiring teachers who wanted to work with Franklin's student population. He summed up his approach this way: "If you're willing to work with me and my program, I'll make you a better disciplinarian. If you have a heart. That's what I'm looking for. I'm looking for academic skills and heart. I'll take care of the rest." Furthermore, he told me, "I want worker bees here. We don't need any queen bees—just good worker bees." Said another way, Campbell is like Carter, very much in charge. Also like Carter at Webster Middle School, he saw the route to school improvement originating with new and dedicated teaching staff—"worker bees"—while he did the schoolwide coordination. Carter and Campbell's strategies are similar, but their conception of teaching is slightly different. First, for Carter it's about visible effort and hard work (ADHD overarchievers). For Campbell it's about "heart."

Like Carla Martin, Campbell is a Springfield native and a graduate of Springfield schools. He is friends with the superintendent, whom he has known since high school. The superintendent's impression of Campbell is that he's charismatic, good at discipline (for which he was hired) but that, frankly, he will be evaluated out of the job in a few years on instruction if test scores don't go up. "Unfortunately," the superintendent told me, "that's part of the way we set people up in this district. Campbell runs a tight ship. But I also need someone there working on instruction." Neither the superintendent's description of the Campbell system nor Campbell's own definition of that system included much direct mention of teaching and learning.

Franklin Middle School serves a neighborhood in East Springfield. Most students live nearby. The traditional, two-story, 1950s-era building is clean and well-maintained. The recreation yard is blacktop and houses several portable buildings. Although the school was almost all African American as recently as 10 years ago, the current student population reflects demographic changes taking place in East Springfield and is now about two-thirds African American and one-third Latino. Half of Franklin's students qualify for free and reduced price lunch. Only 38% of Franklin's teachers are fully credentialed. Franklin's teaching staff is made up of 20 women and 17 men; overall, 19 of the teachers are White, 13 are Black, and 4 are Latino. Campbell's two assistant principals are a White woman in her first administrative position and a Black man who, after 5 years as a teacher at Franklin, is now in his third year as assistant principal.

Here are the takeaway points for Campbell: he is a friendly and charismatic principal. Like Martin, he feels a special connection to some Franklin parents and kids, particularly those who are African American; unlike Martin, he does not let his interactions with parents and families dominate his day or force him into a "frenzy." Like Carter, he is squarely authoritative in his approach to school management, but because he conceives of teachers as little more than "worker bees" and because he devotes little time to direct supervision of teaching and learning, the Campbell System has less to do with academics than it does with discipline.

A Management Vignette

The Campbell System anticipated and addressed many school-site managerial problems. One strategy at the heart of the system was to use the "who you know" strategy to get things done. In the following vignette, Campbell describes a situation where he put that strategy to use. Campbell describes how the district did not hold up its end of the bargain after requiring that Franklin Middle School upgrade its furniture. After responding to the district mandate and timeline to clear things out, Campbell then waited for 5 days for the district to pick things up. He was eventually successful only after using the who-you-know strategy.

> They tell us to get all the broken furniture together in the school site, and they're going to bring a dumpster out. We get all the broken furniture together, we pack it all outside, then they don't bring the dumpster. Then you got all these teachers steady bringing all this stuff out, right, so when the dumpster finally comes, you put it in the dumpster, the dumpster fills up immediately, and they don't remove it and bring another one. So, all this stuff is piled up outside, people going down [the street alongside the school], adding stuff to the pile, making the school look like a junkyard, so you know you've got to call the superintendent. You call the superintendent, you know, "David, pass by my school, look at the crap out there, that's not acceptable." And *then* they jump. If he can do it in 5 minutes, why does it take us 5 days? I'm running the school site. That's crazy.

So, Campbell had to resort to calling the superintendent to request special attention to solve a not-special maintenance issue. That the school couldn't get its garbage collected without the direct intervention of the district superintendent indicates a system in trouble. It also indicates that an urban school principal needs to mobilize a variety of strategies to accomplish even the most mundane tasks, and who you know matters. Campbell relies on personal contacts and networks to get things done downtown. Obviously, he can't always rely on his friendship with the superintendent, so he uses a human-relations strategy in general to get some of the support that he needs. He was very direct about this goal. "It pays to know people in the district office," he told me.

While I shadowed Campbell, I observed him teaching this approach to his administrative team. During a before-school meeting with his assistant principals, for example, he gave this advice to a novice assistant principal who was unable to find a long-term substitute teacher replacement for a teacher who left in the middle of the school year. Campbell told her "You need to get a *live person* on the phone in that office. And then you need to know who you talked to and you need to familiarize yourself with them so that they will handle your work more expeditiously. Otherwise it comes back on you and then you've got more business to take care of." During the weeks that I spent at Franklin, I heard that advice applied in a variety of situations. When counseling the same assistant principal to be persistent in her efforts to get the maintenance department downtown to send someone to remove the graffiti from the front of the school, Campbell told her, "You've got to be friends with them." On a different day, when attempting to solve a payroll issue with one of his custodians, Campbell told him, "Go to payroll, but also go to HR. And be sure that you get names. Not 'somebody told me' but a specific name and title." One strategy for leveraging resources from the large bureaucracy in an urban district, then, is for principals to develop special, personal relationships with the people who can help them get things done. The consequence of an approach like this, however, is that it does nothing to build districtwide capacity. In other words, for every time that the superintendent is working on Campbell's garbage collection, he's not working on one of the equally frustrating things that is taking place in any of the other hundred schools in Springfield. Furthermore, this approach also works best with veterans—and veteran principals are in very short supply in urban districts.

PRINCIPAL #4: CAROLINA MONTOYA AT CHAVEZ MIDDLE SCHOOL: NO ONE'S LIGHTNING ROD

Carolina Montoya is a Mexican American woman and was in her first year as principal at Chavez Middle School when I met her. She has more than 15 years' experience as a school administrator, most of it at the high school level in a large city in another state. She is the fifth principal of Chavez Middle School in 4 years and understands that, naturally, most teachers and school community members are wondering how long she'll last. "The silver lining is that if I offer stability, I think I've outdone my three predecessors! Just hanging in here, just staying put. But there's a lot of work that has to be done." The fact that a basic condition for effective school administration—lack of turnover—is so rare says something about the strained professional working environment at Chavez. The predictability of principal turnover is also one of the urban pieces of school administration in Springfield. Montoya was the only Latino/a principal of a comprehensive middle school in Springfield during the period of this study.

Ms. Montoya is a former physical education and health science teacher and carries herself with straight-backed posture. She is in her 40s and, though younger than Campbell, speaks about her experiences with a similar degree of perspective.

> The most important thing is my attitude and who I am with the kids and who I am with the staff. I feel I have high standards, but I also feel that I don't need to be a horse's ass to get anything accomplished. This is a great job, but it doesn't need to consume you. I mean, the day that I don't like coming to work, then I shouldn't be here.

When I first met Ms. Montoya, she was standing at the counter in the main office explaining enrollment procedures in Spanish to a man whose daughter was seated behind him. I sat down to wait for her to finish with this parent. In fewer than 5 minutes I watched Ms. Montoya be interrupted three times—once by the secretary wanting to know where to send the substitute teacher, once by a security officer stating that a certain class had no coverage, and once by her own phone, which she did not answer. Throughout this encounter, Montoya showed the same composure that I came to recognize as central to her principalling skills—she answered questions when she could but stayed focused on what she decided was the most important task at hand. In this case she was polite and efficient with the parent while also quick to direct interruptions to others on her staff whom she felt could better take care of the concern.

The teachers, security officers, administrators, and other staff that I spoke to about Ms. Montoya were guardedly optimistic about the changes that she seemed capable of making at Chavez. More than once people said, "knock on wood" in the middle of their positive descriptions of Carolina's reliability. One veteran Chavez teacher put it this way:

> My experience with a really good principal here is—well, I think this might be the *first* year that I'm starting to see what a principal can do. I'm afraid to even say it that maybe she's really good. And will she be here next year? I don't know. So we're all a little like holding our breath.

Again in this quote there is evidence that, at Chavez, consistency was so rare as to be worthy of special mention. Montoya emphasized to me the importance of routines and predictable processes for soliciting teacher and parental input and for making decisions. For example, she initiated a standing meeting 20 minutes before the start of each school day with her whole administrative team: the three assistant principals, the security officers, the counselors, and the county mental health counselor (i.e., almost anyone with a schoolwide perspective on students at the school). This mechanism was a built-in way not only to talk about, for example, who was returning from suspension, but also to mention, as I observed one morning, that a student's cousin had been shot over the weekend and that this student could probably use a little TLC (tender loving care). Another example of her attendance to routines and visible, reliable processes for decision making is her approach to site-based shared decision making.

> What we've been trying to do is diversify the membership because faculty council and school-site council and instructional leadership council, I want them to look different, I don't want the same power brokers to be in all of them. The only power broker that's there is me. I'm the only consistent one with all of them. And it's working so far. I mean, we go through some growing pains. But it seems to be more collaborative. They still struggle with trust. They'll probably struggle with trust for a while, a couple years.

In this quote there is evidence that Montoya's approach to site leadership is similar to Carter's and Campbell's—she is firmly authoritative as "the only power broker there." On the other hand, the very acknowledgment of shared decision-making structures distinguishes her from her colleagues. She sees utility in the long run in utilizing these committees, and she acknowledges the difficulties associated with being new but trying to institute shared, collaborative work that requires trust. Montoya recognized the long-term, incremental work ahead of her and she stated that she agreed with the school reform adage that "you have to go slow to go fast."

Also similar to Campbell, Montoya focused on student discipline and, in particular, gangs. With 14 years' experience as a high school principal, Montoya was not naïve about urban school violence. "I have been to a student funeral every year," she told me. Campbell and Montoya, independent of one another, each organized parent meetings to address gang slang, clothes, and other signifiers of allegiance and discussed ways for parents to intervene. Montoya's parent workshop was conducted in the evening and in Spanish and addressed the consequences of gang-identified behavior at Chavez, where the major fights were between American-identified ("Sureño") and Mexican-identified ("Norteño") gangs. Montoya talked a lot about her high expectations for students, and she also talked about setting in place a school climate where teachers will also raise their expectations. "As a Latina, I'm particularly sensitive to the ways that we adults in a school enable kids *not* to perform. There's a '*pobrecito*' mentality among some teachers that they use as an excuse not to teach these kids."

Chavez Middle School is located in a neighborhood that is, yearly, increasingly Latino. As Montoya puts it, "Driving through this neighborhood is like driving through Mexico. From the early, early morning dynamics of a community, it literally wakes up at 6:00–6:30, and people are selling things on the side of the street, and people are stopping and buying them, including me!" The school faces a busy thoroughfare that connects the upper-middle-class hills to the working-class, industrial flatlands of Springfield. Chavez is located in the flatlands. The front of the building is adorned with a colorful, multiethnic mural and the campus includes buildings (the gymnasium and the cafeteria, for example) from the first half of the 20th century.

Chavez Middle School was built in 1922 and is the largest middle school in Springfield, with student enrollment of 1,150. The racial makeup of the student body is 53% Latino, 23% African American, and 16% Asian/Asian American. At Chavez, 72% of students qualify for free and reduced lunch. When describing the challenges facing the school, Montoya mentioned the difficulties associated with being a school that serves communities in transition. "This specific school has a very needy population. It has a high mobility rate, almost 25%. It's a high-density rental community—there's a lot of fluidness and it's not as stable as a suburban community would be."

Chavez' API rank is 1-1. In other words, it is among the handful of very lowest middle schools in the state of California in terms of standardized testing. In the 2001–2002 school year, Chavez employed 41 teachers of whom 20 were White, 12 were African American, 7 were Latino, and 1 was Asian. There were 68% fully credentialed teachers at Chavez during that school year.

The takeaway points for Montoya are that in many ways—as a newcomer to the district, taking over the largest middle school, one with a history of rapid principal turnover and the lowest level of student achievement—she faced the greatest challenges. Because in part of her personal disposition and because in part of the skills developed elsewhere, Montoya stated that she was not overwhelmed by the job but in fact recognized step-by-step ways that she could make an impact. Chief among her responsibilities, as she understood them, was to put in place routines and rituals as an attempt to address systematically the challenges facing Chavez.

A Management Vignette

According to Carolina Montoya, part of an urban school's responsibility is to teach students appropriate behavior. She says that the job of the administrator, then,

> means teaching and training and reinforcing and talking and retalking to the kids about just having a higher level of understanding of what's acceptable and what's not. And for them to be a part of making those decisions because part of the drain is that when only the adults want the students to have a certain change in behavior and the students don't; that's a feuding process. They have to have the same want to change. No doubt about it, I would love for the kids to have higher standards in terms of responsibility for their academic learning,

for them to truly take their learning seriously and to excel with it. Also higher standards for decisions and how those decisions affect them. Oftentimes cause and effect is not even in the same orbit for them. You know it's what I called those stupid decisions that kids make that have more of a detriment to them than they even think possible.

Author: Give me an example.

CM: Oh bringing a knife to class, bringing a knife to school and showing it off without the intent of harming somebody, but being foolish and taking it out and playing knife. I don't know what games they play right now, it used to be like Power Rangers, but now it's that Judo guy. So they have a knife thinking that they're doing that but, you can't do that! So the district has a protocol, here's a knife, if it has a blade of a certain length it's an automatic suspension with a Disciplinary Hearing Panel and before you know it the kid goes into that process and they don't realize that the simplicity of it was not to have brought the knife at all. The consequences that they made a choice to take it out to show it off, and now you have the school process you have to go through. And it's crazy.

Montoya's description of the school's "training" role is similar to Carter's notion of teaching students how to "do school." She also acknowledges that it is a time-consuming process that requires vigilant "talking and retalking." Later in the interview Montoya stated that the students at Chavez were street smart—"they don't see themselves as academically smart, but they're definitely very smart about how they survive in the community"—but they were also ignorant of the ways that certain behaviors, such as showing off a knife, could have serious negative consequences inside the school. Part of Montoya's work, then, was not only to respond to situations where students bring weapons on campus, it was also to educate her student population that "the simplicity of it was not to have brought the knife at all." Although Montoya stated that her attention to student discipline per se was not necessarily urban—"regardless of where you are," she said, "it's important to have a safe school"—Montoya did state that in urban schools addressing discipline is especially important. Montoya's description here reveals that she interprets part of the mission of urban schools to include serving as an antidote to the negative environments that students come from. Montoya says

I think [having a safe school] is more important in the urban setting because so many of our students have already witnessed a substantial amount of violence, either in the home or in the community. And this sometimes becomes their haven, so we have to ensure that the school is safe and give kids specific parameters of what's acceptable and what's not acceptable. So it's kind of like trying to provide a home away from home with a lot more structure.

Montoya implies two things in this quote. First, she states clearly that the job of the school and, by connection herself as principal, is to provide an environment where students feel safe and cared for. The implication of saying that Chavez should be "a haven" with "specific parameters of what's acceptable, or a home away from home with a lot more structure" is that the school has different expectations of how to ensure this level of safety and care than the families or community do. The point to take away from this discussion is that, according to Montoya, the schools have to focus on teaching discipline because those skills may not currently be built outside the school in a way that schools find "acceptable" or "appropriate."

SUMMARY

The preceding vignettes do not compare urban and nonurban school principals. However, they suggest that, at least from the principals' own perspective, being principal in an urban school is especially challenging work, given the simultaneous, urgent managerial and instructional needs that demand principals' time. The four principals reacted to these needs with a combination of strategies—hands-on, who-you-know, clean-house, establishing routines—and management occupied more time than instruction. Some observers of principal leadership have provided frames for thinking about the combination of knowledge, skills, and beliefs it takes to be effective on the job. Hughes (1999), for example, suggested that one must combine the skills of artist, architect, and commissar. Deal and Peterson (1994) called for "bifocal" principals who are able both to manage and lead. Such characterizations provide a useful metaphorical frame for understanding alternative approaches to doing the work of being principal. The experiences of these four individuals show that even when a principal's repertoire is varied, however, management tends to become an end in itself, suggesting that the job of putting managerial tasks to work for important academic goals requires both individual principals' skills as well as institutional and structural support. The guiding questions that follow provide readers with an opportunity to review the four vignettes in order to articulate their own perspectives about the skills and supports that principals need on the job, particularly in urban school districts.

GUIDING QUESTIONS

Read the Table 15.1, and consider the questions in the third column. How would you answer the questions? What questions would you add?

TABLE 15.1   Different Conceptualizations of the Principalship
and the Questions Raised

Principal	Conceptualizations of the Job	Analytical Questions About the Urban School Principalship
Carla Martin	• "hands-on" • "social and emotional piece" but not "the academic piece" • "issues of the African American family" • working with students one by one	By spending time working well with individuals, the school's operations languish; by focusing on "trees" Martin loses sight of the "forest." What combination of bridges and walls—by connecting to other adults at Cruz and protecting at least some of her time on campus—might address the overwhelming "frenzy" she feels?
Carol Carter	• "Ombudsman" who coordinates adults' complaints • "ADHD overachiever" for whom visible hard work is important • manages budget effectively and raises money to increase the number of adults at school with contact with kids • gets rid of clockers and "trade up for a better human"	Webster Middle School was removed from a low-performing schools list. Is Carter's excellent school-based management actually premised on not addressing broader issues? By avoiding conversations about race among adults at school, what opportunities are missed? What tradeoffs would Carter have to make in order to prioritize, say, increasing parental involvement at Webster?
Clark Campbell	• "Campbell System" is about discipline and order, not teaching • teachers should have heart and teach; he'll take care of everything else • uses the who-you-know approach to getting things done downtown	The Campbell System has made Franklin Middle School a safer, happier place. Direct attention to teaching and learning are not part of the System. The discipline/academics split is a version of a Deweyan *Either-Or*—what combination of incentives and sanctions might help Campbell to focus Franklin's attention on classroom instruction? How would you classify Campbell's approach to parents?
Carolina Montoya	• just showing up and being predictable is progress this year • systematic routine check-ins are the way to keep school under control and express concern for students	Montoya states that she needs to "go slow to go fast" with her school improvement work. What are the costs of this approach in a school failing so dramatically as Chavez? Are there some things that, in fact, she should move fast on? Do these systems in fact free up more time for principals to focus on instruction?

1. What managerial tasks occupy your/your principal's time? How you spend your time communicates what your priorities are. When you analyze how you spend your time, what priorities do you see emerging in your day-to-day work? Are these the priorities you want to have?

2. Many new principals in large districts lack the sort of connections to use the who-you-know strategy successfully. What should new principals do in order to get the sorts of support that they need from their district office supervisors? In a time of budgetary constraints, what sorts of district-level support are feasible?

3. In this chapter there is a lot of demographic and background data provided for each school. How, if at all, do you think this kind of data matters to a school principal? Is there any evidence that it mattered to these four principals? What else would be important to know?

4. Is there something "urban" about being principal in a school in a large city? Or, at the end of the day, is the principal's job pretty much the same?

SELECTED READINGS

Anyon, J. (1997). *Ghetto schooling: A political economy of urban educational reform.* New York: Teachers College Press.

Boyd, W. L. (1991). What makes ghetto schools work or not work? In *Advances in educational administration, Volume 2: School Leadership* (pp. 83–129).

Cuban, L. (2001). Leadership for student learning: Urban school leadership—different in kind and degree. Washington, DC: School Leadership for the 21st Century Initiative, Institute for Educational Leadership.

Noguera, P. (1996). Confronting the urban in urban school reform. *The Urban Review, 28*(1), 1–19.

Rury J., & Mirel, J. (1997). The political economy of urban education. In M. Apple (Ed.), *Review of research in education,* Vol. 22 (pp. 49–113). Washington, DC: American Educational Research Association.

REFERENCES

Carter, S. (1999). *No excuses: Seven principals of low-income schools who set the standard for high achievement.* Washington, DC: The Heritage Foundation.

Cuban, L. (1988). *The managerial imperative and the practice of leadership in schools.* Albany: State University of New York Press.

Deal, T., & Peterson, K. (1994). *The leadership paradox: Balancing logic and artistry in schools.* San Francisco: Jossey-Bass.

Edmonds, R. (1979, October). Effective schools for the urban poor. *Educational leadership, 37*(1), 15–24.

Grubb, W. N., & Huerta, L. (2001, April). *Straw into gold, resources into results: Spinning out the implications of the "new" school finance.* Research Series 01-1. Berkeley: Policy Analysis for California Education, Graduate School of Education, University of California, Berkeley.

Haycock, K. (1999). *Dispelling the myth: High poverty schools exceeding expectations.* Washington, DC: The Education Trust.

Hughes, L. (1999). *The principal as leader.* Upper Saddle River, NJ: Merrill.

Chapter 16

Culture, Climate, and School Outcomes

Angus J. MacNeil
University of Houston

Educators who have served in more than one school or who have had the opportunity to serve in a supervisory capacity and visited schools on regular bases can attest that each school is distinctive and unique. Over the years many different names have been used to describe the sometimes subtle, elusive force that makes up the "who we are" phenomena that forms the human behavior in schools. Sometimes terms such *ethos, atmosphere, personality, genre,* and *philosophy* are used in reference to this phenomena characteristic of a school. The terms most often used to describe this phenomenon are *organizational culture* and *climate.*

Gareth Morgan (1998) told us that organizational management theories are based on images and metaphors with differing effects, creating profound insights but also distortions. Theories of organization have been shaped by metaphors such as machine, factory, and other culture phenotypes. School leaders can avoid fads by selecting metaphors wisely and using them to develop new ways of working. School leaders have to understand their schools in different metaphors then the mechanistic principles that have dominated school organizational theory for the last 50 years.

This chapter begins with an understanding of the importance of school culture. Next is a discussion about the building and leading the school culture that will create a school climate that will result in an education that will contribute to the success of its students. The chapter continues with a dialogue about the relationship between school culture and climate and then proceeds to focus on the concept of climate and how school leaders can use climate to improve the school.

This chapter explains that the reform movements have been unsuccessful at improving schools and explores the intricate nature of culture of culture and climate as a foundation of school improvement. There is an examination of the concept of climate and how it is measured and how school personnel can make use of the measurements for climate.

The chapter concludes with some propositions for strategies for improving school leadership that will change the school culture and improve school climate and create a successful learning community for students. The focus of the chapter is to help create a school culture and climate that supports the notion of school as a learning community.

CULTURE

There is substantial evidence in the literature to advise and guide a school leader that he or she must first understand the school's culture before implementing change. Evidence includes:

1. Bulach (2001) suggested that a leader must identify a school's existing culture before attempting to change it.
2. Watson (2001) warned us that if the culture is not appropriate, promising practices will not be successful.
3. Fink and Resnick (2001) reminded us that school leaders are responsible for establishing a pervasive culture of learning and teaching in each school.
4. Leonard (1999) studied the dynamics and complexities of a school culture when teacher values were compatible and in conflict with school culture with predictable results.
5. Mortimore (2001) warned us that we should concentrate on establishing more knowledge about the complex interactions between culture and schooling.
6. Lakomski (2001) studied the claim that it is necessary to change an organization's culture in order to bring about organizational change and concluded that there is a causal relationship between the role of the leader and organizational learning.
7. Taylor and Williams (2001) agued that as accountability through tests has become a threat, school leaders need to work on long-term cultural goals.
8. Fullan (2001) contended that the concept of instructional leader is too limited to sustain school improvement. He promoted that school leaders serve as change agents to transform the teaching and learning culture of the school.

Testimony from successful school leaders suggests that focusing on leading the school's culture is the "way to go."

1. Nomura (1999) advised that school leaders understand their school's culture.
2. Reavis, Vinson, and Fox (1999) explored how a new school leader at a historically low-performing high school brought about changes in the school culture and how it positively affected student achievement.
3. Kytle and Bogotch (2000) examined school reform efforts through a "reculturing," rather than a "restructuring," model with positive results.

Two issues that obviously respond positively to efforts at "reculturing" schools is inclusion and school bullying and/or violence in schools.

1. Zollers, Ramanathan, and Yu, (1999) recommended that a school's culture should be understood when implementing inclusion.
2. King (2000) theorized that a large part of moving from self-contained practices to inclusion was school leadership.
3. Friedland (1999) recommended that if school leaders need to work at violence reduction they must start with the school culture.
4. Lantieri (2001) suggested that more school security and elaborate security hardware will not solve the problem of safety in schools; it will require a cultural change in the school. Schools need to address this challenge by replacing a culture of hostile cliques with a climate of respect (Brendtro, 2001).
5. Carter (2002) suggested that culture of many schools create, condone, and sustain aggression.

School leaders who choose to lead rather than just manage must first understand the school's culture. It is important to realize that culture is complex because it has very unique and idiosyncratic ways of working. When an organization has a clear understanding of its purpose, why it exists, what it must do, and who it should serve, culture makes things work excellently. When the complex patterns of beliefs, values, attitudes, expectations, ideas, and behaviors in an organization are inappropriate or incongruent, culture makes things work badly. Successful school leaders comprehend the critical role that culture plays in developing a successful school.

Building Organizational Culture

One of the more important concepts in organizational theory is authority and responsibility. Responsibility for the execution of work must be accompanied by the authority to accomplish the job. Within the education community there is a constant debate about the level of authority a school leader should have. The concepts of centralization and decentralization are continually in play. School leaders often complain about their powerless condition. Indeed, Goldhammer and Becker (1971) found that successful school leaders were often critical of the central office restraints and found it difficult to live within the constraints of the bureaucracy. Yet as stated earlier, the role of the leader in shaping the school culture is considered critical. The power of leadership for shaping the culture of the school when used wisely can empower the faculty, students, and parents and in return empower the school leaders. Leaders who understand the importance of the relationships in the school and develop those relationships so that faculty, student, and parents function well are truly leaders of the school culture.

Players

Educational leaders need to recognize that to build a strong school culture requires leadership from many different people. Every organization has people who function and perform in different ways. Deal and Peterson (1999) referred to some of the faculty roles found in school organizations as priests and priestesses, storytellers, heros and heroines, and gossips. There are many examples from practitioners that use even more pejorative terms to describe the roles played out by teachers, students, parents, and other administrators in the school. School leaders who effectively use the informal communication networks in their school and understand the roles played by various teachers are effective leaders. Roles and relationships are complex in a school. Someone who may be priest in one situation may be a gossip in another. An example is a teacher who is highly competent in a subject area and on a curriculum issue may be a priest but when the issue changes to something different, he or she may become a storyteller or even a gossip. The roles are never that clearly defined and change with the issues. As wise school leaders are inclined to say "it depends." Most teachers play many roles in the school depending on the issue and their expertise, experience, and respect or trust with the other players in the school. School leaders when focusing on staff development classify the teachers differently than when they are focusing on issues concerning curriculum, assessing and deciding on student placement, discipline—both student and teacher, athletics, student affairs, parent involvement, public relations, staffing, organizing schedules and timetables, balancing accounts, procuring resources, organizing human resources other than faculty, managing the facility, and the many other responsibilities that they are charged to be accountable. As one teacher described it, "one day you're a hero the next day you're a bum." Knowing and using human resources is an effective tool when building school culture.

Stories, Myths, and Legends

School leaders who have had the opportunity to be assigned to a school that has a "wild culture" or a "dysfunctional culture" know that one of the first things they must do is change the talk. If the talk of the school is about Heros and Legends that are dysfunctional, criminal, hostile, or negative, the talk reflects the culture. When the talk is about student success, achievement, accomplishment, civility, citizenship, and sacrifice for the cause, then the players are shaping the culture. The expression they can "talk the talk" but can they "walk the walk" comes from knowing that the real talk comes from people who can "walk the walk."

If the school has sycophants, naysayers, malcontents, and chronically dissatisfied people to reshape, the culture requires a new direction in the talk of the stories, myths, and legends for the school. School leaders are especially important in creating school culture. School leaders communicate values and represent the "stuff that matters" in their school buildings by what they say and do. Teachers emphasize values or the school culture in their words and behavior. Parents add to the culture when they visit school, participate in governance, and celebrate successes. School culture and the leadership of the culture come from many sources.

Rites, Rituals, and Symbols

Another key aspect in creating organizational cultures is the everyday activities and celebrations that characterize the organization. Most successful organizations have people who make extensive efforts to make sure that these rites, rituals, and symbolic actions should be adhered to as well as lead and managed. Through rites and rituals, recognition of achievement is possible. The achievements that represent the values of the organization are encouraged and celebrated and become part of the stories and legends of the organization. The failures and disappointments, although learning experiences, are not celebrated and don't become part of the rites and rituals of the school. Student orientations, grading day, achievement days, pep rallies, and graduation exercises usually have positive symbolic meanings. The symbols of the school—the colors, mascots, crests—are useful to identify the school and when worn on the clothing of teachers and students, they symbolize the pride and commitment individuals have for their school. The importance of symbols in our society cannot be underrated. The Nazi Swastika started as a secret symbol of Christianity and turned into a symbol of hate.

Culture Phenotypes. How is school culture described? There are many examples in the literature that describe types of school cultures. Lunenburg and Ornstein (2004) used many analogous or metaphorical statements from the literature about the school to convey the type of school culture. Practitioners themselves use analogous terms to describe school cultures. School as a machine, factory, prison, or cabaret illustrate some of the analogous terms used to convey the notions of what is right or wrong with the school. Recently, perhaps because of research and the resulting literature, the notions of schools being effective and efficient have been pervasive. These organizational behavioral terms support the business models of the hierarchical, mechanistic machine and factory age that were supported by the scientific management by theorists such as Frederick Taylor and Max Weber. The business of school is not like the business of a factory. The factory model may work effectively and efficiently when building widgets but educating people requires a different culture.

The Greek academies, the Roman lyceum, monastic schools of the Middle Ages, and religious schools of today are based on the concept of community. School as a learning community has a very old and long tradition. Learning communities or schools that are committed to educating all participants and where the joy of learning is celebrated in the rites, rituals, and symbols of the school focus on the civility of the citizens, which Thomas Jefferson advocated was the purpose of public education. Many schools that follow the factory model, when left unattended, take the form of a "wild culture" (Sergiovanni, 2001). Sergiovanni (2001) said that the job of the school principal is to try to unravel and make manifest the wild culture so that it can be examined and understood. This creates a culture that helps those involved understand the values and beliefs that are desired. The first responsibility of any school leader is to "domesticate" this culture so that it emerges as a system of shared values and beliefs that define for all a way of life that is committed to quality teaching and learning. "The goal of domestication of the school is to create community" (Sergiovanni, 2001, p. 182). School as community provides the model for finding and making meaning for the framework of culture building. It is a powerful remedy that can protect the school from negative influences and help it achieve its goals. Researchers have compiled some impressive evidence on the effect school culture has on learning. Healthy and sound school cultures correlate strongly with increased student achievement and motivation, and with teacher productivity and satisfaction.

RELATIONSHIP BETWEEN CULTURE AND CLIMATE

Organizational culture and climate have been described as overlapping concepts by theorists (Miner, 1995). Hoy, Tarter, and Kottkamp (1991) offered a distinguishing view between climate and culture with school or organizational climate being viewed from a psychological perspective and school culture viewed from an anthropological perspective. Differences between school climate and culture are highlighted in organizational studies. Often the climate is viewed as behavior, while culture is seen as comprising the values and norms of the school or organization (Hoy, 1990; Heck & Marcoulides, 1996). Lunenburg and Ornstein (2004) described organizational climate as the total environmental quality within an organization and believed that the recent attention to the effectiveness of public schools and their cultures has shed more interest on the importance of climate.

Even though the notions of school culture and climate are similar and overlap in their meanings and usage, major distinctions between the two exist. One difference is that culture consists of shared assumptions, values, and norms, while climate is defined by shared perceptions of the behaviors of the members of the school or organization (Ashford, 1985). Even though the conceptual distance between culture (shared norms) and climate (shared perceptions) is small, it is still real (Hoy & Feldman, 1999). Hoy and Feldman (1999) believed this difference is meaningful and crucial because shared perceptions of behavior are more readily measured than shared values. They described climate as fewer abstracts than culture (more descriptive and less symbolic) and concluded that climate presents fewer problems with empirical measurements. Climate is the preferred construct when measuring the organizational health of a school.

Climate

Freiberg and Stein (1999) described school climate as the heart and soul of the school and the essence of the school that draws teachers and students to love the school and to want to be a part of it. This renewed emphasis on the importance of school climate is further reinforced by a meta-analysis study performed by Wang, Haertel, and Walberg (1997), which finds that school culture and climate were among the top influences in affecting improved student achievement. Their study also finds that state and local policies, schools organization, and student demographics exerted the least influence on student learning.

According to Hoy and Tarter (1997), unhealthy schools are deterred from their mission and goals by parental and public demands. Unhealthy schools lack an effective leader and the teachers are generally unhappy with their jobs and colleagues. In addition, neither teachers nor students are academically motivated in sick schools and academic achievement is not highly valued. Healthy schools that promote high academic standards, appropriate leadership, and collegiality provide a climate more conducive for student success and achievement (Hoy, Tarter, & Bliss, 1990). Because the culture and climate of the school affects student achievement and the school leader directly influences the culture and climate, the question should be asked: What qualities of strong leadership help to create healthy school climates that support and promote student achievement?

IMPORTANCE OF THE SCHOOL LEADERSHIP

There is substantial evidence concerning the importance of leadership for creating good schools (Sergiovanni, 2001; Snowden & Gorton, 2002; Ubben, Hughes, & Norris, 2001; Donaldson, 2001; Blase & Kirby, 2000; Freiberg, 1999). Ultimately, the relationships that shape the culture and climate of the school are strongly influenced by the school leadership. "In schools where achievement was high and where there was a clear sense of community, we found invariably that the principal made the difference" (Boyer, 1983, p. 219).

The most significant change in school culture happens when school leaders, teachers, and students model the values and beliefs important to the institution. The actions of the school leaders are noticed and interpreted by others as "what is important." A school leader who acts with care and concern for others will develop a school culture with similar values. The leader who ignores the value and input of others places a stamp of approval on selfish behaviors and attitudes.

THE FAILURE OF SCHOOL REFORM

DuFour and Eaker (1998) believed, "Despite persistent attempts to reform public education, there is little evidence to suggest that schools have become significantly more effective in meeting the challenges that confront them" (p. 16). Neither the Excellence Movement of the 1980s nor the Restructuring Movement of the 1990s was successful in achieving meaningful improvement in schools. "The demands of modern society are such that America's public schools must now provide what they have never provided before: a first-rate academic education for nearly all students" (Schlechty, 1997, p. 235). The relationship between the school leadership and the subsequent health of the culture and climate of the school are fundamental issues to be addressed if schools as learning communities are to achieve the goal of improved student learning. An urgent need exists for school leaders to design learning communities that accentuate the learning process for both students and teachers (DuFour & Eaker, 1998).

Considering the connection among the school leadership, the resulting climate of the school, and the level of student achievement, it is worthwhile to question the leadership skills needed to positively affect climate and increase student achievement. Fairman and McLean (1988), in their work with dimensions of organizational health, believed that diagnosing the climate or health of schools in order to capitalize on existing leadership strengths and for identifying improvement priorities should be the goal of every school leader.

Despite numerous attempts at reform and a one-third increase in educational funding, in November 1990 the National Testing Service issued a report that summarized the results of what seemed to be the "education reform decade" of the 1980s: Student achievement had not improved (Fiske, 1992). Fiske further summarized that the reforms of the 1980s failed because public schools were never designed to prepare students for the demanding, fast-paced jobs of the future. The rigid, bureaucratic structures of schools used were designed for the early Industrial Age. The goal was to turn out well-trained workers. Unlike schools of the Industrial Age, the schools of today must prepare students to think for themselves, negotiate huge amounts of information, and think creatively. With schools being required to meet a different set of needs for a very different set of students, the current industrial factory model of today's schools is no longer effective.

Lunenburg (2001) contended that past reform efforts have failed because they fail to reach the classroom where learning occurs. He further suggested that in an ideal school, improvement efforts should focus directly on the classroom and not simply the organizational structure of the school or system itself. Even the famous five-factor model for effective schools of Edmonds (1979) was dropped into schools in a top-down bureaucratic fashion (Creemer & Reezigt, 1999). The reason for their lack of sustained affect in student improvement is that these improvement strategies were too strongly related to the content of school improvement and too loosely related to the environmental climate of schools (Scheerens, 1992). Successful changes in the effectiveness factors must be aligned with changes in the school climate in order for lasting improvement to occur (Freiberg, 1999).

Ogawa, Crowson, and Goldring (1999) suggested that one of the foremost reasons for the failure of current reform efforts is that many of the main structures and roles of schooling have remained stable and unchanged over time, even in the face of elaborate and expensive reform efforts to change them. The resulting changes in schools fit into existing organizational structures but have not penetrated to the classroom where learning occurs (Cuban, 1988, 1992; Tye, 1987).

DuFour and Eaker (1998) suggested the following reasons for the failure of the reform and restructuring movement to effect meaningful improvements in schools: (a) the complexity of the task, (b) misplaced focus, (c) lack of clarity on intended results, (d) lack of perseverance, and (e) failure to appreciate and attend to the change process.

The relationship between the school leadership and the subsequent health of the climate of the school are fundamental issues to address if schools as learning communities are to achieve the goal of improved student learning. Even today policy makers are demanding that the main focus of schooling be improved teaching and learning (Elmore, 2000).

Successful leaders have learned to view their organizations' environment in a holistic way. This wide-angle view is what the concept of school culture offers school leaders. It gives them a broader framework for understanding difficult problems and complex relationships within the school. By deepening their understanding of school culture, these leaders will be better equipped to shape the values, beliefs, and attitudes necessary to promote a stable and nurturing learning environment.

Researchers have compiled some impressive evidence on school culture. Healthy and sound school cultures correlate strongly with increased student achievement and motivation and with teacher productivity and satisfaction.

The overwhelming majority of studies on school climate focus on adults in the form of teachers and leader-teacher relations and subsequent issues of job satisfaction. In fact, school climate has rarely been studied in relation to its effect on student achievement (Miller, 1993). In recent years, the emphasis on climate has shifted from a management orientation to a focus on students (Sergiovanni, 2001). The reform efforts of the last 30 years have failed to improve student achievement in schools because they failed to adequately address the importance of the culture of the school. The first major purpose of a school is to create and provide a culture that is hospitable to human learning (Barth, 2001). Structural changes made to improve schools without addressing the culture and organizational health of schools have failed as well.

Deal and Peterson (1999) defined symbolic leadership as the ability to understand and shape the culture of the school. A school leader who creates a culture that promotes and encourages learning is absolutely essential in order to improve student achievement in schools. The connection between effective schools and strong leadership is supported by educational research.

FOCUS ON CLIMATE

School leaders who care and focus on the specific aspects of the dimensions of school climate that affect the culture of the school promote student achievement (Pellicer, 2003). Stated in more precise and descriptive language, healthy schools are schools that exhibit the following types of cultures:

1. The school staff share strong support for the goals and objectives of the school. The mission and vision of the school are clearly stated and supported by the school leader and the staff.
2. Members of the school's staff communicate effectively both horizontally and vertically. Information is relatively distortion free and accurate.
3. A balance of power exists between the school leader and the teachers. Teachers and staff feel empowered to make decisions and exert influence within the school.
4. The work of the school involves the staff in a cooperative fashion and is relatively free of conflict and strain.
5. The staff of the school have a clear sense of identity. They want to be a part of the school; they share its mission and are willing to sacrifice their personal needs for the improvement of the school.
6. The staff of the school enjoy a sense of job satisfaction and professional motivation and feel their needs are being met.
7. The staff of the school feel free to take professional risks. They are allowed to be creative and inventive in their work.
8. The external demands of the environment do not negatively affect the goals and ideals of the school.
9. The school culture is effective in tolerating the stresses of the external environment and remains stable under stressful situations.
10. The staff of the school are able to identify problems and solve them with minimal energy.

The comparisons between school climate and student achievement can help school leaders to focus their efforts to improve student achievement. Saranson (1996) stated that if we want to change and improve the outcomes of schooling for both students and teachers, there are features of the school that must be changed.

The efforts of policy makers and school leaders to improve student learning in American schools has had less than expected results; Education leaders need to reframe and refocus their leadership efforts. Simply altering the structure and expectations of schools has failed over the last 50 years. Schlechty (1997) suggested that structural change that is not supported by cultural change will fail because it is in the culture that any organization finds meaning and stability. Educational studies of school change have isolated the organizational culture of schools as a critical factor to the successful improvement of teaching and learning (Fullan, 2001). Deal and Peterson (1999) stated that study after study confirms that the culture of the school and its resulting climate must support reform or improvement will not occur.

Improvements in student achievement will happen in schools with positive and professional cultures that reflect positive school climate.

SUMMARY

Strong school cultures have better motivated teachers. Highly motivated teachers have more success with student performance and student outcomes. School leaders seeking to improve student performance should focus on improving the school's culture by getting the relationships right between themselves, their teachers, students, and parents. Measuring school climate and using these assessments to focus the school's goals are important for the process of improving the schools' academic performance.

GUIDING QUESTIONS

1. Explain the concept of organizational culture and climate.
2. What influences the creation of an organizational culture?
3. Why should school leaders focus on the school's culture?
4. Explain what is meant by organizational climate.
5. What are the differences between organizational culture and climate?
6. How do culture and climate relate to performance in schools?

SELECTED READINGS

Deal, T. E., & Peterson, K. D. (1999). *Shaping school culture: The heart of leadership.* San Francisco: Jossey-Bass.

Freiberg, H. J. (1999). *School climate: Measuring, improving and sustaining healthy learning environments.* Philadelphia, PA: Falmer Press.

Fullan, M. (2001). *Leading in a culture of change.* San Francisco: Jossey-Bass.

Pellicer, L. O. (2003). *Caring enough to lead: Schools and the sacred trust* (2nd ed.). Thousand Oaks, CA: Corwin Press.

REFERENCES

Ashford, B. E. (1985). Climate formations: Issues and extensions. *Academy of Management Review, 10,* 837–847.

Barth, R. S. (2001). *Learning by heart.* San Francisco: Jossey-Bass.

Blase, J., & Kirby, P. C. (2000). *Bringing out the best in teachers: What effective principals do.* Thousand Oaks, CA: Corwin Press.

Boyer, E. (1983). *High school: A report on secondary education in America.* New York: Harper & Row.

Brendtro, L. K. (2001). Worse than sticks and stones: Lessons from research on ridicule. *Reclaiming Children and Youth, 10*(1), 47–49.

Bulach, C. R. (2001). A 4-step process for identifying and reshaping school culture. *Principal Leadership, 1*(8), 48–51.

Carter, C. (2002). Schools ethos and the construction of masculine identity: Do schools create, condone, and sustain aggression? *Educational Review, 54,* 27–36.

Creemer, P. M., & Reezigt, G. J. (1999). The role of school and classroom climate in elementary school learning environments. In H. J. Freiberg (Ed.), *School climate: Measuring, improving and sustaining healthy learning* (p. 37). Philadelphia, PA: Falmer Press.

Cuban, L. (1988). Constancy and change in schools. In P. W. Jackson (Ed.), *Contributing to educational change.* Berkeley, CA: McCutchan Deal.

Cuban, L. (1992). The corporate myth of reforming public schools. *Phi Delta Kappan, 74,* 157–159.

Deal, T. E., & Peterson, K. D. (1999). *Shaping school culture: The heart of leadership.* San Francisco: Jossey-Bass.

Donaldson, G. A. Jr. (2001). *Cultivating leadership in schools: Connecting people, purpose, and practice.* New York: Teachers College Press.

DuFour, R., & Eaker, R. (1998). *Professional learning communities at work.* Bloomington, IN: National Educational Service.

Edmonds, R. (1979). Effective schools for the urban poor. *Educational Leadership, 37,* 15–24.

Elmore, R. F. (2000). Building a new structure for school leadership. *American Educator, 23*(4), 6–13.

Fairman, M., & McLean, L. (1988). *Organizational health: Implications for the Springfield Public Schools.* Fayetteville, AK: University of Arkansas.

Fink, E., & Resnick, L. B. (2001). Developing principals as instructional leaders. *Phi Delta Kappan, 82,* 598–606.

Fiske, E. (1992). *Smart schools, smart kids: Why do some schools work?* New York: Simon & Schuster.

Freiberg, H. J. (1999). *School climate: Measuring, improving and sustaining healthy learning environments.* Philadelphia, PA: Falmer Press.

Freiberg, H. J., & Stein, T. A. (1999). Measuring, improving and sustaining healthy learning envirnoments. In H. J. Freiberg (Ed.), *School climate: Measuring, improving and sustaining healthy learning environments* (p. 11). Philadelphia, PA: Falmer Press.

Friedland, S. (1999). Violence reduction? Start with school culture. *School Administrator, 56*(6), 14–16.

Fullan, M. (2001). *Leading in a culture of change.* San Francisco: Jossey-Bass.

Goldhammer, K., & Becker, G. L. (1971). What makes a good elementary school principal? *American Education, 6*(3), 11–3.

Heck, R. H., & Marcoulides, G. A. (1996). School culture and performance: Testing the invariance of an organizational model. *School Effectiveness and School Improvement, 7*(1), 76–96.

Hoy, W. K. (1990). Organizational climate and culture: A conceptual analysis of the school workplace, *Journal of Educational and Psychological Consultation, 1*(2), 149–168.

Hoy, W. K., & Feldman, J. A. (1999). Organizational health profiles for high schools. In H. J. Freiberg (Ed.), *School climate: Measuring, improving and sustaining healthy learning environments* (p. 85). Philadelphia, PA: Falmer Press.

Hoy, W., Tarter, J. C., & Kottkamp, B. (1991). Open school/healthy schools: Measuring organizational climate. London: Sage.

Hoy, W. K., & Tarter, C. J. (1997). *The road to open and healthy schools: A handbook for change, elementary and middle school edition.* Thousand Oaks, CA: Corwin Press.

Hoy, W. K., Tarter, C. J., & Bliss, J. (1990). Organization climate, school health, and effectiveness: A comparative analysis. *Educational Administration Quarterly, 26,* 260–279.

King, S. (2000). Principals influence culture of inclusion. *High School Magazine, 7*(7), 45–46.

Kytle, A. W., & Bogotch, I. E. (2000). Measuring reculturing in national reform models. *Journal of School Leadership, 10*, 131–57.

Lakomski, G. (2001). Organizational change, leadership and learning: Culture as cognitive process. *International Journal of Educational Management, 15*(2), 68–77.

Lantieri, L. (2001). An ounce of prevention is worth a pound of metal detectors. *Reclaiming Children and Youth, 10*(1), 33–38.

Leonard, P. (1999). Understanding the dimensions of school culture: Value orientations and value conflicts. *Journal of Educational Administration and Foundations, 13*(2), 27–53.

Lunenburg, F. C. (2001, August). *Improving student achievement: Some structural imcompatibilities.* Paper presented at the annual meeting of the National Council of Professors of Educational Administration, Houston, TX.

Lunenburg, F. C., & Ornstein, A. C. (2004). *Educational administration: Concepts and practices* (4th ed.). Belmont, CA: Wadsworth/Thomson Learning.

Miller, S. K. (1993). *School climate.* Reston, VA: National Association of Secondary School Principals.

Miner, J. B. (1995). *Administration and management theory.* Brookfield, VT: Ashgate.

Morgan, G. (1998). *Images of organizations: The executive edition.* San Francisco: Berrett-Koehler.

Mortimore, P. (2001). Globalization, effectiveness and improvement. *School Effectiveness and School Improvement, 12*, 229–249.

Nomura, K. (1999). Learning to lead. *Thrust for Educational Leadership, 29*(2), 18–20.

Ogawa, R. T., Crowson, R. L., & Goldring, E. B. (1999). Eduring dilemmas of school organization. In J. Murphy & K. S. Louis (Eds.), *Handbook of research of educational administration* (2nd ed.), pp. 277–295.

Reavis, C. A., Vinson, D., & Fox, R. (1999). Importing a culture of success via a strong principal. *Clearing House, 72*, 199–202.

Saranson, S. (1996). *Re-visiting the culture of the school and the problem of change.* New York: Teachers College Press.

Scheerens, J. (1992). *Effective schooling: Research, theory and practice.* London: Cassell.

Schlechty, P. (1997). *Inventing better schools: An action plan for educational reform.* San Francisco: Jossey-Bass.

Sergiovanni, T. J. (2001). *The principalship: A reflective practice perspective* (4th ed.). Needham Heights, MA: Allyn & Bacon.

Snowden, P. T., & Gorton, R. A. (2002). *School leadership and administration.* New York: McGraw-Hill.

Taylor, F. W. (1911). *Principles of scientific management.* New York: Harper.

Taylor, R. T., & Williams, R. D. (2001). Accountability: Threat or target? *School Administrator, 58*(6), 30–33.

Tye, B. B. (1987). The deep structure of schooling. *Phi Delta Kappan, 69*, 281–284.

Ubben, G. C., Hughes, L. W., & Norris, C. J. (2001). *The principalship: Creating effective leadership for effective schools* (4th ed.). Needham Heights, MA: Allyn & Bacon.

Wang, M. C., Haertel, G. D., & Walberg, H. J. (1997). Learning influences. In H. J. Walberg & G. D. Haertel (Eds.), *Psychology and educational practice* (pp. 199–211). Berkeley, CA: McCuthan.

Watson, N. (2001). Promising practices: What does it really take to make a difference? *Education Canada, 40*(4), 4–6.

Weber, M. (1947). *The theory of social and economic organizations* (Talcott Parsons, Trans.). New York: Oxford University Press.

Zollers, N. J., Ramanathan, A. K., & Yu, M. (1999). The relationship between school culture and inclusion: How an inclusive culture supports inclusive education. *International Journal of Qualitative Studies in Education, 12*, 157–74.

Chapter 17

Professional Development and Education Improvement?

C. M. Achilles
Seton Hall University and Eastern Michigan University, both part-time

Christopher H. Tienken[1]
Monroe Township School District

Is professional development (PD) a panacea for perceived shortcomings in the educational system? To begin answering that question one must accept the view that the education system is broken and likewise accept that PD has helped, or will help to fix the system. The literature on professional development as a method to increase student achievement reads like a mystery novel. The mystery is determining what really works. The PD archives are replete with mixed results based on feel-good surveys or on studies with questionable methodology. The few quality studies that do exist provide professional development possibilities and clues but are small in scale.

This chapter examines the idea that professional development is an effective education-improvement tool and raises questions about its ability to change teacher behavior and impact student achievement. The first section provides an overview of the logic behind a claim of professional development efficiency and a summary of high-profile attempts to legislate PD to fix perceived deficiencies in the American education system. A second section questions researchers' ability to connect professional development to (a) changes in teacher behavior or (b) to improved student outcomes. A third section presents two small-scale, experimental studies that have demonstrated teacher change and student gains and might serve as approaches to job-embedded PD efforts. The efficiency and viability of such

---

[1] Portions of this material are from Achilles (2003, Winter) and from Tienken (2003).

limited studies for large-scale improvement remain to be seen. The chapter concludes by reviewing proven strategies and often overlooked alternatives to professional development that do increase organizational effectiveness to help teachers teach and improve student achievement. As shown in the fourth section of the chapter, these alternatives are logical, effective alternatives to expensive, ineffective PD that often removes teachers from their students and classrooms.

MORE PROFESSIONAL DEVELOPMENT! WHY?

The constant focus on and funding for professional development, nearly to the exclusion of other education-improvement strategies, has derailed education improvement. This focus wrongly blames teachers and (indirectly) teacher preparation for presumed education deficiencies and shields other possible causes, such as inept school administration activities, a lack of careful goal setting and problem definition, or poor research and evaluation work.[2]

Challenging Professional Development As Presently Done for Capacity Building

Constantly renewing one's knowledge and skills requires professional development. In some fields (e.g., medicine, dentistry) the impetus for improvement and renewal comes from and is primarily supported by the person. In education, however, professional development is often mandated with specific days allocated as part of the educator's work year. Typically, students do not attend school on these days.

Professional development has huge commercial interests with a deeply embedded infrastructure, often manifest as entire departments in central offices dedicated to PD and human resources and featuring experts in any fad. PD is driven by a national organization, a thriving textbook market, cadres of staff developers (many professors "moonlight" heavily in this), and hordes of special projects—many untested and unproven as to student benefits. Some projects promise to address any actual or perceived need (Have I got a project for you!)—but only after the project's developer has given potential users ample inservice exposure. Federal, state, and local funds fuel much professional or staff development and inservice events.

---

[2]This paper does not deny a need for professional development. It raises questions about various approaches to capacity building and improvement, including PD for all ills.

Nevertheless, the emphasis on PD-type events in education seems top-heavy and out of balance when assessed against three criteria:

1. Those who receive the professional development (e.g., teachers) will demonstrate positive change in skills, knowledge, attitudes, and behaviors.
2. The desired changes and improvements should be measurable and observable in the short term and in the long term: They become the norm until better knowledge, skills, and the like are available.
3. Because the ultimate beneficiary of professional development should include the clients (i.e., students), the results of PD should lead directly to observable, measurable positive change in student outcomes on clearly defined criteria.

Definitions Are Important.   Because research and professional discussions should be clear and precise, and because words may mean different things to different people, we provide a definition of relevant terms in Table 17.1. As used here, professional development excludes advanced degree work. However, an unpopular study by Haller, Brent, and McNamara (1997) called into question the value of advanced preparation in education administration (Ed Ad).

Some Empirical Evidence.   Teachers seldom clamor for more professional development. Regardless of self-reports and surveys, scant, if any, replicable, scientific-based research (SBR) relates PD to (a) changes in teacher behavior and (b) improved student outcomes. Articles and ideas for education improvement perpetuate, with unsupported assertions, that professional development is required. However, many studies that have demonstrated improved student outcomes do not find concurrent and observable teacher changes even if teachers self-report them. The absence of such a finding is particularly notable in relation to organization changes, such as class size or school size that do provide replicable student gains. Because professional development has been around a long time and has received huge expenditures of time, funds, and effort, one might expect demonstrable, replicable SBR evidence of PD successes. The depth and ubiquity of the problem are evident in the question "Can you provide two or more high-quality, replicable, independent, empirical studies (SBR) of the positive effects of professional development on teacher behavior and especially of its effects on student short- and long-term success as usually measured?" Table 17.2 data demonstrate the dearth of evidence supporting professional development outcomes as "scientific" research.

TABLE 17.1   A Glossary of Terms as Used in This Chapter

Inservice training refers to one-time or short-term training, usually a specific workshop or large-group session to present information or a basic skill, easily learned, usually delivered primarily via one-way communication. The training may include job-embedded elements, but there typically is no follow up.

Job-embedded staff or professional development is planned and continuous training that in education specifically emphasizes teaching or instructional skills and knowledge related to student outcomes. Examples include action research and evaluation, structured study groups, peer coaching, and mentoring.

Professional development (PD) is ongoing, planned, continuing education through which certified, qualified teachers, and other education professionals improve skills, knowledge, and attitudes/dispositions related to assisting students achieve the goals of the organization (i.e., improved student performance and outcomes). A primary interest is to improve the professional's long-term value in workplace performance. Interaction and two-way communication are an integral part of the long-term effort. PD (as distinct from personal improvement) should have at least two levels of observable, measurable impact: (a) to improve the participant's observed professional practice when measured against stated criteria, and (b) to influence positively the achievement of students when measured against desired outcomes. The new professional practice will be sustained as part of the professional's armamentarium.

   Note that PD, as defined here, excludes formal advanced work, such as for a degree or certification. Experience, a type of on-the-job training (OJT), is also excluded.

Staff development (SD) involves workshops, training, and knowledge related to the workplace and is offered to both professional and support personnel. The focus may not be on classroom performance but rather on personal and job-related topics of interest and value to staff and to organization maintenance or health (e.g., retirement planning, first aid training, diversity training, conflict resolution, policies/procedures related to law, etc.).

Note: Definitions are adapted from Covert (2003, pp. 16–17); Tienken (2003, pp. 14–15); and Tienken & Achilles (2004, pp. 153–154). In these studies, the researchers explained the connection of PD to observed changes in teacher behavior. Tienken connected the job-embedded work to measured student improvement in writing (experimental design); Covert sought to determine if changes in teacher behavior persisted at least a full year in the use of running records, the emphasis of the PD.

Does History Repeat Itself?

Recent history of professional development includes 50 years of legislated spending by state and the federal governments. Social forces and ideologies produced multiple requests for improved teaching and student achievement. National and international events combined with a narrowly test-driven view of learning led to increased scrutiny of teachers, student achievement, and education leaders.

Russia's launch of Sputnik in 1957 prompted American legislators to criticize public education vehemently and demand reforms in mathematics and science education. Sputnik's political ramifications brought funding through the National Defense Education Act (NDEA). (Remember,

TABLE 17.2 Sample of Studies That Support Professional Development
(PD) But Fail to Find Empirical Evidence of Teacher Change or
Student-Improvement Gains

Source/Focus/Design	Title/Outcome/Quote
Guskey, T. R. (1997)	Research needs to link professional development and student learning. (Title of Article)
Haller, Brent & McNamara (1997) Advanced training in EdAd.	No measurable difference on "Effective Schools" indicators of advanced training.
Carpenter (2000) reviewed school reform efforts (1990–2000).	Professional development (and other reforms) have had little impact on student achievement or on school improvement.
Newmann et al. (2001, January). Broadly theoretic and conceptual paper. School capacity focus.	"The case for substantial investment in [professional development] is vulnerable because of an absence of research that links specific forms of [professional development] to changes in teacher learning and practice and to student achievement gains." (p. 53).
Garet, Porter, Desimone, Birman, & Yoon (2001). Focus on teacher learning.	National probability sample (n = 1027). Teachers self-reported on a survey. No evidence of student gains.
Bodilly et al. (2003). RAND Evaluation of New American Schools (NAS) implementations.	"[R]eforms such as NAS—including teacher-reported collaboration, professional development, and revised instructional practices—were *not* related to student achievement." (p. 6)
Covert, S. L. (2003, p. 25). Review of research for a dissertation on professional development (Eastern Michigan University)	"Given the lack of studies which demonstrate professional development effects on teachers or student outcomes." (p. 25) Argues for attention to theory to guide professional development.
Tienken, C. (2003). Review of research for a dissertation on professional development (Seton Hall University).	Minimal evidence of professional development changing teacher behavior or student achievement. Job-embedded professional development seems promising.
Guskey, T. R. (2003, p. 79). Review of 13 lists of "effective professional development." Dearth of SBR work and evidence of outcomes. Mostly "surveys of opinions." (p. 749)	[L]ists could be described as 'research based.' But that research rarely includes rigorous investigations of the relationship between the noted improvements in instructional practice or learning outcomes." (p. 749).

education is a state function until national security or abridgment of constitutional rights brings federal action.) Although much NDEA funding focused on mathematics and science, foreign language, guidance, and professional development in general received great attention.

The Elementary and Secondary Education Act (ESEA) of 1965 (PL 89-10), the education cornerstone of President Johnson's War on Poverty, called for professional development to promote high-quality teaching. The Emergency School Assistance Act (ESAA) was an education response to civil rights and desegregation issues because it targeted low-achieving, poverty-stricken students. In some ways ESEA and ESAA helped to create and support the belief that professional development would help teachers overcome the numbing impacts of poverty and deprivation. Multiple studies have shown that ESEA programs failed to make good on promises of meeting the needs of poor children (Borman & D'Agostino, 1996; Wong & Meyer, 1998; ABT Associates, 1997). By extension, part of the blame for failure can be attributed to how the funds were spent.

A focus on education intensified after *A Nation at Risk* (National Commission on Excellence in Education [NCEE], 1983). The NCEE—without data, of course—recommended professional development for teachers as one means of raising student achievement (1983). The fact that the report was a political tool rather than an education critique has clearly been identified by subsequent writers and researchers (e.g., Bracey, 2003; Berliner & Biddle, 1995) and even by a systems analysis of education conducted at the Sandia National Laboratories (Carson, Huelskamp & Woodall, 1991).

The Eisenhower funding program, Title II of ESEA, was implemented in 1985 to improve math and science instruction. The program extended the NDEA of 1957 and allocated funding for professional development in mathematics and science. Although PD to improve student outcomes appeals to educators and politicians, the impacts of this multibillion-dollar program have yet to be determined by scientific studies, or even evaluated thoroughly.

In 1989, President Bush, business executives, and governors held an "education" summit to discuss the education progress made since *A Nation at Risk*. Educators were not invited. The meeting led to six broad education goals to be attained by the year 2000 (National Education Goals Panel, 1991). Even though some goals were only remotely the responsibility of schools, such as requiring all children to come to school ready to learn, the goals became policy in 1994 under the "Goals 2000: Educate America Act" that provided PD funds. Results of the increased spending and focus on the Goals 2000 professional development efforts have not yet been determined. However, when narrative writing results for the National Assessment of Education Progress (NAEP) were released for 1998, 45% of the 19,816 fourth-grade students who took the exam were rated in the bottom three categories of "uneven," "insufficient," or "unsatisfactory" (NAEP, 1999). As a sidebar, the 2002 NAEP results showed improvement for fourth graders but not for eighth graders. Does PD only work in elementary grades?

The preceding reports, policy initiatives, and ideological issues brought about calls for national curricula standards, tests, and professional development to improve teaching and increase student achievement. President G. W. Bush signed the No Child Left Behind (NCLB) Act into law on January 8, 2002. Section 1001 of NCLB recommended increased PD to elevate the quality of instruction delivered to students.[3] By 2002, many states had core curriculum content standards, tests to monitor their implementation, and professional development requirements for teachers.

Professional Development in Schools

Historically, professional development for teachers consisted of single-day inservice events or workshops with little follow up. Loucks-Horsley, Hewson, Love, and Stiles (1998) defined a workshop as a structured approach to staff development that usually occurs outside of the classroom and involves leaders with some form of expertise and teachers who attend specific sessions. As early as 1983, Joyce and Showers stated that one-day events were largely ineffective relative to classroom implementation. Teachers did not include the content of the inservice activities in future lesson planning or implementation. Achilles, Dickerson, Dockery-Runkel, Egelson, and Epstein (1992) identified an alternative to single-day training and wrote that, "Successful in-service is not an add-on; it occurs during the day in the laboratory of the classroom. Some type of continuing 'renewal' is needed if educators are to stay current and vibrant" (p. 3). Another point on the professional development continuum included PD as school reform. Garet and colleagues (2001) included study groups, mentoring, and coaching as reform-types PD. Although traditional and general workshops tend to occur outside a teacher's classroom and outside the regular teaching day, focused reform activities occur within classrooms (embedded), during school hours (e.g., during the teacher's daily preparation period). Activities generally relate to actions teachers can take to remedy or enhance instruction.

Wood and Thompson (1993) examined assumptions about professional development. They identified 11 faulty assumptions and practices. The most common faulty assumptions included: (a) Inservice training does not need to be ongoing; (b) teachers do not learn from their involvement in teaching,

---

[3]The report *Improving Educational Achievement* (National Academy of Education, Committee on Testing and Basic Skills, 1978) seemed to be the foundation for the NCLB legislation (2002). The 1978 report refocused the attention on accountability and student achievement originally brought on by the launch of Sputnik. The authors of the report called for changes in schooling. They recommended a return to basic skills, increasing achievement-test scores as a goal of government, improving teacher quality, and increased accountability on schools and administrators as ways to "improve" education. The report cited a 14-year drop in SAT scores beginning in 1963. The authors of the report identified factors they believed caused the decline: proliferation of courses, confusing pedagogy, less time on task, and an overall lack of academic excellence. Conspicuously left out of the discussion were the social upheavals of the late 1960s and early 1970s, the increasing rates of students taking standardized tests and staying in school until graduation, increasing enrollments, and growth of class sizes. All of this sounds much like the "new" NCLB!

planning teams, or peer observation; (c) inspirational speakers get teachers motivated; and (d) teachers will automatically transfer what they learn in workshops into the classroom without assistance. Showers and Joyce (1996) confirmed that a low percentage of teachers implement what they encounter at inservice training sessions.

DOES PROFESSIONAL DEVELOPMENT CHANGE TEACHING OR IMPROVE STUDENT OUTCOMES?

Professional development activities certainly should have goals and objectives. These should logically be able to be measured and supported. Two such goals should be to refine teaching practice and to improve student success. How's the evidence look?

MIXED RESULTS ARE THE NORM

The National Staff Development Council (NSDC) recently stated that districts need to change how they view and plan for professional development. The NSDC recommended that districts allocate 10% of their budgets and 25% of teacher time to PD (Kelleher, 2003). Well, that might work, but it would represent a large expenditure and a huge investment in faith given weaknesses found in the current research on the effectiveness of professional development.

Results of almost 50 years of legislated spending on teacher improvement and its impact on student achievement have not yet been determined by consistent, replicable, empirical studies. The literature landscape is strewn with studies that possess one or more of the following characteristics: (a) The study is based primarily on teachers' self-reported perceptions of the impacts of PD on their teaching behavior or student achievement; (b) mixed, neutral, or negative impact on student achievement and teacher behavior; and (c) flawed methodology (see Table 17.2). Even some of the stronger studies have one of the weaknesses listed.

Garet and colleagues (2001) used a national probability sample of over 1,000 mathematics and science teachers in 358 districts to examine PD characteristics that significantly impacted teachers' learning as reported by teachers. Requirements for teachers to qualify for the survey included participation in a PD activity sponsored by Eisenhower funds during the 1997–1998 school year. The researchers reported a teacher survey response rate of 70%, or 783 out of 1,113 teachers who qualified for the survey.

Results of the study by Garet and colleagues (2001) were based on teachers' self-reported change; the researchers did not observe teachers to validate the self-reported changes. Without an independent evaluation, the teachers' perceptions of skill enhancement cannot be confirmed. Connections to student achievement were not part of the study. These study results left approximately 85% of the variance unaccounted for by PD. What else could possibly account for the missing 85% of the variance in an organization's success? Deming (2000) provided a clue. He originally postulated that administratively mutable (that is, factors that the administrator has the power, resources, and ability to change) aspects of an organization account for up to 85% of its effectiveness. Later, Deming revised that estimate to 94%. If professional development does not (a) result in observed changes in teacher behavior, and (b) positively impact student achievement, then what has it accomplished?

Cohen and Hill (1998) examined the impact of California's instructional policy initiatives on fourth-grade students' performance in mathematics. The California Department of Education (CDE) used the state assessment, California Learning Assessment System (CLAS), as an incentive for teachers to change their instructional strategies. The state made available new student curriculum units, provided PD related to the units, and provided information about the CLAS test and its relationship to the new curriculum units. The state tests were aligned to the new curriculum units. The CDE directors reasoned that the teachers involved in professional development would learn new things about mathematics and implement new kinds of instructional strategies. Hence, student achievement on the mathematics portion of the CLAS would increase. Teachers attended state-sponsored workshops taught by consultants. Approximately 29% of the teachers attended 1 day or less of training while approximately 14% attended 2 to 6 days; fewer than 3% attended more than 6 days. Results did not show a strong relationship between PD related to mathematics curriculum and increased student achievement as measured by the CLAS. However, teachers learning about the CLAS test had a positive relationship to student achievement. One may hypothesize that teachers who learned about the CLAS were able to align their instruction and assessment to the test and were able to prepare their students better for CLAS than were those teachers who did not learn about the test. The training related to learning about CLAS could have included aspects such as: (a) question formats, (b) skills tested, and (c) levels of difficulty for subject matter tested, information that commonly is found in directories of test specifications. Such directories cost much less than several days of professional development. This led Cohen and Hill (1998) to conclude:

> This study confirms that neither teachers' practice nor students' achievement was changed by the professional development most California teachers had experienced. Still, very large amounts of money are spent every year on just such activities. Our results therefore challenge those who make policy for

and practice professional development: can they design programs, policies and requirements that focus more closely on improved teaching for improved student learning? (p. 33)

Harwell, D'Amico, Stein, and Gatti (2000) attempted to determine the effects of professional development for teachers on student achievement over a 10-year period. Researchers looked at student reading and mathematics achievement in grades 3–5 during 1988–1998 and found only one area to which PD seemed related: reading. Students of teachers who reported engagement in activities such as professional discussions with colleagues and their principals about literacy instruction had higher classroom average test scores in reading as measured by the California Test of Basic Skills (CTBS) than did students of teachers who reported little or no engagement in such activities.

In reviewing 13 lists on "effective professional development all published within the last decade," Guskey (2003) came to three "related conclusions." In summary, the conclusions were: (a) there is little agreement about criteria for effectiveness, (b) most studies offer "yes, but . . . statements," and (c) "the promise of research-based decision making in professional development has been largely unfilled" but . . . (pp. 748–750; paraphrase and quote). The last statement serves to exemplify the "yes . . . but" model after the documented years of effort and money. Wow!

The preceding represents outcomes of much professional development research and literature. The next section presents small-scale experimental studies demonstrating a link between PD and student achievement. Small studies, however, should not be generalized to the entire education system. Large-scale replications are needed before major recommendations can be made.

SMALL-SCALE PROFESSIONAL DEVELOPMENT WITH POSITIVE RESULTS

Caulfield-Sloan (2001) examined the effect of professional development on student achievement and found that pupil performance and teacher behavior could be influenced by teacher PD. Caulfield-Sloan randomly divided 27 teachers into groups of 13 and 14 and provided ongoing training in the use of higher order questioning strategies for science instruction. Students of teachers who were trained scored significantly higher (p < .001) on an open-ended science question assessment than did students of teachers who had not been trained. Caulfield-Sloan stated that, "Staff development directly influences instructional practices and pupil performance. The instructional practices of teachers do in turn have a significant and measurable impact on the performance of students" (p. 62). On a small scale, Caulfield-Sloan demonstrated the ability of professional development to influence student achievement in the area of answering open-ended science questions at the third-grade level. The training was conducted with small groups of teachers (in effect, in small classes).

In another small-scale experimental study, Tienken (2003) demonstrated that professional development could impact teacher behavior and student achievement positively. Students in classes taught by teachers who received training performed better on narrative writing assessment than did students taught by teachers in the control group. Tienken conducted classroom visitations of teachers in the experimental group to determine how effectively the participants implemented the strategies they were taught (fidelity). The experimental-group teachers wrote reflections after the 7th and 14th weeks of training. Analyses of the classroom observations and reflective logs indicated a shift in the experimental-group teachers' instructional mode from "presentational" to "environmental" (Hillocks, 1986). By the end of the study, the teachers in the experimental group taught differently from when they started and from the control group. The shift in the teachers' instructional mode may demonstrate a link between professional development and a change in teaching behavior in this study.

Students of the experimental-group teachers self-assessed three of their writing pieces during the study. The teachers also scored each paper. By the third scoring, students in the experimental groups achieved agreement with their teachers at a rate of 72%, a positive gain. The students and teachers agreed about the criteria of quality writing. The level of agreement achieved by the experimental-group students and teachers by the end of this study demonstrated that the students responded to the writing instruction, were able to think critically about their own work and make positive revisions, and outscored the students of the control-group teachers ($p \leq .05$).

Findings of some small-scale efforts suggest that professional development can change teachers' instructional behaviors when (a) implemented in a deliberate and planned manner, (b) embedded in the teacher's job and class, (c) conducted with small groups of teachers, and (d) guided by change and communication theory. Changes in teacher behavior can lead to changes in student outcomes, but change in student outcomes cannot be assumed without prior teacher change.

Group size could be a positive factor. The experimental-group teachers in both studies received professional development in small groups. Caufield-Sloan's (2001) groups were $n = 14$ and $n = 13$; each of Tienken's groups (2003) included only $n = 2$ teachers. Teachers, and not just students, may benefit from structured, small-group, and individual instruction.

Professional Development to Impact Student Achievement?

Is professional development a viable tool for school improvement? Maybe, under very specific conditions. As stated earlier, in order to be considered viable, we believe that PD must have two measurable levels of impact: (a) to improve the participants' observed teaching performance and (b) to improve measurable student achievement. Two experimental studies (Caulfield-Sloan, 2001; Tienken, 2003) and one quasi-experimental study (Achilles & colleagues, 1992) possessed characteristics that may have enhanced the positive impacts on student achievement and teacher behavior. The instructional groups were small (n = 2–14) and activities included action research, peer coaching, structured study groups, mentoring, and administrative support. The Tienken (2003) study also included lesson and assessment calibration (Wilson & Tienken, 2002). The training and processes were designed specifically to impact student achievement and teacher behavior and followed a job-embedded format.

The training provided by Achilles and colleagues (1992) and by Tienken (2003) followed a theoretically based communication change model (e.g., Achilles, Reynolds, & Achilles, 1997, pp. 130–135) to structure and deliver the job-embedded professional development. Communication is embedded in the change process and in the training by attending to the presenter, audience, message, and transmission processes. Diffusion of an innovation such as training teachers how to teach students to revise and self-assess writing based on criteria is predicated on someone communicating a new idea or knowledge to others in the system who accept the change (Rogers & Shoemaker, 1983). Learning is a form of change. Once a person learns something new, by definition, that person changes. The theory and model suggest that the change-agent's ability to manage the structure and medium of the communication effectively impacts the successful adoption of an innovation. As an individual moves toward acceptance of the proposed innovation, the communication elements become more personalized the closer the individual gets to independent use of the PD. Small-group settings and personalized communication help the PD provider to build rapport and to overcome teacher resistance.

Time and Money

Job-embedded professional development is labor-intensive and is costly to implement on a large scale. The impacts are limited to the specific area of training and should not be generalized to other areas. For example, Caulfield-Sloan's (2001) experimental results should not be generalized beyond questioning techniques to improve student performance on open-ended science questions. Effective job-embedded training requires small groups and continuity (time). Groups of up to seven participants produce good results and increase the probability that changes will become self-sustaining and self-renewing. Many school districts routinely employ more than 100 certified staff, so simple division shows that job-embedded PD can be extremely expensive.

If the definition of professional development includes continuing higher education credits, costs grow exponentially if districts reimburse teachers for university courses and also move teachers higher on the salary scale. The salary scale move represents a permanent expenditure to the district. That is, when a teacher moves from BA to MA, the jump in pay for the same year of experience could be considerable. If that staff member achieves that pay increase during the 5th year teaching and then stays in the district for 20 more years, the district may spend $75,000–$100,000 on that staff member. Even if there were empirical research to demonstrate its effectiveness, professional development as traditionally delivered would become a very costly alternative.

PROVEN AND UNDERUSED STRATEGIES TO IMPROVE EDUCATION OUTCOMES

Should professional development be emphasized to the extent that it overshadows other organizational improvement strategies, especially when little or no substantive SBR outcomes support the extensive investment? What are some logical alternatives?

SBR Alternatives

Many SBR-supported innovations consistently show teacher change and student improvement and are well within the sphere of an administrator's control—they are administratively mutable factors such as scheduling, program design, coordination, school size, organization for instruction, and other elements (see Table 17.3). These are factors that school administrators can manipulate to set the conditions needed to improve organizational outcomes. In education, outcomes would be student achievement. The ways that administrators structure schools can enhance student achievement (Bolman & Deal, 1997). Consider once again Deming's proposal that workers account for only 6% to 15% of an organization's effectiveness. If this is true, professional development for teachers would have to be 100% successful (quite unlikely) to improve organizational effectiveness 6% to 15%. Doesn't the

TABLE 17.3   A Sample of Proven Innovations and Administratively Mutable Organization. Factors that Influence Teacher Behavior and Student Achievement Positively (The emerging list has more than 35 entries already. Add others that meet SBR criteria.)

A. Administratively Mutable Organization Factors

1. Class size: where the class is the unit for instruction; tutoring
2. School size: School within a school, small learning communities, etc.
3. Reduced retention in grade
4. Multigraded or nongraded schools
5. Quality pre-K programs
6. Looping and cohorts
7. Structures to generate program and instruction coherence
8. Hands-on structured learning opportunities
9. Full-day kindergarten
10. Effective schools organization
11. Alternative uses of time, such as year-round schooling
12. Models of parent/adult involvement

B. Curriculum and Instruction Supported by Organization Structures

1. Developmentally appropriate practices
2. Appropriate uses of homework
3. Matching teaching to learning style
4. Problem-based learning; projects, service, and community learning
5. Participation; cooperative learning

idea of professional development as the primary capacity-building effort for education begin to lose its luster?

SUMMARY

The recent NCLB directive for using scientifically based research (SBR) should motivate administrators to review the list of SBR-proven education improvements in Table 17.3 closely before settling on professional development as the answer to every organization's problem: Very little replicable, empirical, independent research shows that professional development impacts student achievement positively. However, many large empirical studies support that organization changes, such as reducing school size and class sizes do improve student achievement.

We are not advocating that schools discard completely their professional development activities. Professionals strive for lifelong learning and continue to hone skills. Would you go to a doctor or lawyer who has not updated her or his skills in 5, 10, 20 years? Of course not! You would not want your child with a teacher who teaches based on outmoded ideas. Unquestionably, professional development is an integral part of being a professional, but it is not the primary focus. Achilles (2003) wrote:

> Because of the dearth of SBR evidence that PD provides teacher change and student improvements in education, PD should follow the model set by fields such as medicine and law and rely on user (e.g., teacher) choice in a market model: Teachers will select their PD needs and delivery system. They will pay for PD directly to the provider. There will be minimum state or district payout for mandated SD days, although there may be required in-service days to implement policy or legal mandates.... The PD time frame would usually occur so that practitioners did not lose time instructing the students for whom they are responsible. (p. 115)

Billions of federal dollars are allocated for professional development each year. Grants and state funds add billions more and yet the impact on student achievement has not been clearly determined. Should we stop funding PD? No. Ongoing PD is needed to keep abreast of the latest research but why continue to place large bets on a horse that has only a 15% chance, at most, of winning? Professional bettors call those odds a long shot. It is time to stop wagering our children's futures while waiting for the payoff that may never come.

GUIDING QUESTIONS

1. The NCLB Act mentions SBR more than 100 times. Considering professional development, what is your position on the SBR idea for (a) the content of PD efforts and (b) evaluating the efficacy of the professional development?

2. What would you consider as convincing evidence of the (a) efficacy and (b) utility of a professional development initiative? How is professional development initiated and evaluated in your district?

3. Develop a list of criteria for SBR. Match education practice and PD in your setting against the criteria. Add to the list in Table 17.3 of SBR alternatives to PD. Entries to the list should be "administratively mutable" and not status variables such as gender or age. Criteria for SBR might include: Objectivity, Evidence, Comparisons, Persistence (effect lasts), Replicability/Reliability, Credibility/Validity.

SELECTED READINGS

Because many professional development books are "how-to" texts or advocate a particular position and seldom provide independent, replicable, empirical evidence (SBR) of success (as we ask for in the early pages of the chapter), we hesitate to recommend specific books. The interested reader might pursue the research on PD, keeping in mind reasonable criteria for success. References for this chapter provide a sample of studies on PD.

Carpenter, W. A. (2000, January). Ten years of silver bullets: Dissenting thoughts on education reform. *Phi Delta Kappan, 81*(5), 383–389.

Garet, M. S., Porter, A. C., Desimone, L., Birman, B. F., & Yoon, K. S. (2001). What makes professional development effective? Results from a national sample of teachers. *American Educational Research Journal, 38*(4), 915–945.

Guskey, T. R. (2003, June). What makes professional development effective? *Phi Delta Kappan, 84*(10), 748–750.

Loucks-Horsley, S., Hewson, P. W., Love, N., & Stiles, K. E. (1998). *Designing professional development for teachers of science and mathematics*. Thousand Oaks, CA: Corwin Press.

Showers, B., & Joyce, B. (1996). The evolution of peer coaching. *Educational Leadership, 53*(6), 12–16.

REFERENCES

ABT Associates. (1997, June). *National impact evaluation of the comprehensive child development program*. Cambridge, MA: St. Pierre, R.G.

Achilles, C. M. (2003, Winter). Thoughts about education administration and improvement *Journal of Thought, 38*(2), 105–121.

Achilles, C. M., Dickerson, C., Dockery-Runkel, L., Egelson, P., & Epstein, M. (1992). *Practical school improvement: The Mary Reynolds Babcock Project at Moore School*. Paper presented at the annual meeting of the American Educational Research Association, San Francisco, CA. ED 343221.

Achilles, C. M., Reynolds, J. S., & Achilles, S. H. (1997). *Problem analysis: Responding to school complexity*. Larchmont, NY: Eye on Education.

Berliner, D., & Biddle, B. (1995). *The manufactured crisis: Myths, fraud, and the attack on America's public schools*. Reading, MA: Addison-Wesley.

Bodilly, S. J., Gill, B. P., Berends, M., Kirby, S. N., Dembowsky, J. W., & Caulkins, J. P. (2003). Hard lessons learned from educational interventions. *Rand Review, 27*(1): 1–10. Retrieved May 1, 2003, from http://www.rand.org/publications/randreview/issues/spring2003/crashcourses.html.

Bolman, L. G., & Deal, T. E. (1997). *Reframing organizations*. San Francisco: Jossey-Bass.

Borman, G. D., & D'Agostino, J. V. (1996). Title I and student achievement: A meta-analysis of federal evaluation results. *Educational Evaluation & Policy Analysis, 18*, 309–326.

Bracey, G. W. (2003). April foolishness: The 20th anniversary of a Nation at Risk. *Phi Delta Kappan, 84*(8), 616–621.

Carpenter, W. A. (2000, January). Ten years of silver bullets: Dissenting thoughts on education reform. *Phi Delta Kappan, 81*(5), 383–389.

Carson, C. C., Huelskamp, R. M., & Woodall, T. D. (1991, May 10). *Perspectives on education in America. Annotated briefing*. Albuquerque, NM: Sandia National Laboratories.

Caulfield-Sloan, M. (2001). *The effects of staff development of teachers in the use of higher order *questioning strategies on third grade students' rubric science assessment.* Unpublished PhD dissertation, Seton Hall University, South Orange, New Jersey.

Cohen, D. K., & Hill, H. C. (1998). *Instructional policy and classroom performance: The mathematics reform in California* (CPRE Research Report Series RR-39). Philadelphia: University of Pennsylvania, Consortium for Policy Research in Education.

Covert, S. L. (2003). *Transferring professional development in the classroom.* Unpublished EdD dissertation, Eastern Michigan University, Ypsilanti, MI (pp. 16–17).

Deming, W. E. (2000). *The new economics for industry, government, education* (2nd ed.). Cambridge, MA: MIT Press.

Garet, M. S., Porter, A. C., Desimone, L., Birman, B. F., & Yoon, K. S. (2001). What makes professional development effective? Results from a national sample of teachers. *American Educational Research Journal, 38*(4), 915–945.

Guskey, T. R. (2003, June). What makes professional development effective? *Phi Delta Kappan, 84*(10), 748–750.

Guskey, T. R. (1997) Research needs to link professional development and student learning. *The Journal of Staff Development, 18*(2).

Haller, E. J., Brent, B. O., & McNamara, J. H. (1997). Does graduate training in educational administration improve America's Schools? *Phi Delta Kappan 79*(3) 222–227.

Harwell, M., D'Amico, L., Stein, M., & Gatti, G. (2000). *The effects of teachers' professional development on student achievement in community school district #2.* Paper presented at the annual meeting of the American Educational Research Association, New Orleans, LA.

Hillocks, G. (1986). *Research on written composition.* Urbana, IL: ERIC Clearinghouse on Reading and Communication Skills, National Institute on Education (ED 265552).

Joyce, B., & Showers, B. (1983). *Power in staff development through research on training.* Arlington, VA: Association for Supervision and Curriculum Development.

Kelleher, J. (2003, June). A model for assessment-driven professional development. *Phi Delta Kappan, 84*(10), 751–756.

Loucks-Horsley, S., Hewson, P. W., Love, N., & Stiles, K. E. (1998). *Designing professional development for teachers of science and mathematics.* Thousand Oaks, CA: Corwin Press.

National Academy of Education, Committee on Testing and Basic Skills (1978). *Improving educational achievement.* A Report to the Assistant Secretary. Washington, DC: Department of Health, Education and Welfare.

National Center for Education Statistics. (1999). *NAEP 1998 writing: Report card for the nation and the states* (NCES Publication No. 1999462). Washington, DC: U.S. Government Printing Office.

National Commission on Excellence in Education (NCEE). (1983). *A nation at risk.* Washington, DC: United States Department of Education, U.S. Government Printing Office.

National Education Goals Panel. (1991). *National education goals report: Building a nation of learners.* Washington, DC: U.S. Government Printing Office.

Newmann, F. M., King, M. B., Yongs, P. (2001, January) *Professional development that addresses school capacity:* Lessons from urban elementary schools. Madison, University of Wisconsin.

Rogers, E. M., & Shoemaker, F. (1983). *Communication of innovation* (2nd ed.). New York: Macmillan.

Showers, B., & Joyce, B. (1996). The evolution of peer coaching. *Educational Leadership, 53*(6), 12–16.

Tienken, C. H. (2003). *The effect of staff development in the use of scoring rubrics and reflective questioning strategies on fourth-grade students' narrative writing performance.* Unpublished doctoral dissertation, Seton Hall University, South Orange, NJ.

Tienken, C. H., & Achilles, C. M. (2004). Changing teacher behavior and improving student writing. *Planning and Changing, 34*(3–4), 153–168.

Wilson, M., & Tienken, C. H. (2002, Winter). Using standards to improve instruction. *Kappa Delta Pi Record, 38*(2), 82–84.

Wong, K. K., & Meyer, S. J. (1998, Summer). Title I school-wide programs: A synthesis of findings from recent evaluations. *Education Evaluation and Policy Analysis, 20*(2), 115–136.

Wood, F., & Thompson, S. (1993). Assumptions about staff development based on research and best practice. *Journal of Staff Development, 14*(4), 52–57.

Chapter 18

School Finance: The Russian Novel

Augustina Reyes
University of Houston

Gloria M. Rodriguez
California State University, Hayword

> *School finance is like a Russian novel. It's long, it's tedious, everybody gets killed in the end, and no one knows anything about it!*
>
> —Unknown

Public policy in Western societies was designed around five core values: liberty or freedom, equality or equity, fraternity or citizenship, efficiency, and economic growth (King, Swanson, & Sweetland, 2003). The purpose of this chapter is to address the financial issues related to the challenge of balancing expectations of higher levels of education with the values of equity, efficiency, and economic growth. Section one discusses the social context of school finance in the United States. This section discusses the history of school finance in the United States including equity issues. Section one also shows how the school funds are spent. Section two discusses traditional funding structures and state funding policies. Section three discusses decentralization and site-based budgeting, including the use of charters, vouchers, and contracts. The conclusion focuses on how restructuring school budgeting can improve instruction and student performance. This chapter provides class activities for reflection and for using school experiences to develop budgeting case studies.

BRIEF HISTORY OF SCHOOL FINANCE

The roots of school finance can be found within a broader history of educational reform and the proceedings of the *Brown v. Topeka Board of Education* case. Although the public financing of schools has been a feature of education in the United States since the turn of the last century, the reform efforts that began in the 1960s are perhaps the most instructive for students of school finance today. Indeed, school finance reform over the past 35 years has incorporated the multiple demands that Americans of all walks of life place on their school system, and the ability to serve such diverse constituents with state school finance policy is a perennial challenge. This section therefore provides a brief history of school finance reform in the United States and includes a discussion of the key debates and policy issues emanating from the court cases that helped to shape the school finance systems on which we currently rely. This section outlines how school finance reforms produced by various court challenges have increasingly brought attention to the classroom and the need to support strong teaching practices designed to interrupt patterns of educational inequity.

The history of contemporary school finance reform has come about in three iterations or "waves." The impetus for the first wave was the *Brown* decision, which abolished "separate but equal" schools and set the stage for seeking equal treatment for all students; however, many communities continued to experience segregated schools, inequitable schooling conditions based on racial and wealth differences, as well as a mix of unsuccessful strategies intended to comply with the *Brown* decision. Yet it was nearly a decade before the Elementary and Secondary Education Act was passed in the United States, and the federal government provided initial resources to ameliorate the negative impact of various social factors on the academic success of low-income communities and students of color.

Supported by the momentum of the *Brown* decision and subsequent federal initiatives designed to address the extremes of extant schooling conditions in the United States, school finance reform efforts began in the late 1960s and early 1970s. This first wave of school finance cases was focused on intervening in systems that relied almost exclusively on local property taxes that produced wide disparities in both available revenues and associated educational expenditures.

The earliest cases in California (*Serrano I*) and Texas (*Rodriguez*) brought to light the existence of extreme disparities in funding among districts, as well as the direct relationship between such disparities and the reliance on local property tax systems that were quite regressive. The lowest property wealth districts were taxing themselves at extremely high rates to generate revenues for schools that paled in comparison to the revenues that much wealthier districts were able to generate with relatively minimal tax effort. Using both the federal equal protection clause (and the state equal protection clause, in the case of California), the constitutionality of these disparate systems was challenged. In the Texas case, the U.S. Supreme Court ruled that education was not a fundamental right guaranteed by the federal constitution protected by equal protection clause of the 14th Amendment and upheld the system's constitutionality, despite acknowledging disparities among school districts.

The Rodriguez test led to the second—and quite lengthy—wave of litigation in school finance. In this second wave, school finance reformers had to rely on state constitutional provisions, both for equal protection and for specific guarantees related to public education. Given that the majority of states' constitutions contained language with such provisions, the strategy shifted to using the states' "education clauses" as the basis for seeking remedy from the extreme disparities in quality of education among school districts (Heubert, 1997; Odden & Picus, 1992; Vandersall, 1998). New Jersey (*Robinson*) led the way in the use of state education clauses with its provision calling for a "thorough and efficient system" of public education. There is a challenge in relying on state education clauses as there is little understanding of how such vague language can translate into enforceable standards for education—much less how the clauses can be used to provide relief for variations in revenues available to support public schools.

Legal scholars throughout the 1960s and 1970s contributed greatly by developing an understanding of how the reliance on local property taxes for school funding directly related to the existing disparities in educational expenditures, and presumably, the quality of education associated with varying expenditures (Minorini & Sugarman, 1999a). Perhaps the most widely used concept during the second wave of litigation was that of fiscal neutrality, or the idea that the quality of a child's education should not be dependent on the level of local property values of his or her community. Legal scholars John Coons, William Clune, and Stephen Sugarman introduced the premise and concept of fiscal neutrality, and the notion had staying power during the decades of litigation that followed its introduction (Vandersall, 1998).

According to Minorini and Sugarman (1999a), plaintiffs challenging state school finance systems actually won their cases in 19 states, many resolved only after several iterations lasting well into the 1990s. Of the 21 cases in which the states (defendants) prevailed, several filed additional complaints, so efforts to seek relief from the variety of inequitable funding conditions continues in many parts of the United States (Minorini & Sugarman, 1999a). In terms of their broader educational impact, it appears that despite the efforts in school finance reform since the 1970s, the educational arena is still characterized by extreme variations and disparities within and among districts in terms of various resources (e.g., qualified teachers) and outcomes (dropout rates, test scores, etc.).

Certainly advocates for school finance reform were interested in more than just the equalization of funding among school districts within the states, even though this in itself was to be a hard-fought battle for many communities (Gittell, 1998). However, without equalization as a starting point, disparate school systems throughout the country would no doubt continue to offer variously situated students an inappropriately wide range of educational quality. Interestingly, as Gittell (1998) pointed out in an analysis of school finance reform in several states, the lack of attention to state politics surrounding the implementation of reforms in this field is a contributing factor to the length of time it seems to take to see the positive impact of court victories. Indeed, as Minorini and Sugarman (1999a) discussed, even the oft-cited *Brown* decision in desegregation took at least a full decade before the implementation and institutionalization of desegregation actually took place. Similarly, one might argue that the persistent disparities one sees in public education may be perpetuated by continuing resistance to enacting the necessary changes that translate the additional financial resources into systems that better serve an increasing population of low-income students and students of color.

In fact, the lack of progress in terms of academic achievement and other outcomes in public education seems to surface as a key concern within the more recent third wave of school finance litigation. In the third wave, having experienced the impact—however positive or limited—of arguing for fiscal neutrality in the courts on behalf of low-property wealth districts, many school finance reform advocates have chosen to build on the spirit of state education clauses to address broader educational concerns. To the degree that educational outcomes continue to vary significantly and to the degree that even students who leave as graduates of public school systems seem ill-prepared for college or other post–high school options, school finance reform advocates have turned to issues of "adequacy" in education. In this instance, adequacy refers to how educational inputs, long the focus of school finance litigation, can be tied directly to specific academic outcome expectations (Minorini & Sugarman, 1999b; Rethinking Schools, 1997).

Although there were earlier references in fiscal equity cases to the notion of adequacy, most states currently involved in adequacy cases have followed the example set by Kentucky, in which not only the state's school finance system but also the entire educational system was deemed unconstitutional using a specified adequacy standard (Minorini & Sugarman, 1999b). Although it was unusual for the courts to assert specific educational standards as part of a decision, in the Kentucky case the court defined an adequate education as one that developed in each child seven basic capacities: (a) oral and written communication skills; (b) knowledge of social, economic, and political systems; (c) knowledge of governmental processes; (d) knowledge of mental and physical wellness; (e) grounding in the arts; (f) adequate training for life work; and (g) sufficient academic and vocational training to compete with students in surrounding states (Verstegen, 1998).

Interestingly, as Verstegen (1998) illuminated in her analysis of recent policy and legal treatments of the adequacy standard, its strength and potential impact lie in how it is conceptualized. If adequacy refers to a high minimum standard for academic outcomes and achievement, then the resources needed to support the high minimum can be identified and allocated accordingly (depending, of course, on the political will within the states). However, if adequacy is a standard reflecting a state's conceptualization of the basic minimum education it must provide to avoid future litigation, the resources associated with the basic minimum will likely become the ceiling for public educational spending.

In addition, the perennial challenge in the field of school finance has been to understand the differences between dollars and achievement. Many scholars have reached the conclusion that dollars alone are not enough. Indeed, without a clearer picture of how best teaching practices, classroom organization strategies, community engagement, and other school community features are brought to bear on the learning of students in public schools, the disparities in educational outcomes may persist despite the strides that have been made in increasing the available funds for public schools of all types (Rethinking Schools, 1997).

In addition, as Verstegen (1998, 2002) discussed, there exist challenges in determining the level of funding that would be necessary to fully support a high minimum standard of adequacy in public education. An adequacy standard is, in effect, not only a question of how much money is enough but more accurately, a question of how much education is enough. Such standards therefore involve more than the expertise of school finance researchers, reform advocates, and policy experts, but also the involvement of educators who understand the day-to-day operations of schools and the instructional imperative that is required to accomplish a high minimum standard of education for all students in public schools (Rethinking Schools, 1997).

Basic Funding Structures and State Policies

In school finance theory and policy, there are a number of terms and concepts that are commonly used to discuss the mechanisms for directing funds to public schools. This section provides a brief definition of each term or concept and a discussion of how it is used in policy and theoretical treatments of school finance issues.

One key component of any state or local system of school finance is *revenues*. Revenues are the dollars that are generated by either fees for various services or taxes on certain goods and services. At the state level, revenues are largely produced from a variety of taxes that are levied on things such as income, the sale of merchandise, and capital gains. To a lesser degree, states also collect fees for licensing, professional certificates, and so forth. Revenues are distributed to local governments and school districts and are referred to according to the level of government from which they originated. For example, all school districts will generally have some combination of revenues from local, state, and federal sources, and they can either be referred to by source or by program (e.g., State Compensatory Education or Federal Title I).

Over the past 30 years, there has been considerable legal, legislative, and grassroots activity to address the disparities that exist among districts in terms of the revenues they are able to generate from property taxes. Indeed, the interdistrict variations in property wealth disparities have been at the crux of most school finance equity cases as discussed in the first section of this chapter. State policies designed to ameliorate the disparities among school districts in terms of property tax revenues generated are referred to as *equalization* policies.

Equalization policies include state methods for ensuring the there is provision for a basic level of educational funding supported by a combination of local and state revenues. In cases where large disparities exist relative to the local property tax revenue-raising capacity among districts, the state provides funding for school districts in inverse relationship to their capacity to raise revenues. By doing so, states are able to ensure that low-property wealth districts have access to at least a basic minimum level of funding for their schools, although high-property wealth districts are able to maintain their basic funding from primarily locally raised revenues.

Very often, the starting point for figuring the available funding for schools is the *foundation program* or base amount that is allotted as a minimum basic level of funding for schools. In some cases, states may include a variety of adjustments to the funding distributed to districts based on factors that relate either to higher costs of education or variations in student needs among districts. For example, a state constitution may provide originating language guiding the state legislature or other agency to ensure that each district receive a *flat grant* or equal dollar figure in total or per pupil. The flat grant usually reflects the starting point of the funding available for all districts within a given state.

Next, the state may add funding to support the additional costs associated with transportation, special educational services, and so forth. Such adjustments may be made using an index or using *weighted pupils*, which is a method for counting students eligible for special services in a way that reflects the additional costs associated with providing them with a basic education. Although a state or district may determine the amount that reflects a minimum basic education, the student with special educational needs is typically assigned a weight that indicates the extra costs associated with his or her education. For example, it may be determined that a student who is eligible for certain extra educational services costs twice as much to educate as a student who is not eligible. Such a student would count as two students in a weighted pupil system.

The funding most states distribute to local school districts is typically some balance of local, state, and federal support, with the latter often filtering through state-level structures. In cases where the local share is nearly or completely nonexistent, it is referred to as *full state funding*. This means that the revenues that schools use to support their operations are composed virtually or entirely from state-collected taxes, fees, and other sources. The concept of full state funding is also used to describe situations where, because of equalization efforts at the state level, local districts are no longer able to exert the same control over the generation, distribution, and/or expenditure of such funds.

The intricate mechanisms that determine the level of funding that public schools receive are referred to as *funding formulas*. Indeed, the structures used to systematically determine how much and what sources of funding districts and schools receive are generally very complex sets of mathematical operations grouped together and applied as a formula. The mathematical operations involve each of the different types of adjustments—upward and downward—that reflect the various factors that are acknowledged as necessary in appropriately distributing available funding to local school districts that exhibit wide variation in characteristics and challenges.

As mentioned earlier, revenues that states receive are in turn distributed to school districts for support of local educational services. When the revenues are distributed to districts, they are referred to as *district revenues*. Several factors can affect the level and variation of available district revenues. For example, in most states revenues are distributed to districts based on some measure of students in attendance the previous year, including actual attendance or average daily attendance (the methods used to determine how many students a district can count for funding purposes can likewise vary significantly). This is why for many educators attendance in school is such a huge concern—indeed, it drives district revenues to a great degree in many finance systems.

Within state school finance systems, considerable attention is paid to the tax policies that help to support reforms to ensure increased equity in the distribution of funding to school districts. In particular, one concept that has been useful to policy makers is the notion of *district power equalization*. District power equalization refers to state policies or structures that intervene in situations where large disparities exist in the property tax revenue-raising capacity among school districts. The idea is to enable districts with lower capacity to raise property tax revenues, especially in cases where the average property values are significantly lower than in other districts, to benefit from policies that enable them to more easily generate property tax revenues. Another term that is often used to refer to district power equalization is *guaranteed tax base*, where states ensure that districts can generate property tax revenues as though they had access to higher average property values.

One key component associated with a policy of district power equalization or guaranteed tax base is *guaranteed tax yield (GTY)*. The guaranteed tax yield feature is tied to a district's taxpayers' willingness to tax themselves at higher levels in order to generate sufficient support for local schools. Under some state finance schemes, when a district's taxpayers approve a certain tax rate this enacts a policy that guarantees a certain yield (level of revenues) given a certain tax rate—regardless of the average property wealth in the district. Typically, such features are only applied to lower property wealth districts using a very specific property value threshold to qualify for participation. In addition, the guaranteed yield is usually stated in dollar terms tied to specific tax rates. For example, in a given state system, low-property wealth districts may have the option of taxing themselves at a slightly higher rate per $1,000 of property wealth, which in turn generates a set dollar amount in yield for every extra percentage of tax rate levied. That is, if a district taxes itself at $1.55 per $1,000 of property value and the GTY is enacted above a rate of $1.50 per $1,000, the district would enjoy the enhanced yield guaranteed for the additional $.05 levied. In this way, districts are able to generate extra revenues at the margin that would reflect higher average property values in the absence of the GTY.

Finally, another concept that is often used in the distribution of funding to schools is the *categorical program*. Categorical programs—also referred to as targeted programs—are designed to address either a particular or targeted educational policy goal or the special needs of a "category" of eligible student populations. Very often the existence of categorical programs within a school finance formula reflects an acknowledgment by policy makers that additional resources are needed in districts with several schools exhibiting certain characteristics or serving students with certain special needs. In other instances, the categorical programs through which resources are distributed to districts fall outside of the regular state school finance formula and are therefore under the scrutiny of other parties, such as the federal Department of Education. Some categorical programs operate as entitlements, meaning that the dollars follow the students who qualify under the programs' guidelines. In other cases, categorical programs are doled out to schools on a competitive basis, requiring a carefully presented school district (or state) proposal for the use of funds to advance the particular purposes of the program.

DECENTRALIZATION

Decentralization proposes to restructure bureaucratically centralized school systems by redistributing decision-making authority and funds to the local campus. Decentralization promotes the decentralization or devolution of management, budgeting, curriculum, and instruction to the school site. Decentralization is accomplished by redistributing traditionally centralized authority to those closest to the decisions, by making schools more efficient when those closest to decisions become more committed to schools by being involved in the decision-making process, and by allowing schools to develop curriculum that is matched with the needs of students, including the use of a cultures of learning model (Weiler, 1990).

According to the theory, schools become more efficient when those closest to the decisions become more committed to schools by being involved in the decision-making process (Weiler, 1990). Theoretically, decentralization puts all the decision-making authority in the school campus. It allows school communities to meet their unique needs. Decentralization also meets the political needs of the state by providing a system of conflict management that meets the unique poverty, desegregation, religious, and other political needs of communities (Weiler, 1990). School decentralization is identified with the redesign of school systems or school districts to a site-managed education system (Odden & Busch, 1998). Charter schools and vouchers are components of the decentralization efforts. This section discusses the research in school system decentralization, charter schools, and vouchers.

Decentralization is a part of a management movement to develop flatter, more flexible forms (networks, spider webs, and the like) of organizational structure (Bolman & Deal, 1997). The management goal of decentralization is to design a structure that fits the organization's goals, task, and contexts (Bolman & Deal, 1997). Decentralization provides an opportunity to change an outdated vertical system into a lateral system that allows coordination at the campus level. According to Bolman and Deal (1997), changing an organization from a hierarchical system to a flatter participatory system requires consideration to the following six structural parameters:

1. size and age of the organization,
2. core processes or core technology for transforming raw material,
3. environments as stable or uncertain and turbulent,
4. strategy and goals,
5. information and technology.

The theory of organizational decentralization is best aligned with contingency leadership theory or leadership theory with a focus on context and situation, incorporating aspects of Fiedler (1967); Hersey and Blanchard (1977); Argyris and Schon (1978); Mc Gregor (1967); Likert (1967), and Deming (1986). The conflict for decentralization of public schools is which goals, tasks, and contexts will drive the decentralization process, the state, the local district, or the campus. How will a system and its leaders who have been socialized to operate in a hierarchical culture transform their operational behavior to leaders of quasi-independent units?

The most common example of school decentralization referred to as the local management of school (LMS) is found in the England (King et al., 2003). In the period starting in 1988, the English started an organizational decentralization process enacted under the Education Reform Act of 1988. The reform served as an impetus to budget decentralization or school-based decentralization. The English school system is comparable to the U.S. education system. In the United States, the states are responsible for state funding and state constitutional and legislative policy. The school districts serve as the local education agency. Schools operate under the umbrella of the local school district. In England, the central government is responsible for central policy and funding generated from tax assessments. The local government is responsible for the local education agency or agencies (LEA) within their jurisdiction. The local government generates school funding from local property taxes.

The English LEA is fiscally dependent on the local government similar to some U.S. fiscally dependent schools. Schools operate under the LEA. England has a national curriculum, performance-based testing, student choice, and a decentralized management system that largely eliminates curricular innovation at the school level but encourages organizational variety (King et al., 2003; Odden & Busch, 1998). The English system with a policy-based student tracking system is also different from the U.S. system. The English system funds "selective comprehensive schools, single-sex and mixed schools, and schools sponsored by religious and other organizations" (King et al., 2003), (p. 21). Students between the ages of 16 to 19 years of age are accommodated by secondary schools and academic, technical, or tertiary colleges (King et al., 2003).

In addition to the state schools that must include a religious curriculum, there are independent schools for those who can afford the tuition (King et al., 2003). The size of the English system is radically different from the size of the U.S. system. The English central government reports 8 million students with 132 local education agencies (Odden & Busch, 1998). In Texas alone there are 4 million students with 1,145 local education agencies or school districts. In England, education is provided by the local government through a fiscally dependent LEA (Odden & Busch, 1998). The cost of English education is shared by central government taxes and local government taxes, exclusively local domestic property taxes (Odden & Busch, 1998).

In 1988, the English Reform Act of 1988 enacted the use of grant-maintained (GM) schools. These are like U.S. charter schools. Local site-based councils and parents were allowed to take a vote to opt out of their LEA and become a quasi-independent school (Odden & Busch, 1998). Under this system decentralization was reduced to two layers of bureaucracies.

The English decentralization system progressed but did not address cost of education for student differences across LEAs and created several equity issues.

In an effort to address spending variations and equalization issues, the English government converted the school revenue system from a 50% local funds and 50% central government funds to 80% central government and 20% local funding (King et al., 2003; Odden & Busch, 1998). The new revenue system increased the central government's role, decreased the role of LEAs, put caps on local spending, changed in how the central government provides aid for the local service functions, and reduced spending per capita (Odden & Busch, 1998).

The central government budgeting process is made up of the role of the central government, the role of the LEA, and the role of the school creating a three-layer system; however, in the case of grant-maintained schools that are similar to U.S. charter schools, it is a two-layer system or a state-to-school-site funding system (Odden & Busch, 1998). Grant schools receive 100% of their funding directly from the central government.

The general government revenue grant is the central government's revenue package to the local government agency (Odden & Busch, 1998). The LEA funding system consists of a foundation amount per pupil for every school in attendance. The formula uses an age-based equation that gives a greater weight and larger per pupil reimbursement for secondary school students. The second set of central government-generated formulas provide additional funding for categorical needs, including single-parent family, poverty, limited English proficiency, free lunch, sparsity, and area-specific cost adjustments or cost of living index factor.

The central government established guidelines specifying that LEAs must use a three-level school budgeting process that consists of the general school budget (GSB), the potential school budget (PSB), and the aggregate school budget (ASB). Under the general school budget, the local education agency (similar to U.S. local school district) maintains mandatory budget exceptions and discretionary budget exceptions as specified by the state government.

Some of the LEA mandatory budget exceptions include capital expenditure and financing, welfare services like attendance, educational psychology services, statutory assessments for disabled students, premature retirement and dismissal costs, and central grants for special purposes (Odden & Busch, 1998). Discretionary budget exceptions retained by the LEA include school meals and milk, transportation, pupil support, liability insurance, LEA initiatives, and contingencies (Odden & Busch, 1998). The services retained by the LEA are subtracted from the general school budget to make up the potential school budget. The goal is to send 95% of the potential school budget to the school site (Odden & Busch, 1998).

The second LEA budgeting process level is the PSB. The PSB is made up of major school-level functions, like instruction, school administration, school operations, and minor maintenance (Odden & Busch, 1998). Under the PSB, the LEA retains locally determined functions but primarily the following typical functions including management and administration, curriculum advisory and inspection services, special education, peripatetic staff services, library and museum services, operational services (excluding special needs), substitute teachers, salary safeguarding, professional development, insurance, structural repairs and maintenance, and other costs (Odden & Busch, 1998).

The third LEA budgeting process level is the aggregate school budget. The ASB is the lump sum or money budgeted to the school site. The ASB process requires that 80% of the ASB must be distributed to students based on pupil weighted formulas including a cap of 5% for high-cost students, like low-income and at risk (Odden & Busch, 1998). The LEA may allocate the remaining percentage of the ASB using formulas based on nonpupil-related objective factors including school size, salary protection, premises-related funding, transitional adjustments, and other special-needs funding (Odden & Busch, 1998).

There are several differences and similarities between the English system of decentralization and the U.S. system of funding schools. According to Odden and Busch (1998), one difference is that the central government provides 80% of the school funds and the local government or the LEA provides 20%. In addition, increases in local property taxes are limited by central government policy; however, there are some U.S. states, including Texas, that cap school district taxing authority (TEC 42.252, 2001). Central government policy requires the LEAs to send the bulk of their funding to each school site (King et al., 2003). Another difference is the way that money flows from the central government to the school sites. According to central government policies, the budgetary framework flows the overall budget for the primary and secondary per pupil funding to the local government. Funding from the state flows from the central government to the local school districts. The local government develops a general school budget or the total amount appropriated by each local government authority to its LEA for expenditures for all the schools in the LEA cluster. The English central government uses funding formulas very much like U.S. systems use.

The Odden and Busch (1998) research identified concerns over equity issues. Headmasters believed that the weighted per-pupil flat reimbursement formula used by the state favored secondary students and penalized primary students. They felt that primary students required more money than the secondary students. The second equity issue raised was the differences in funding between the LEA schools and the grant-maintained schools or the charter schools. Overfunding policies provided more money for grant-maintained schools.

Grant-maintained schools expressed concerns about their lack of access to capital funding. The issue of equity in general emerged as a concern over interschool funding differences. Why should one similarly situated school receive more money than another school (Odden & Busch, 1998)? Class size was also a concern. Possibly because one of the few ways to increase revenue is to decrease personnel, that is, hire fewer teachers by increasing the class size. Schools believed that there was not enough staff development for teachers and headmasters. Concerns were expressed in the lack of investment in maintenance and facilities (Odden & Busch, 1998). Although the political right argues that the English school reforms encourage the growth of different types of schools responsive to the needs and interests of particular groups, the political left argues that there is evidence that they are re-creating a selective school system that is highly inequitable to the lower classes or the poor (King et al., 2003).

Although the English decentralization provides some interesting models, it also raises questions. Although the English budgeting process is labeled as a decentralization process, it really is a very elaborate system that at five different policy levels reduces the amount of money that will be funded to the school. Theoretically decentralization implies that the layers of sifting funds from the state to the school site will be reduced as in the two-layer system or a state-to-school-site funding system used for grant maintained or charter schools. Each policy level identified in the English system sifts out funds intended for schools.

The major difference identified by the research is that the state centralization was increased by state efforts to convert state revenues from 50% to 80%. There is no evidence that the local schools actually received more money under a decentralized system when compared with a decentralized system. As with U.S. funding systems, there are concerns about the kinds of funding formulas to be used to develop decentralized school funding systems. For example, what data or research will be used to determine adequate resources for the regular education program in a cost-effective, ideally sized elementary, middle, or high school campus (Augenblick, 1984)? What kind of research will be used to determine appropriate weights for categorical programs (Augenblick, 1984; Rossmiller, 1987; Webb, McCarthy, & Thomas, 1988)? When using a foundation pupil reimbursement system, what kind of formula will be used: full-time equivalence (FTE), average daily membership, average daily attendance (ADA), peak enrollment (Augenblick, 1984)? Who loses and who wins? An ADA system rewards middle-class communities with regularly attending school populations. Conversely, the ADA system penalizes urban and other kinds of school districts with a predominance of low-income students and lower attendance rates (Hooker, 2001). How will the per-pupil cost for regular education by school level be calculated to establish the basic unit cost with the numerical unit cost of $1.00? Will the base of the weight system be developed on reliable research on the cost of achieving program goals or will backroom political horse trading be used to maintain the existing state funding levels (Hooker, 2001)? Although the English decentralization model provides interesting lessons, it also poses many questions.

LINKING DECENTRALIZATION TO INSTRUCTION

Although the purpose of decentralization is to improve school efficiency by allowing those closest to classroom instruction to participate in decision making, the goal of site-based budgeting has to provide a link between instruction and school budgeting to improve instruction, to improve student achievement, and to hold schools accountable for student performance. The research on school decentralization provides several working examples of how principals and assistant principals are developing budgeting strategies to improve instructional results, including the following: (a) the more efficient use of personnel, time, and information; (b) the use budget reallocations; and (c) the phasing-in of affordable instructional improvements (Matthews & Crow, 2003; Miles & Darling-Hammond, 1997; Odden & Busch, 1998). In a study conducted by Miles and Darling-Hammond (1997), the following five resource-allocation strategies were used to improve instruction and student performance:

1. Increase the number of regular classroom teachers and reduce class size (core education services) by trading out expensive positions for regular classroom teacher positions.
2. Provide varied class sizes for different subjects, like eight students per reading class.
3. Group students differently from traditional age-grade groups.
4. Expand common teacher planning periods to give teachers more time to plan as instructional teams.
5. Increased teacher professional development.

Decentralized budgeting or campus-based budgeting allows instruction to drive the school budget rather than some central office.

CHARTER SCHOOLS AND VOUCHER PROGRAMS

Decentralization has been spurred by the movement to provide choice in public education. In an effort to meet the demands to provide parental choice, school districts have offered magnet schools, site-based management, regulation waivers, inter district vouchers, inter- and intradistrict options to transfer out of a failing school, and contracting for educational services with for-profit and nonprofit organizations (NPOs) (Reyes, 2002). Contracting for educational services with for-profit organizations include contracts with educational maintenance organizations (EMO) like the New American Schools Development Corporation; Education Alternatives Incorporated in Minnesota; the Edison Project in New York City; Public Strategies Group; Beacon Education Management, formerly Alternative Public Schools in Tennessee; SABIS Educational Systems, Inc., founded in 1886 in Beirut, Lebanon; Noble Education Dynamics, Inc.; Advantage Schools, Inc., based in Jersey City, New Jersey; and Hope Academies owned by Ohio industrialist David Brennan (*Education Daily*, 1998; Furtwengler, 1997).

Charter schools and vouchers represent a major effort to reintroduce market competition in public schools. The market-driven philosophy is driven by deregulation or allowing schools to operate in a regime where, to the greatest extent, they are judged by outcomes (achievement scores) and not inputs (who they hire, who the student population is, where they operate, which curricula they use) (Dilulio, 1994). Market-driven philosophy is accompanied by the notice that private business can do it better and cheaper (Dilulio, 1994). Because neither full decentralization nor full deregulation is in the interest of the state, choice movements like charter schools and vouchers will have rules and centralization.

The school choice movement is based on the notion that parents should be allowed to choose the public school that best suits their child, regardless of where they live (Chubb & Moe, 1990; Elmore, 1987). In reality, wealthy parents have always exerted their choice rights by shopping for houses on the basis of the quality of the school (Frug, 1998). Poor Whites and minorities do not choose bad urban schools; they just cannot afford to choose better schools (Frug, 1998).

Charter schools are an experimental concept based on market-driven theories of choice that allow parents, teachers, business people, universities, government agencies, or other groups to set up their own public schools under an existing school regulatory agency, such as the state education agency or a local education agency (Cohen, 2002). Charter schools may also be operated by nonprofit organizations or for-profit organizations (Hart & Burr, 1996). Charter schools operate on the basis of a charter or a contract between organizations (parents, teachers, NPOs, for-profit organizations) and sponsors by the local district board or the state education agency (Reyes, 2002). State charter school legislation typically relieves charter schools of most state and local regulations so schools can have autonomy and flexibility while they are free to innovate and experiment (Cookson, 1994; Wohlstetter & Griffin, 1997). Charter school contracts do not provide relief from criminal acts, special education, bilingual education, or other responsibilities specified by state charter schools laws (Heubert, 1997; Texas Education Code Annotated, 2001).

Charter schools, like vouchers, have attracted constituents who are dissatisfied with the public school system. Dissatisfaction with public schools particularly by minorities has led to the search for educational alternatives, like community controlled schools, charters, and vouchers. Alternative schools outside the public school system included free schools and other community controlled schools like the Afro-centric alternative schools of the 1960s (Cohen, 1969). Cohen (1969) recommended the use of Afro-centric alternative schools as an approach to improve segregated education for African American students using a decentralization plan. In 1997, a Texas Hispanic legislator supporting charters commented, "Sure as hell, we couldn't do any worse" (Dubose, 1998). The community controlled schools gave minority groups a tool with which to achieve self-determination and control of their destiny (Cohen, 1969). The policy of controlling one's destiny through the control of one's schools is long-standing and has been practiced by many religious groups, including Irish and other Catholic groups and Jews (Tyack, 1974).

In 2002, there were 2,400 charter schools in the United States (Finn & Kanstoroom, 2003). According to Bulkley and Fisler (2002), the early proponents of charter schools outlined five outcomes of charter schools: (a) Charter schools would lead to the creation or reinvention of public schools. (b) Deregulation would produce more autonomous and flexible organizations. (c) Autonomy and market forces would challenge public schools to be more innovative or provide a higher quality education for the students left behind in public schools. (d) Parental commitment would produce greater charter school accountability. (e) Autonomy, innovation, and accountability would lead to improved student achievement, high commitment and satisfaction from teachers, parents, and other clients.

The funding theory for charter schools is that the money follows the student. Many states use a per-pupil funding base (King et al., 2003). States use one of three basic funding mechanisms to flow money to charter schools. Funding goes directly from the state to the charter school. Funding goes from the local school district to the charter school. Funding is negotiated locally between the charter school and the school district (Odden & Busch, 1998). In some states based on the state charter school legislation, funding may use two or all three mechanisms. The Texas legislation outlines three kinds of charter schools and three funding mechanisms. Arkansas, Georgia, Kansas, and Wyoming do not address funding in their state law (Odden & Busch, 1998). In 1998, charter school students in Texas received approximately $5,000 in state dollars per student while the per-pupil cost at the Renaissance Charter in Boston was $7,500 (Farber, 1997; Walt, 1998).

Many states have developed charter school finance formulas that distribute local and state funds from the state to the local district to charter schools. For funding purposes, most states treat charter schools like independent school districts. They receive their share of the state foundation program and their share of local property taxes. For example, in Texas the charter school legislation prescribes that charter schools will receive funds from the state school foundation program and their share of local tax property taxes (Texas Education Code Annotated, 2001). Categorical program allotments include career and technology, bilingual and English as a second language, compensatory education, gifted and talented education, and special education. The local district tax payment is equal to the maintenance tax revenue collected in the district divided by the sum of students enrolled in the school district (including charter school students).

Charter schools are eligible for all federal funding, including Title I and Individuals for Disabilities Education Act. In addition, they receive federal start-up funds and special facilities financing or $300 million in 2003 (National Charter School Alliance, 2003). Only six states and the District of Columbia provide funding for facilities while federal legislation and a few states provide start-up grants (King et al., 2003).

Vouchers

Vouchers are another form of decentralization introduced in 1950s by Milton Friedman (Friedman, 1962). The state issues vouchers in the form of certificates from the state to parents as some portion of tax dollars earmarked for their child's public education, usually toward the cost of authorized private schooling (Koppick, 1997; & Levin, 2002). The theory is that once the vouchers are issued to parents, private and public schools would compete for students and the vouchers. Some voucher systems call for allowing public schools to accept vouchers so that education dollars flow from the child instead of automatically being funneled into a particular school district (King et al., 2003). Some voucher proposals target students most disadvantaged by the current public education system; however, vouchers do not assure that private schools will accept the vouchers of the most disadvantaged or whether the tuition of voucher-approved schools would exceed the public voucher. Vouchers come in the form of public and private grants. The size of vouchers varies from one state plan to another. Partial vouchers will disproportionately benefit middle- and upper-income families while widening the achievement gap between middle- and upper-income and low-income and minority students.

Public vouchers were initiated in 1991 in Milwaukee and in 1995 in Cleveland. Private vouchers were initiated in 1991 by J. Patrick Rooney,

CEO of the Golden Rule Life Insurance in Indianapolis, and in 1994 by Walton Family Foundation in San Antonio (King et al., 2003). By 2000, private voucher programs were operating in 41 cities paying for private school tuition for over 50,000 children (King et al., 2003). Although private school vouchers have expanded, the goal of the voucher movement is to legitimize publicly funded vouchers.

The Milwaukee voucher program targeted 15,000 low-income Milwaukee families for state tuition grants equivalent to the per-pupil aid for the Milwaukee Public Schools (about $5,550 in 2001) to send their children to private schools, including religious schools. The 1995 Milwaukee legislation was challenged in the courts and in 2003, the U.S. Supreme Court declined to hear the case, upholding the Wisconsin Supreme Court ruling that the law did not violate the establishment clause (King et al., 2003).

The Cleveland voucher program began operating in 1996 for K–8 students, providing up to 90% or up to $2,250 of private schools and religious schools. Smaller grants are available for higher income families. The grants or scholarships are distributed by a lottery that gives higher priority to low-income families (King et al., 2003). In 1999, the Cleveland voucher program was challenged in the Ohio Supreme Courts for its support of over 4,000 recipients of which 96% were enrolled in religious schools. In the spring 2003 the U.S. Supreme Court ruled that the Cleveland case was not in violation of the establishment clause.

The Florida voucher program is the first statewide voucher program (Herrington, 1999; and King, Swanson, & Sweetland, 2003). The Florida Opportunity Program provides a $4,000 grant for students who receive failing grades for any two out of four years (Herrington, 1999; King et al., 2003). The receiving school cannot charge more than the state grant. The program qualified 136 students, of which 58 selected private schools and 78 transferred to other public schools (King et al., 2003). In a second voucher program, Florida provides vouchers for children with disabilities (King et al., 2003). In an interesting twist, the Florida voucher program has been challenged on the basis of the state constitution.

PRODUCTIVITY

Levin (2002) offered a comprehensive framework for evaluating educational vouchers that focuses on the following four criteria: (a) freedom of choice, (b) productive efficiency, (c) equity, and (d) social cohesion. Freedom of choice gives parents the right to choose based on values, educational philosophy, religious teachings, and political outlook. Productive efficiency provides maximization of educational outcomes given the resource constraint.

Equity is a quest for fairness in access to educational opportunity, resources, and outputs. Social cohesion incorporates the pubic policy of fraternity or citizenship (King et al., 2003; Levin, 2002). The major purpose of schooling in a democratic society is to provide common educational experiences that will prepare citizens who are able to participate in the social, political, and economic institutions of society (Levin, 2002). According to Levin (2002), given the vast differences of voucher plans, the four criteria of freedom of choice, productive efficiency, equity, and social cohesion, these plans can be constructed with particular features to address each criterion by using three design instruments: (a) finance, (b) regulation; and (c) support services.

SUMMARY

The history of school finance has evolved from the Equal Protection Amendment of the 14th Amendment of the U.S. Constitution to state constitutional equal protection clause to adequacy or sufficiency of funds allocated to students and to schools. Defining adequacy for future school finance policy may be totally dependent on the political will of a state. If a state defines adequacy as a high minimum standard for academic outcomes and achievement, then the resources needed to support the high minimum can be identified and allocated accordingly; however, if adequacy is a standard reflecting a state's conceptualization of the basic minimum education the resources associated with the basic minimum will likely become the ceiling for public educational spending. Adequacy may signal the end of a Russian novel "and in the end everybody dies."

The answer to school finance concerns may lie in the understanding the differences between dollars, achievement, the conclusion that dollars alone are not enough, and a clearer picture of how best teaching practices, classroom organization strategies, community engagement, and other school community features bear on student learning in public schools. Defining adequacy or the level of funding necessary to fully support a high minimum standard of adequacy may be a question not only of how much money is enough but how much education is enough.

In the current era of school reform, the purpose of school finance and school budgeting is to more equitably distribute resources while more productively using school dollars to increase student performance in the face of increasing standards and shrinking state budgets. Decentralized budgeting or campus-based budgeting allows instruction to drive the school budget rather than some central office business manager with districtwide budget allocations; however, there is little evidence of successful budget decentralization models. Although charters and vouchers provide a more common model for decentralization, the research on the effects of academic achievement, choice, access, integration, and civic socialization show some improvements; however, there is no consistent evidence (Gill, Timpane, Ross, & Brewer, 2003). There is some evidence on vouchers showing that when charter schools compete with local public schools, there are improvements in academic performance for students who remain in the public schools with vouchers (Gill et al., 2003; Ladd & Fisk, 2003). Some of the evidence suggests that only in comparison with underperforming public schools are vouchers and charters effective (Gill et al., 2003).

Regardless of whether school leaders use traditional budgeting techniques, decentralization, charters, or vouchers, practitioners need a conceptual understanding of educational productivity. What is the best mix of resources to:

1. enhance curriculum and make sure students are engaged in high academic standards, and programs?
2. focus adequate school resources on high-poverty students and schools?
3. focus on resources?
4. make student learning and achievement the school's primary goal and the impetus for resource allocation (Consortium for Policy Research in Education, cpre@nwfs.gse.upenn.edu)?

CRITERIA FOR SCHOOL BUDGET CASE STUDY

The purpose of this activity is to develop your own case study for school budgeting. You should select a finance/budget budget organizational event or experience that was significant or challenging to you. The event should consist of two or more budgeting issues that directly impact the quality of instruction in your school. Your case should pose questions or challenges to improvement in instruction and student performance. You case study should be one to three double-spaced pages. Your case study should be a description of one event or your qualitative interpretation of one major event and related issues, including sequence, issues, and direct quotes or language used by the participants.

Because this is a budgeting or school finance case study you may use more data. For example, "Mr. Troutman is a former bilingual teacher who, for the last 3 years, has been an elementary school principal in a large urban school with a 60% bilingual student enrollment and 80% low income. Last year Mr. Troutman's school was rated exemplary for their passing rates in the state accountability test. This is the second year that Zavala Elementary school is rated exemplary. The other day another principal made the following comment, 'Mr. Troutman is able to improve achievement and provide all the extra after-school and weekend fine arts activities because his school is a magnet school. Magnet schools receive special grants from the school district that pay for a lower teacher/pupil ratio and a magnet school coordinator.' Mr. Troutman replied, 'I'm not a magnet school, I just read the entire school district finance manual and figured out how I can more creatively use existing district funds. I also wrote a grant to fund my parent center. I took a teacher aide position and converted it to hire part-time college and high school students to teach violin, baile folklorico, and music after school and on Saturdays. I traded a counseling position so that I could hire extra reading teachers and reduce the reading class size to one teacher per ten students. I received the same budget amount as your campus.'"

Organization of School Budget Case Study

1. In paragraph one, set the stage for your budget case study. You many want to provide some school demographics and describe the funding system used by the state, school district, and the school. Remember you're writing a short story.
2. Use qualitative research skills and focus on actual events describing the event and the language by scripting the event. In the example above, campus data and the language of the major event were captured in the paragraph.
3. Think about the following budget elements:

   a. Budget system used by the district and the school, like traditional centralized budgeting, decentralized budgeting, charter school, or vouchers.
   b. School revenues generated from ADA/ADM, state student categories, federal revenues, and private revenues.
   c. School expenditures in the form of teacher FTEs.
   d. The links between instruction and budgeting.
   e. Budget program evaluation techniques or how do you measure efficient and effective use of school revenues?

4. Consider ending your case study with a question on what you do next to solve your problem.
5. In writing your case study, consider school confidentiality and disguise your case study by using creative names. For example, the school could be named "Hogwarts Middle School," the principal could be

"Ms. Dumbledore," etc. Be creative. If you do not wish your case study to be public, you should indicate it as "Confidential."

6. You will present your case study in class and will receive feedback from students, your principal mentor, and the professor.

GUIDING QUESTIONS

1. Identify a highly effective and efficient school. Make an appointment with the principal and let the principal know that you are doing research on school budgets for highly effective and efficient schools. You will want to collect the following data from the school: (a) a copy of the school budget, (b) a school staffing roster, including FTE data, (c) student attendance data, including ADA/ADM, (d) categorical student data, including special education, bilingual/ESL, at-risk students, vocational education, gifted and talented, and other state student categories, (e) external funds, including Title I, School Safety, special program funds, and private funds, and (f) student performance data for the 3 previous years. Check with the principal to find out how student full-time equivalences (FTE) are used.

For the second part of this activity, gather the same budget data on your school budget. Respond to the following questions:

2. How can some schools improve instruction and student performance and do so under the same budget that restrains others?

3. How do principals and assistant principals use the following budgeting concepts to determine the school budget: average daily attendance (ADA), average daily membership (ADM), and teacher full-time equivalence (FTE)?

4. How is school budgeting connected to the quality of instruction?

5. How is budget reallocation used to improve instruction? How can some schools increase the number of regular classroom teachers and reduce class size by focusing on core education services? Which positions can the converted or traded for classroom teachers? List ways that reallocation can be used to provide varied class sizes for different subjects. List ways that students can be grouped differently from the traditional age-grade groups to improve instruction. How can teachers be scheduled for common team planning periods?

SELECTED READINGS

King, R. A., Swanson, A. D., & Sweetland, S. R. (2003). *School finance: Achieving high standards with equity and standards.* Boston: Allyn & Bacon.

Matthews, L. J., & Crow, G. M. (2003). *On being and becoming a principal.* Boston: Allyn & Bacon.

Levin, H. M. (2002, Fall). A comprehensive framework for evaluating educational vouchers. *Educational Evaluation and Policy Analysis, 24*(3), 159–174.

Miles, K. H., & Darling-Hammond, L. (1997). *Rethinking schools resources in high performing schools.* Madison: University of Wisconsin, Wisconsin Center for Educational Research, Consortium for Policy Research in Education.

Odden, A., & Busch, C. (1998). *Financing schools for high performance.* San Francisco: Jossey-Bass.

REFERENCES

Argyris, C., & Schon, D. A. (1978). *Organizational learning: A theory of action perspective.* Reading, MA: Addison-Wesley.

Augenblick, J. (1984). *Providing incentives in the allocation of state aid for schools.* Denver, CO: Education Policy Planning Services.

Bolman, L. G., & Deal, T. E. (1997). *Reframing organizations.* San Francisco: Jossey-Bass.

Bulkley, K., & Fisler, J. (2002, April). A decade of charter schools: From theory to practice. *CPRE Policy Briefs.* Philadelphia: University of Pennsylvania.

Chubb, J., & Moe, T. (1990). *Politics, markets, and America's schools.* Washington, DC: Brookings Institution.

Cohen, R. M. (2002, March). Schools our teachers deserve: A proposal for teacher-centered reform. *Phi Delta Kappan, 83*(7), 532–537.

Consortium for Policy Research in Education. (1996). *Public policy and school reform: A research summary.* Philadelphia: Pennsylvania Graduate School of Education.

Cookson, P. W. Jr. (1994). School *choice the struggle for the soul of American education.* New Haven, CT: Yale University Press.

Deming, E. (1986). *Out of the crisis.* Cambridge, MA: MIT Press.

Dilulio, J. J. Jr. (Ed.). (1994). *Deregulating the public service: Can government be improved?* Washington, DC: Brookings Institution.

Dubose, L. (1998, March 27). Deschooling Society. Who's paying for public school vouchers? The Texas Observer, pp. 4–7.

Education Daily. (1998, December 3). *California charter system too loose, study says, 31*(23), 1–12.

Elmore, R. (1987). Choice in public education. *Politics of Education Association Yearbook 1987.*

Farber, P. (1998). The Edison project scores—and stumbles—in Boston. *Phi Delta Kappan, 79*(7), 506–511.

Fiedler, F. E. (1967). *A theory of leadership effectiveness.* New York: McGraw-Hill.

Finn, C. E. Jr., & Kanstoroom, M. (2002, September 2002). Do charter schools do it differently? *Phi Delta Kappan, 84*(1), 59–62.

Fox, J. L. (2002, March). Organizational structures and perceived cultures of community charter schools in Ohio. *Phi Delta Kappan, 83*(7), 525–532.

Friedman, M. (1962). *Capitalism and freedom.* Chicago, IL: University of Chicago Press.

Frug, J. (1998, April). City Services. *New York University Law Review, 73*(1), 23–96.

Furtwengler, C. B. (1997, March). *For profit educational firms: Their probable impact on U.S. educational system.* Paper presentation at the annual meeting of the American Educational Research Association, Chicago, IL.

Gill, B. P., Timpane, M. P., Ross, K. E., & Brewer, D. J. (2003). What we know and what we need to know about vouchers and charters. In W. J. Fowler Jr. (Ed.), *Developments in school finance: 2001–02.* Washington, DC: National Center for Educational Statistics, U.S. Department of Education, Institute of Education Sciences.

Gittell, M. J. (Ed.). (1998). *Strategies for school equity: Creating productive schools in a just society.* New Haven, CT: Yale University Press.

Hart, G. K., & Burr, S. (1996). The story of California's charter school legislation. *Phi Delta Kappan, 78*(1), 37–40.

Herrington, C. D. (1999). Performance-based budgeting for public schools. In M. Goertz & A. R. Odden (Eds.), *Florida School-based financing.* Thousand Oaks, CA: Corwin Press.

Hersey, P., & Blanchard, K. H. (1977). *Management of organizational behavior.* Mahwah, NJ: Prentice-Hall.

Heubert, J. P. (1997). Schools without rules? Charter schools, federal disability law, and the paradoxes of deregulation. *Harvard Civil Rights-Civil Liberties Law Review, 32*(2), 301–353.

Hooker, R. (2001). *Funding students, not schools: Houston ISD efforts to decentralize school funding.* Paper presented at meeting the grade conference, University of Houston.

King, R. A., Swanson, A. D., & Sweetland, S. R. (2003). *School finance: Achieving high standards with equity and standards.* Boston: Allyn & Bacon.

Koppich, J. E. (1997, Winter). Considering nontraditional alternatives charters, private contracts, and vouchers. *The Future of Children, 7*(3), 96–112.

Ladd, H. F., & Fiske, E. B. (2003, Spring). Does competition improve teaching and learning? Evidence from New Zealand. *Educational Evaluation and Policy Analysis, 25*(1), 97–120.

Levin, H. M. (2002, Fall). A comprehensive framework for evaluating educational vouchers. *Educational Evaluation and Policy Analysis, 24*(3), 159–174.

Likert, R. (1967). *The human organizations: Its management and value.* New York: McGraw-Hill.

Manno, B. V., Finn, C. E., Bierlein, L. A., & Vanourek, G. (1998). How charter schools are different. *Phi Delta Kappan, 79*(7), 492.

Mc Gregor, D. (1960). *The human side of enterprise.* New York: McGraw-Hill.

Matthews, L. J., & Crow, G. M. (2003). *On being and becoming a principal.* Boston: Allyn & Bacon.

Miles, K. H., & Darling-Hammond, L. (1997). *Rethinking schools resources in high performing schools.* Madison: University of Wisconsin, Wisconsin Center for Educational Research, Consortium for Policy Research in Education.

Minorini, P. A., & Sugarman, S. D. (1999a). School finance litigation in the name of educational equity: Its evolution, impact and future. In H. F. Ladd, R. Chalk, & J. S. Hansen (Eds.), *Equity and adequacy in education finance: Issues and perspectives* (pp. 34–71). Washington, DC: National Academy Press.

Minorini, P. A., & Sugarman, S. D. (1999b). Educational adequacy and the courts: The promise and problems of moving to a new paradigm. In H. F. Ladd, R. Chalk, & J. S. Hansen (Eds.), *Equity and adequacy in education finance: Issues and perspectives* (pp. 175–208). Washington, DC: National Academy Press.

Monk, D. H., & Rice, J. K. (1999). Modern education productivity research: Emerging implications for the financing of education. In W. J. Fowler (Ed.), *National Center for Educational Statistics: 1997–1999 Selected Papers in School Finance.* Washington, DC: National Center for Educational Statistics, U.S. Department of Education, Institute of Education Sciences.

National Charter School Alliance. (2003). Federal policy update. Retrieved July 21, 2003, from http://www. charter friends.org/.

Odden, A., & Busch, C. (1998). *Financing schools for high performance.* San Francisco: Jossey-Bass.

Odden A. R., & Picus, L. O. (1992). *School finance: A policy perspective.* New York: McGraw-Hill.

Rethinking Schools. (1997). *Funding for justice: Money, equity, and the future of public education.* Milwaukee, WI: A Rethinking Schools Publication.

Reyes, A. H. (2000). Alternative education: The dark side of education or new tools for Latinos to achieve self-actualization? *Bilingual Review, XXV*(3), 539–559.

Rossmiller, R. A. (1987). Achieving equity and effectiveness in schooling. *Journal of Education Finance, 12*(4), 561–577.

Texas Education Code Annotated (2001). Chapter 11, 12. 25, 41, 42, 43, 44, and 45. St. Paul, MN: West Publishing.

Tyack, D. B. (1974). *The one best system.* Cambridge, MA: Harvard University Press.

Vandersall, K. (1998). Post-Brown school finance reform. In M. J. Gittell (Ed.), *Strategies for school equity: Creating productive schools in a just society* (pp. 11–23). New Haven, CT: Yale University Press.

Verstegen, D. A. (1998, Summer). Judicial analysis during the new wave of school finance litigation: The new adequacy in education. *Journal of Education Finance, 24,* 51–68.

Verstegen, D. A. (2002, Winter). Financing the new adequacy: Towards new models of state education finance systems that support standards based reform. *Journal of Education Finance, 27,* 749–782.

Walt, K. (1998). Education board tries to limit charter schools. *Houston Chronicle,* Section A, p. 38. November 14, 1998

Webb, D. L., McCarthy, M. M., & Thomas, S. B. (1988). *Financing elementary and secondary education.* Columbus, OH: Merrill.

Weiler, H. (1990). Comparative perspectives on educational decentralization: An exercise in contradiction? *Educational Evaluation in Policy Analysis, 12*(4), 433–448.

Wohlstetter, P., & Griffin, N. C. (1997). First lessons: Charter schools as learning communities. Philadelphia: University of Pennsylvania. Consortium for Policy Research in Education Policy Briefs.

Chapter 19

Charter Schools

Liane Brouillette
University of California, Irvine

Debate over the nature and purpose of public education began early in U.S. history. Thomas Jefferson argued that if his countrymen were to protect their newfound liberties they had to be literate and able to learn from the lessons of history. In his "Bill for the More General Diffusion of Knowledge" (1779), Jefferson proposed that Virginia offer 3 years of free schooling to every child. Although his colleagues rejected this proposal as too costly, Jefferson provided future generations with a compelling rationale for a comprehensive state system of education:

> Whereas it appeareth that however certain forms of government are better cal-
> culated than others to protect individuals in the free exercise of their natural
> rights, and are at the same time themselves better guarded against degeneracy,
> yet experience hath shewn, that even under the best forms, those entrusted
> with power have, in time, and by slow operations, perverted it into tyranny;
> and it is believed that the most effectual means of preventing this would be, to
> illuminate, as far as practicable, the minds of people at large. (1904, p. 414)

Horace Mann and other 19th-century reformers argued that public schools would help build community based on common knowledge and common values. However, in his "Twelfth Annual Report" to the Massachusetts Board of Education (1848), Mann offered a quite different rationale for public schooling than did Jefferson: "if all the children in the community, from the age of four years to that of sixteen, could be brought within the reformatory and elevating influence of schools, the dark host of private vices and public crimes, which now embitter domestic peace and stain the civilization of the age, might, in ninety-nine cases in every hundred, be banished from the world" (Johnson, 2002, p. 95).

The views of Mann and Jefferson were shaped by their differing backgrounds. Among the Puritans, who had dominated the Massachusetts Bay colony in its early years, knowing how to read, understand, and comply with God's law had been considered a necessity. In 1635, 6 years after the first settlers landed, the first Latin Grammar school was established in Boston. A year later Harvard College was founded. In 1647, the general court of the colony enacted a law ordering every town of 50 or more households to offer instruction in reading and writing. The rationale was clearly stated in the law: "It being one chiefe project of that ould deluder, Satan, to keepe men from knowledge of the Scriptures." Mann's vision of schools as antidotes to the unraveling of the social fabric and to moral decline drew on that Puritan legacy.

Tension between the "bottom-up" view of public schools (epitomized in Jefferson's view of education as the safeguard of individual liberty) and the "top-down" view of education (inherent in Mann's vision of a common school that would provide moral guidance for the masses) has continued to pervade debates on public education. Even the meaning of the word "public" has been a subject of controversy. For example, universities may be considered "public" even if they charge tuition that many people cannot afford. Neighborhood schools are considered "public" even when they admit only children whose families can afford the costly down payment on a home located within that school's attendance area (Areen & Jencks, 1971).

Affluent parents have the alternative of either moving to an area with "good" public schools or paying to send their children to a private school. Less affluent parents who think that their children are not getting an adequate education can take their grievances to the local school board, but mounting an effective campaign to change local schools takes an enormous investment of time, energy, money. Few parents have the political skill or commitment to solve their problems this way. Voices from every portion of the political spectrum have, at one time or another, complained that the political mechanisms set up to make public schools accountable to their clients have proved ineffective. The charter school movement is but the latest attempt to provide a solution to this dilemma. However, it has been the subject of much public debate.

GENESIS OF CHARTER SCHOOL MOVEMENT

Charter schools are publicly sponsored autonomous schools that are substantially free of direct government control, but are held accountable for achieving certain levels of student performance and other specified outcomes (Cookson, 1994). The first such schools were created in Minnesota, where a provision was passed in 1991 that allowed licensed teachers to create innovative schools, essentially on contract to a public school board. These schools could be either existing, but redesigned, schools or new schools. The idea had been suggested by Albert Shanker, president of the American Federation of Teachers, in a 1988 speech to the National Press Club, where he commented:

> I hear this all over the country. Somebody says, "Oh, Mr. Shanker, we tried something like that 15 years ago. We worked around the clock, and we worked weekends.... I never worked so hard in my life. And then a new school board was elected or a new principal or superintendent came in and said, 'That's not my thing.'" And that's the end of the school or program. You'll never get people to make that kind of commitment if our educational world is just filled with people who went through the disappointment of having been engaged and involved and committed to building something only to have it cut out from under them. (Nathan, 1996a, p. 63)

Public school choice already had a strong base in Minnesota; Minneapolis and St. Paul had offered alternative schools and magnet schools since the 1970s (Nathan, 1996b). Prior to passage of the first charter school legislation in 1991, Minnesota Governor Rudy Perpich, a Democrat, had introduced proposals for several other public school choice programs. State residents had learned that thoughtful competition could stimulate improvements. As Joe Nathan (1996b) points out:

> In 1985, only 33% of Minnesotans favored cross-district public school choice, while 60% opposed it. By 1992, polls by major education groups found that 76% of the state's residents supported the idea, while only 21% opposed it. Support grew because 1) thousands of students who had dropped out used these laws to return to school; 2) the number of advanced courses in high schools more than doubled, as schools responded to the competition provided by the postsecondary options law; 3) public school choice brought families back into public education; and 4) choice allowed educators to create new, distinctive schools. (p. 19)

Minnesota State Senator Ember Reichgott Junge, a Democrat, and several local activists heard Shankar's call for a new kind of public school and refined the idea to fit Minnesota. The charter school bill that finally was passed was far weaker than supporters had hoped. However, a door had been opened, allowing for the establishment of a new kind of public school. Within 5 years, 25 states had adopted charter school legislation, although the details varied widely.

Characteristics of Charter Schools

Charter school founders typically seek to implement an alternative vision of schooling, one they believe requires the creation of a school with greater autonomy than is traditionally allowed in the public school system. Unlike magnet or alternative schools, charter schools exist outside the normal school district hierarchy. They operate under a written contract, or charter, from a state or local government agency. In most states, administration of charter schools is limited to nonprofit organizations (although some states do allow profit-making organizations to operate charter schools). Although regulations governing charter schools vary greatly from state to state, charter school advocate Nathan (1996b) points out that, broadly speaking, charter school laws share the following elements:

- *The state authorizes more than one organization to start and operate a public school in a community.* The state thus withdraws what Ted Kolderie (1990) has called the "exclusive franchise" that has historically been given to public school districts. Elimination of this exclusive franchise "removes from the district its ability to take its students for granted." Organizers of charter schools may approach either a local board or some other public body to be their sponsor.
- *The newly organized (or converted) schools would be public schools.* They would not charge tuition and would be open to all kinds of students, without admission tests.
- *The schools would be responsible for improved student achievement.* Each school would negotiate a 3- to 5-year contract (or "charter") with the sponsoring agency, specifying (a) areas in which students would learn more and (b) how that learning would be measured. Schools that failed to achieve their contracted improvements would be closed by the sponsoring organization.
- *In return for this accountability for improved results, the state would grant an up-front waiver of virtually all rules and regulations governing public schools.* Aside from health, safety, and other specified regulations, charter schools would be exempt from state regulations about how to operate.
- *The charter school would be a school of choice.* No one would be assigned to work in or to attend the school who had not chosen to do so.
- *The school would be a discrete entity.* The school would be a legal entity, with its own elected board. Teachers could organize and bargain collectively. However, this bargaining unit would be separate from, and not bound by, the contracts negotiated by any district bargaining unit.
- *The full per-pupil allocation would move with the student.* The amount would be roughly equal to the average state per-pupil allocation or the average

allocation from the district from which the student comes. If the state provides extra funds for students with disabilities or for students from low-income families, these funds would also follow the student.

• *Participating teachers would be protected and given new opportunities.* The state would permit teachers to take a leave from their public school systems and retain their seniority. Teachers could stay in local or state retirement systems.

The Debate Over Charter Schools

Since 1991, charter schools have received support from Democrats and Republicans, teacher organizations, business groups, and parent associations. Reasons for this support vary. Three underlying belief systems have been seen as motivating charter school supporters—*antibureaucracy, market-based education,* and *teacher professionalism* (Garn, 1999). The antibureaucracy view holds that, by legislating an ever-growing number of "best practice" methods and penalizing deviation, various government agencies have created a top-down educational system that chokes out innovations. Educators, parents, and community activists who start charter schools argue that, freed from such restrictions, they can more effectively address the real needs of the students they serve. The amount of freedom from local and state regulations that charter school laws grant varies from state to state; but, in states with strong charter school laws, charters enjoy significantly more freedom in regard to choosing faculty, curriculum, and methods of self-governance than do regular neighborhood schools in the same districts.

Those who hold a market-based view contend that district schools continue to go on as they always have, regardless of educational outcomes, because they have a monopoly on public school students. Charter schools, which do not have a captive population, are forced to compete for the allegiance of parents and students. Those with market-based views also believe that, by injecting competition into the public school environment, the quality of education is improved. Having to compete with charters forces other public schools to adapt, in order to retain their students. Another group of charter school supporters are motivated by a belief in teacher professionalism. For them, charter schools are about valuing the expertise of teachers and giving teachers control over decisions that affect learning in the classroom. They see charter schools as collaborative enterprises, where teachers and parents work together for the good of the child.

Wells, Grutzik, Carnochan, Slayton, and Vasudeva (1999) pointed out that bipartisan support for charter schools often masks opposing viewpoints regarding the purpose of initiating autonomous schools. Based on interviews with more than 50 policy makers in six states, they identified three conflicting themes that emerged from policy makers' explanations of their support for charter schools. The first theme was voiced by policy makers who saw charter schools as the beginning of a move toward vouchers. The second theme was articulated by policy makers who saw charter school reform as a "last chance" to save the existing public school system. A third theme arose in interviews with policy makers who saw charter schools as one of many (but not necessarily the central) reforms that could strengthen the public schools. According to Wells and colleagues (1999), passage of charter school legislation has been the result of a fragile bargain between political adversaries who sought different ends.

CHARTER SCHOOL DEBATE AS A REFLECTION OF A SOCIAL DIVIDE

The eddies of rhetoric that have swirled around the charter school issue are described by Wayson (1999), who notes the polemical tone of much of the debate:

> Each side of the issue uses "red flag" phrases to rally support or opposition. For example, teachers' groups speak of the rights of employees as though they did not know that defining teachers' responsibilities as hours spent rather than results achieved is guaranteed to lower achievement.... Licensed teachers are equated with quality instruction as though no one knows the deficiencies of present-day licensure. Proponents of choice unashamedly laud "privatization," "free-market competition," and "entrepreneurialism" as though they know nothing about the failures of private operations in the early 1970s or, more recently, in Baltimore. (pp. 447–448)

How is it that this network of more autonomous public schools has excited such passionate support—and opposition? There is a widespread perception that U.S. public education may be at a crossroads. Criticism has come from many quarters.

The achievement levels of U.S. students do not compare well to those of other countries. For example, in the first grade, the math skills of American and Asian children are similar. Yet by fifth grade, the gap in achievement has expanded to where there is virtually no overlap in the scores of American children and their peers in Japan, China, and Taiwan (Stevenson, Lee, & Stigler, 1986). At eleventh grade, only 14.5% of Chinese and 8.0% of Japanese students attain scores below the *average* American score (Stevenson, Chen, & Lee, 1993). Results from TIMSS, the Third International Mathematics and Science Study, revealed that U.S. fourth graders scored among the best in the world in math and science, but U.S.

eighth-grade scores were mediocre, and U.S. twelfth grade scores were among the lowest. The decline in the relative standing of the U.S. students as they progressed from elementary school through high school was startling and disturbing to many educators, parents, and policy makers.

Ever since the report *A Nation at Risk* was published by the National Commission on Excellence in Education in 1983, there have been worries that a "rising tide of mediocrity" was threatening the nation's longtime preeminence in commerce, science, and technology. The report argued that "If an unfriendly foreign power had attempted to impose on America the mediocre educational performance that exists today, we might well have viewed it as an act of war." Implicitly, such a critique defined the national well-being primarily in terms of the economic position in the world markets. As a consequence of framing the school reform dialogue in this manner, certain conclusions were drawn. Those nations where scores on international tests were highest had a planned curriculum, driven by standardized tests. Soon pressure was brought to bear to make greater use of standardized testing in the United States. State legislatures moved to tighten graduation requirements and mandate high-stakes tests, which would be used to judge the effectiveness of public schools.

Feeling beleaguered, teachers' groups asked: Were school personnel expected to take the blame for decades of social change? Teachers already had to tend to an ever-growing list of nonteaching duties arising from a host of state- and district-mandated programs, many having little to do with the central tasks of teaching and learning. In high-crime areas, teachers also had to be on guard against intrusion, robbery, assault, and vandalism. As one urban principal pointed out:

> Most people agree that the central goal of the public schools is to teach students to read, write, and compute. Urban schools today simply have too many other things to accomplish under too many unfavorable conditions. The urban school is no longer merely an academic institution: it is also a social and welfare institution. Among the necessary services it provides are recreation, cultural growth, emotional development, basic health care, food service, voter registration, draft registration, driver education, sex education, employment service, immunization, and the collection of census data. (Crosby, 1999, p. 300)

Most often, the added responsibilities had come without sufficient funding or essential personnel. All this added responsibility, without the means to carry it out, had drained time and energy while increasing feelings of futility among public school personnel. Teachers and administrators felt alone, on the front lines, struggling to deal with problems that others ignored. Given the hardships under which they often worked, demands for school reform, made by outsiders, can easily be interpreted as attacks. Similarly, talk about encouraging competition among schools could seem a cynical joke to educators who felt that existing bureaucratic regulations have put them at a distinct disadvantage.

The Need for Alternatives

Our form of government assumes that any governmental institution derives its powers from the consent of the governed. This implied social contract lies at the root of the charter school debate. What happens when the interests of a child are not well served by the schools that the child is legally required to attend? Is there not a sense in which an implied social contract has been breached? Should there not be some obligation to provide that child with an opportunity to go elsewhere? The goal was to offer alternatives to students who were not satisfied with the sort of education they were being offered in their current schools.

Charter school supporters point to the fact that two students sitting next to one another in class might be inhabiting vastly different social and emotional worlds. To insist upon a one-size-fits-all formula for public schools thus means that some children are given tremendous advantages over others—from the moment that they enter kindergarten. Such favoritism triggers profound questions about how a society that proclaims its goal to be "freedom and justice for all" could justify requiring children to attend schools that systematically advantage some over others. Why should children who are not succeeding in their present schools not be given the chance to search out a school that better fits their needs?

This chapter has its roots in just that question. As part of a study of a high school equivalency program that enrolled many inner-city youth (Brouillette, 1999), the author interviewed many former high school dropouts. They described the stark choices that confronted many urban youth. Recalling their high school experiences, former gang members described the difficulty of concentrating on math, knowing that someone sitting behind them had a knife—and a grudge of some sort. Young people with no gang involvement spoke of picking their way through neighborhoods criss-crossed by the territories of rival gangs. By the time they arrived at school, their ability to concentrate had been shattered by tensions reminiscent of those experienced by soldiers on the battlefield.

What these students liked about the high school equivalency program in which they were enrolled was that it allowed them to escape an environment permeated by fear. Many found that, for the first time since elementary school, they felt free to focus their full attention on what they were learning. This is not to say that this same level of stress was felt by all students. During the same period of time when the interviews with the GED students were being carried out, I was also supervising administrative interns—in some of the same schools. These were large, complex urban schools with many different "tracks." The higher "tracks" offered excellent educational programs, of which the gang-involved future GED students had not taken advantage.

Yet the existence of such academic programs, seemingly within their reach, did not make the problems encountered the students who would eventually drop out any less real. Among the GED students there were many who needed a smaller, more controlled learning environment where they could step outside their accustomed "tough guy" facade and be seen to be putting real effort into their schoolwork. Given these facts, the most pressing question was not "What is wrong with these high schools?" but "Why had these young people not been offered viable alternatives that would allow them to start anew without dropping out of school?"

Research Findings Differ Concerning Charter Schools

Although charter schools are too new for it to be possible to assess their long-term impact on educational outcomes, the early evidence would seem to confirm neither the greatest hopes of charter school proponents nor the greatest fears of opponents. There is evidence that these schools are serving as a laboratory for educational innovation but no dramatic educational strategies have yet emerged (Geske, Davis, & Hingle, 1997). Charter schools enroll similar proportions of low-income students and have a racial composition roughly similar to statewide averages (Office of Educational Research and Improvement (OERI), 1999), although charter schools in some states (Connecticut, Massachusetts, Michigan, Minnesota, North Carolina, and Texas) serve significantly higher percentages of minority or economically disadvantaged students.

Wells and colleagues (1998) conducted 17 case studies in 10 school districts in California (a state that initially enacted a weak charter school law but also the state that had the most students enrolled in charter schools), comparing claims made by charter school advocates with the experiences reported by educators, parents, and students. They found claims that greater autonomy led to greater satisfaction and decision-making capacity were supported, in part, by their data. Yet the degree of autonomy charters enjoyed varied greatly across schools and districts. Many charter schools had relied heavily on the support and services available to them through local districts or other entities. Unsure how to hold charter schools accountable for academic performance, school districts had been more likely to hold them fiscally accountable. In addition, charter schools often depended heavily on strong, well-connected leaders and on supplemental private resources.

Becker, Nakagawa, and Corwin (1996) analyzed survey data from California's charter schools and comparison schools in the same communities.

They also examined parent contracts in use at the charter schools. Becker and colleagues found that, in order to build parent participation, some California charter schools were experimenting with having parents sign agreements or "contracts" promising a certain amount or type of involvement. Their study reported that charter schools did have greater levels of parent involvement, but that this involvement may have been because of selectivity in the kinds of families participating in charter schools. The parent contracts might have had the effect of restricting enrollment to children whose parents demonstrated the desired willingness to meet school expectations.

Finn, Manno, Bierlein, and Vanourek (1997) visited 60 schools in 14 states and interviewed more than 1,300 individuals about the start-up difficulties that charter schools face. They identified six major categories of start-up problems:

1. Governance: mostly internal difficulties having to do with tensions and turmoil within and among governing boards, principals, parents, teaching staff, and other major school constituencies.
2. Funding: mostly external fiscal woes, centering on lack of money but sometimes involving cash flow, budgeting, and the like.
3. Students: trouble attracting (and sometimes retaining) enough students of the sort the school intended to serve and/or the arrival of many who pose challenges that the school was not expecting.
4. Staffing: difficulty engaging enough teachers and other staff members who are suited to, and prepared for, the school's program.
5. Instruction: includes problems with curriculum, materials, pedagogy, assessment, and other issues pertaining to educational content and its delivery.
6. Facilities: difficulty obtaining a suitable building or other site for the school program.

Schools that had reached their second or greater year of operation in 1996–1997 were found by Finn and colleagues to experience fewer or less severe problems than during their start-up year. In several important categories (governance, students, instruction), it appeared that, the longer these schools were in operation, the more likely they were to have eased or solved their start-up problems. Yet as is common with new schools, many charter schools continued to face significant problems in their second or third (or more) year of operation. Governance remained a concern in a third of the "veteran" schools; money was a problem for two-thirds; students for more than a third; staffing for one in seven; instruction for three-fifths of these schools. Facilities were fully satisfactory for barely one school in four.

TWO COMPETING VISIONS OF EDUCATION

The current school reform debate has its roots in decisions made during the closing decades of the 19th century. At that time, the United States was just emerging as a world power. Until the years just prior to World War I, Germany was seen as the European country to emulate. Impressed by the growing industrial might of Germany, businessmen worried about the ability of the United States to hold its own in the global marketplace.

> Of particular concern was the excellence of Germany's manufactured goods, an advantage manufacturers attributed to the German system of vocational education. What America needed in their view was a plentiful reservoir of skilled labor similar to what presumably existed in Germany. (Kliebard, 1999, p. 27)

Educators from kindergarten teachers to university professors flocked to Germany to study the pedagogical ideas being developed and taught there. German schools and universities were widely considered to be the best in the world.

The groundwork for the German educational system had been laid down by Frederick the Great of Prussia. An enlightened despot, Frederick had in 1763 issued general school regulations establishing compulsory schooling (then a radical idea) for boys and girls from 5 to 13 or 14 years of age. Frederick's minister, Freiherr (Baron) von Zedlitz, supported centralization of school administration under a national board of education. A school-leaving examination for university entrance (the *Abitur*, which still exists in Germany) was introduced. In 1807 Fichte drew up a plan for the new University of Berlin, which Humboldt was able to realize 2 years later. The university was dedicated to a scientific approach to knowledge, to the combination of research and teaching, and to the proliferation of academic pursuits. By the third quarter of the 19th century, the influence of German *Lernfreiheit* (freedom of the student to choose his own program) and *Lehrfreiheit* (freedom of the professor to develop the subject and to engage in research) was felt throughout the academic world.

German industry reaped the benefits of new scientific discoveries. Americans felt that the United States was forced to play "catch up." The 19th century had brought a steady expansion of scientific knowledge, yet the curriculum of most established universities had remained virtually untouched. Although this was the century of the scientists Michael Faraday, Charles Darwin, and Louis Pasteur, most significant research had been done outside the walls of universities. In Great Britain, for instance, it was the Royal Society and other such organizations that fostered advanced studies. The basic curriculum of most colleges and universities remained nontechnical and nonprofessional, with an emphasis on the study of the liberal arts.

Concerns about international economic competitiveness helped to mold educational policies in the United States. The Morrill Act of 1862 established land grant colleges. Federal lands were distributed to support and maintain at least one college in each state. In contrast to the liberal arts tradition that had heretofore dominated American higher education, the instructional focus of the land grant colleges would be agricultural and mechanical. The Morrill Act of 1890 broadened the focus to include federal assistance to the states for instructional purposes. In 1917 the Smith–Hughes Act provided categorical aid to public schools for vocational education.

The new vocational and professional emphasis constituted a radical departure from the traditional liberal arts curriculum of American secondary schools and institutions of higher education. The liberal arts curriculum had its roots in ancient times. In the Hellenistic world, created by the conquests of Alexander the Great, a "liberal education" had meant the kind of learning that makes the mind free, not subject to the influence of others. In ancient Rome and during the Middle Ages, grammar, rhetoric, logic (the trivium), arithmetic, geometry, astronomy, and music (the quadrivium) composed the *artes liberales*, or the arts befitting *liberi*, or free men. In contrast, education for "servility" included all subjects intended to prepare students for a practical trade, as opposed to political or cultural leadership.

In more modern times, the liberal arts had been understood to consist of subjects studied for their cultural and intellectual value, rather than for immediate practical use. A liberal education emphasized intellectual development rather than preparation for business or a profession. Students were exposed to the work of philosophers, historians, novelists, artists, and dramatists whose work encouraged them to ponder such questions as the nature of love and courage, the meaning of death, the proper balance between private and public life, and the consequences of good intentions and mistaken judgments. The arts of expression were taught through enabling students to experience the highest quality work in the visual and performing arts, in literature, and in speech.

Germany under the Kaiser emphasized other concerns. Social mobility was limited and the aristocracy remained firmly in charge. The educational system was structured so as to efficiently provide highly trained human resources to serve the needs of a booming economy. In the United States, however, a policy of sorting children into separate educational programs (to be trained for very different adult vocations) could not be mandated simply on grounds of economic efficiency. Many questioned the assumption that human intelligence was just another natural resource, to be harvested in whatever manner seemed to best serve the nation's economic well-being.

Supporters of the liberal arts tradition opposed defining education primarily in terms of vocational training, arguing that education should be designed to support the freedom of the mind. Charles W. Eliot, president of

Harvard University, argued in 1893 that educators should not differentiate between "education for college" and "education for life" (Kliebard, 1987). A liberal education was seen by its supporters as that type of schooling most suitable for a free human being, quite apart from any consideration of work or vocation. Educators were seen as the guardians of the finest elements of the Western heritage, entrusted with using the teaching of this heritage to develop the reasoning power of students—thus enabling students to express their thoughts clearly, concisely, cogently.

However, supporters of the liberal arts curriculum found themselves fighting an uphill battle. Many powerful economic and social forces were at work. The transformation of the nature of work and the workplace created a new imperative:

> With apprenticeship in steep decline as a source of training, it seemed obvious to educators, parents, social reformers, business and industrial leaders, and labor alike that education tied to the new workplace was required. The family alone could no longer mediate between the world of childhood and the new and puzzling world of work. A social agency had to intervene, and the schools were the logical choice. (Kliebard, 1999, p. 117)

A growing cadre of professional educators saw in the prospect of an expanded vocational education a chance to make the public school curriculum more visible in the lives of Americans. Not incidentally, the status of educators would be enhanced in the process:

> Education would become not merely a way to master a restricted range of academic subjects and thereby in some vague way promote intellectual development; at one that the same time, public education would become an indispensable instrument for addressing matters vital to the national interest and to individual success. (Kliebard, 1999, p. 28)

By the end of the 20th century, these new initiatives and priorities would transform public education in the United States. Yet the goals that professional educators had so enthusiastically embraced as the century began would never be satisfactorily achieved. To understand the reasons why, it is important to understand how things have changed—and why.

Redefining Who Should Control the Schools

> During the nineteenth century the country school belonged to the community in more than a legal sense: it was frequently the focus for people's lives outside the home. An early settler of Prairie View Kansas, wrote that its capitol "was a small white-painted building which was not only the schoolhouse, but the

center—educational, social, dramatic, political, and religious—of a pioneer community of the prairie region of the West." (Tyack, 1974, pp. 15–16)

A century ago, one-room schools across the nation served as natural gathering places where ministers met their flocks, politicians caucused, itinerant lecturers spoke, families gathered for hoe-downs, and children competed in spelling bees. School and community were organically related. "Most rural patrons had little doubt that the school was theirs to control (whatever state regulations might say) and not the property of the professional educator" (Tyack, 1974, p. 17). Local citizens provided both the school building and the teachers' salary. Parents had a strong influence on how the school was run. Cultural memories of this era still inform the attitudes of many Americans, creating considerable ambivalence vis-à-vis the more hierarchical and bureaucratic administrative practices that, a century ago, had already begun to dominate urban school districts.

As the 19th century ended, leading educators had begun to argue that a community-dominated form of education could no longer equip young people to deal with the complex nature of citizenship in a technological, urban society. The transition had been gradual. Beginning in the late 1830s, reformers like Horace Mann and Henry Barnard had led campaigns to reorganize public schools. Age-graded classrooms, a uniform curriculum, special training for teachers, and organization of schools into a hierarchical system run by professional administrators were among the reforms introduced. Reformers met with most success in cities, where concentrations of population made age-graded classrooms possible. However, governance remained in the hands of the community members who served on the school board. Urban school boards tended to be large, linked to party politics, and representative of local wards and districts.

In the 1890s businessmen and professionals became disillusioned with the perceived inefficiency of the existing system and sought, instead, to put the governance of schools into the hands of disinterested experts. By 1920, professional school superintendents had gained considerable power at the expense of city school boards. As urban school systems continued to grow in size and complexity, they came to resemble the large business corporations whose efficiency many school reform advocates admired. Meanwhile pressures to equalize educational opportunity led to increased state control over local school districts. Gradually larger consolidated schools replaced small schoolhouses, even in rural areas. As the decades passed, all public school districts came to increasingly resemble big city schools in their organization.

Yet the reorganization of public schools along bureaucratic lines brought problems not foreseen by the urban reformers who, during the first quarter of the 20th century, had sought to free schools from the widespread fiscal and policy abuses of 19th-century patronage politics (Iannaccone,

1967). The reformers' aim—embodied in the slogan "Get politics out of the schools and get education out of politics"—was to put policy decisions in the hands of politically neutral educators. Uniform, centralized public school systems gradually evolved out of haphazard educational alternatives. However, much was lost in terms of variety, responsiveness, individual choice, and local control (Kaestle, 1983).

Urban school superintendents began to use the language of social engineers as they sought to replace traditional forms of school governance (in which community members participated in decision making) with a new bureaucratic model where professional educators controlled schools. From classroom to central office, new controls were instituted over pupils, teachers, principals, and other subordinate members of the school hierarchy. Like a factory manager, the superintendent of schools was expected to supervise employees, keep the enterprise technically up to date, and monitor the uniformity and quality of the product (Tyack, 1974).

THE SEARCH FOR ALTERNATIVES TO THE "DRAFTEE MENTALITY"

Charter school parents who were interviewed for this book often mentioned the lack of motivation their child had displayed while attending her or his previous public school; their comments recalled the findings described in *The Shopping Mall High School: Winners and Losers in the Educational Marketplace.* Powell, Farrar, and Cohen (1985) described the situation of the "unspecial" middle 70% of high school students who are left out of the special programs school districts have developed for their most highly motivated as well as their "at risk" students:

> Few characteristics of the shopping mall high school are more significant than the existence of unspecial students in the middle who are ignored and poorly served. Teachers and administrators talk a great deal about the problem. (p. 173)

One reason the "unspecial student" can slide through with only a cursory knowledge of the subject matter is the existence of classroom treaties that allow the "unspecial" to avoid work. Little is usually expected of these students, and little is done to change their lot. In such an environment, there is little encouragement to excel:

> For the middle students, a school's neutral stance on pushing students has the effect of making minimum requirements maximum standards. (Powell, Farrar, & Cohen, p. 180)

Such classroom treaties may result from tacit recognition that U.S. public schools have become caught in a contradiction. On the one hand, there are laws that make school attendance compulsory. On the other hand, once students are in the building, there is comparatively little teachers can do to compel a high level of performance. Most children progress through the school system, passing from grade to grade, whether they choose to do much in the way of schoolwork or not. A few may have to repeat a grade. But, on the whole, penalties for academic failure are far lower than in school systems where "seat time" counts for little and where a school-leaving test is used to determine whether or not a student qualifies for university entrance.

The difference is made strikingly clear when one compares U.S. schools to those of other nations. For example, in post–World War II Germany the period of elementary education covers eight or nine grades. After this period, three options have traditionally been available to pupils. They may, after counseling by the elementary school teacher and on the request of the parents, be placed in a *Realschule*, a *Gymnasium*, or a *Hauptschule* (the last representing a continuation of elementary education). After completion of studies at the *Hauptschule*, the pupil typically enters apprenticeship training. The *Realschule* offers pupils further general education, some prevocational courses, and English-language study. At the age of 16, *Realschule* students conclude their studies and transfer to a vocational school or enter apprenticeship training. If academically qualified, the pupil may also transfer to the *Gymnasium*.

The *Gymnasium*, the third alternative for German youth, offers rigorous academic preparation for higher education. Like the *lycée* in France, the *Gymnasium* is designed for those students who have shown the most academic promise; and its curriculum, emphasizing languages, mathematics, natural sciences, and social sciences, requires a high degree of diligence throughout all of the nine grades. Students in the *Gymnasium* must pass an examination, the *Abitur*, if they are to be admitted to a German university. The content of the *Abitur* is adjusted to the focus of the students' studies, such as classical languages or mathematics-science.

Given this curriculum, the role of the teacher in a German *Gymnasium* is rather different than the role of teachers in American schools. In the German system an external exam, over which the teacher has no control, is used to appraise student performance. The teacher's role resembles that of a coach, working together with the student to help the latter acquire the knowledge and skills needed to pass the school-leaving examination. The American teacher, in contrast, must serve both as teacher and as judge, deciding on the adequacy of student academic performance. If a student receives a passing grade for a semester's work, no further proof of achievement in that subject is required. This can result in a subtle (or not-so-subtle) negotiation process, as students attempt to "wear down" the teacher, subtly bartering good behavior for passing grades, resulting in the kind of "class-room treaties" described in *The Shopping Mall High School.*

Because teachers are evaluated by their principals, there is considerable pressure to avoid situations that may cause trouble or embarrassment. When a teacher gives a large number of students failing grades, uncomfortable confrontations with parents can result. The parents may talk to the school principal. If parents do not get the reaction they desire from the principal, they may go to the superintendent's office. If the superintendent does not react in the desired manner, parents may contact members of the school board. Given that the school superintendent serves at the pleasure of the school board, all district staff employees who are dependent on the good will of the superintendent generally strive to avoid such an eventuality.

The Legacy of Conflicting Reform Efforts

In most states, local school districts have extensive power to make curriculum decisions (Metz, 1978). Yet the multilayered structure of the U.S. political system—plus the fact that most states and local school districts are in need of federal funds—makes schools simultaneously answerable to federal, state, and local regulations (Bennett & LeCompte, 1990). This division of authority has often put schools in the position of simultaneously attempting to meet two different and partially contradictory reforms or goals. For example, a school district might be directed both to tighten graduation requirements and to lower the dropout rate or a school might be directed to teach a more rigorous core curriculum while at the same time mainstreaming children with ever more profound handicaps.

Goodlad (1984) pointed out:

> Current expectations for schools constitute a hodgepodge, resulting from ac-cumulations of piecemeal legislation. New legislation takes little or no account of existing requirements in the education code. In fact, most legislators are virtually ignorant of these requirements and the potential impact of new bills on the finite time and resources of schools. Principals and teachers are often caught in a paralytic inertia created by the bombardment of changing and often conflicting expectations. (p. 275)

Such a situation can easily become an open invitation to cynicism. Because true compliance is impossible, a premium is put, not on effectively accom-plishing a clearly defined task, but on protecting oneself and one's school from any punitive measures that might result from noncompliance.

Even when the school does accomplish one of the assigned goals, what constitutes success to the partisans of one educational goal often constitutes failure to the partisans of another. Therefore, when the tide of public opinion causes one of two competing goals to be strongly emphasized, the partisans of the goal that has been ignored tend to do their best to focus media attention on this perceived failure, thus turning the tide of public opinion in their direction. As a result there is a tendency for the emphasis of educational policy to lurch from one goal to another, giving the recurrent crises in education a cyclical nature (Kirst & Meister, 1985; Cuban, 1990).

Not only does this turbulence encourage an attitude that dismisses attempts at reform as mere shifts in educational fashion, but it produces another unfortunate side effect. Few educational reforms last long enough for a solid research base to be established on which further rational progress could be built. Thus, when the debate circles around once again, the same debating points are repeated, with everyone hanging onto their original opinion and finding no rational way to settle differences through appeal to mutually acceptable empirical evidence. The constant churning effect created by politically motivated change helps explain why the large sums of money that have been spent on educational research have not brought about meaningful improvement in the way schools are run.

THE DEEPER ROOTS OF THE CHARTER SCHOOL DEBATE

The charter school movement represents a different approach to educational reform. Instead of attempting to hold together a districtwide consensus (or even persuade a diverse and opinionated high school faculty to agree on a single reform), the charter school movement allows individuals to gravitate to those programs for which they feel a natural affinity. An assumption is made that different students have different needs and an approach that does not work well for one may work well for another. In the charter school movement, proponents of different types of educational reform are not put into the position of having to defeat those with differing beliefs in order to put their own ideas to the test. The hope is that school reform can, in this way, be made into a win/win proposition. Although new to education, this approach has deep historical roots.

In medieval Europe, monarchs issued charters to towns, cities, guilds, merchant associations, universities, and religious institutions; such charters guaranteed certain privileges and immunities to those organizations, sometimes also specifying arrangements for the conduct of their internal affairs. Simply put, a charter is a document granting specified rights, powers, privileges, or functions to an individual, city, or other organization by the state (or sovereign). Even today the document that lays out the organizational structure of a city is called a "charter." Therefore, when a city wishes to make changes in its municipal form of government the debate will commonly center on provisions in the charter.

The most famous charter, the *Magna Carta* ("Great Charter"), was a compact between the English king John and his barons, specifying the king's grant of certain liberties to the English people. In England, the Petition of Right (1628) and the Habeas Corpus Act (1679) looked directly back to clause 39 of the charter of 1215, which stated that "no free man shall be ... imprisoned or disseised [dispossessed] ... except by the lawful judgment of his peers or by the law of the land." In subsequent English statutes, the references to "the legal judgment of his peers" and "laws of the land" are treated as substantially synonymous with due process of law. Drafters of the U.S. federal Constitution adopted the due process phraseology in the Fifth Amendment, ratified in 1791, which provides that "No person shall ... be deprived of life, liberty, or property, without due process of law."

Virtually all the British colonies in North America were established through charters that granted land and certain governing rights to the colonists, while retaining certain powers for the British crown. Similarly, when a U.S. city incorporates, the state government allows a charter to be drawn up, allowing the people of a specific locality to organize themselves into a municipal corporation (i.e., a city). Such a charter delegates powers to the people for the purpose of local self-government. A municipality is therefore the response of the state government to the need for certain public services (i.e., waste disposal, police and fire protection, water supply, health services) in addition to the services available from the county or from other local governments in the area. When the state grants, a charter to a school this allows parents and teachers to organize in such a manner as to provide educational services in addition to those that are available from the school district and existing schools.

Just as cities exist within, but are distinct from, the surrounding county and state, charter schools can be seen as distinct educational communities, each having the advantage of coming into existence already possessed of a nascent social contract, in the form of the school's charter. The establishment of charter schools can thus be seen as a movement, within the field of public education, toward the separation of responsibilities that has long characterized other arenas of public life. For example, constitutional government in the United States has traditionally been characterized by a division of powers (between the local, state, and federal levels of government, as well as between legislature, executive, and judiciary). This complex system of "checks and balances" restrains the unchecked use of power by government, safeguarding individual freedom. Nor is it only within government that such restraints have played a pivotal role.

CHARTER SCHOOLS AS MEDIATING INSTITUTIONS

> Government and the market are similar to two legs of a three-legged stool.
> Without the third leg of civil society, the stool is not stable and cannot provide
> support for a vital America
> —Bradley (1995, p. 95)

For much of the nation's early history, the exercise of government power was
viewed with considerable wariness. This sense of caution can be seen clearly
in the U.S. Constitution, which carefully limits the powers allotted to the
legislative, administrative, and judicial branches of government. There also
existed a more informal system of checks and balances, also with a tripartite
character. One part of this informal system consisted of the government,
in the election of which each voter (ideally) had an equal voice. A second
part was made up of the nation's economic institutions, where the laws of
supply and demand held sway. The third part consisted was formed by civil
society, which brought citizens together in voluntary associations to carry out
common tasks and to pursue common interests. As Alexis de Tocqueville
pointed out in *Democracy in America* (the first portion of which appeared in
1835):

> The Americans make associations to give entertainments, to form seminaries,
> to build inns, to construct churches, to diffuse books, to send missionaries to
> the antipodes; in this manner they found hospitals, prisons, or schools. (1990,
> vol. 2, p. 106)

Tocqueville predicted that the time was drawing near when individuals
would be less and less able to produce—of themselves alone—the necessities of life. Without voluntary associations, the tasks of government would
perpetually increase. In Tocqueville's view, the more government "stands
in the place of associations, the more will individuals, losing the notion of
combining together, require its assistance" (1990, vol. 1, p. 108). In contrast,
when people formed associations to carry out a task, their ability to direct
their own affairs grew:

> A government can no more be competent to keep alive and to renew the
> circulation of opinions and feelings amongst a great people than to manage
> all the speculations of productive industry. No sooner does a government
> attempt to go beyond its political sphere and enter upon this new track than
> it exercises, even unintentionally, an insupportable tyranny; for a government
> can only dictate strict rules, the opinions which it favors are rigidly enforced,
> and it is never easy to discriminate between its advice and its commands. (1990,
> vol. 1, p. 109)

It was Tocqueville's belief that voluntary associations, composed of individuals who had banded together in defense of mutual interests, were of pivotal importance in mitigating the imbalances of power found in every nation. He noted that, despite their many advantages, democratic governments also have certain weaknesses. "In aristocratic nations the body of the nobles and the wealthy are in themselves natural associations which check the abuses of power" (1990, vol. 1, p. 195). Whereas even though the citizens of democratic nations might be independent, most individuals were, by themselves, able to wield very little political influence. Therefore it was only by joining with others that the citizen of a democracy could make sure his or her voice would be heard in the citadels of power.

Where such associations did not exist, Tocqueville argued that the interests of individuals would be at risk unless some "artificial and temporary substitute" could be found. This argument closely mirrors sentiments that have been voiced by many charter school supporters. Typically, stakeholders at charter schools point to their schools as examples of "democracy in action." At both parent-led and teacher-led schools there was a perception that, by going outside the usual bureaucratic channels, the founders of the school had not shortcircuited the democratic process. They felt that they had, instead, enhanced it (Brouillette, 2002).

Like Tocqueville, former United States Senator Bill Bradley has argued that government and the market are not, by themselves, sufficient to support a healthy democratic culture:

> Civil Society is the place where Americans make their homes, sustain their marriages, raise their families, visit with their friends, meet their neighbors, educate their children, worship their God. It is in the churches, schools, fraternities, community centers, union halls, synagogues, sports leagues, PTAs, libraries, and barbershops. It is where opinions are expressed and refined, where views are exchanged and agreements made, where a sense of common purpose and consensus is forged. It lies apart from the realms of the market and government, and possesses a different ethic. The market is governed by the logic of economic self-interest, while government is the domain of laws, with all their coercive authority. (1995, p. 95)

Two centuries ago the fledgling United States faced the challenge of consciously creating a new set of social and political institutions. The influence of the social contract theory put forward by the 17th-century English philosopher John Locke pervaded the era leading up to the War of Independence and is easily recognized in the language of the *Declaration of Independence* and the *Bill of Rights*. Comparing the advantages of social order with the disadvantages of the state of nature (a hypothetical condition characterized by a complete absence of governmental authority), Locke set out to show why, and under what conditions, government is useful and ought to be accepted by reasonable people as a voluntary obligation, a "social contract." Moreover, Locke's defense of liberty extended to the educational process: "The rod, which is the only instrument of government that tutors generally know, or ever think of, is the most unfit of any to be used in education" (Locke, 1705).

Charter school supporters put forward a similar argument, suggesting that the resistance, or "draftee attitude," exhibited by many students today is a natural reaction to the element of coercion that has become an integral part of public education. Although the parallel should not be overstated, it is interesting to note the similarity between the rationale currently put forth for a unifying "common school curriculum" and the argument put forth, in an earlier era, that uniformity of religious belief was necessary to social cohesion. In the case of religion, the opposite has proved true. Although the United States has never had an established church, it has the highest rate of church attendance among industrialized nations, yet has remained remarkably free of the violent religious conflicts that have tragically divided other countries.

Such observations do not, of course, get to the core of the issue. The pivotal importance of the separation of church and state lies in the protection afforded to freedom of conscience, through assuring that the power of the state will not be used to coerce belief or stifle inquiry. These same considerations must be taken into account whenever there is a possibility that the free development of the individual may be turned aside from its natural course as a result of mandates put in place by the collective will of the majority. Regarding this issue, it is instructive to return to Tocqueville, who argued eloquently that the strongest lessons of democracy are learned on the grassroots level:

> The native of New England is attached to his own township because it is independent and free; his co-operation in its affairs ensures his attachment to its interests; the well-being it affords him secures his affection; and its welfare is the aim of his ambition and of his future exertions. He takes a part in every occurrence in the place; he practices the art of government in the small sphere within his reach; he accustoms himself to those forms without which liberty can only advance by revolutions; he imbibes their spirit; he acquires a taste for order, comprehends the balance of powers, and collects clear practical notions on the nature of his duties and the extent of his rights. (1990, vol. 1, p. 68)

SUMMARY

Charter schools offer the opportunity to make a commitment to a specific educational program and to a specific school community. As in marriage, there is some risk involved. Not all marriages (nor all charter schools) work out as the participants had initially hoped. Yet there seems to be something about commitment that engages the vital energies of human beings in a special way. A new level of effort is brought forth. A different set of expectations is created, leading in turn to an awareness of a new range of possibilities. Whether the culture that evolves out of the new relationship exists only within the confines of a single home or involves all the stakeholders at a school site, it can heighten the resiliency and resourcefulness of all involved.

Children benefit from such involvement; so do other stakeholders, who soon realize that they are able, collectively, to exercise a kind of power that none would have been able exercise alone. The strength of the charter school movement is that young people and their families are able to shape their lives through their own choices, while those community members who recognize an educational need are empowered to offer a remedy. As a result, new ideas, new energies, new perspectives are brought into the nation's public schools. School reform becomes an effort in which all can take part.

Although the charter school movement may not be *the* answer to what ails the nation's public schools, it suggests a pathway along which the answer may be found. Through the charter school movement new ideas, new energies, new perspectives have been brought into the nation's public schools. School reform has become an effort in which all can take part. Those who recognize an educational need have been empowered to offer a remedy. By allowing a wider range of citizens to make their own characteristic contributions to the improvement of the nation's public schools, charter schools have shown how education might, once again, be made a community affair.

GUIDING QUESTIONS

1. What problems were the people who advocated and/or supported charter school legislation attempting to address?

2. Although regulations governing charter schools vary greatly from state to state, what elements do the charter school laws in most states share?

3. Describe the major arguments put forth by charter school advocates and opponents.

4. Compare the competing views of education associated with the liberal arts tradition and the German tradition of linking education to vocational training and research.

5. How do charter schools and bureaucratic controls differ as approaches to school reform?

SELECTED READINGS

Brouillette, L. (2002). *Charter schools: Lessons in school reform.* Mahwah, NJ: Lawrence Erlbaum Associates.

Fuller, B. (2000). *Inside charter schools: The paradox of radical decentralization.* Cambridge, MA: Harvard University Press.

Nathan, J. (1996). *Charter schools: Creating hope and opportunity for American education.* San Francisco: Jossey-Bass.

Sarason, S. (1998). *Charter schools: Another flawed educational reform?* New York: Teachers College Press.

REFERENCES

Areen, J., & Jencks, C. (1971). Education vouchers: A proposal for diversity and choice. *Teachers College Record, LXXII,* 327–335.

Becker, H. J., Nakagawa, K., & Corwin, R. G. (1996). Parent involvement contracts in California's charter schools: Strategy for educational improvement or method of exclusion. *Teachers College Record, 98*(3), 511–536.

Bennett, K. P., & LeCompte, M. D. (1990) *The way schools work.* New York: Longman.

Bradley, B. (1995, Spring). America's challenge: Revitalizing our national community. *National Civic Review, 84*(2), 95.

Brouillette, L. (1999). Behind the statistics: Urban dropouts and the GED. *Phi Delta Kappan, 81*(4), 313–315.

Brouillette, L. (2002). *Charter schools: Lessons in school reform.* Mahwah, NJ: Lawrence Erlbaum Associates.

Cookson, P. W. (1994). *School choice: The struggle for the soul of American education.* New Haven, CT: Yale University Press.

Crosby, E. A. (1999, December). Urban schools: Forced to fail. *Phi Delta Kappan, 81*(4), 298–303.

Cuban, L. (1990, April). Reforming, again, again, and again, *Educational Researcher,* 3–13.

Finn, C. E. Jr., Manno, B. V., Bierlein, L. A., & Vanourek, G. (1997). The birth-pains and life-cycles of charter schools. *Charter Schools in Action Project, Final Report, Part II.* Hudson Institute. Retrieved August 12, 2004, from http://www.edexcellence.net.

Garn, G. (1999, October). The thinking behind Arizona's charter movement. *Educational Leadership, 56*(2), 48–50.

Geske, T. G., Davis, D. R., & Hingle, P. L. (1997). Charter schools: A viable public school option? *Economics of Education Review, 16,* 15–23.

Goodlad, J. I. (1984). *A place called school: Prospects for the future.* New York: McGraw-Hill.

Hogan, J. (1985). *The schools, the courts, and the public interest* (2nd ed.). Lexington, MA: Lexington.

Iannaccone, L. (1967). *Politics in education.* New York: Center for Applied Research in Education.

Jefferson, T. (1904). Bill for the More General Diffusion of Knowledge. In P. L. Ford (Ed.), *The works of Thomas Jefferson* (pp. 414–426). New York: Knickerbocker Press.

Johnson, T. W. (2002). *Historical documents in American education.* Boston: Allyn & Bacon.

Kaestle, C. F. (1983). *Pillars of the republic: Common schools and American society 1780–1860.* New York: Hill & Wang.

Kirst, M. W., & Meister, G. (1985). Turbulence in American secondary schools: What reforms last? *Curriculum Inquiry, 15,* 169–186.

Kliebard, H. (1987) *The struggle for the American curriculum 1893–1958.* New York: Routledge.

Kliebard, H. (1999). *Schooled to work: Vocationalism and the American curriculum, 1876–1946*. New York: Teachers College Press.

Kolderie, T. (1990). *The states will have to withdraw the exclusive*. Minneapolis, MN: Center for Policy studies.

Locke, J. (1705). *Some thoughts concerning education* (5th ed., sect. 47). London: Printed for A. and J. Churchill.

McCarthy, M. M. (1992). Judicial decisions. In M. C. Alkin (Ed.), *Encyclopedia of Educational Research* (6th ed., pp. 677–689). New York: Macmillan.

Metz, M. H. (1978). *Classrooms and corridors: The crisis of authority in desegregated secondary schools*. Berkeley: University of California Press.

Nathan, J. (1996a). *Charter schools: Creating hope and opportunity for American education*. San Francisco: Jossey-Bass.

Nathan, J. (1996b, September). Possibilities, problems, and progress: Early lessons from the charter movement. *Phi Delta Kappan*, 18–23.

National Commission on Excellence in Education. (1983). *A nation at risk: The imperative for educational reform*. Washington, DC: U.S. Government Printing Office.

Office of Educational Research and Improvement (OERI). (1999, May). A study of charter schools: Third-year report executive summary 1999. Washington, DC: U.S. Department of Education.

Powell, A. G., Farrar, E., & Cohen, D. K. (1985). *The shopping mall high school: Winners and losers in the educational marketplace*. Boston: Houghton Mifflin.

Stevenson, H., Chen, C., & Lee, S. (1993). Mathematics achievement of Chinese, Japanese, and American children: Ten years later. *Science, 259*, 53–58.

Stevenson, H. W., Lee, S., & Stigler, J. W. (1986). Mathematics achievement of Chinese, Japanese, and American children. *Science, 231*, 693–699.

Tocqueville, A. (1990). *Democracy in America* (2 volumes). New York: Random House.

Tyack, D. (1974). *The one best system: A history of American urban education*. Cambridge, MA: Harvard University Press.

Wayson, William W. (1999, August). Charter Schools: Franchise for Creativity or License for Fractionation? *Education and Urban Society, 31*(4), 446–464.

Wells, A. S., Artiles, L., Carnochan, S., Cooper, C. W., Grutzik, C., Holm, J. J., Lopez, A. L., Scott, J., Slayton, J., & Vasudeva, A. (1998). *The UCLA charter school study*. Los Angeles: University of California, Los Angeles.

Wells, A. S., Grutzik, C., Carnochan, S., Slayton, J., & Vasudeva, A. (1999). Underlying policy assumptions of charter school reform: The multiple meanings of a Movement. *Teachers College Record, 100*(3), 513–535.

Index